HOW TO WORK IN
STAINED
GLASS

THIRD EDITION

Anita & Seymour Isenberg

**krause
publications**

700 E. State Street • Iola, WI 54990-0001
Telephone: 715/445-2214

www.krause.com

**700 East State St., Iola, WI 54990-0001
Telephone 715-445-2214
www.krause.com**

Please call or write for our free catalog of publications. Our toll-free number
to place an order or to obtain a free catalog is 800-258-0929 or please use our regular telephone
715-445-2214 for editorial comment and further information.

Manufactured in the United States of America
Library of Congress Cataloging in Publication Data

Isenberg, Anita and Seymour
How to work in stained glass
ISBN 0-87341-628-7
1. stained glass   2. glass staining and painting   3. title
Includes index   82-73537
CIP

Cover window panels from Miguel's Restaurant in Siesta Key, Florida,
designed by Patricia Daley, Kaleidoscope Studio.

This third edition
For Ariana and Brielle
First editions

Contents

Preface

It is amazing to us to recall the origins of this book, from lectures at various art classes and social organizations to articles in *The Glass Workshop Magazine* published by the now defunct Stained Glass Club, to the tentative outline submitted to various publishers, all of whom (with one exception) declined it with the rationale that there was not enough interest in the subject to warrant a work of this nature. That was back in 1971. The exception was the Chilton Book Co., whose far-seeing editor, John Marion, thought there *was* enough interest. This third edition, 27 years and many thousands of copies later, of what many working in the field call the "bible" of the stained glass craft, has more than justified his faith.

Although we have written 12 other stained glass books, many of which enjoyed years of popularity, they are presently out of print; however *How to Work* has, since its inception, maintained its primary position as a guide and teaching modality for beginners as well as advanced workers in the field. Our goal initially was to hold nothing back, to describe to the best of our abilities the techniques and procedures inherent in working in stained glass, yet to provide a work that was, first and last, readable and appealing to hobbyist and professional alike. That first edition is now a collector's item; we've seen copies of it in studios and workshops ready to hand, if practically disabled from constant use.

The second edition, over ten years ago, brought the newer techniques and materials up to date. With that edition, we began to incorporate chapters by experts in specific fields, since by that time the craft had grown to such an extent that it was difficult to be knowledgeable and adept in all its forms. We have continued this procedure in this third edition, regretfully deleting for lack of room many of our past contributors. We have also updated and redefined the materials and procedures chapters and reshot or replaced almost all the photographs, adding more sequential pictures to amplify textual description which, under the best of circumstances, can be hard to follow on its own.

Of necessity, there must be some repetition of discussions in various chapters due to overlapping of materials and techniques. When we discuss soldering, we must relate it to leading and foiling even though these procedures are addressed in other chapters. When we discuss the nature of lead came in its separate chapter, we find ourselves redefining it in a chapter on leading up a window. Hopefully, this will serve to heighten the information by its use in very different contexts. We have found with previous editions, that such reiteration helps to emphasize the close-knit nature of all tools and devices involved in stained glass work. The fact that we have made artificial divisions of these intertwined elements is somewhat negated by just this overlapping. The point is, that any craft as far reaching as stained glass incorporates many facets all at once. The overall purpose of this book is to align them as a unit while focusing on them one at a time.

This book is not meant primarily to be a tract or manual, though to be serviceable it must have characteristics of both. It is meant to be a teacher and companion and hopefully, a source of inspiration. That it has served the craft for so long is something we are very proud of.

No work of this nature is the product of a single enthusiasm. Without the help and encouragement of Patricia Daley, this book might still be in limbo. Getting it on the printed page is largely her doing and she is responsible for any of its merits and none of its flaws.

From the first edition to the present one, we have received many helpful suggestions from our readers on how to make the book more effective. Where feasible, we have tried to incorporate such suggestions in the general scheme. We are also indebted to aids and comforts from the various manufacturers who have contributed their knowledge and materials as specified herein; and of course to our contributors who have waited so patiently for this third edition to be completed. As specific instances, we would like to thank:

For the use of their studios for demonstrations and photo sessions, thanks to Al and Irene Brum of The Stained Glass Connection and Brum Studios of Sarasota, Florida.

Also to Glasscrafters of Sarasota, Florida, for allowing us to photograph many of the newer tools and devices, in some instances taking them right out of customer's hands.

Teaching stained glass aboard the Pacific Far East Line's cruise ship Mariposa bound for Tahiti. To our knowledge, this was the first time stained glass was taught aboard a cruise ship. The voyage lasted six weeks and the classes were filled to capacity. Everyone went home with a stained glass object of their own fabrication.

Thanks as well to the Pacific Far East Line passengers and officers who taught us that you can teach novices to cut glass even when dealing with a rough (is it ever smooth?) crossing of the Tasman Sea.

And for his far-seeing intervention by putting one of us on the agenda to speak at the 1976 meeting of the Stained Glass Association of America, thus with one stroke opening the field for hobbyists, E. Crosby Willet deserves not only our thanks, but the thanks of all connected with the industry.

With this third edition there is yet another change. The Chilton Book Co., with whom we have worked so long, has passed into history. Our new publisher, Krause Publications, has been most patient and understanding during this period of toil.

Lastly, of course, the most thanks go to our readers. Their judgments and evaluations have allowed this third edition to head for the 21st century. Go with it!

Si and Anita Isenberg
Sarasota, Florida
Ellenton, Florida

Introduction

By E. Crosby Willet and Helene Weis

E. Crosby Willet has been President of the Willet Stained Glass Studios since 1964. The studio, started by his grandparents in 1898, has done thirteen thousand plus commissions in new stained glass and restorations in the past ninety nine and one half years. Helene H. Weis is a freelance consultant for historic stained glass research and is the author of many technical articles on the subject.

"Stained glass" has become an all inclusive name for various kinds of glass cut in shapes to form specific designs joined with lead, copper, foil, zinc, cement, epoxies, and all types of space-age adhesives. It can be etched, sandblasted, fused, and manipulated in a myriad of ways.

What makes it unique, contrasted with other art forms, is its particular relationships with light. When viewed from a darkened area with intense exterior light, it glows with sensuous beauty. When the light changes, so does the appearance of the glass, including the relationship of the colors. The cool colors are at their best on cloudy or rainy days while the hot rubies and golds sparkle and vibrate when the sun is out. With reflective light, the window dulls and the darker colors become almost opaque.

Because of its unparalleled ability to stimulate and create moods for the viewer, stained glass has been used for more than ten centuries to decorate churches and cathedrals in Europe. The Gothic Age, the 12th through 14th

A sectional church window. The bottom portion would open outwards. The three top portions would be fixed. Note the heavy separations, probably wood.

The heavy lead or zinc lines dominate these windows so the background stained glass is seen through a grid, almost like a fence and rather like an afterthought.

Here the painted figures are in the foreground even though there are many more lead lines than the previous example. These windows, with their regular rectangular components, act almost as if they are tiles. However, the tiled effect recedes into the background as the strength of the work comes through due to the foreground painting.

The earliest documented church windows to contain subject matter made in America were by William Jay and John Bolton. Much time and effort has been expended to restore their scheme of windows in St. Ann's and Holy Trinity Church in Brooklyn, New York.

As the 19th century advanced with rising prosperity and increasing taste for more elaboration, domestic windows began to display ornaments based on natural forms. An assortment of bevels and pressed jewels made them sparkle. In 1884, approximately 2,000 people were employed making stained glass in the New York area. Onto this scene burst the entrepreneur Louis Comfort Tiffany. He first organized his business following the pattern set by William Morris in England to provide homogeneous interiors for churches and luxurious dwellings. Stained glass was only one of his products. His company produced ceramics, metals, fabrics, mosaics, and jewelry.

centuries, is considered the highest peak of the art. Sometimes stained glass is called a lost art, although the process was never lost. A few people in the world kept the craft alive but tastes changed and it went out of style.

A return to the Gothic style of architecture in the mid-19th century created a renaissance in stained glass. At that time most stained glass work was insipid enamel colors that were not permanent, being fired on clear glass. The beautiful blown glass of earlier times was no longer made. In 1849, lawyer and stained glass enthusiast Charles Winston had fragments of medieval colored glass chemically analyzed and encouraged English manufacturers to begin again to make comparable glass. From that time, stained glass production prospered in the British Isles and today the work of English studios fills many American churches.

In the beginning, Tiffany used outside glass houses for his sheet glass, principally Heidt in Brooklyn, where John LaFarge had developed opalescent glass. LaFarge was no businessman although a fine artist, and soon Tiffany's business had overtaken him. Tiffany employed a number of designers, some of whom also worked for other studios. Many other studios at the time used opalescent glass; some even bought glass from Tiffany. This makes an unsigned opalescent window very difficult to ascribe to the Tiffany studios. Tiffany outlived his popularity—again taste in domestic interiors had changed.

For church windows, the neo-Gothic style was taken up by pioneers like William Willet and Charles Connick and others who felt, like the architect Ralph Adams Cram, that it was the only appropriate style for religious buildings. Under Cram's aegis, the only "suitable" stained glass imitated medieval windows. The shapes were tall pointed arches and elaborate rose windows; the predominant colors red and blue with smaller accents of secondary colors. The subjects were illustrated in a flat style and were often enclosed in medallions. Windows like this are still being made today.

Just before World War II there was a move in Europe to include the work of the famous secular artists of the time in the churches. Among these were Swiss artists Alexandre Cingria and Augusto Giacometti and French artist Georges Rouault. After the war, partly to replace the many broken windows caused by bombing, partly to experiment with and enlarge the form to their own purposes, artists Fernand Leger, Alfred Manessier, and Marc Chagall began to design windows. The famous Jerusalem Windows of Chagall belong to this period.

Also before World War II the technique of using thick faceted glass set in cement or epoxy was developed in France. This technique became extremely popular in America (see Working with Slab Glass). The influence of contemporary secular art is also evident in England, notably in Coventry Cathedral, a modern structure joined to the ruin of the old cathedral which was wrecked by bombs.

Stained glass had been a thriving art in Germany, which sent many pictorial windows to American churches in the late 19th and early 20th centuries. A pioneer in German expressionist-designed stained glass was Johann Thorn-Prikker. Thorn-Prikker taught Anton Wendling who in turn taught Ludwig Schaffrath. Schaffrath, Schreiter, and other contemporary German artists had (and continue to have) great influence on post World War II North American stained glass artists. Their technique is demonstrated in simpler forms of non-representational design that is linear and architectonic in feeling with generally muted palettes.

While some craftspeople were promoting the German "simplified" style, Americans began to take up stained glass as a hobby. Text books began to appear to teach those who wanted to learn the process but were not near one of the rare schools that taught stained glass or who could not spare the time for a traditional apprenticeship. These individuals began to make suncatchers, lampshades, and small autonomous panels. Stained glass began lending color to public and private spaces. Much of this hobbyist work initially showed the influence of the late 19th century (Victorian period?) in a concentration on flowers, birds, and natural scenes, although it has gradually become more sophisticated. By now, some practitioners of the 1960s have turned to other occupations and new generations have taken their place.

In fact, stained glass as a hobby appears to be here to stay, confounding those naysayers who viewed this aspect of the craft as a fly-by-night fad. The hobbyist faction has as many enthusiasts as ever, producing an even wider spectrum of work. New books keep appearing and disappearing that are devoted to various aspects of stained glass. And the craft is beginning to flourish in many countries such as Japan, Saudi Arabia, and Israel which have no ancient tradition of the art.

A new generation of art historians is adopting stained glass as a serious field of study. The work of compiling a census of stained glass in America has begun and it is finally joining the mainstream of artistic endeavor.

A type of rose window—the pictorial portion nicely in partnership with heavy linear commentary.

Part I

Equipment and Materials

"The right tool in the right hands can accomplish miracles."

**Ancient Glass Paintings
by Winston**

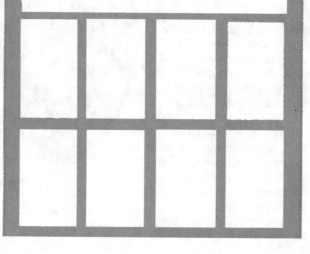

CHAPTER 1
Please Don't Call It "Stain" Glass

You'd be surprised how many people do. It is properly called stained glass. There's no such thing as "stain" glass.

Actually, there's no such thing as stained glass either. What we are really talking about is not stained at all, since that would indicate the material was covered with some sort of overlay. The color of stained glass is imparted before the glass even becomes glass.

Which leads us to believe that anyone working in the field should understand certain concepts about glass itself. The propensities of this material establish and guide the techniques that can be employed with any glass, stained or not. Imparting color to the glass modifies its physical capabilities to some extent, so stained glass has certain requirements of its own. But to design with glass, the worker must keep the characteristics of the medium very much in focus. All most people know about glass is that 1) it cuts you and 2) light comes through it clearly. But in working with stained glass, this is not always the case. The principles here are 1) you "cut" it (though it certainly can cut you back) and 2) you cannot always see through it clearly nor would you want to.

Glass is a vitreous substance, which means when liquid glass right from the furnace cools, it does not crystallize. Most other liquids crystallize. The word crystal itself can be confusing. Most people visualize crystal as being translucent (quartz being a familiar example) and they assume that glass is similar. In fact, the word crystal is often applied to glass but it is used only in a comparative sense to distinguish exceptionally clear glass from muddy or colored varieties or a highly leaded glass. In a true crystal state, the atoms composing any substance have a regular arrangement rather like a military lineup. When they break, crystalline objects are likely to do so along specific planes of cleavage. Such objects constitute true solids.

But when a vitreous substance cools, it does not crystallize so it does not have the properties of a true solid. The atoms composing this "frozen liquid" we know as glass are randomly arranged and allow microscopic fractures that do not follow the clean cleavage planes of true solids. If it is maintained for a long period at a temperature somewhat above its softening temperature, any vitreous substance will devitrify—that is, crystallize. In this state, it will have a frosted and muddy appearance.

The American Society for Testing Materials, through its Committee on Glass and Glass Products, has adopted the following as the standard definition of glass: "An organic product of fusion which has cooled to a rigid condition without crystallizing. It is typically hard and brittle. It may be colorless or colored, and transparent to opaque."

THE STAINING PROCESS

Stained glass is actually impregnated with color in the factory while still in raw chemical form. In medieval times the colors or metallic oxides were added to the batch while it was molten, but most factories today mix the elements before putting them into the furnace. Adding color is an integral part of the entire process. Stained glass is composed of silica sand with approximately 1% iron, soda ash, limestone, and some borax. The percentage of iron in the sand is important. Sand can contain up to 10% iron. The iron content has to be checked—too much will give a greenish cast to the glass rather like the color of a Coca-Cola bottle. Such an overlay could be disastrous to the factory's product.

To put color into the glass, the factory mixes in various metallic oxides at the very beginning of the operation. Each color has its own formula and may be mixed by a special worker who is an expert in the particular mixture. Some of the chemicals used for coloring glass are sugar and sulfur for amber; dichromate for green; copper oxides for blues; and the addition of cobalt for still stronger blues. Red colors, including rubies, oranges, and yellows (the entire royal family), come from selenium or from gold salts which explains the higher cost of this glass. Cadmium is another element whose oxides give the glass a yellow color. Other common elements used in an oxide state are nickel and iron.

Coloring glass is not so simple as mixing pigments into sand and limestone and applying heat. Humidity and temperature play a great part in the end result, as does the thickness of the furnace and the coefficient of expansion (COE) of the different oxides within the molten glass. It is because of this last factor especially that the finished stained glass sheet may behave more peculiarly than regular window glass when you cut it. The internal stresses and strains can be immense, especially in sheets with more than one color such as "streakies."

Since glass is a homogeneous liquid, it is susceptible to the laws of hydraulics just like other liquids. That means if you put pressure on one particular part of it with a glass cutter, you may set up a strain pattern through the sheet that causes a fracture some distance away. This can be a bit unnerving, and not only to beginners. The force transmitted is similar to that of the hydraulic brake in a car. The larger the sheet, the greater the possibility of this happening. Regular window glass will almost always transmit the pressure equally in a radius surrounding the moving cutter and generally behaves itself much better than stained glass with its nervous oxides. Some highly neurotic stained glass sheets fly apart at the merest touch of a cutter. Fortunately they are in the minority, but even people who have worked in the medium for years have times when a sheet of glass will insist on running its own way no matter how coerced it may be to follow orders.

TYPES OF STAINED GLASS

Stained glass sheets can be broken down into two main categories: antique and cathedral. Within these are individual characteristics involving the transparency and texture of the finished sheet. Although the mixing of pigments basically follows the same process in all stained glass manufacture, from then on the process varies depending on what the end result is going to be.

Antique Glass

Like glass in medieval times, antique glass is mouth-blown. Once the glass has become molten in the furnace, the glass blower picks up a certain amount of it on the end of his pontil and blows it into a long cylinder. Sometimes the cylinder is blown into a mold. Such a mold can be made of apple wood and may have designs carved into it to give the finished glass a pattern. However, most of the "seeds," "bubbles," and other "movement" within the glass that are so characteristic of antique hand-blown glass come from the art of the glass blower. "Trapped sunlight" is the way one admirer expressed his pleasure at these small air pockets, which resemble miniature reflectors when the light flashes among them.

Once the antique glass cylinder has been blown, the ends are cut off and it is sliced down the center with a hot knife. It is then placed on its side in an oven, cut side up, and allowed to fall flat with the heat, thus making it into a sheet of glass. Such a blown cylinder can be done free-form (without a mold) and it will be extremely uneven in thickness and very difficult to score and cut. Even the ones blown in a mold may vary in thickness from 1/4" to almost 3/4" in the same sheet.

In the past, hand-blown glass was made mostly in factories in France, Germany, and England, and its purchase in America entailed the additional expense of any imported item. With today's increased demand for the transparent hues and tones of all possible varieties, factories in this country have set up a determined challenge to what was for years mostly a European enterprise.

It is not exaggerating to say that a revolution in thinking about glass has led to a revolution in its manufacture. Glass has become more than "decor" for its own sake. Even when a stained glass piece is commissioned primarily for ornament, the range of material now available can transform it into an aesthetic statement. The eye of the beholder may be the final judge, but the plentiful choices of glass exercise a range of subtleties that influence such judgment. And antique glass is no longer the only glass category where these subtleties are found.

Cathedral Glass

All glass that is not mouth-blown is, at least by our definition, cathedral. Cathedral glass encompasses a wide variety of machine-made vitreous sheets. Its manufacture is either by a single- or double-rolling process in which the glass is forced between rollers or impressed in its molten state against a flat surface by a top roller alone. These rollers may be embossed with a texture to be impressed on the glass sheet. The glass is of a uniform thickness, usually 1/8", and in general is easier to score and cut than antique glass, although this isn't always the case.

Opalescent Glass: A large proportion of cathedral glass is opalescent glass, which is opaque. However, the opacities vary. Rather than allowing light rays to pass directly through, it spreads them within its surface, giving the effect of being lighted from within. Opalescent glass is seldom of one color except when it is pure white or pure black. Even when it is pure white, it is usually a white-on-white design. Dramatic mixtures of colors are spread throughout the sheet in whorls and darting lines that give movement and life when light illuminates the glass from behind. Opalescent, alone among stained glasses, also reflects light. Because of its dense makeup, it does not lose its hues and tones with the disappearance of back lighting as do most stained glass windows when the sun goes down. This quality makes it a natural choice for objects with consistent color tone, such as lamps and room dividers which are not always provided with back lighting. In lamps it is a particularly happy choice because opalescent glass hides the bulb which, through transparent glass, would be seen as a "hot spot."

Because of the linear flow of color across an opalescent sheet, beginners can be misled into thinking that the glass has a grain somewhat like wood. The question then arises whether to cut with or against the grain. In fact, glass has no grain whatsoever and the appearance is misleading. Opalescent glass is somewhat more difficult to cut than other types of stained glass; it is harder and requires a special cutter and generally more pressure than antique or other cathedral glass.

SPECIALTY STAINED GLASSES

Within the broad categories of antique and cathedral; opalescent and semitransparent are specific features which categorize types of glasses according to their physical makeup and specific uses. Here we find streakies, glue chip, flashed glass, reamy, and so forth. It is well for the stained glass craftsman to be familiar with such names, even though they are subjective terms coined by the manufacturer. Waterglass, for instance, is not made from water. There are new types of glass constantly coming on the market and, occasionally, some older types are discarded.

In some cases, names are confusing. Machine streaky glass, for example, is similar to opalescent glass, but instead of using an opal base, it begins with a flint (clear) glass base. Both opalescent and machine streaky are available in a wide variety of color combinations. Opalescent glass can be either machine- or hand-rolled and is formed by mixing an opal glass (white as opposed to clear) with one or more colors.

These ranges of specialty glasses can't all be touched on here. Some are considered more aesthetically sophisticated than others, but that depends on who is doing the considering. As we have noted, there is also a practical basis to specialty glasses, some being more appropriate to certain uses than others. It is profitable labor to experiment with the different glass varieties, although it is not always necessary to purchase entire sheets of each particular type just for experimental use. That can become expensive. Small pieces will do for a start. It is wise not to overburden yourself at the beginning with an extensive stock of different glasses that you may not get to use for some time.

Flashed Glass

Flashed glass is a form of antique glass usually made with one color layer on top of another by "flashing" a finished sheet with a secondary color. Flashed glass is only bi-colored on one side. The other side is considered the white or basic color. Various combinations are available. For example, blue flashed on yellow, red on white, red on yellow, and blue on orange, etc. You can tell a piece of flashed glass by scratching a corner of the flashed side with a glass cutter or chipping a small bit away. The underlying color will show through. Any color flashed on white or clear glass is particularly easy to tell by holding an edge of the glass up to the light. You should make out the clear underlying portion with the thin layer of top color.

Flashed glass has two main purposes. The first is to combine two colors to get a melding of both that will add yet another hue to the color range; the second is for etching purposes. By using the proper etching materials (hydrofluoric acid is best), it is possible to dispense with portions of the flashed upper layer according to a predetermined design and thus allow the bottom layer to show through. The procedure can be prolix or simple—from etching out the eye of an animal on a suncatcher to the Jeruselam Windows of Chagall.

Streakies

Streakies follow their name—sheets of colors are streaked across the glass surface. Streakies are similar in this to opalescent glass, but being transparent, they have an airy delicacy that can be breathtaking when the light streams through. Some of the best streakies—many of them English—could be put in a frame as they are. In fact, unless you are cutting fairly large pieces of such glass, you can mar more than you make since you may lose much of the color flow. Many of the English streakies, in addition to combining a colorful palette, add a rippling of the glass itself—a textural component that lets the colors dance across the sheet, though it makes for uncertain cutting. We have in our studio several German streakies that we have never been able to bring ourselves to cut. There seems to be no way to improve on the beauty of the glass as it is.

Streakies are particularly effective as sunsets, cloud-filled skies, ocean waves, landscapes, rainbows, or perhaps the Manhattan skyline. They also serve well as mountains or abstract colorations in nonspecific works. They may be employed in freeform objects and for animals—butterfly wings made from them are especially alluring.

Textured Glass

Granite-backed glass: This is a low-relief rough-back glass so treated on what is usually considered the back side. The granite texture disperses light more effectively than non-textured glass if this is the effect you want. A common question is whether the "right" side should face outward or inward? The right side of any glass is the side you think is best for your purpose; there are no hard and fast rules. Don't try cutting on the granite side. Just one look at it may make your glass cutter's wheel fall off. If you cut on the smooth side, remembering to reverse your pattern if you want the granite side up, you should find granite-backed glass no more difficult to work with than any of the other cathedral glasses. It does scare some beginners though.

Granite ripple: This is a heavier granite-type backing to which is added a rippling of the glass surface itself. This traps the light at the same time it is diffused and so conveys a sense of spread to the illumination as well as added texture to the glass.

Drapery: This is the heaviest of the ripple glasses and is used, as the name implies, mainly for clothing, room furnishings, and waves—any object that requires a three-dimensional projection. Tiffany windows make use of drapery glass. Its use can point up a dramatic situation or provide necessary relief from a non-contrasting backdrop. Used to best effect, it emphasizes the work overall, rather than standing out itself as a novel element.

Pebbled glass: The surface of pebbled glass displays a smooth facing rather than a granulated one with deep, irregular indentations.

Pebble ripple: A combination of pebbled glass and granite ripple. This unusual, indented glass gives a peculiar irregular light diffusion that can be highly dramatic. It's a pretty idiosyncratic glass, however, used only for specific statements.

Cutting textured glass: Although textured surfaces tend to look awesome to those not used to working with

them, they can be cut with relative ease by employing a few simple procedures. Try these hints from the folks at Uroboros Glass the next time you are face-to-face with a textured surface:

1) Make sure your cutter is clean and sharp. Carbide cutters work best, and we recommend the MacInnes with a #4 wheel.
2) Lubricate the cutter by dipping it in kerosene before each score. A dry cutter produces an uneven score and causes extra wear on the wheel.
3) Place the sheet of glass on a thin dense foam pad, such as the 3/8(Ensolite pads used by backpackers. This evenly distributes the pressure of the cutter over the entire sheet.
4) Score on the smooth side of the sheet and avoid applying too much pressure.
5) With the ball end of the cutter, tap the textured side along the length of the score. For particularly difficult cuts, develop the crack visibly by tapping along the entire length of the score. (Experts can tell by the sound of the tapping if the crack is adequately developed.)
6) With fingers or grozzing pliers, gently separate the glass in the usual manner for smooth glasses.
7) Extremely acute angles with thick textures can be easily cut with a small diamond band saw.
8) Remember to be patient. Every glass manufacturer makes glass of different hardness and cutting qualities. It sometimes takes a while to develop a feel for each of the different glasses.

Hammered Class

Another type of cathedral glass, hammered glass looks as though it had been textured by a small, persistent ball hammer. The indentations are uniform and when the light hits them they act like facets. There is a rough and a smooth side to this glass and the choice, as usual, is yours as to which side you put forward.

Crackle Glass

Crackle glass is an antique glass that is dipped quickly in water immediately after being formed. The shock of this contact forms definite fracture lines throughout the sheet. The glass is removed from the water before the sheet can self-destruct. As the glass slowly cools, these fracture lines become embedded in the subsurface. Crackle glass comes in almost all colors, although ranges within a specific color may not be always available. This is a type of "figured" glass with the figurations—the crackling—running throughout the sheet. There is usually no problem cutting this glass but be careful since you are dealing with a rather fragile type.

Flemish Glass

Flemish glass has deep channels running helter-skelter throughout the sheet. These channels are caused by the rollers of the pressing machine, and while the color may change, the indentations are all alike. This gives a lack of individuality to Flemish glass that is not noticed as much with either hammered or granite-backed glass, perhaps because the indentations are monotonous and so readily apparent. Our advice would be to not use Flemish in great quantity because it cheapens other types of glass used with it. Used alone it is unimaginative. With Flemish glass, more than with any other type discussed so far, a little bit goes a long way.

Fracture Glass

Fracture glass was created by fusing thin glass flakes or fractures to a glass sheet during the rolling process. The best fracture glass was an artfully designed color collage, utilizing fractures of a variety of sizes and in a range of hues. The result was surprisingly organic and three-dimensional. Uroboros Glass is one of the companies (Bulls Eye is another) that has redeveloped true fracture streamer glass. The technique fuses an artfully designed palette of fractures onto a carefully selected range of sheet glass colors. Streamers are thin glass strings that in the past have been used in conjunction with fractures to suggest vines, twigs, or even pine needles. Today's artists also use them in conceptual designs.

One advantage to using this type of glass lies in the nonlinear color you have to work with. Standard sheet glasses are limited to streaks and swirls, even though nature's colors are often spotty or blotchy. Fracture glass visually suggests nature's nonlinear aspects. That is one reason it works so well for foliage backgrounds and abstracts.

When used on the front surface of a work, fracture glass provides a distinct and bold aspect, since the shiny edges of the flakes are evident. By placing the fractures on the back surface, you can soften the effect and cause the colors to fade into the background. Another common technique is to "plate" the fracture glass behind the front surface of the work. This is done in as many as four layers and it creates a superb three-dimensional effect.

Fracture glass is only one of the recently developed "design glasses" that the imagination of the manufacturer and advances in technology have made available to the hobbyist and professional alike.

Ring-Mottled Opalescent Glass

Like fracture glass, ring-mottled glass was reconstituted by Uroboros Glass Studios. The mottled opalescent effect was a glass making secret thought to be lost with Louis Comfort Tiffany. Research by Uroboros into the use of gold as a colorant has opened up a range of hues that includes fuchsias, purples, and hot pinks. These exuberant colors can be used as a base for the creation of wildly exotic special effects, many of which are employed to the full by contemporary artists in the "new wave" of glass design. This glass also adds flair and know-how to the works of beginners with very little effort. The difficulties beginners may run into with these glasses is through their overuse. If a little bit is good, a lot is better doesn't work here.

Slab Glass

Slab glasses or dalles de verre, often just called dalles, are thick chunks of glass approximately 1" thick by about 6" to 8" wide and 12" long. To produce them requires a precise annealing system that relieves such masses of the innate stresses of cooling. This, of course, allows for easier cutting of the dalle and less chance of it fragmenting. In turn, this means less waste, more usable glass, and a lot less frustration.

To work with dalles requires special materials, mainly epoxy or cement, special hammers and anvils, as well as special occasions to suit their characteristic design potential. They may be employed just as they come from the factory or, more likely, in broken or cut pieces acquired either by using a glass cutter or a slab glass wedge.

Chunk glass is the term often used for the broken pieces of dalles. These chunks, made to varying thicknesses by the worker, break up light along their various cleavage planes or facets and so provide yet another stained glass luminescence, especially formidable when seen within a large cement or epoxy background support. Light filtering through these chunks makes them look like so many precious stones.

Iridized Glass

This glass has a specially formulated surface that reflects light in a manner similar to Tiffany's glass. A chemical process is used to impart rainbow-like colors on the surface of the glass; colors are usually blue, gold, green and pink. It is dramatic when it is incorporated as part of an overall design, but like Flemish glass, it can become monotonous if used too much. Certainly it is one of the more spectacular of the opalescents. It offers no special cutting problems and is fun to work with.. Dichroic glass, which many confuse with iridized glass, is a totally different glass made by a totally different process. (See the chapter on dichroic glass.)

Glue-Chip Glass

This glass is patterned on one or both sides, but the pattern is not impressed by a roller. Today, it is used for office doors, partitions, glass tabletops, room dividers, as parts of stained glass windows, and sometimes as bordering pieces.

Further specifics on this glass and its uses are given in its own chapter. To chip glass you first need a special animal-product glue. Other glues will not work. You will also need a desiccant such as silica gel. If the surface of the glass is smooth, you must roughen it either by sandblasting or by grinding it to allow the glue to adhere. The glue is then heated in a double boiler and spread on the glass with an ordinary paint brush. The glue now must be encouraged to dry. To do this as efficiently as possible, you must fashion some sort of drying or chipping chamber—anything from a plastic bag to a kiln. The desiccant is placed in the drying chamber to remove the moisture from the glue. During this process, the glue literally tears itself away from the glass surface, taking with it some of the surface flakes. Indeed, the force of this tearing away can send chips of glue-laden glass flying if the chamber is not enclosed. It is the curling of the glue away from the glass that forms the distinctive pattern on the glass surface.

Waterglass

Waterglass is a trade name rather than a specific type of glass. Made by the Spectrum Glass Co., this non-mechanical rippled glass has gained enthusiastic acceptance by artists and craftspeople in the stained glass field. Its high luster as well as the feeling of liquidity it projects makes its name almost automatic. Spectrum also produces Wispies, its name for translucent mixes.

It is interesting to note that Spectrum Glass is the only glass factory (at least to our knowledge) to use large electric furnaces to feed molten glass in a continuous ribbon through a 200-foot digitally controlled annealing lehr. This unique process attempts to assure uniformity of composition and minimal internal stress within the glass.

All glass factories do their best to make their glass readily workable. Workable glass scores easily and breaks along the score line precisely. It does not shatter in one portion of the sheet when another part is being worked on. It also grozzes smoothly and does not tend to chip and flake. In short, it works *with* rather than *against* the craftsperson.

WHICH GLASS IS BEST FOR YOU?

Glass workers establish individual preferences based on experience, but they also pay attention to manufacturers' claims. And glass manufacturers are very much attuned to their response. This provides a give and take to the industry that is not present in most others. When a particular glass does not live up to expectations, it is generally taken off the market and reconsidered. As you make your initial acquaintance with the material, you do not have to assume that it is always right and you are always wrong. You may have purchased a sheet of glass that is poorly annealed. If this happens, always discuss it with your retailer. He is there not only to sell you glass. It is to his advantage that you be happy with it. Then you will be back for more.

The boundary between what makes a generic type of glass made by all companies and an individual tradename item is not well defined. In a nomenclature that is growing rapidly and that many workers individualize according to their own rules, it is easy to get confused. When ordering glass by any particular manufacturer, it is well to study their catalogue and terminology. Such information is readily available from retailers who sell these brand names and who are (hopefully) knowledgeable enough to point out differences between the glasses of specific manufacturers.

WORKING WITH STAINED GLASS

To achieve its true measure of power, stained glass must be back-lighted. But this is not a limiting factor, as many prospective clients suppose. In fact, it is dramatically advantageous. During the day, stained glass windows are infused with light. As the daylight changes, so does the character of the stained glass and the nature of the design. Diminishing daylight does not have to diminish the effect of the stained glass. Instead, as the waning light strikes the glass from a different aspect, certain features and colors that were muted before now become highlighted. Many people have favorite hours for viewing a particular panel or window; for some it is not the noon hour, but the meditative light of afternoon or even the solemn perspectives induced by gathering twilight.

Once night comes, the window or panel is extinguished from within. But outside the window glows, providing a different aura courtesy of the electric company. This is a lot of activity for a single art form, and the designer of stained glass must be prepared to deal with it. But you don't have to make an entire window to get your effects. A small panel or small freeform objects will also light up your chosen spaces. Stylized animals, flowers, and insignias will do the trick. Placing objects in the window is simple enough. They can be suspended from the wooden molding or hung from plastic suction hooks attached to the clear glass of the pane. Make sure the window surface you are going to use for a suction hook is clean, or the hook may shortly gasp and fall, taking your pride and joy with it. It is best to use a clear fish line to attach your pieces, since metal wire is noticeable and looks awkward.

Stained glass mobiles also give an intriguing effect to a space. It is not necessary for these to be constructed entirely of glass pieces; stained glass hangings can be interspersed with many other materials, from pieces of forged metal to lengths of bamboo.

THE STAINED GLASS LIGHT BOX

A light box is a nice way to show off stained glass, especially if you are out of walls and windows. It need not be expensive—it's easy to make one yourself for about the cost of a reasonably priced frame. The light box should be made of a type of wood that will set off the panel. It should stand away from the wall as unobtrusively as possible, leaving only enough space to accommodate the fluorescent lights in their crafted recesses. The back of the box is usually covered with silver foil. A 1/4(wood molding will serve to hold the stained glass. When building, it is important to screw the back panel of your light box into place rather than nailing it. Sometimes it's easy to forget that the light bulbs will eventually have to be changed, and of course it's easier to remove screws than nails.

The light box should weigh only slightly more than a framed picture of approximately the same size. If it is much heavier than that, you have either used too dense a wood or provided more space within than necessary. You can make the light box lighter by using frosted plastic for the diffusing screen rather than frosted glass. The diffusing screen supports the stained glass piece and allows the fluorescent light to diffuse from within. Although it's best to make the screen light, if it is somewhat heavy, you can allow for the extra weight by providing a stronger hook for suspending the box. To turn the light box off and on, a line switch will do, or you can set a small toggle switch into the box itself.

The most ornate type of light box is the stained glass lampshade. The glass used in lampshades is generally of an opalescent or granite-backed cathedral variety—both to diffuse the light and to hide the bulb.

Room dividers and fireplace screens—a type of modified room divider—have been produced by stained glass workers as well as clock faces, three-dimensional panels, double-glazed hangings to give the effect of glass on glass, self-supporting abstracts, figurines (in one case, a full orchestra), triptychs, and entire ceilings. The interaction of light and color produces a vivacity that seems to enhance the imaginative powers of those working with the material, so almost anything becomes a possibility. As you will see as you read on.

CHAPTER 2
Sand Into Glass

Methinks you are my glass.
Shakespeare, Comedy of Errors

GLASS IN THE EGYPTIAN AND GREEK WORLD

The transformation of sand into glass is one of the miracles of the planet. We take this process for granted today, what with glass in all its forms hardly uncommon. This was not the case in the past. The process of making glass was expensive and, in the case of stained glass in Italy, a state secret. Artisans were practically prisoners on the island of Murano and if one escaped, an assassin was sent after him.

No one knows who discovered the process. It may have been accidental. According to Roman historian Pliny, Phoenician sailors going ashore to cook their meal found nothing to rest their pots on and returned to their ship to bring back blocks of niter. When heated, this substance, sodium bisulfate, united with the sand on the beach to form a crude sort of glass.

Glass and glaze have an almost identical chemical content. If we consider glazed tile as a forerunner to glass, we can trace the material to prehistoric Egypt. Among early glazed objects of this civilization is a vase bearing the cartouche of a ruler of the First Dynasty.

From the glaze in which clay objects were dipped, beads came about. Beads were made by taking a fine rod of hammered bronze and dipping it into the molten glaze and twirling it around rapidly until it cooled. The ball that formed could be slipped off the rod, which contracted when it cooled. Cylindrical beads known as bugles were made of a tube of glass cut into lengths. Such a technique is still used today for certain types of tube glass. Beads are the most widespread and hence the most frequently found of all historical glass objects since they were used as coins. Glass beads were usually opaque and made in many colors with varying degrees of skill. Most early beads give no clues to date or place of origin but they were in common use by the fourth millennium B.C. Beads were prized for their color and stringing beads was both child's play (literally) and a business endeavor. Strands of beads were made into necklaces, collars, and fringes for clothing and headdresses. Some mummies are covered with a fine network of beads over the linen wrappings.

The Egyptians did not aim to make colorless glass. They sought primarily to use glass to imitate the hues of precious stones. Pliny calls such early attempts at cheating customers "a far more lucrative deceit than any devised by the ingenuity of man." The coloring of these forgeries possessed a rare brilliancy, the workers copying with astonishing perfection the characteristics of the natural stones.

As with today's colored glass, metal was used extensively as a coloring agent. Copper was a favorite. Turquoise blue is a dominant color in glass and glazes of all periods. Genuine stones in blues and greens were rare and perhaps these colors were used in glass to make up for this deficiency. The characteristic glaze was made of a silicate of soda, lime, and copper. Intensity of color was governed by firing temperature, the lighter tints being produced from hotter exposure. Cobalt is used in semitransparent blue glass even today. Transparent ruby tints were not perfected until the Middle Ages. An opaque red glass seems to have been used almost exclusively for inlay work, probably because this color had a strong tendency to oxidize. Purple was derived from manganese and used in glazes of the First Dynasty. Manganese was used for brown but was not a color extensively employed. Yellow, a popular color, probably came from iron or antimony.

This imitation of precious stones seems to have been of more consequence to the glassworkers than the making of glassware. Expert renditions of amethyst, emerald, sapphire, lapis lazuli, jasper, carnelian, and diamond were produced by the Egyptians.

Probably the next step beyond the manufacture of beads and "gems" was the making of small glass vessels to contain perfumes and other liquids. Before the blowing iron (blow pipe) was devised, vases were probably made over an iron tube to which a bag of sand was firmly tied in the shape desired. Molten glass was poured on the metal and sandbag and colors introduced in a zigzag or crescent effect upon each layer of the hardening glass. The object was kept in motion until the shape became defined. As it cooled, the metal contracted and could be removed. The sandbag was then punctured and allowed to empty. In this process, the metal served to shape the neck. It is assumed that as the workmen developed a familiarity with the process they realized the sandbag was unnecessary. The vitreous substance was finally discovered to be able to be blown through a tube by hand or with bellows.

The discovery of the blowing iron is to glass manufacture what the potter's wheel is to pottery. With this device, glass objects could be made much more easily and use of this instrument became universal. Still today, the blowing iron is just a long hollow tube. A mass of molten glass is fixed upon its end (gathered) and is shaped by the amount of air blown into it. The general appearance of the object as well as the thickness of its walls, its character, and its aesthetic appeal is determined by the force of air applied, the rhythm of the reheating, and the shaping tools and processes, all under the skill of the worker. Very little air is actually necessary. Once the blowing iron came into use, more variety of shapes was possible, many of these having very long necks and elliptical bodies.

The Egyptians also understood the processes of glass cutting, engraving, and grinding. What they did not seem interested in, however, was making sheet glass. Nor were the Greeks much interested in this process—or in glass at all to any great extent. Instead, they were preoccupied with ceramics. The Greeks, who had a word for everything, had none for glass, awkwardly calling the material "melted stone."

It was the Romans who, fascinated by glass, built large furnaces to work the material. They made a multitude of vases but they also used glass for much of their intricate mosaic work, employing gold leaf to back transparent pieces of glass to provide a glittering effect—again, a very modern approach. While the Romans used sheet glass for windows, these were essentially small surfaces; they also used mica, alabaster, and shells for windows. Probably they cast their glass on a flat stone, with consequent unevenness and defects throughout the sheet. Although such glass was capable of transmitting light, it must have given a unique view of the outside world.

THE MEDIEVAL WINDOW

A medieval stained glass window ablaze in sunlight seems to splinter that light into a shower of colors that are

Portion of a medieval window.

augmented and muted as the light brightens and dims. Unlike those in a painting, the colors in stained glass are never static. For many stained glass fanciers, the medieval window epitomizes the craft.

There are a number of reasons to substantiate the claims made for the supremacy of early medieval stained glass. Every writer on glass points to the 12th and early 13th century windows as incomparable. The early Chartres windows are referred to as perfect and irreproachable. While it cannot be doubted that not only were the choices of colors and their placement aesthetically masterful, there was the superiority of the glass itself. For many, its color has never been surpassed.

At least, others would argue, until recently. Today's glass need not take a back seat to any century's product. But, having said that, there is something admittedly mystical about these early windows. Rough and uneven in texture, this very crudeness brought about prismatic effects and added enormously to the overall effect. The phrase "imprisoned sunlight" sums it up.

Medieval designers relied on action and rhythm as well as the mystical quality of the medium, tied in as it was with a religious overlay. Perhaps quaint, even awkward by today's standards, but always sincere in his direct and unstudied manner, the glass artist of the day was unique. His designs grew out of the shapes of the pieces of glass at hand, since the process of making glass was expensive. His technique belonged to his medium in a manner that is rare today, considering the tools and procedures at our disposal.

The earliest known representation of a stained glass window, the Wissembourg Disk with the head of Christ, goes back only as far as the late 11th century. Stained glass likely has some of its antecedents in the miniature paintings of Charlemagne's era. These "illuminated" portions of manuscripts do bear a certain resemblance to stained glass windows.

As we mentioned, the subjects of medieval windows—indeed the windows themselves—were religious in nature. For the medieval churchman, stained glass had a mystical significance. He saw in this substance that transformed the light passing through it a parallel to the divine word, transforming man by passing through his spirit. This religious overlay categorized the medium and left it imprisoned for centuries as a non-secular art form.

THE VICTORIAN PERIOD

Much of the stained glass work done in this country toward the end of the 19th century and quite a lot done right up through the 1920s and '30s might be classified as neo-Victorian.

The name does not so much represent a style as a convenience—there was a pragmatic aesthetic involved. In Victorian homes, stained glass windows were meant to fit a specific opening and to let in light. There are a limited number of such areas. Staircase landings offered a particularly good opportunity for stained glass. Front door panels were also considered appropriate, especially since the obscuring effect of the colored glass would offer a degree of privacy. Glass was intended to harmonize with other decorative features of the surroundings.

Many people today equate the term Victorian with old-fashioned, if not antiquated. What they are probably judging are mass-produced imitations of Victorian style. The Victorian ideal—nature and natural forms—still presents ever-fresh and lovely motifs, certainly as far as stained glass is concerned.

Detail from a design by Edward Burne-Jones for a window. Rottingdean Parish Church, England. Note the calm, almost dreamy expression of these ethereal creatures and the lovely flow of line, both painted and leaded, the one complementing the other.

A great number of Victorian windows demonstrate this. The medallion window was an especially popular design. It had a squared background in the center of which was a round area of glass containing some type of central focus, either a detailed leaded design or a painting. Ultimately these windows were so duplicated and imitated that their vitality was diluted. But it was from this style that the great works of John LaFarge and Louis Comfort Tiffany came into being.

THE TIFFANY ERA

For the new glass aesthetic that emerged from the Victorian period, Louis Comfort Tiffany's name is recognizably the standard bearer. The Victorian concept, frozen in a dead end of stained glass by-the-yard, was fading fast, unable to evolve further. Commercialism had ended its pretensions of validity as an art form. Studio after studio was grinding out variations of the same theme under the marketplace imperative that what had sold well once was worth repeating indefinitely.

Tiffany was more aesthete than handcrafter. He was also a practical businessman whose interests covered many decorative media. While not setting himself up as a representative of American glassworking, he did visualize himself as the man of the moment to enhance American tastes in art. This new art, or art nouveau, was his field of reference.

To extend the boundaries of expression through plastic forms, he began to investigate the possibilities of widening the range of his materials. For his experiments with glass he used not the European transparent glass, but the American opal or "milk glass" which had come into being as a substitute for china. By the 1870s there was a great deal of opal glass being used in decorative windows as well as in cups and saucers. It was available in a wide assortment of colors, textures, and densities. Eventually it became so popular that it threatened to outsell the imported "antique" variety.

Portion of a Tiffany window.

Whether it was Tiffany or LaFarge who invented the process of applying a distinctive iridescence to glass in addition to extending its hues and tones, is hard to say. Christopher Durand, another famous artist of the period, was also experimenting in this area, but Tiffany got the credit and this then brand new iridized glass now goes by his name. He called it "favrile glass," from the Latin "faber" for "smith" or "hand-worked."

The strength of color and variety of form finally achieved in favrile glass for many is still unequaled, although one would be hard put to say certain of the modern day glass companies have not come very close in their own output. Tiffany used his glass in vases and lamps as well as in windows. Many of his windows also incorporate details painted with enamels. He also used rocks, seashells, pebbles, and a host of other materials to enhance a specific effect. But these details never overwhelmed the glass. His employment of filigree overlays and even his ornate lamp bases were enhancements, never diminutions or compromises, of the basic medium of glass.

Graceful designs characterize his work, based mainly on a quantity of undulating break lines allowable by small pieces of glass. To achieve these he used—and possibly devised—a method of joining his small glass pieces together with copper foil. The more supple foil could preserve the multiple irregular borders of individual glass pieces in a more lace-like manner than lead came and, when these pieces were soldered to neighboring pieces, the double edges of foil were not as bulky as lead would be. Foil was also better suited to double and triple glazing, another Tiffany hallmark.

Foil provides a natural adaptation to the three-dimensional form. Each piece of glass wrapped in its thin edging, no matter how many surfaces it has, can be made to conform to its neighbor. Copper foil also solders well. Making such designs of small pieces of glass held together with copper foil and involving extreme technical skill has become known as the "Tiffany foil method."

STAINED GLASS AND YOU

We invite you to enter the exciting world of stained glass through the pages of this book. If you have never worked in stained glass or if you tried it and found you didn't have proper guidance to keep you going, you can start from scratch right here. If you are already working in the medium, you can add to your techniques and knowledge.

Few other crafts offer such rewards. The material is so dramatic that even as a beginner you can fabricate an end result that will give you a sense of fulfillment. In fact, it has been said that even terrible stained glass work still looks good because the glass itself makes such a powerful statement. That doesn't mean that terrible work should be your norm. It does mean that you can effect a working compromise with your material: do the best you can and the glass will take up the slack. As you get better your personality, rather than that of the glass, will come forth. But unless you try hard to make it happen, the final result can never be a total disaster. This means you will never waste time, material, or effort. Time spent is always beneficial as part of a learning process. Material can always be reused in another project as you advance in technique. Effort builds on effort and no step in this craft is ever taken in vain.

While the techniques involved in working in stained glass are exacting, the work itself (excepting certain specialized areas) is not difficult. It requires only the willingness to learn, the patience to follow directions, and the incentive to create. Since there are many good techniques, we cannot assume that our way of working with or teaching stained glass is the only way. We can say that it is the best way we have found over the years. In this regard, we caution that stained glass is both art and craft. Thus it becomes a discipline. You should follow instructions in sequence. To attempt any stained glass project with no idea of what steps to take can lead to disappointment and waste. There are beginners who thrive on plunging in without preparation.. Trial and error is their middle name. If you are one of these, you should probably stick with painting by numbers.

Often we have heard people say, "I really would like to try stained glass but it looks so hard. And I'm not artistic." It isn't, and you don't have to be. Anyone can learn to cut glass in half an hour. And some of the newer cutters practically do the job for you anyway. Believe us, once you've experienced the fun of scoring glass and having it break precisely where you want it to, you will have trouble letting the cutter out of your hand. As for not being artistic, that's no problem at all. In fact, it can be an advantage. Artists in other fields coming to glass attempt to apply principles that are ineffective where glass is concerned. Lastly, don't assume that because you "can't draw a straight line," you can't design. Anyone can design for glass. Use a ruler to draw some straight lines, a compass to produce a circle, and put them all together. Draw a square, put a diamond in it, and a circle around it. You now have a design that, transposed into glass colors of your choice, will make you proud.

From there, as one student said, "I can create a world."

A more contemporary stained glass window design.

CHAPTER 3

Cutting, Scoring, Running, and Breaking Glass

HAND CUTTING

Many individuals are afraid of handling glass, much less cutting it. An experienced glass cutter scoring and breaking glass so the piece comes out as calculated can be a marvel to observe. Most commercial shops work not with stained glass, but with clear window glass which is usually easier to deal with.

Yet anyone can learn to cut glass in a matter of 30 minutes or less. Timidity in dealing with this material is not a bad thing; too often familiarity breeds, if not contempt, at least carelessness. We have successfully taught elderly people on shipboard to cut glass in 30 minutes on a rough sea with the ship heaving and yawing.

The first thing to learn about glass cutting is that there is no right or wrong way to do it. Preferences abound, especially determined by the strength of your hand or arm, whether you are right- or left-handed, how good your eyesight is, your age and overall strength, whether you are sitting or standing, what kind of cutter you are using, and, above all, what is most comfortable for you. Professional glass cutters tend to use straight cutters and draw the hand toward, rather than away from the body. But that's not the only way to go, as we shall see.

Paradoxically, the primary objective in glass cutting is to keep from breaking the glass. This means you don't want to use so much strength moving the cutter over the surface that the material flies to pieces under you. Enthusiasm is a fine thing, but where glass is concerned, moderation is more apt to provide a result to your taste. You must make a score deep enough to allow the line to run, but not so deep that the glass breaks from the pressure or results in cut edges that are chipped and nicked. Such edges will be difficult to deal with later.

SCORING THE GLASS

What do we mean by scoring? Keep in mind that the term glass cutting is a misnomer. Glass is not really cut, although there are individuals who claim they can actually cut glass with a scissors under water. (We've never actually seen this done.) In fact, glass—being a liquid not a solid—is subject to the laws of hydraulics: a pressure supplied on one portion gets transmitted overall. This is especially true where such pressure is defined. A glass cutter, then, does not cut glass in the sense of shearing or sawing. Rather it is a force generator. The wheel of the cutter plows a furrow or fissure in the glass surface, weakening the surface along that line. This first step is called scoring. Step two is applying the proper secondary force to make the glass break out along that line. You can see how important it is to make a good score. If you fail, the force you apply to break out the piece can cause the glass to break badly or not at all.

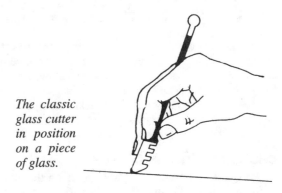

The classic glass cutter in position on a piece of glass.

Interestingly, the score that yields a good strong edge may be, if not invisible on the glass surface, at least difficult to see. This depends to an extent on the type of glass you are scoring. Opalescent glass will show a score line more readily than more transparent antique or hand-blown glass or window glass. Many times the score you make will only be seen by looking into, not over the surface. A good score should stand the fingernail test—running your fingernail over it should let you feel it as a definite fissure, not just a scratch. Such a fissure should reflect light and appear as a continuous narrow band from one border of the glass to another.

You should not apply so much pressure when you score as to have glass chips or dust fly out along the final result. In other words, you can't be too emphatic or too timid and it will take you a little time to find the proper amount of pressure to use for a good score. Practicing with window glass will give you an idea of how much pressure is best, though even here you will find that pressure will vary with the types of stained glass you'll be scoring later. (Practice on scrap single strength window glass from a commercial shop in your area.) The same pressure you use on opalescent glass may well cause a more fragile French antique to shatter under the cutter or an English streaky may not be affected enough to break the score out at all.

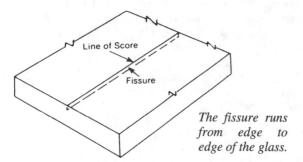

The fissure runs from edge to edge of the glass.

This does not mean that a deep score won't be effective in breaking glass along its length. Glass can be broken out along a gouge or sometimes even along a scratch. But the edges will not usually be clean. Such edges should be ground or belted to remove the nicks that will inevitably appear and make the glass harder to work with later.

CHOOSING A GLASS CUTTER

There are a multitude of glass cutters on the market. Before you commit to one, try out the various types. Your supplier may have samples for this purpose; you should at least ask to see a couple of styles. The day of the single cutter used by everyone is long past. For many individuals, the pistol-grip oil cutter is ideal—it allows even pressure on the forearm and wrist and provides a more natural grasp for the hand than the classic straight cutter (though we prefer the latter). There are several styles of pistol-grip cutters, some heavier than others.

The pencil type cutter allows the hand a familiar grip since it is held, as you might imagine, like a pencil. The classic straight cutter used by most professionals takes a bit more practice to master. It is held with the index and third finger on the flat spot on the handle and is supported by the thumb underneath. Such cutters may also have an

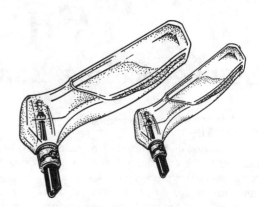

One type of pistol grip cutter which has since been improved upon. The clear plastic handle contains an oil reservoir as is usual with these types of cutters. The handle is most effectively gripped with the thumb on top and the other four fingers around it.

oil reservoir while others do not. The choice is yours, but remember that the cutter is your most important piece of equipment and a poor choice, while not necessarily committing yourself to discomfort, will cost money to replace. The average price for a good oil cutter runs $20 to $30, so it would behoove you to get it right from the start.

Using the pistol grip cutter. If you use two hands (and many elderly people find this easier), make sure the glass you are cutting is positioned so it will not move. Glass may be cut either by pushing the cutter or pulling it toward the body with the pistol grip cutter.

To further complicate your choice, there are soft glass cutters and hard glass cutters. This designation applies to the wheel, not the cutter itself. Any cutter will usually

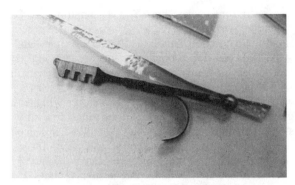

The classic cutter with ball for tapping and grozzing bar teeth. This cutter also has been fitted with a palm rest so it supports your hand. (Courtesy Fletcher-Terry Co.)

score any piece of glass; it's a question of pressure and wear. If you attempt to score opalescent (hard) glass with a soft glass cutter, you will have to use more pressure (thus more labor) to do the job, and even at that you may get a poor score. Cutters are labeled according to the type of wheel attached. All cutters score from a wheel attached to an axle. Such wheels or "heads" are replaceable. For general cutting, a carbide wheel is best. Such a wheel will do equally well on opalescent as on cathedral glass; on plate as on single strength or double strength window glass. Carbide cutters are generally more expensive than steel-wheel cutters but in the long run they are worth the money.

CUTTING WHEELS

Cutting wheels are honed to various angles. Standard cutters offered in hardware stores have wheels honed to 120° or 124°. This is a good angle for glass ranging in thickness from .063 to .093 inches.

While flaking during a score can occur with any wheel, sharp-angled wheels (under 120°) are most likely to cause it. Flaking (or chipping) can be delayed by wiping the area of the score line with a cloth dampened with kerosene or light oil. Oil cutters do this automatically, which is one advantage to their use. It is important to avoid flaking during scoring because flaking will affect the quality of the fissure and can lead to chipping which can cause problems with the edge later.

To determine the best wheel angle for a specific glass, start with any cutter, say with a standard 120° wheel. Score the glass using the maximum non-crushing force. If you are cutting thin glass and the wheel crushes it, switch to a sharper-angled wheel. The maximum non-crushing force will be less. If the score seems right but a good breakout doesn't occur, use a higher-angled wheel. Here the maximum non-crushing force will be greater, but a deeper fissure will be made. For those doing work that requires the best cutter wheel for the best result, testing is a very practical matter. For the hobbyist, it's probably not worth the time involved, though as you progress to save time and energy in the cutting work, you might refer back to the test results.

To get the best results from the cutting wheel, maintain the cutter in as vertical a position as you can, allowing the wheel the best purchase on the glass surface. Holding the cutter at a slant will give you a very poor score which can be extremely frustrating. All cutters should be held straight up and down no matter how you grip the handle.

CUTTING FORCE AND SPEED

The force applied to the cutter is not the only factor in the scoring equation. The applied pressure is affected by the wheel angle and the condition of the wheel. A cutter wheel in poor shape (from going over scores or other misuse) will yield a disappointing (unusable) score every time. Regardless of the wheel angle, the maximum force that can be applied through the cutter is easily defined: it is the greatest force that can be used without breaking the glass. This does not mean when the score becomes a white gritty line, or that if chips and glass dust are foaming up from below you have not exceeded the maximum force. We consider this condition equivalent to breaking the glass. Most beginners don't have this problem because they are wary of applying too much force. In their case, the force may be so far below maximum that it is practically useless. The best score is clean of glass chips and barely visible when looking at it from above.

Obviously practice is essential to get the feel of applying the maximum cutting force without destroying the glass. Not only must the proper force be applied, it should be maintained uniformly for the full length of the score. If the force varies, the depth of the fissure will vary and the quality of the break will be affected. The score should be made continuously from one edge of the glass to another—you can't stop in the middle to get a fresh grip on the cutter or blow your nose. When you get to the opposite glass edge, the wheel should run off but the force should be considerably less. You don't want the wheel bounding off the glass so hard that the cutter hits the table with a thonk. A few cuts like this will disable the cutter wheel and may well break the entire piece of glass. It's wise to lessen the force of the cut as you approach the glass edge.

The speed of the cut will also affect the force you apply. In general, the faster the cutting wheel rolls, the deeper the score will be. However, there is an inverse relation between force and speed. As the speed is increased, the force must be decreased to avoid breaking the glass or gouging it. At the same time, again in general, the faster the score is made (below maximum non-crushing force), the better the score. There is less wavering of the hand in this instance and that means a truer score line. Again, maintain uniform speed throughout the scoring process.

If the score is inadequate (if the breakout does not occur or if it occurs badly), attempt a new score with increased force. Never redo the same score. A score can be made only once. Going over a score line will damage the cutting wheel, can fracture the glass when you least expect it and cut you, and will almost always give a bad breakout.

THE CUTTING SURFACE

A piece of rug or the wood of a work tabletop may be used as a cutting surface. Any work surface should be flat and clean of glass chips from prior scorings. This is extremely important because glass chips will not only scratch the piece you are working on, but just one, acting as a little fulcrum, can break the work into unplanned pieces as you apply pressure to score. One ingenious surface is provided by The Morton System and consists of a plastic grid with multiple boxes where glass chips from prior cuttings fall, so the surface remains smooth and clean. If you are using felt to cover the work surface, the felt should not be more than 1/16" thick. If the surface cover is too thick, it will hamper your cutting because most of the force will be absorbed by the covering.

The height of the work surface should suit your height: too high and your arm will soon tire, too low and your back will begin to give out. The work surface height should allow you to score comfortably without having to strain or constantly change position. Average work surfaces measure 36" to 38" from the floor. Measure what is comfortable for you by standing at an invisible table surface and raising your arms from the elbows down to feel what is comfortable.

CUTTING STANCE

We recommend that glass cutting be done standing, though it is certainly possible to cut from a sitting position, even from a wheelchair. You'll get optimum force in a standing position and the work surface, where possible, should be chosen on this basis. If you are right-handed, stand with your left foot slightly forward and your right foot turned not quite at right angles to it. This will shift your balance toward your right arm which is where you want your cutting strength to be. This stance will also angle your body so you don't pull the cutter toward your stomach (assuming you are using the pull rather than push method). The free space allows your wrist to move smoothly from the initial point of the cut to the end of the cut line. If you are left-handed, reverse this stance.

If you must cut from a sitting position, use the weight of your torso rather than your whole body to get pressure. This is a bit more difficult and takes more practice but will work. Try not to use too much wrist pressure by itself because your arm will quickly tire. The force should come from your shoulder, backed by the weight of your upper body. Whether sitting or standing, experiment to find the most effective way to coordinate weight, balance, and wrist and arm motion. Generally all these factors fall into place at one time.

SCORING BY PUSHING OR PULLING

We like to use our cutter by starting at the far border of a piece of glass and pulling the cutter toward us while holding the glass steady with the other hand. This way we can see where we are coming from. Where we are going is partially obscured by the hand holding the cutter, but this is not an obstacle. With the pushing method, start at the border nearest you and push the cutter away from your body toward the far border. When pushing, it is not always necessary to hold the glass in place because the pressure applied at more of a right angle will generally keep the glass from moving. With pushing, you have a completely unobstructed view of where you are going. The choice is a matter of individual comfort and training, as long as the pressure is uniform and the glass surface is clean. If the glass is dusty or wet or (heaven help us) oily, the cutter will be impeded along its way and the glass very likely ruined.

It's always a good idea to clean the glass before pushing or pulling the cutter along its length to prevent skipping on the score line and other unfriendly maneuvers. Use a residue-free cleaner to remove lint, dust, and the protective coating manufacturers sometimes add. Probably the best cleaner is soap and water with crumpled newspaper to wipe the surface dry. The glass cutter wheel should also be clean and should revolve easily on its axle. If you are using an oil cutter, the lubrication will take place automatically. If you are not using an oil cutter, keep the cutter in a baby food jar with a piece of steel wool soaked in kerosene at the bottom. The steel wool cushions the cutter wheel from hitting the glass bottom and becoming damaged and the kerosene keeps the wheel clean. With this type of storage, the cutter (or cutters, since such a jar can accommodate any number of cutters) will be easily accessible and remain usable for a long time.

If you are not using an oil cutter, you may want to brush a special cutting oil on the glass along the line of the projected cut. There are several cutting oils on the market, though since the advent of the oil cutter, this technique has pretty much diminished. The remains of this oil will have to be cleaned off the glass before leading or foiling. A thin water line over glass that has been thoroughly cleaned will also tend to lubricate the wheel of the cutter as it moves along. Having said all this, we feel that if the glass surface is clean, you should be able to make precise and effective score lines using the cutter by itself as long as you are using the correct wheel for the type of glass.

WHICH SIDE TO SCORE?

Before scoring any piece of glass, examine it to make sure you are cutting on the "right" side. Unlike window glass, some stained glass has an easy and a difficult cutting surface. Obviously a granite-backed or pebbled surface should not be chosen unless you are a masochist. Most stained glass has one side that is easier to score than the other. It depends on how the glass is made. The general rule is that the smoother of the two sides is usually the best for scoring, but it is sometimes difficult to decide which side is smoother. Remember, glass is a liquid and has no grain. If you are uncertain which is the best side to score, make a test score on each side of the glass and break it.

This test is especially recommended on sheets of flashed stained glass where one color has been laid on top of another. Here you want to cut on the white or under-color side. To find which side is which, hold the glass edge up to the light so you can see which side has had color applied. If you still can't tell, chip away a small corner. Keep in mind that flashed glass doesn't always have a color placed on white; red could be flashed on yellow, for example, in which case the yellow side might be the best cutting bet.

PRACTICE, PRACTICE, PRACTICE

Get some clear window glass scraps from the local glazier (glaziers throw away a lot of scrap) and practice scoring with the glass cutter. First practice straight lines, moving the cutter slowly at first and increasing your speed gradually while keeping the cutter under control. After straight lines, try wavy lines, curves, and inside curves (half circles against a glass edge). Remember to keep the cutter as perpendicular as possible and listen for the "cry" of the glass. If you don't hear the noise the cutter makes over the surface, chances are the score is inadequate. Single strength window glass is very easy to cut so this procedure will not only provide you with the necessary practice, it will also give you the confidence to approach the more difficult process of scoring stained glass.

Remember to clean off the work surface each time (with a brush, not the back of your hand) and to have a waste basket ready to catch the debris. It also helps to have a bandage or two handy in case you scratch yourself (looking for one while dripping blood on the rug is counter-productive).

SAFETY FACTORS: HAS ANYBODY SEEN MY FINGERS?

All of us who teach glass have had students who appear to utilize the material for self-destruction. The most common carelessness is brushing glass crumbs off the work table with your hand. This will quickly provide multiple puncture wounds of a nice span and variety.

Putting your eyeball directly to the score line you are tapping can make you the center of attention in no time. If the splinter of glass that flies into your eye doesn't allow you ample pain, the glass you were holding at the time that drops on your foot probably will.

The act of bending over in front of the glass bin where the corner of a sheet is sticking out can parallel the usual backside crease with one even more extensive.

Here are a few common possibilities:

1) You've cut a piece of glass in a nice square shape. You can't resist running your finger around the edges to see if they are sharp. They always are.

2) Trying to find the perfect color to go with one already chosen, you hold several pieces of glass up to the light at the same time. This puts them right over your face. One is cracked and falls apart. Bingo, you become the creative blend.

- **Don't** wear sandals or any open footwear.

- **Don't** wear gloves. Glass can slip from gloves.

- **Do** wear comfortable clothing.

- **Don't** eat or drink at the work table

- **Don't** work in an enclosed space, especially when soldering.

- **Don't** hand break a piece of glass if the corners or edges are facing your palms.

- **Do** wear safety glasses when at the grinder.

- **Don't** do any soldering if you are pregnant.

- **Do** wash your hands thoroughly when finished working.

- **Do** keep the workspace uncluttered and clean of glass crumbs. Use a brush for this purpose.

- **Do** keep the stored glass sheets level with the floor, not stacked.

- **Do** check with your doctor about any allergies or other health problems that may be associated with working in stained glass.

3) A variation of #2. You have looked at five or six pieces of glass but none of them is just right. You select another and pile the rejects on the table in front of you. As the pile grows, it becomes more and more unstable. One of two things happens. Either you can move very quickly or you can't.

4) You select a large sheet from the bin. It sounds cracked but it looks okay and you know you can get it to the table on time. Guess who's on the table?

5) On the surface of the scrap glass bucket is the perfect piece for your new creation, but as you reach for it, it slides just a bit below the hundreds of pieces there. You grab for it anyway because time is short. So are your fingers.

6) Though the top bin is higher than you can reach, you don't bother to stand on something to pull out the sheet you want. It comes out smoothly in your grip, along with its sneaky neighbor and you find you are literally beside yourself.

It isn't only glass that can be useful for discovering how extensive your hospital benefits are. Many practitio-

ners of self-destruction prefer the soldering iron. Grasping it by the broiling barrel while paying attention elsewhere will allow you to entertain everyone with some of your favorite dance steps. The variant here is hot solder under a fingernail.

Taking food or drink into the workspace nourishes only a latent death wish. I've heard of the individual who drank his flux instead of the scotch and soda he'd placed alongside it. Quite possibly he said, "Here's how," before going into spasm. Liquids can also become contaminated by oxides in the air.

This all sounds as if working with glass is tantamount to putting in time in a fireworks factory. Not so. Most beginners approach glass with timidity, expecting to find it dangerous. When they find it isn't, they themselves become dangerous. They forget that glass doesn't so much act as react. The notion of taking glass for granted affects advanced workers and professionals as well. An acquaintance who is an expert in glass one day carelessly reached into the scrap bin and cut all the tendons in his hand, putting him out of action for almost a year.

The point is, you have to realize what you are doing and think before you cut, tap, break, solder, foil, or lead. And keep an eye on what your neighbor is doing as well. He may be dangerous to others as well as himself. It is true that working with glass can be a tremendous emotional release, one that takes you out of yourself and the workaday world. But while it's fascinating to be carried away by the creative experience, it's not so fascinating to be carried away by ambulance.

SUMMARY ON GLASS CUTTING

1) Use a good cutter that you feel comfortable with.

2) Have a flat, firm support under the glass. This is particularly necessary for some antique sheets that may not lie flat. In such cases, you will have to rock the glass as you score.

3) Make sure the glass is clean with no glass crumbs from prior cuttings. If you use a mat under the glass, give it a good shaking over the wastebasket before cutting on it a second or third time.

4) Never go over a score.

5) Score from one glass edge to another and don't come off the glass with unnecessary force.

6) You may start a cut from slightly below one edge but then you must go back and continue the score line off the glass edge.

7) Use only enough pressure to make the score. On many glasses you will hear the cry of the glass as the cutter moves along its surface; that usually (though not always) indicates a successful score. However, on some glasses—particularly antique reds, oranges, and yellows—the cutter may make no noise even though the glass is being scored. Here you may have to use your fingernail to see if the score is there.

8) The cutter should move along the glass evenly. Many beginners cannot seem to control a side-to-side waver. This will give you an uneven score and a poor break.

9) It is not so much the pressure of your wrist that gives the requisite force to score properly as it is the pressure from your shoulder and body. Pressure will also depend on your cutting speed.

10) The glass thickness shouldn't influence the amount of pressure needed to score properly as much as the angle of the glass cutter wheel. With the proper wheel angle, pressure can be mostly constant. If you are not using the proper wheel angle, certain glasses, particularly opalescents, will require more scoring pressure than other types of stained glass. Cutting a thin antique tint (1/16" or less) or a thick, uneven English streaky (some portions of which can exceed 1/4") is more a matter of the proper cutter than the amount of force.

11) Lubricating the score line can be done manually (if at all) or automatically with an oil cutter.

12) For safety's sake, break each score line as you make it and before making another score. Scoring a piece of glass weakens it and too many score lines may cause the glass to break where you least expect it.

BREAKING THE SCORE

Okay, you've learned all there is to know about scoring and you've got an entire studio full of glass with score lines going every which way. What's next?

Just scoring glass isn't the end result, of course. You have to break out the piece you want and use the excess for some other project. There are several ways to go about this.

Tapping

The most effective tapping method is to hold the glass securely in one hand with the score line uppermost between your fingers. Swing the tapper (usually the ball end of a glass cutter) against the bottom portion of the score line in quick firm strokes. Don't allow the glass to swing away as the ball hits it or you will lose most of the force of the tap. Tap along the entire length of the score line. As you tap you will see the score begin to run—deepening and becoming more apparent. Another reason to hold the glass firmly is that the two portions may separate when you least expect it. If the glass has not separated by the time the entire score has run, chances are the glass fracture is now so strong the two pieces can easily be separated by hand. Do not tap recklessly, holding the glass by a single edge. Chances are it will fall apart and one piece will hit the floor or your foot.

The tapper need not only be the ball end of a cutter. You can use the cutter's grozzing teeth (those notched edges) to tap with. This will not give as much of a blow as the ball, but for more delicate glass it might be just right. If you have scored a large piece of glass, tapping requires you to have your hand and part of your arm below the surface. It is imperative that you hold the glass with a good solid grip so you don't get cut when the pieces separate.

As you tap, if you see the run line begin to wander from the score line the piece may well be ruined. In this case your score line was probably not strong enough to support the tap. All you can do is try again and this time make your score line deeper.

Unfortunately, the tapping method is over-emphasized in many beginning classes and taught badly in the bargain. Most beginners simply either 1) peck at the glass or 2) whack it from the top as it sits on the table. All this will accomplish is 1) nothing at all and 2) smashed glass. Like most procedures in stained glass work, tapping takes practice and a sense of how glass reacts.

The Fulcrum Method

The fulcrum method is demonstrated by placing the handle of the straight cutter under the furthest end of the score away from you. Equal pressure is applied by hand to the surface of the glass on either side of the score.

This is a useful technique for moderate-to-large pieces of glass where a straight line or a very gentle curve is to be broken out. Raise the piece of glass on one end and place about 1/4" of the fulcrum directly beneath the score line. The fulcrum can be almost anything, from the back of a straight glass cutter to a straightened paper clip, depending on the thickness of the glass in question. With the fulcrum in place, press the glass firmly by hand from both sides equidistant from the score. The score will run and the glass will break at the proper line.

The thickness of the fulcrum is important here. For long scores, a thicker fulcrum may be necessary. Especially in the case of long scores you may hear a satisfactory crack only to discover that the score has not run all the way across. In this case you can turn the glass around, reposition the fulcrum on the other side, and redo the procedure.

No procedure is foolproof. Among the things that can go wrong are: too much pressure, too thick (or thin) a fulcrum, too shallow a score line, glass that was cracked, a fulcrum too far under the score or not far enough, or just plain bad luck. Any of these might cause the glass to go to pieces instead of nicely separating. If this happens, take a break rather than try another one right away.

Breaking by Hand

Essentially this is another fulcrum method. Hold the glass with your thumbs on either side of the score line and your other fingers folded into your palms. The corners of the glass should be well away from your body. The pressure during the breaking process is out and down, almost a rolling of the knuckles of one hand against those of the

other. If the glass won't break, don't force it, try a different method.

The Tabletop Method

With this method, open-toed sandals are definitely not advised. Place the glass over the edge of the table until the score line is parallel to the table edge. Raise the glass and snap it smartly downward. The piece you are holding will break off neatly as the leverage of the tabletop snaps the score. Large sheets of glass may be broken in this fashion with very little effort. Of course this is strictly for straight line cuts.

Breaking With Running Pliers

Running pliers are shaped to break out straight lines, especially when you are dealing with long thin pieces, though they can be used on any score that doesn't involve sharp curves. There are several different makes of running pliers on the market and before buying, try to test out the various types. The better running pliers have a set screw which enables you to set the jaws to compensate for various thicknesses of glass.

Running pliers are positioned with the center line of the pliers over the score. Not only for straight breaks, wavy lines and inside curves can be broken by gently squeezing the score from both ends.

Running pliers break out score lines by applying equal pressure to either side of the score. A line atop the pliers guides the placement of the tool to the score line. The jaws are applied with the convex upper one against the

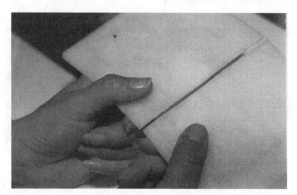

Hand breaks with the fingers curled underneath the glass to hold it firmly and snapping upwards.

upper glass surface, the concave jaw below; pressure is applied to the handles in a firm, steady grip, and presto, the score will run and the glass will break just where you want it to. Usually. If it doesn't, you may be applying too much pressure, the score is weak, the glass may be too thick, or the jaw spacing may be wrong. It takes more practice than you might think to get the hang of using running pliers, but once you find how convenient a tool they are, you'll wonder how you ever got along without them.

Breaking with Pliers

Pliers can be employed to good effect when the pieces are too small to be broken by any other method. Two pliers, one on either side of the score line, can break out the smallest piece of glass.

Grozzing the glass with pliers is a snipping-like action to chew the edge of the glass up to the score if it did not properly break or to remove sharp edges left by tapping.

Jaws are placed against the score in the center of the glass to apply a downwards pressure to that side of the glass. Two pairs of pliers can act as an extension of your fingers where very small pieces of glass are involved.

Some glass pliers grip the glass firmly with wide flat jaws and hold it securely. When used to break large pieces of glass, the technique is usually to lay the glass flat on the table and move it so the score line is just at the table's edge. Place the glass pliers' jaws at right angles up to the

score line, apply firm pressure, and pull out and down. If you've made a good score, the glass will break just where you want it to. It's best to use the tabletop as a stabilizer rather than holding the glass in your hand where it can't help but waver as you apply pressure. When using the tabletop, keep one hand firmly on the glass to immobilize it.

To some degree you can use any glass pliers as grozzing pliers since they all have sharp ridges cut into either jaw. However, the width of some jaws makes grozzing more awkward than when using grozzing pliers made for this purpose. The act of grozzing (filing, chewing, nipping away small pieces of glass from the edges) is an art in itself. Taken to the nth degree, grozzing isn't much different than carving. However, grozzing pliers are rarely used to break out score lines on large glass pieces because their jaws are too narrow for the job. Here wide-jawed glass pliers are best.

Breaking Plate Glass

Occasionally you may find a use for plate glass in your stained glass work, either to emphasize a portion of a design, to employ a clear thick surface, to act as a double-glazed unit, or to bevel. Again, several breaking methods can be applied, though success with any of them depends on the thickness of the glass. Ideally, plate glass can be broken by placing it flat on the table with the score line down and tapping from the unscored surface. Or you may want to double score (score the piece on both sides). Needless to say, the score lines must be precisely on top of one another or the piece will break unevenly.

A much more accurate method is to use the Fletcher Co.'s Plate Glass Breaker, a most unique tool. Here's how it's done:

1) Run the score on glass anywhere from 3/4" to 1". Fletcher recommends using a carbide cutter for the purpose (CA-B). The thicker the glass, the more essential it is to have a good score. The glass must be clean and the score continuous and uniform. Once the score has been made, pull the sheet of glass a few inches over the edge of the cutting table in the same direction as the score was made. Place the breaker tool on the glass with the screw knob down. Spread the two upper anvils as far apart as the glass permits, but keep them equidistant from the score.

2) Locate the center fulcrum directly under the score. Turn the lead screw with the knob so the fulcrum presses upward on the glass from below.

3) When splitting long narrow pieces (lengths six or more times the width) place a second breaker tool at the terminal end of the run and tighten the fulcrum screw slightly.

4) To break smaller pieces of glass, set the breaker tool on the table with the knob up. After scoring the glass, turn it over so the score is on the underside. Insert the glass in the breaker, align the score, spread the sliding anvils as far apart as possible, and turn the knob.

Caution: Always wear protective glasses and arm covering when running a break on heavy plate. We don't suppose anyone would try to break out a score in plate over their knee but don't kid yourself. We've seen two beginners try it. You're liable to be wearing a plate with this technique.

Breaking Out Circles

Circles are fun, but in order to best enjoy scoring and breaking them, you should first practice on single strength window glass. Circles can be cut freehand or by using a circle cutter. Circle cutters are of two basic types:

The suction cup circle cutter will let you concentrate on the score pressure as you move the cutter head on the glass and not be afraid of losing your anchor point on the glass halfway around the sweep. You can cut up to 23" diameter circles with ease.

those that use a central pivot with a variable arm, and those that use a stand with an arm that limits the diameter to the length of that arm. Either one will cut accurate circles.

Scoring the circle is not difficult with circle cutters but that's only half the battle. The more lengthy procedure is breaking the circle out of the glass. Here's where glass pliers come in handy. Breaking out a circle can be accomplished as follows:

1) Score the circle using whatever method you prefer.

2) Score tangential score lines to the major one. These lines should reach from the edge of the circle to the edge of the glass.

3) Use glass pliers to break these lines away.

Some workers add a step—after scoring their circle they turn the glass over and press firmly with their fingers all around the cut line. The purpose is to start a run. With thin glass, you may even be able to break out the circle completely, leaving the outside portion intact (this is a nice maneuver). However, with many stained glasses this procedure may only weaken the circle score line. When pressing on glass in this manner, make certain it's on a firm flat surface and that you don't press so hard that the glass shatters under you. Don't count on always being able to run the score in this manner, though it is certainly always worth a try.

You can break out the excess glass surrounding the circle easily enough with glass pliers, provided you don't try to get too much off at one time. How much is too much? If the circle breaks from the pressure of taking off the outside glass, that's too much. Next time, try scoring a few more tangential lines.

Don't be concerned about saving the glass you break away. Waste not, want not is not a proverb that applies to glass. To spend the time tapping out a circle is fine if you have that kind of time, but if you are involved in other projects or are running a commercial studio, you won't have the time. Besides, assuming the glass runs properly and, depending on the glass being used, it's not always

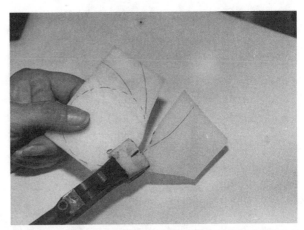

Turn the glass to position the running pliers on the opposite end of the same score and slowly squeeze again. If the glass doesn't break, do it again more firmly.

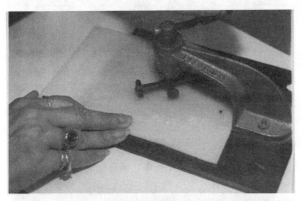

The lens type cutter will limit the size of the circle but will apply pressure on the wheel when you move the shaft downwards and turn the handle. It is best to brush oil on the glass where the score will be to lubricate the wheel. (Colurtesy Fletcher-Terry Co.)

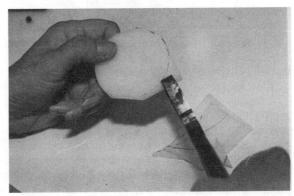

Finish removing glass around the circle with the breakers/grozzers.

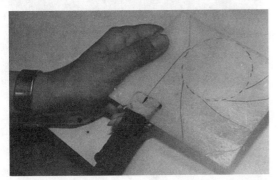

Slowly squeeze the running pliers to run the score from the edge back to the circle. Listen for a slight ping which will be the score moving back towards the circle.

The rough circle after using the runners and breakers/grozzers.

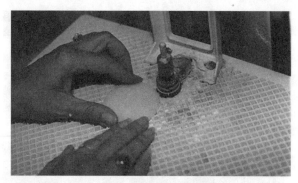

Grinding the jagged points to smooth the circle for foiling and accurate fitting.

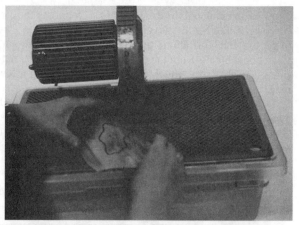

A saw is a luxury for those scores that would normally be impossible to make by hand and take too much time to grind. (Above and below: Courtesy Gemini Saw Co.)

easy to get glass to run in a circular fashion by tapping; usually a lot of irregularities are left on the edges which then must be sanded away. You'll get a much cleaner result using the pliers.

Breaking Out Inner Curves

These are probably the most difficult cuts to break out and in extreme cases only a glass saw will do the job. Whereas outer curves (such as circles) allow the pressure you apply to cause them to run to left and right pretty freely, inner curves will destroy the glass portion you desire by doing just this. Remember, glass is a fluid and pressure applied to one spot can transmit all over the surface. The best way to break out inner curves is to take out small pieces of glass, inching up to the final score line. Of course it depends on how extreme an inner curve you are dealing with. Gradual curves may be broken out in one piece and sometimes an entire section of an inner curve may be broken out by tapping, but usually tapping is dangerous in this situation since you are transmitting force that you are not fully controlling. In a sharp inner curve, the tap may cause the glass to run off the score and ruin the work.

The best procedure we have found for dealing with inner curves is to cut duplicates of the inner curve within the hollow of the curve itself. Run these mini curves into one another. Then, with grozzing pliers, break out each individual mini curve until you have cleared the entire area and are left with just the inner area you want. When breaking out the curve, grasp it with pliers at its narrowest portion and allow the tension to flow to the wider part which can better handle it. That will provide a more controlled break. The tendency is to grasp the mini curve at its center and pull it away. That can break everything. Use

If the sheet of glass is a problem to hand cut or that's the highlight piece of the project and it's the only piece you have, the saw such as the Taurus Ring saw shown, can be an invaluable aid to help you.

more and more care as you break out these little curves and get further and further into the hollow of the major curve. When you get to the point where you are close to the original score line, proceed even more cautiously. Here you may want to use grozzing pliers precisely for that purpose and grozz or nip away small pieces of excess just as if you were carving.

Of course if you have a glass saw the procedure is simpler, but even then you can't take the glass for granted. Using a saw, especially to cut inner curves, can try your patience. Besides, not too many beginners have a saw immediately to hand. A saw is a fine thing to use when making cuts that are impossible to cut by hand, but to depend on one for routine designing and production is, in our estimation, defeating the purpose of establishing your own skills and techniques. In the extreme case, you might as well just go out and buy someone else's work and save yourself any production problems whatsoever.

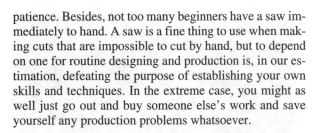

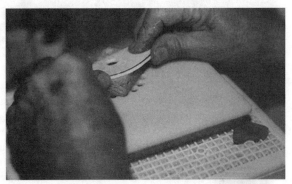

A hole can be made in a piece of glass by using bits on the grinder. Start by placing a wet sponge under the glass and holding the glass at a 45° angle and press it onto the edge of a 1/4" bit. The sponge will keep the glass cool and bit lubricated. Seat the bit into the glass. Rock the glass slowly around on the bit until it pops down over the shaft.

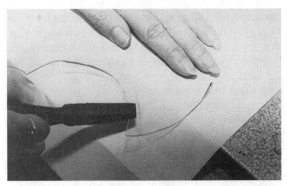

You can grozz the glass up to the score line or position the glass off the edge of the bench and carefully apply downward pressure almost to the breaking point on each end and in the middle of the score. By doing so you will start a subtle run at these three areas.

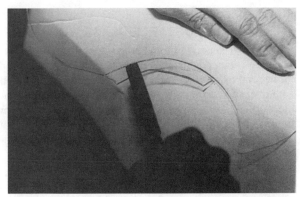

The inside curve has had enough pressure applied at the right end to partially break off. The left side is ready for breaking. By holding it off the edge of the bench you will be able to snap downwards and backwards to complete the break.

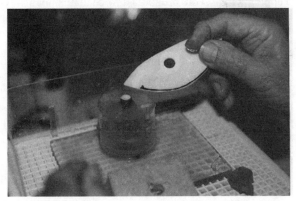

The completed hole with the center glass remaining in the open top of the bit.

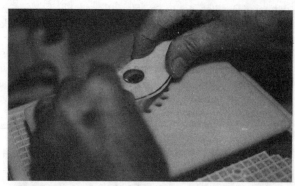

The hole can be enlarged to the required size by circling around the shaft of the bit.

For less extreme inner curves, use the same procedure, reducing the number of inside cuts. The cuts can also be larger and you can break them out right up to the actual score line without grozzing. As usual, successful scoring and breaking depends on the glass. Greens, reds, and yellows tend to follow a score line poorly (depending on the manufacturer), especially with inner curves. On the other hand, certain French antique glasses will break perfectly. In stained glass work, as in so many other artistic endeavors, it can be the luck of the draw.

Breaking Out Long Strips

As we mentioned earlier, long strips are usually the province of running pliers or small fulcrums; we mention them here to caution against tapping long score lines. Tapping a long score produces a force that is not always under your control. You may find the run line varying on and off the score line (leading to very jagged edges that you have to grind forever) and possibly running in its own direction entirely. This can be pretty frustrating. If you insist on designing with long strips, don't put yourself in a bind by also insisting on tapping them out. Get a good pair of running pliers instead and above all, make steady firm scores using a ruler or some other straight edge. (See Tools)

INCOMPLETE SCORING AND OTHER PROBLEMS

Each score you make *must* go from one edge of the glass to another edge, with the exception of an inside curve. Certainly don't consider making a score and stopping in the middle of the glass. As a beginner you should avoid difficult cuts such as C cuts and certainly V cuts (best done with a saw if you insist on doing one). There are ways to break V and C cuts without a saw, but it's best not to throw yourself this kind of curve right away. Many glass professionals don't believe C and V cuts belong in the glass field anyway.

Points and Thin Cuts

One of the more common beginner designing errors is clustering a lot of points together. It's common because initially you may not be thinking glass-wise. If you design seven or eight converging lines and hope to establish a common meeting place, the end result is going to be a big blob of solder. If you must have converging lines, keep them to a maximum of three. If you want lines to cluster, leave enough room for each to remain clearly visible when soldering, whether you intend to lead or foil them. Foiling is more design-friendly with converging lines (depending on your cutting technique) but even foil has its limitations and when soldered, the foiled glass is going to crowd its neighbor at their points.

Not thinking such thin cuts through to the final glass result is a common error and leads to a lot of adjusting later on. Not all this adjusting can be considered an artistic achievement when you finally get done backing and filling. It's best to do all your considering beforehand, since adjusting lines on paper is much easier than trying to do so in glass later.

THE MORTON PORTABLE GLASS WORKSHOP

There isn't enough room here to describe in detail this ingenious device which has been modified and extended far beyond its original boundaries. When it first appeared a number of years ago, it was a method of creating portable working space especially for the apartment dweller or homeowner with limited space. Today it continues that original purpose but has grown to be practically a complete workshop on its own.

The plastic grid base forms pockets that serve as locking devices for a number of special tools. The pockets also provide receptacles for glass chips (rather than the floor). This system allows very odd shapes to be cut and broken out with ease while the egg-crate surface holds debris such as chips and glass dust. To clean out the plastic pockets, use a vacuum cleaner or just tip the plastic over a piece of newspaper.

Also from the Morton Co. is the Safety Break System, which allows you to break out almost impossible cuts by a clever slow process, using pressure over the surface at multiple contact points. The control possible with the system means less scrap and less grinding or grozzing of the final piece.

The basic components of the Morton System are the running button and the pressure block. It is also possible to cut plate glass with the Morton System using a special tool for the purpose. If you are a beveler, you will find this very helpful. Using their plate glass breaker, we were able to cut both 1/4" and 3/8" plate into curves and angles that were quite spectacular. Naturally, plate glass takes more time and multiple pressures than does regular glass, but when the glass finally does break, the resulting edges are usually flush (except for a possible slight fringe of glass on the back surface from surface tension, which can be readily wiped away with the small abrasive stone that comes with the tool).

Morton's booklet gives a thorough schooling in its methods, tools, and philosophy—from the basic glass surface to the light box they can supply, including their layout blocks and plate glass cutter. While these devices are subsidiary to more extensive endeavors on your own, the Morton System, with its ingenious additions, is a good glass introduction.

CHAPTER 4
The Soldering Process

Soldering is a process for joining specific metals through heat. Not all metals will solder: steel and aluminum are examples of two that will not. In general, metals do not adhere directly. Instead, an alloy (a mixture of metals) is used to bind them. The amount of heat necessary to accomplish this process varies with the process. Brazing is one such method, requiring a special brazing rod and blow torch; soldering is another, requiring a special iron. Solder, an alloy of tin and lead, "wets" the particular metals we use in stained glass and enables them to join firmly together. Lead, copper, brass, and tin are some of the metals we use in stained glass, and soldering is the process we use to "glue" them together in a tight unbreakable bond.

SOLDERING PREREQUISITES

In order for the soldering process to take place, certain things are necessary.

Solderability: The metal must be solderable. If it is not, it may be coated over with a secondary metal for the

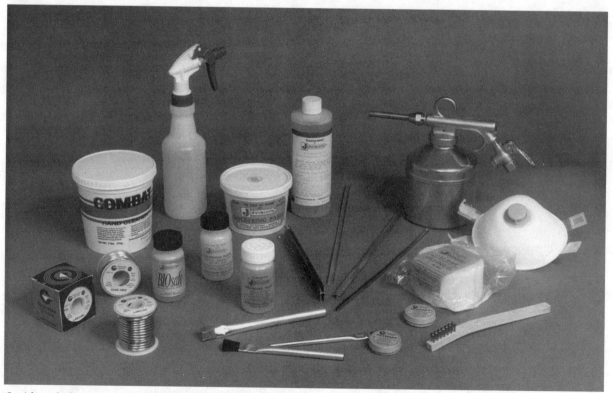

Incidentals for use with the soldering process: in the foreground are flux brushes for applying flux and a wire brush for cleaning the lead. There is a mask for fumes and various fluxes (pastes and liquids) and several strips of lead came. (Courtesy Gardiner Metal Co.)

purpose. Steel, for example, is not solderable but when coated over with zinc (galvanized), it becomes solderable. Reinforcing rods or bars used in stained glass have been so treated to make them usable. Tin, sheet metal, bronze, copper, brass, and white metal are solderable. The surfaces of the metals to be joined must be clean or the soldering process will not take place.

Heat: The soldering process occurs when the metal pieces to be soldered are heated above the melting point of the solder itself. The heat source must rapidly reach a temperature of about 100° over the melting point of the solder. Since lead has a fairly low melting point, care must be taken when soldering to heat lead came without melting it. Holes in the came from overheating during the soldering process is a common cause of frustration among beginners.

Flux: Flux is a chemical that loosens the oxides from the metal to be soldered and allows the molten solder to flow onto the surfaces of the metals to be joined. A good flux must fulfill a number of requirements:

- It should be readily applied, preferably with a brush. Flux is easier to use in liquid form than as a paste and affords quicker maximum penetration of the metal surfaces in this state.
- It should rapidly deoxidize the metals to be joined. Deoxidizing begins as soon as the flux is applied and should be complete in a few seconds, depending on the thickness of the oxide coat that has built up on the metal surfaces. If the metals to be joined have particularly dirty surfaces, flux alone may not clean them. You may have to scrub the surfaces with a stiff metal bristle brush, then apply flux.
- A good flux will reduce the surface tension of the molten solder, permitting it to flow freely over the deoxidized surfaces of the metals to be joined. In this way, a smooth wide bond of solder is laid down. Flux permits solder to flow on its own so it needn't be "chased" with the soldering iron.
- It should not smoke, fume, bubble, hiss, steam, or spit. There should be no evidence of harsh or toxic odors.
- It should never be so strong as to pit the soldering iron tip. Therefore, acid core fluxes are not recommended or necessary in stained glass work.
- It should clean up easily and should not leave a cloudy layer on the glass or a sticky scum on the

lead joints. It should leave as little residue as possible. You will appreciate this at cleanup time.
- It should not leave dangerous elements behind as byproducts of the soldering process.
- It shouldn't be caustic to the skin. This doesn't mean you should treat flux as an indifferent chemical. If you get it on your skin, wash it off immediately. Different skins react differently and yours might not like being fluxed.

Solder: The solder alloy percent is the tin to lead ratio. We use either 60/40 or 50/50. The more precious metal (tin) is always placed first in the ratio. It's a matter of choice which you prefer. The less ratio of tin to lead allows the solder to set up faster once the proper soldering temperature is reached.

The solder flows over the surfaces of the opposing metals by capillary action to produce (hopefully) neat smooth joints. A proper solder for the purpose should flow smoothly over the heated surfaces. It should not be necessary to keep going over a joint with the iron to even out solder that has points sticking up or that is flowing more on the table than the work, or that is flowing unevenly. If you have to keep fussing with a solder joint to make it functional and professional looking, something is wrong with the solder, the flux, the metals to be joined, the soldering equipment, or (more likely) your technique.

Welding is another process for joining metals, but it is not used in stained glass work. Brazing is closely associated with welding because of the high temperatures required to do the job. Both brazing and welding involve joining metals of higher melting points than lead. The only way lead strips can be joined together in a metal-to-metal bond is through soldering.

CHARACTERISTICS OF SOLDER

When we use the term "solder" or "soldering," we are not speaking of so-called "liquid solder" or "cold solder." Both of these are really glues and have no place in stained glass work.

A 60/40 solder is one containing 60% tin and 40% lead. A 50/50 solder contains equal amounts of lead and tin. Either or both can be used, depending on how fast you want the metal bond to appear. A 50/50 solder allows less time to fuss with a joint than the slower 60/40. It depends on what you get used to, but beginners should become familiar with the idiosyncrasies of both types, which can only be done by working with them.

Melting Points of Tin-Lead Alloys

Composition % Tin % Lead	Complete Liquidation Points Degrees F.	Solidification Points Degrees F.	Composition % Tin % Lead	Complete Liquidation Points Degrees F.	Solidification Points Degrees F.
0–100.0	620	620	52.5– 47.5	403	358
2.5– 97.5	608	570	55.0– 45.0	392	358
5.0– 95.0	597	522	57.5– 42.5	381	358
7.5– 92.5	586	475	60.0– 40.0	370	358
10.0– 90.0	576	435	62.5– 37.5	361	358
12.5– 87.5	565	397	63.0– 37.0	358	358
15.0– 85.0	554	358	65.0– 35.0	360	358
17.5– 82.5	545	358	67.5– 32.5	363	358
20.0– 80.0	536	358	70.0– 30.0	367	358
22.5– 77.5	525	358	72.5– 27.5	372	358
25.0– 75.0	514	358	75.0– 25.0	378	358
27.5– 72.5	504	358	77.5– 22.5	383	358
30.0– 70.0	496	358	80.0– 20.0	390	358
32.5– 67.5	486	358	82.5– 17.5	396	358
35.0– 65.0	477	358	85.0– 15.0	403	358
37.5– 62.5	468	358	87.5– 12.5	410	358
40.0– 60.0	460	358	90.0– 10.0	415	358
42.5– 57.5	448	358	92.5– 7.5	424	358
45.0– 55.0	437	358	95.0– 5.0	432	358
47.5– 52.5	424	358	97.5– 2.5	441	358
50.0– 50.0	414	358	100.0– .0	450	450

COMPLETE LIQUIDATION POINT: Point at which all is liquid.
SOLIDIFICATION POINT: Point at which the alloy begins to change from the solid to the liquid.

Lead melts at 621°F and tin at 450°F. However, combined in solder form, they melt at 361°F. To get a completely molten state of combinations of the two is to run a gamut of temperatures between the solid to partly solid, partly liquid, to the fully liquid state. For example, a solder of 20/80 (20% tin, 80% lead) would have to be heated to 531°F to be completely liquid. This is a very high temperature for use in stained glass, indeed almost as high as the melting temperature of lead. This particular ratio (20/80) liquefies slowly and sluggishly and has a temperature range of 361°F to 531°F before it is entirely liquid. Such a ratio forms more of a paste than a liquid and is used for plumbing work, although it is really too sluggish even for that. Certainly it is too unwieldy for the pin-point soldering of lead joints, which requires a fast melt and fast freeze with as little heat as possible. On the other hand, a 60/40 solder need be heated only to approximately 370°F before it achieves a completely liquid state; 50/50 solder a little less. A 60/40 becomes solid again at 361°F, leaving a working zone temperature of 9°F. This is exactly right for some stained glass professionals, but too long a working zone for others who prefer the shorter melt/freeze zone of 50/50 solder.

One extreme combination of tin and lead goes immediately to a liquid from a solid with no working zone at all. It is practically instantaneous and therefore useless in stained glass. This is a combination of 63% tin and 37% lead. The instant shift from solid to liquid is called the "eutectic point" of the solder. We mention it merely to round out this discussion.

SUMMARY

The more tin you add to lead, the lower the melting point of the tin/lead combination and the shorter the workable zone of the solder; that is, the time it takes to go from completely solid to completely liquid. A solder of 63/37 would have no workable zone at all, since it would go solid-liquid, liquid-solid instantaneously. The solder with a 9°F workable zone is 60/40, about ten to 12 seconds. The addition of tin beyond this point will raise the working zone gradually between 361°F to 450°F, the melting point of tin. Less tin, as in 50/50 solder, lowers the workable zone to 4°F, about five to eight seconds. Workers who prefer 50/50 solder like the quick melt/quick freeze it supplies, whereas those using 60/40 like the additional seconds to get the joint in order. It's strictly a matter of choice.

Solid core spool solders of varying compositions with a spool of lead free solder in the foreground. Lead free solders contain other metals to make up for the missing lead and require higher iron temperatures than do solders of 60/40 or 50/50 composition to melt and flow readily. This takes a little getting used to if you haven't used lead free solder before. Kester Corp. (who bought out the Gardiner Co) makes a lead free solder that is 95% tin and 5% antimony. The Canfield Co. makes a pewter finish solder which is lead free and composed of 95% tin, 4% copper, and 1% silver. (You need to steel wool this finish to get it to shine after the usual cleaning. Once you do this, it stays shiny.) The point is that lead free doesn't mean you can ignore all safety precautions as you are still dealing with heavy metals.

SHAPES OF SOLDER

Solder is generally sold as bar or wire forms. Wire solder comes in different dimensions. The best shape of solder for stained glass is 1/8" solid-core wire solder. This width allows the maximum amount of solder to flow onto the iron tip (where a chisel tip is used) and thence to the lead to give the neatest joint. Using a solder with a diameter less than 1/8" is inefficient since it provides too small amounts. Bar solder is totally inadequate for stained glass work since the iron melts it too slowly, if at all, in sufficient quantities to work with.

CORE SOLDER

These solders contain a core of material, usually a resinous flux. They should be avoided because the resin will eventually gum soldering tips and leave a gummy residue on the glass. The resin may continue to ooze from the soldered joints long after the piece has been finished, making it difficult to keep clean.

WHAT'S A GOOD SOLDER JOINT?

While it is the soldered joints that hold the stained glass work together, they should stay modestly in the background. Bulges of solder arthritically sitting in great humped masses over the joints of a panel or lamp add nothing to the artistic effect. On the other hand, lead ends that have been pitted and burned in an attempt to use as little solder as possible aren't the answer either. The procedure for making a neat, substantial solder joint involves five steps:

1) Clean all joint surfaces with a wire brush.
2) Make sure the lead cames are properly mitered—that they abut one another as closely as possible.
3) Make sure you use the correct soldering flux for the particular work.
4) Keep the iron at the proper temperature and use a solder you feel comfortable with.
5) Make sure each joint is clean and smooth after you have soldered it.

CLEANING THE JOINT SURFACES

A clean surface is half the battle. And battle it can be. Any particles of dirt or grease or any oxides covering the lead will interfere with the soldering process. Do not use a cleaning solution on lead came. Instead, clean it with a copper wire brush. Copper wire will not scratch the glass but will have enough abrasive quality to strip the oxide coat from the lead.

In cases where the lead is so old and oxidized that even a wire brush will not remove the coating, you may have to scrape it off with the blade of the leading knife so the shiny under portion appears. Only this surface is solderable. Of course the soldering tip should also be clean or it will not only refuse to pick up solder, but its application against an otherwise clean joint will dirty it and make it unsolderable. Do not use strong inorganic acids such as hydrochloric or sulfuric acid as cleansing agents. These acids release highly toxic fumes and the acids themselves are extremely dangerous.

FITTING THE LEAD CAMES

The lead cames should be fitted together in such a way that the solder can be easily drawn over the ends with one touch of the iron tip. If the leads are widely separated don't try to solder them, re-cut them. The cames should be mitered or cut to correspond closely with each other so they touch. Gaps invariably lead to problems with joints. Leads should be sliced with a sharp instrument, preferably a leading knife, which allows a clean and true end-to-end meeting of the separate cames. Attempting to bridge a gap between the leads will not only result in a messy solder joint, but will waste solder, time, and temper. It is better to do a leading job correctly step-by-step from the beginning than to try to make up for an inadequate job with solder later on.

USING THE RIGHT FLUX

Liquid flux is best. There are a number of these on the market—some work better on lead than on foil, others work better on foil. We prefer an oleic acid flux for lead, but you should try a few different fluxes to see which you prefer. The one that cleans the joint surfaces best is the one to use. And if the joint surface is really dirty, no amount of flux will help; you'll have to hand clean it. Remember, the flux is not strictly a cleaning agent. Its main purpose is to act as a vehicle for the solder to flow.

The flux is best applied to the joint by brushing with a fairly stiff paste or acid brush. Don't just dab it on, scrub it in. A cotton swab is useless for this work. Use a stiff bristle brush that is impervious to the flux. We cut ours down practically to the ferrule to make the bristles as stiff as possible. This stiffness is essential to work the flux into the lead surface and through any remaining oxide coat. The better you work the flux into the surface of the lead came, the more readily the solder will flow. It is not necessary to flood the area with flux. That will only make a mess on the glass. A small amount properly applied will work better than an ocean of it merely poured on.

KEEPING THE SOLDERING IRON AT THE RIGHT TEMPERATURE

The soldering iron is the tool of choice for a good joint. Select an iron of sufficient heat capacity to perform its function at a reasonable rate of speed. We recommend a 100 watt iron. Such an iron (or any iron for that matter) may well overheat. An overheated iron won't pick up solder and will melt the lead surfaces. This cratering of the

lead cames is unsightly and such lead must be replaced. Don't try patching the burned surfaces with solder. Unless you're an expert (in which case you wouldn't have burned the lead to begin with), you'll only make the situation worse. Watch the iron. Don't let it get so hot that it takes over the job. On the other hand, if the iron is not hot enough, you will end up "dragging" the solder, with the end result showing waves of frozen solder in peaks and valleys over the joint. Attempting to remedy this with the iron tip now at a hotter temperature may end up burning the lead. At that point, you may get a little burned up yourself.

Soldering lead came is different than soldering other material. No matter how much soldering you may have done in wiring circuits, plumbing, or other work around the house, you will find that soldering came is unique. Practice on scrap lead for 15 or 20 minutes until you get the feel of the material. You will be amazed at how rapidly the lead melts away from the overheated soldering iron or how reluctant the solder is to flow from an underheated iron.

CLEANING THE JOINTS AFTER SOLDERING

Flux residues make the glass tacky and smudged. Organic solvents may be used as cleaning agents. *Do not* use carbon tetrachloride. We mention this specific agent only to condemn it. While it is an excellent solvent, it is so dangerous that it should be ruled out completely, no matter how well your studio is ventilated. Unfortunately, simple soap and water will not clean away flux residues and oxide coatings from the glass, nor will any of the standard glass cleansers like Windex, which itself may leave a film.

The best material is a combination of two dry powders—we call it cleaning and polishing compound—which you can make yourself. It's a 75/25 mixture of calcium carbonate and diatomaceous earth. You can get the two substances at most hardware stores. Wear a mask when you mix it—the stuff flies around easily. The mix can be used either wet or dry over the entire glass surface, though we prefer it dry. Close the workshop doors if you are working with it in your house so you don't get it in your breakfast cereal. Used wet, it forms a paste which takes more elbow grease to apply properly but doesn't produce as much dust.

Plain whiting is also good. The cleaning agent should be sprinkled over the entire finished work on one surface and then the glass and lead alike scrubbed with a heavy bristled floor brush. The cleaner should not only pick up all flux residues and dirt that have collected on the glass and lead, but it should also dry the putty with which many finished stained glass panels are impregnated.

ALL ABOUT FLUX

Without flux the solder will roll off the lead surface. Not only does flux remove oxides from the metal surface, it prevents any oxidation of the molten solder. A flux must be readily displaced by the solder so as not to interfere with the wetting and bonding of the solder to the underlying metal. The flux must remain stable over the soldering range.

A good soldering technique calls for the selection of the mildest flux that will do the job. Fluxes fall into three main classes: corrosive, intermediate, and non-corrosive. Non-corrosive fluxes are too weak, and corrosive fluxes are generally too strong for stained glass work. A non-corrosive flux, such as is used in resin "core" solder, will ooze from the lead joints. A corrosive flux, one containing an inorganic acid, eventually attacks the lead, resulting in pitting of the surfaces.

One basic disadvantage of liquid flux is how easily the jar tips over, fluxing the work table and perhaps your neighbor in the process. To prevent this, keep only a small amount of flux in the bottle or bottle top so that when the soldering iron cord tangles with it or something bumps against it you will not have a mess on the table.

The aim of most manufacturers has been to develop a flux that promotes rapid activity on the work surface. It's nice to have one that also can do several jobs on both lead and foil. A good one is Royal Flux, made by Kierco, which works well on lead, copper, brass, and zinc. This company also makes Golden Flux, a real friend when it comes to taking off thick oxide coats from leaded windows that need to be repaired. Only a minimum of wire brushing is needed. Golden Flux requires Kierco's flux neutralizer to inactivate it. This renders harmless the residues that are left on the work, and will also clean the glass to some extent. This neutralizer will work on almost all brands of flux to clean up the remains of soldering activity.

Glasflux, made by the Glastar Co., can be used with copper foil, zinc, or lead soldering. You may prefer to use specific fluxes for individual metals. Traditionally, this has been the case, with one flux for lead, one for copper, and one for everything else. However, Glasflux will not corrode copper foil or discolor lead, the basic problems leading to the two-flux situation. Glasflux, a gel, permits a smooth brush-on application without unpleasant fumes or the use of a strong cleaner such as alcohol to clean up the soldering residues afterward. And it can be added to tip-cleaning sponges. It cleans the soldering iron tip from all the dross that accumulates during soldering.

Fluxes, like most of the tools and supplies in stained glass work, are individualistic. Workers develop their own preferences based on experimentation. Local distributors or mail-order suppliers will carry a number of fluxes; try several to see which is best for you.

One of the best ways to test a wide variety of fluxes is to attend a stained glass trade show. Manufacturers offer samples of their products, both old and new, for you and the retailer to test. The Canfield Co. has developed what it calls Instant Solder, a solder and flux formulation that allows preplacement of the exact amount of solder necessary for a particular joint. Other chemicals from Canfield are Action Tin, a tinning paint for applying a coat of solder on metals before joining; Sil-Can White Creme Brazing Flux for use with their brazing alloys; Copper-Mate, a soldering paste flux; and Solder-Mate liquid soldering fluxes. The Plato Co. produces its own brand of flux, which rounds off a complete list of soldering products for this company, including soldering irons. Some workers feel secure with a product from a manufacturer that hits all the bases this way. Other workers prefer a company that deals in a particular product.

Lake Chemical Co. concentrates on flux products. Its La-Co liquid flux is recommended for general soldering of lead and zinc. It is water-soluble and has an easy cleanup. La-Co also works well for cleaning and tinning soldering irons and is readily brushed onto the joint. Lake Chemical also produces a high-heat resistant flux paste, used mainly for copper-foil work. The La-Co Flux Stik is a unique item. Resembling a crayon, it can be applied in pinpoint areas and it's good for overhead soldering, which is always a frustrating endeavor. La-Co Flux, according to the manufacturer, requires no hazardous warning.

The Kester Solder Co. makes several good fluxes, among other soldering items. Its oleic acid flux is an old standby. After trying many of the varieties, you will settle down with a few favorites. (Perhaps "settling down" is not the phrase to use for a field that is in a state of flux.)

THE HEAT SOURCE

The best heat source for soldering is one that will assure a strong bond between the metals in a fast, efficient manner. A torch is certainly fast but would melt the lead. A small heat source that takes many minutes to heat the solder is obviously too slow. For the type of soldering done in stained glass, there is only one real option—the electric soldering iron. But first, here are several soldering irons that you **do not** want to use in stained glass.

The Featherweight: This particular iron costs somewhere between $1 and $3 and is available on the bargain counter of the hardware store. The tip is not replaceable. Wattage varies between 25 and 50 watts. Such an iron is strained beyond its capacity when it comes to melting solder over a wide unit area such as a lead joint. The pinpoint soldering of electrical connections is more in its line. The result of using it on lead joints is an impatient dragging rather than an even flow of solder over the joints. The beginner compensates for this by pressing harder with the iron against the joints in an attempt to flatten them. Novel and haphazard effects can be achieved in this manner, although none of them will be what you want.

The Heavyweight: Here is the other extreme—an iron with overabundant electrical vivacity and a tip large enough to fry an egg. For some reason, workers who use this iron invariably attempt the most delicate joint soldering. This iron gobbles solder at an alarming rate and generally spews it in absentminded dribbles over the tabletop, floor, and shoes, and only seldom on the work in progress. One can barely touch a joint with it lest it evaporate. Thickets of fumes and a residual hacking cough mark its operator's position in the studio.

The Antique: Occasionally a beginning student appears in class proudly displaying a soldering device that has been in the family for generations but that still "has a lot of life in it." Sometimes the handle is in several pieces held loosely together with tape. The tip, on the other hand, is tight, frozen to the barrel, pitted, and rusty. When plugged in, this medieval memento may cause the electric company to go into shock. Nevertheless, the owner is insistent on saving money and may finally turn out some work despite the handicap. He may even insist that he is having fun. Certainly he will have a lot of space in which to work, with his neighbors shying away for fear of electrocution. Such devices often end up showing more sense than their operators. They know when to quit, and often do so right in the middle of an extensive project. Technology being what it is, and common sense being what it is, owners of such antiques spend more money to get them fixed than it would ever cost to buy a new one.

Soldering Guns: In the past we have been emphatic about classifying soldering guns as ineffective. Then we received a number of letters, some irate, from people who insisted that they used soldering guns with no compromise to the quality of their work. To be fair, we tried to find at least one type that could be reasonably used in the craft, the Lenk Co. soldering gun which is similar to an iron with a pistol grip but no trigger. The tip is copper, pyramidal, and not interchangeable. It tends to corrode rather rapidly and must be retinned at intervals. Heating capacity is 75 watts, which is reasonable for soldering moderate joints. The balance of this tool is comfortable, and its use is not unreasonable if you must use a gun. But the question remains, why must you? Irons are where the action is when the latest developments and efficiency of production are concerned. Our original prejudice against guns still stands, although we direct it at those products made for circuitry soldering and those with trigger on/off switches and thin tips. They have achieved amateur status only because some workers have one lying around the house and see no reason not to use it. Unfortunately, there can be no changing of tips in such an instrument, no mobility in the soldering of different joints, angles, or objects, and no wide overlay of solder because of insufficient surface heating. As for tinning (drawing a line of molten solder over a joint), it is difficult with a gun. There's no fast draw with a soldering gun. It's interesting that in our survey we note fewer workers attempting to use guns.

SOLDERING IRONS

The first thing to look for when choosing a soldering iron is the Underwriters Laboratory (UL) listing. Many people forget this little item. All the irons produced for the stained glass field are so listed, so you don't have to worry there. But if you have an iron at home that is a strange brand, make sure it has a UL listing before you use it.

Other than that, the choice of a soldering iron depends on how up to date you want to be. It's a good idea to check that all the parts of the iron are easily interchangeable. We like to have maximum flexibility for selecting the exact combination of handles, temperatures, and tips for any stained glass soldering application. The Unger iron, with its thread-together design, is strong in this regard and makes changing heaters, tips, or handles a fast and easy operation. Of course, you want to keep the cost down, and the most logical way to do this is not to throw away the iron when a part goes bad. You should be able to replace any worn out component, not have to replace the entire iron.

Since you will be using the soldering iron over long periods, the fatigue factor comes into play. The heavier the iron, the greater the fatigue. You want a device as light as possible and one that is easy to use, not one that fights you and throws you off balance every time you pick it up. Comfort is the key here. In this regard, the handle and shape of the iron are modifying factors. Handles are as diverse as the Unger cork or plastic finger grip to the streamlined Esico design that serves both their bent and straight irons so well. Speaking of which, it is the tip of the iron, not the handle, that is supposed to heat up, and companies have spent a lot of time on design and material to provide this discrimination.

The Hexagon deflector is designed to keep the heat where it should be—in the tip—as is Esico's stainless steel stem, which ensures cooler handles. Handle streamlining varies from "pen grip" to "fist grip," depending on the delicacy or rugged character of the soldering.

Irons come in "bent" or "hatchet" styles as well as straight. Even here, the design can make or break your relationship with the iron. Esico offset or hatchet irons are offset 70° to form an included angle of 110°. You may find that this shape is the most comfortable to work with over a period of time. Hexagon provides a hatchet style of 90°, a more acute angle than Esico, and you may prefer this kind.

The wattage is an important consideration, as is the length of time it takes for the iron to heat up. What you want is an iron engineered for quick heat production, transfer, and recovery. The acceptable wattage range is between 75 and 125 watts. Less than 75 watts provides sluggish heat and slows down the work. More than 125 watts slows down the work because you must be so cautious about not burning the came or, if you are using foil, overheating the solder so it rolls off the metal. This explanation is an oversimplification because most soldering irons (regardless of wattage) just get hotter and hotter. What you really want is a tempered heat that peaks rapidly and stays put. Standard irons operate on 120 AC and DC. Most of the plugs can go only into the socket one way for proper grounding.

The tip of an iron can be held in the barrel by a set screw or it can be threaded. We've never had good luck with a threaded tip. Invariably it freezes in place and the flexibility of the iron, which depends on the ability to change tips for different projects, is lost. Even a set screw may freeze. However, you can drill it out if all else fails. But you cannot drill the frozen tip out of a threaded barrel.

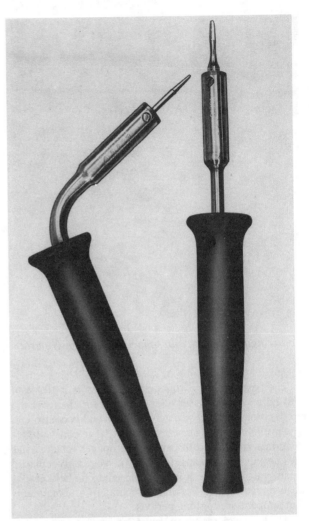

Esico straight and bent irons. Many people prefer the bent to the straight. On the market now are irons that are straight but have bent tips. There is something for everyone.

Our Preference

There are some things to look for in a soldering iron, or at least to know about, that most people never consider. When you go comparison shopping, our experiences may help as follows.

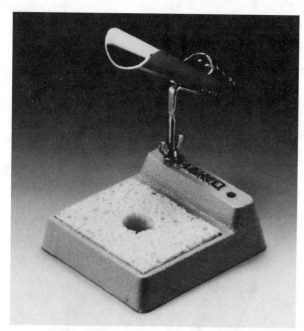

Soldering iron holder with sponge tip cleaner. (Courtesy Hakko Co.)

The best soldering iron we have found is a 100 watt 3/8" bore iron with a set screw to allow for changing the tip. It comes straight or hatchet shaped and is controlled. The iron is designed and constructed to give constant production performance. Its handle does not get hot and it has the latest in heating elements which can be easily replaced should one burn out. It is light enough to be held easily, heats up readily to a workable temperature, and maintains that temperature for long periods.

The tendency for any uncontrolled iron is to get too hot to work with, so a certain amount of plugging in and unplugging becomes necessary to maintain a constant temperature. A controlled iron will save you excess wear and tear by maintaining the ideal heat and allowing work to proceed unhindered by continual stooping and searching for the outlet. Such an iron employs a rheostat control which is a necessity if you are doing any extensive soldering. More about that in a moment.

The set screw on the iron is particularly important. Screw-in tips tend to freeze into place with the continued expansion and contraction as the iron heats and cools. The hammering, oiling, squeezing, twisting, and sweating that result when you discover that a tip cannot be removed from the iron provides a colorful break in routine, but

generally results in the purchase of another iron. The set screw in a new iron should be loosened after the first few uses to keep it from freezing. Once the iron has been broken in, you should have no trouble changing tips.

One way to avoid plugging and unplugging the iron to maintain constant temperature is to put a line switch on the cord. This is easy to do and less expensive than a rheostat control. Providing you remember to use it, you won't wonder why the lead is melting or the solder isn't. Plan the switch placement—if you place it too close to the iron, it will clatter against your work. If you place it too far away, you will have to stoop and bend to find it. Putting it in the middle of the cord will probably have it catching the edge of the table and pulling the iron out of your hand. A fairly safe rule of thumb is to put the switch approximately 12" from the end of the iron and check it before cutting the cord to make sure that is where you want it.

Irons generally come equipped with a stand to rest on during work. It's a good habit to use the stand, even for a cold iron. We've seen stands with Bakelite collars—these can overheat and smell from the heat of the iron. Some workers plug in their iron and leave it on the tabletop just for a moment to warm up while they arrange their equipment. Somehow the stand is the last thing they locate and charred wood is the result. The stand is one of the easiest items to lose. If you misplace it, get another one. Trying to rest the iron on a hammer or wrench or pair of pliers as a temporary stand only results in the iron rolling off and burning either the table or yourself. There is no room for improvisation here.

THE RHEOSTAT CONTROL UNIT AND TIP CLEANERS

For the serious worker in stained glass, the rheostat control unit is more effective than any other heat controlling method. It effectively controls the amount of heat going through the iron and does away with the need to plug in and unplug or switch on and off that is the plague of beginners. We find it more effective than an iron with a built-in control. Such a unit provides manual control of soldering iron tip temperatures with automatic corrections for voltage fluctuations up to 80% of the full wattage of the heating element. It also allows operation without control at 100% of full wattage. A pilot light on the instrument indicates cycling of the current. Rheostat control units are not inexpensive, but they last indefinitely. The only part that may need to be replaced is the small fuse.

A number of companies make rheostat controls, among them Glastar, Inland, and Esico. On its Model 222, Esico has incorporated a self-contained electronic solder station for the rheostat, soldering iron stand, and tip cleaner. It is a compact combination.

The tip cleaner is designed to clean a Vitacote or copper soldering tip quickly and efficiently. A stroke across the wet vertical sponge removes undesirable residues, which fall into the tray at the base. Solder on the tip's working surface is not destroyed. The top cover lifts off to refill the water reservoir that keeps the sponge wet at all times. It is certainly a more conservative way of cleaning the tip than shaking the iron across the floor as we have seen some workers do.

In this tip cleaner from the Hakko Co., the material is similar to a kitchen scrubber—thin coiled continuous metal strips that scrub the iron's tip without the use of water, as in sponge tip cleaners. There are two advantages to this: there is no steam produced which is composed of vapors you don't want to breathe, and second, water may eventually corrode your tip or cause iron seizure where the tip actually adheres to the barrel due to corrosion and can't be removed.

Esico Co. rheostat control unit. A number of companies make similar units; we have tried those which appear in this book and which we can recommend. That does not mean others are not equally fine. That's also true of the soldering irons we discuss.

A number of other tip cleaners are available from Inland and other manufacturers. Ingenuity is contagious, and we have Esico Model HC-4 Iron Holder and Tip Cleaner combined as the round cleaner or with a flat tip cleaner. Esico also makes an under-the-bench iron holder/tip cleaner combination that is easily installed with only two screws. This quality unit is convenient, safe, and compact (especially nice for workers with limited space). Low sulfur content, heavy-duty sponges are used in all Esico tip cleaners.

The Plato Co. makes rotating tip wipers, claiming (sounds reasonable) that soldering tips last longer when they are wiped on clean, damp, sulfur-free cellulose sponges. You can't overwipe a tip when you use a rotating wiper because the design causes the sponges to rotate through the water reservoir when pressure is applied. This is a nice touch. Sponges sear when they are dry. Plato also makes a tip-wiper iron-holder stand. This convenient holder stand for pencil-type soldering irons is a heavily plated double-steel coil-cage construction that protects the worker against burns. A stable base of four rubber-capped legs keeps the holder where you place it.

SOLDERING TIPS

Tips for soldering irons come in all thicknesses and shapes; if you cannot find a shape that suits what you have in mind, you can have one made. However, it's unlikely that you'll conceive a shape that has not already been made.

Diverse as the choice of tip dimensions and shapes is, the material they are composed of is limited to copper—either pure or plated. Not many workers use pure copper tips anymore, unless a specific necessity calls for them, such as not having a plated one of requisite shape. Although the pure copper tip is cheaper than the plated one, it is difficult to maintain in even moderately pristine condition, and the number of styles available are limited. Time was when the plated tip was a novelty, but no longer. At this point, the pure copper tip is becoming less and less the tip of choice, though a few beginners may start off with several of these rather than investing in the more expensive plated tips, and some experienced workers still insist that they get a better joint with a pure copper tip than a plated one. One of the inconveniences of the copper tip is the frequency of retinning.

Tinning involves scraping off the dirt covering this bare copper surface and then covering it with an even layer of solder. This layer should remain in place until the next tinning is required. There are several steps to the tinning operation. Allow the tip to cool if you have been using the iron. To clean the tip well, you may have to remove it from the iron, though tinning can be done with the tip in place. Remove scaly oxides from the working surface. Use a file, an 80-grit abrasive polyurethane foam stick available from the Plato Co. or 100 grit emery cloth. While sanding or scraping, be careful to maintain the tip's original shape (you don't want to change a pyramid to a chisel shape). Once you have filed the copper tip down to a shiny surface, it must be fluxed and retinned. Put the tip back in the iron and coat the working surface of the tip with flux, either liquid or paste. Do this before turning on the iron. Turn on the iron and let the tip get to working temperature, then run solder over the surface. If the tip does not accept solder, it is probably too hot. Cool it until it will accept the solder. If the tip is not completely tinned, apply more flux and solder while the tip is hot. As you work with this newly tinned tip, you will see it gather up more and more oxides until you will have to repeat the tinning process.

Plated Soldering Tips

Plated soldering tips last longer than plain copper ones by far. They need only moderate care—wiping with a sponge—and give maximum performance uninterrupted by the need for retinning. The cores of plated tips are made of highly conductive copper. The working surface and shank are iron-plated. The tips are pre-tinned and the entire shank is alloy-plated and ready for immediate use. These tips are considerably more expensive than the plain copper ones, but they are far more convenient. They do not require (indeed manufacturers warn against) rough filing even if/when retinning becomes necessary, since filing can remove the iron coating and ruin the tip. These handy devices reduce soldering time and add neatness and a great sense of satisfaction to the soldering process.

You should have a number of different shapes of soldering tips in your working area so you can choose one that best fits the needs of the moment. If you have two different size bore irons, you may want to stock two sets of tips. Most workers stay with a single bore, usually a 3/8", even if they have more than one iron, and avoid having to stock a double supply of tips. Both copper tips and plated ones are available for all size bores. We keep several bores of irons on hand, including a 5/8" for extra heavy joint soldering, and one for pre-tinning sheet foil for special projects. This iron uses copper tips and they are, believe us, hard to find.

Tips to Keep the Tips in Shape

Even plated tips are subject to wear. To keep yours in tiptop condition:

1) Inspect all tips periodically to make sure they are clean and that the tinning has not worn away. Plated tips occasionally require tinning, and the procedure is the same as for copper tips, except that with plated tips you never use a file and never grind them against any gritty surface.

2) Flood the tinned working surfaces of a plated tip with solder before using it. This will provide a fresh protective surface on the tip.

3) Clean the tip on a wet cellulose sponge as necessary.

4) Avoid excessive pressure of the tip to the joint surface. Rubbing a tip over a joint does not improve heat transfer or make the solder flow better. The best solder joint all but creates itself. All you furnish is the material for it to do so.

5) In the process of making a solder joint, apply fresh solder to the metals being joined, not to the hot tip.

6) Apply fresh solder on the tip before placing the iron back in the holder after soldering.

THE DESOLDERING PROCESS

You may not think so, but sooner or later you will make a mistake. We all do. Moreover, you will not only make it, you will solder it. But don't despair. A soldered area can be unsoldered without burning away the leads, cutting away the joint, or breaking out the glass.

Several companies make solder removers just for this purpose. Plato makes one of the best, called Soder Wick, and with a spelling like that you might wonder about its effectiveness. It works very well. All you need do is place

Using a desoldering wick (Plato-Wick) to remove excess solder from a joint. The solder is drawn up the copper fabric braid from the joint quite rapidly. Once that portion of the braid has done its work, you cut that part off the spool and you are ready for the next excess.

a small portion of the wick (it comes on a spool) directly on the solder to be removed and put the hot iron tip on top of that. As the solder melts, it is drawn up the wick and off the joint. You just keep cutting away the used wick and replacing it until all the solder is gone. It beats the old method of melting unwanted solder and then shaking the iron to get it off. Hexagon Co. makes a solder remover with the same type of tinned braid, and it also uses the same type of capillary action to pick up the solder. In addition, Hexagon makes a Solder Sucker, a Teflon tiplet attached to a rubber ball, similar to a plastic eyedropper. The idea is to melt the solder and, when it is molten, dip the tip of the tiplet into it and release pressure on the rubber ball. The suction then absorbs and gathers the molten solder into the ball. This technique also works, although we find the wick method more effective.

SUMMARY

The soldering process, including the use of an efficient soldering iron, is an integral part of working in stained glass. The finished product reflects the tools you used. While we do not recommend that beginners immediately

purchase professional soldering irons and a complete set of iron-coated tips, we do feel they owe it to themselves to use equipment that will give the best performance for the time spent.

Approach the entire matter of soldering cautiously at first. Initial attempts may look delightful, only to look second rate under critical appraisal. This will lead to the urge to acquire the proper tools for the job.

Use 60/40 or 50/50 solid core solder. If you use a "resin core" solder, you will have sloppy joints; the resin will ooze over the glass and be almost impossible to remove. It will also eventually gum up the soldering tip.

Use an iron that is hot enough. Irons below 80 watts are not recommended because they take too long to heat up and don't last. Also, the tips available for such irons are too small for use on large joints. There is no question that a small iron will eventually do the job, but you will spend too much time on this one procedure. And by the time you have gone through several small irons, you will have paid for a large one. So, if you intend to do any extensive work in glass, why not get the right iron to begin with?

Make sure the soldering tip is clean. If you are using an ironclad tip, occasionally wipe it on its sponge to remove excess flux and solder. You will notice a considerable difference in solder flow if you do. If you prefer a copper tip, check to see that it is properly tinned and fluxed. The tinning and retinning that are necessary with a copper tip is a nuisance, but more of a nuisance is solder that keeps rolling off the soldering tip because of the barrier of dirt on its surface. Refile the copper tip, flux it, and tin it with solder. If the tip is clean and still won't pick up solder or the solder rolls off and away from the tip, the iron is too hot. Allow it to cool somewhat. Ideal heat is when the solder instantly melts and clings to or is picked up by the tip to be transported to the work.

If the soldering leaves sharp pointed ends on the joints, either you are dragging the solder and the iron is not hot enough or you are not using enough flux. Solder properly applied should flow smoothly.

Do not solder with your nose directly in the work area. Breathing soldering fumes can make you sick.

Use a good liquid flux and flux brush.

CHAPTER 5
Tools

The object of this chapter is not to cover every tool and device on the market. A book could be written about that alone and revised for new material almost immediately. We have no intention of competing with the numerous catalogs your local supplier has on hand. We want to introduce some of these devices to you, either in words or pictures or both, so that when you go to purchase one you will have an idea of what you need for the type of work you will be doing. You certainly won't need everything mentioned, although it may be tempting to think so. You should purchase a little at a time and acquire more tools as your technique requires them and your budget can stand it.

Certain tools you won't be able to do without (glass cutters, lead knives, pliers, soldering irons, etc.) if you want to accomplish any work at all, much less professional work. A good hand tool is an investment that pays for itself many times over. No tool, regardless of how ingenious or sophisticated it is, creates by itself (at least, not yet). Only you can do that. But the efficiency of the tools you acquire will allow you to create more effectively and enjoy it more.

The stained glass field has seen several revolutions in tools and equipment. We will try for the basics as well as some of the more provocative newer ones and we apologize in advance if we've left out one of your favorites. Alas, some of the tools described here may be history by the time this book is published; hopefully not many. Some tools make working with stained glass possible; others make it productive. For example, glass grinders were not around when we began working in the field but it's hard to imagine working without them now.

Because of the overlap of tools and topics, some repetition in other chapters is unavoidable. We'll try to keep such repetition brief.

GLASS CUTTERS

This device consists of a handle attached to a hard steel or carbide wheel rotating on a bronze axle. As the cutter is pushed or pulled along the surface of the glass, the wheel turns and plows a groove through it. This causes a fracture over the surface and a weak area along the length of the score. Pressure applied properly along this weakened area will break the glass into two pieces. Pressure applied improperly, or if the score line is imperfectly made, will result in glass pieces you have to discard or redo. The type of cutter you use is the first element toward the successful or unsuccessful end result.

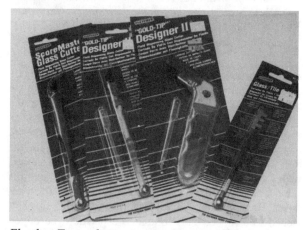

Fletcher-Terry glass cutters to fit every method of scoring glass. From left to right, wide contoured grip, slimline version of oil filled cutter, leak-proof pistol grip and standard straight cutter with tapping ball and grozzing teeth.

Probably no tool is as personal to the stained glassworker as the glass cutter. More shapes and styles have come and gone than you could shake a piece of glass at since hobbyists have entered the field. When this book was first published, the choice was limited to the classic model manufactured by the Fletcher-Terry Co. which is still the choice of a great number of professional workers today. Many of us first got to know glass through our fingertips guiding one of these cutters and see no reason to change from a device that has become so much a part of ourselves. But the classic design can take some getting used to. Unable or unwilling to learn to grip this style of cutter, thousands of individuals new to glass created a mass market and a powerful voice for change. New designs, such as cutters with center holes for the index finger, palm cutters, finger cutters, cutters that would also open tin cans and cut your lawn, oil-reservoir cutters and pistol-grip cutters were developed.

The ones that are still with us today (many are just in personal collections) are the oil cutters and the pistol grips as well as the tried and true and the redesigned classic cutters. Today the Fletcher-Terry Co. and the Toyo Co. are among the leading manufacturers of oil cutters and pistol grips. Both these companies produce cutters with replaceable heads that cost about half the price of the cutter itself.

The term cutting is not accurate when applied to glass. Glass can only be scored, scratched, or grooved. The word cut is legitimized by the name glass cutter, but this instrument should more accurately be called a glass scorer. Scoring means to fracture the glass along one of its surfaces. To "run" the score is to deepen this fracture through to the other surface. To break the glass means to separate the two pieces along the line of the score.

Don't skimp on stained glass tools, least of all on your glass cutter. If you buy a cheap cutter, you will only be fighting the glass. Good glass cutters, especially carbide cutters, are not cheap. At the start, decide what your outlay for tools and supplies can be. If you must cut costs, at least initially, the glass cutter is not the tool to cut. Purchase less glass or lead or foil, or do without one of the pliers, but don't hamper your efforts by not getting a good cutter or two.

The Classic Cutter

The classic glass cutter design is a product of the Fletcher-Terry Co., first manufactured in 1869 as the Bristol Diamond steel-wheel glass cutter. The design, with some modifications, is still in its line of Gold Tip glass cutters. Most of us who have been involved with stained glass for many years still use and cherish our Fletcher Gold Tips. We use other cutters as well, but it would be impossible for any new cutter design, even Fletcher's own Scoremaster, to replace these tried and true friends.

With the classic cutter, the fingertips grasp the cutter and guide it; the upper portions of the fingers, toward the web of the hand, supply stability.

Fletcher-Terry also makes a line of carbide wheel cutters. Carbide cutters, if treated properly, will last about five times as long as steel cutters. Beginners in stained glass should have at least two steel-wheel cutters: an 08 pattern-cutting small wheel cutter and an 06 hard cutter. One of them should be ball-ended. To make things easy for yourself, add a general purpose carbide cutter to these two.

The ball on the end of a cutter allows you to tap a "score line" into a "run line." Only one of your cutters need be ball-ended. This will leave you a hard straight end on the second cutter to use as a fulcrum for breaking a straight score.

The Wheel Size

The smaller the glass cutter wheel, the more readily the cutter will steer. When following pattern borders, a small wheel makes life easier. A 5/32" wheel is a good size. Larger wheels are useful for scoring straight lines. A large wheel might last longer than a small one, but when cutting to pattern, a small wheel tends to allow your hand more dexterity.

The Beveled Angle

The angle at which the wheel was ground is important as far as the kind of glass it is meant to score. In general, broad beveled cutter wheels are designed to score soft glass while steeper beveled ones are meant for hard glass. Plate glass, despite its thickness, is really a soft glass. The best cutter to use on it is an old one, one where the wheel has been dulled by use and consequently has a broader angle. Thus it plows a wider score line.

Handles

The Fletcher-Terry cutters we prefer have metal handles. However, their line has been so expanded that you should have no difficulty finding a cutter with any type handle that has just the proper width and design to fit your hand.

Remember that a good tool often demands a learning process, during which time it may also be learning about you. Tools have personality. Our experience has been that some people want to impose their personality on tools, glass, and teacher all at once. The tools and glass may not stand for it.

Some individuals complain about the thinness of some cutter metal handles and may decide wood handle cutters are more to their liking. Wood handles are stout and fill the fingers more securely. These cutters are somewhat lighter than metal handle ones. Be careful how you hold the wood handle cutter or you may chafe your fingers. Experiment with these various cutters to see which type of handle works best for you before you buy.

Ball-Ended Cutters

The ball is used to tap a score and cause it to run, thus deepening the fracture of the glass and making it easy to separate into (hopefully) two pieces. It is possible to tap the score with the tooth side, the underside of the cutter, but this doesn't work as well and requires more skill and more force in tapping. If the ball on the cutter is not smooth, sand or file it smooth for good tapping results. Some cutters have a small ridge around the ball that interferes with accurate tapping. This should be sanded down. *Never* tap with the cutter wheel unless you want to buy a new one.

Grozzing Teeth

If the glass didn't follow the score line, leaving some excess, or if the piece was a little too large, grozzing is the process that will chip off small pieces of glass to let you get exactly the shape you want. It also smoothes the edge. The three slots found on the underside of classic straight cutters were once used for grozzing.

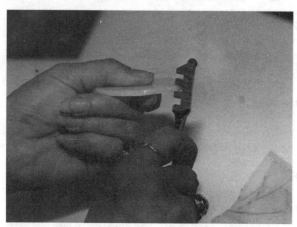

Grozzing glass with the teeth of a classic straight cutter.

Today, grozzing teeth are a thing of the past except on the classic straight cutter where they are made of hard metal and they can break more glass than they grozz. Instead of using grozzing teeth, get a good pair of glass or grozzing pliers, which are made of special soft iron. There are no grozzing teeth on Toyo or Fletcher oil or pistol-grip cutters.

Carbide Glass Cutters

Some carbide cutters have the word "carbide" engraved on the cutter handle. Others may be color coded. Since a Fletcher carbide cutter can look like any other Fletcher cutter, mark yours so you will be able to distinguish it from your regular cutters. Carbide cutter wheels are made of silicon carbide and can be sharpened by the manufacturer for a nominal charge. Carbide glass cutters are a pleasure to use.

Sharpening Glass Cutters

A glass cutter can be sharpened, but it takes patience and the right type of stone—an Arkansas whetstone. The cutter is held at a slant to match the original angle of bevel of the wheel and run back and forth over the stone while using a lubricant. It's not usually a good idea to sharpen cutters, especially steel-wheel cutters. Once you sharpen one, it seems to dull quickly. Buy a new cutter when the time comes or replace the head if possible. A poorly sharpened cutter may ruin glass instead of saving you money.

Cutter Wheel Lubrication

Keep your cutter wheel lubricated if it is not self-lubricating. This will make it score better and last longer. Otherwise you can ruin it in one stroke. Store the classic cutter in a heavy jar or glass (baby food jars work well) and place a pad of steel wool at the bottom so the cutter wheel doesn't rest against the glass. This padding will also turn the wheel as the cutter is moved, causing the lubricant to circulate over the axle. About 1/4" of kerosene in the bottom of the jar or glass will work well as a lubricant. Don't use oil or turpentine; turpentine especially will gum up from the friction of use and immobilize the wheel. If the wheel is stuck when the cutter is used, a flat spot may burn into the wheel and take it permanently out of round. There are special cutter lubricants that are less volatile than kerosene and will last longer, but kerosene is probably the handiest and cheapest.

Testing for Sharpness

Test a glass cutter for sharpness by comparing the way it scores to a new cutter. As you learn the feel of your cutter and cut more glass, you will be able to tell when a cutter is going dull. When your old cutter seems sluggish and you don't get that "singing" from the glass as you move the cutter wheel across the surface, try a new one. A dull cutter may make a score, but that doesn't mean the glass will separate cleanly. When the glass is difficult to separate and when your break line looks ragged, the cutter is probably getting dull.

Always keep a few new cutters on hand. It's no fun trying to cut glass with a dull cutter and it's also expensive in terms of broken glass. A cutter can also get flat spots and dents in the wheel from cutting on dirty glass or from rough handling. Such a cutter will "tic, tic, tic, tic" as you make a score. No matter how good the cutter is otherwise, it is useless with this defect. Such problems are generally caused by dropping the cutter on its wheel end or from inadequate lubrication. If you take care of your glass cutter, it will serve you well for a reasonable length of time.

The Palm Rest and the Scoremaster III

Both from Fletcher-Terry, these are calculated to make glass cutting easier, especially for individuals who have trouble gripping the classic cutter. The Palm Rest is actually a modification of the classic cutter. The Palm Rest handle attachment improves the conventional holding technique by putting the entire palm to work instead of three fingers. Made of spring steel, it fits snugly in the palm of the hand, maintaining a constant and firm contact throughout the scoring procedure. For beginners, it offers a secure guide to the process, as well as a steady grip and better cutter stability and control with less hand fatigue.

The Palm Rest is easy to attach to the regular Fletcher cutter by sliding the clasp on or off the handle. You can adjust the support to the size and shape of your hand. The device works equally well for straight line or pattern cutting.

The Scoremaster III glass cutter differs in a number of ways from Fletcher's Gold Tip classic design. Instead of the thin stem handle (which tends to wobble between inexperienced fingers) which flattens as it approaches the grozzing teeth, this cutter has a contoured handle and no grozzing teeth. The finger grips allow for comfortable placement of the fingertips. There is no danger of chafing at the web of the fingers. The Scoremaster is an anatomically pleasing cutter; it is hand-sure. There is a precision-made head assembly to keep the wheel firmly in place, allow full wheel visibility for accurate pull or push scoring, a replaceable carbide wheel and axle that gives the cutter a sense of permanence, and a lubricating wick that can be dipped in light oil so no oil reservoir is needed. Altogether, the Scoremaster seems to know the score in

more ways than one. A ball end tops off the handle, providing both a tapping mechanism and a balancing function. At the other end, serrated indentations provide nonskid fingertip control just above the head. The cutter can be used for flat clear glass and all types of stained glass for pattern or straight cutting.

You can hold the Scoremaster any way it's comfortable, but make sure the wheel is straight up and down and the handle perpendicular to the glass. The amount of force applied depends on the type of glass you will be cutting. The basic rule for cutting is to apply as much force as you can without crushing the surface of the glass. If you find a white, gritty score line developing, you may be pushing too hard. Try to maintain uniform speed and force until the wheel runs gently off the edge of the glass. Never retrace the line of cut.

The Oil Hand Cutter

Glass Accessories International (distributor for the Toyo cutter) revolutionized the glass cutting market with its series of Supercutters. Its design, the TC 600, unlike the pen grip Supercutters, is a palm grip cutter (pistol grip) with an oil reservoir located in the plastic handle. The serrated lower surface of this lightweight transparent tool provides comfortable finger grips. The cutting head itself is magnificent. The cutter may be held either in a fist grip with the thumb on top resting as a guide or in a palm grip with the index finger acting as the guide. Don't hold this or any other palm grip cutter with all fingers completely wrapped around it. Such a grip limits wrist mobility. Use one finger as a guide on top.

Circle Cutters

Toyo circle cutter with flex arm.

Circles can be cut freehand with a regular glass cutter (why bother?) or with a device that can cut circles to almost any dimension. For circles from 3/8" to 5" in diameter, Fletcher-Terry's compact rotating handle Lens Cutter can be used. Once the circle is inscribed, it is broken out of the glass by scoring lines at right angles to it and pulling off the pieces with glass pliers.

For larger circles from 2" on up, a suction-cup circle cutter can be used. Several companies produce these. Fletcher, Glastar, and Inland all have their own versions though this is such a foolproof design that all these devices look (and act) pretty much alike. There are three pieces: a suction cup (in Inland's case a small tripod you have to hold), a movable turret with a screw gauge, and a rod on which the turret travels. The further the turret is placed from the center suction cup, the wider the diameter of the circle will be. The cup must have good suction which is applied by a small handle that also releases it. The cutting wheel is similar to that on a regular cutter and should be lubricated and kept clean. With any circle cutter (or any glass cutter), if you don't lubricate the wheel, you can lubricate the glass by brushing a very thin coating of cutting oil (kerosene or any commercially available product).

When the wheel becomes dull, attach a replacement wheel. Usually all you have to do is loosen and tighten a single screw to replace the wheel. Breaking the circle out with these larger varieties is easier than with the smaller lens cutter. After scoring the glass, turn it over on a flat surface and press around the circumference just over the score line. You will see the score line immediately begin to run (if you've made an adequate one) and by following it along with pressure, the circle will pretty much drop right out of the glass.

The Odd-Shaped Cutter

A logical next step from a machine that cuts circles is a machine that cuts curved shapes. The hobbyist making one-of-a kind items may have little use for this, but the hobbyist/businessperson who is producing multiple items may find this machine to be a real help. With this machine each piece will be exact and each will be scored in a minimum amount of time. Bilco Co. makes such machines for commercial use. Many hobby oriented ones have disappeared. We still use one—the Fassglass, a German machine. We have been unable to discover whether it is still produced, but we assume it is.

The Fassglass cutting machines are efficient, rugged, and accurate. Fassglass I will cut virtually any shape you can cut by hand, even squares and triangles. The cutting head rides against a template and raises out of the way in an instant to make changing templates easy. The machine comes with a template layout tool and easy instructions. The Fassglass II does the same work but has five times more cutting area. It measures only 24" by 24". Templates are easy to make.

Strip Cutting Devices

Cutting glass into long narrow strips using a ruler can be tedious. The ruler invariably slips, no matter how securely you hold it, and it's hard to keep the cutter moving with the same force along the entire length of the cut. When the time comes to break out the glass strips, the uneven pressure may provoke a break line that is not quite even with the score line or the break won't run the entire length of the score line. This, in turn, gives you uneven strips that have to be ground either on a wet belt or a disc grinder or grozzed by hand—and that means a lot of extra work even if you manage to straighten out the borders. Strip cutters make such a project a lot easier.

A strip and circle cutter combination made by Glastar Corp. can cut squares, rectangles, and diamonds from l/2" to 12" wide. The circle cutter attachment cuts circles from 3" to 24" in diameter with accuracy to a fraction of an inch. This time saver is especially useful in cutting repetitive border pieces. It is lightweight, constructed of extra hard, glass-filled Acetel, and contains three pieces: a 12" t-bar with a 6" cutter wheel turret, a circle cutter base, and a stripper base. The t-bar attaches to either base. To provide durability, the six cutting wheels are on the t-bar turret. By turning a screw, a fresh cutting blade rotates into place, replacing the worn blade. The circle cutter is held

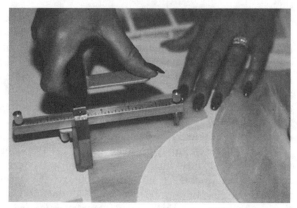

Toyo strip cutter.

by three small rubber points that anchor securely to the glass.

To cut strips, nail a standard 1" x 2" board to the work table and place the glass against the board. The stripper rides on the edge of the board as you draw the cutter over the glass. Thus all glass pieces are cut to exactly the same size.

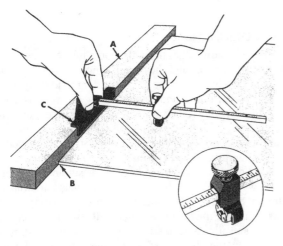

Toyo circle cutter with flex arm.

Glass Saws

So far we've been discussing cutting by hand. You can also cut by machine with a glass saw. Glass saws are more expensive than glass cutters, as you might imagine; they are similar to wood band saws in style and in that they allow the cutting of any glass shape you could possibly desire, the majority of which would be impossible or impractical to cut by hand. They all use water as a cooling agent for the blade so as little heat as possible will be generated against the glass; you can add router/grinder coolant to the water for additional insurance. The 36" continuous blade is pressure fitted against rotating wheels top and bottom; and the bottom wheel (at least in the older versions; many saws now use a continuous drip bottle) sits partly in a water bath in a base container. This can be a problem since water can ride up the blade onto the glass surface and wash off your pattern marks. (The water bath is aptly named as far as the operator is concerned as well.) A new product on the market, Mark-Stay, rubbed on the glass as a thin coating prior to placement on the saw can prevent the loss of pattern marks.

Once you try one of these saws and feel the power of cutting a glass shape you couldn't cut otherwise, it's hard

Diamond Laser series band saws are capable of cutting virtually any glass shapes including curves with radii as short as 3/16". It's also great for stack cutting up to four pieces at one time. This is the DL 3000 model.

The Taurus II Ring saw has a round omni-directional cutting blade which makes intricate inside curves a delight.

to imagine life without one. The cutting process is guided by a variable speed control. Several companies have had glass saws on the market for some time and continuously upgrade their models, among them Gryphon Corp., Diamond Tech International, and Gemini Saw Co. Advanced Machinery Products has modified a scroll saw to cut glass that has throat sizes of 14", 18", and 22" with a round omni-directional blade to allow cutting very large glass pieces. Since the blade in this instance is straight, not circular, attaching to cleats top and bottom, by drilling a hole in the glass and passing the saw blade through it you can cut out the center and drop a different glass element into that space. This machine is very expensive and is mainly used by large studios specializing in this kind of work.

Our Diamond Laser from Diamond Tech International is now over five years old and has a diamond-coated stainless steel flat blade similar to a band saw blade for wood. The tightest inside curve you can make with a blade saw of this nature is 3/16". The blade is somewhat limited (as compared to the Taurus Ring Saw from Gemini Saw Co.) because you can basically only go forward as you cut; some minimum sideways movement is allowable to move your blade around on the glass but you have to be careful about twisting the blade to any extent or it will snap. The original work surface for the glass to rest on is roughly 6" square but add-ons to this table have become available.

With all these saws, you can stack glass pieces up to 1/2" high (four pieces is probably pushing it) and cut them simultaneously. Caution: stacking means movement so if you attempt this, glue the stack together as one piece. Use a water soluble glue such as Elmer's and put thin scrap paper between each layer, then let it sit overnight. To separate the layers after cutting, soak in water to break the glue down.

Our Diamond Laser 1000 needs to have the blade pitched perfectly on both the top and bottom wheels so it doesn't walk off them in the midst of use (this has been a problem). Tension and torque must be exactly right or frustration takes over. The problem has been solved in the Diamond Laser 3000 series by raising a rim on the wheels to secure and center the blade. This works perfectly and allows an excellent machine to function to capacity.

The remarkable Taurus Ring Saw uses a round blade rather than a flat one so you can cut in all directions. The company claims it cuts everything but fingers. There are diamonds all around the blade, not just on the edge and the blade (actually a rod) is advertised to last four times longer than other diamond coated blades and cost less. It

also provides a smooth surface to the cut edge, smoothing the glass as it cuts it. At least three models of this saw are on the market, from hobbyist use to commercial.

These saws are not limited solely to cutting glass. They will cut all types of glass but will also cut plastic, metal, tile, silver, and stone. Your local retailer will have information and descriptions of all the saws we mentioned and more.

DISC GRINDERS

To our knowledge, the only company making a disc grinder is Glastar, and they really know how to take the edge off. As experts in the glass grinding field (they make beveling machines and sandblasters as well as router/grinders), they can save you a lot of time truing up straight edges on your glass, especially if you are turning out a lot of work requiring absolute straight edges such as boxes, lampshades, and panels with a great number of squares or rectangles. Most large glass studios, including our own, have used belt sanders for years to true up straight edges. A belt sander is cumbersome compared to this efficient little machine which will also grind rock, ceramic, and tile. Not nearly as well known as the router/grinder, the disc grinder is ingenious and equally simple in design. The disc, which is water cooled, rotates horizontally and you simply hold your glass vertically

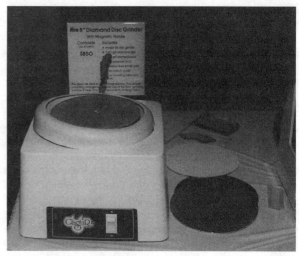

Glastar flat disc grinder for beveling and grinding straight edges.

against the horizontal work surface and the machine will do the rest. An internal fan helps cool the motor, but the whole idea is pretty cool.

GLASS PLIERS

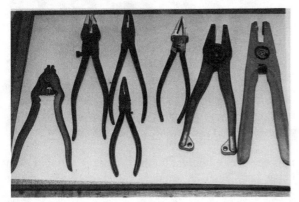

Metal and plastic running pliers with breaking and breaker/grozzer pliers. On the left end are chain pliers used to open and close links.

Glass pliers have a number of specialized applications, although one pair of pliers may be used for various operations without too much trouble. This means that you can probably buy a single pair of pliers initially. Glass pliers go by various names, such as grozzers, breaking pliers, running pliers, and lead-cutting pliers, and there are various categories within each of these according to manufacturing characteristics. Many are manufactured by the Fletcher-Terry Co. and Diamond Tools. Your local retailer should have more extensive descriptions and prices of all these pliers.

Glass or Breaking Pliers

These all-purpose pliers can be used for breaking and grozzing—trimming away pieces of glass that extend beyond the bordering edge of a cut portion too small or too awkward to remove by hand. Some breaking pliers are made with underslung jaws to grip the glass below the score line and nowhere else. Others are made with parallel jaws so as not to pinch the glass, but rather to apply even pressure above and below.

Such pliers are made both with and without grooves in the jaws; grooved pliers have an advantage because they also can be used for rough grozzing. To be used in this fashion, the jaw of a grooved glass plier is worked over a glass edge more or less like a file. Be careful—if too much pressure is applied, the glass will splinter and the edge will be in worse shape than before. Grozzing takes practice and fine grozzing should only be attempted with special grozzing pliers. Only the more obvious points and imbalances can be aligned with a breaker.

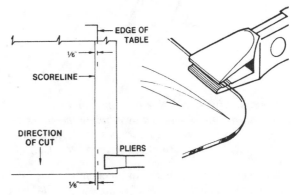

Breaking pliers can either break glass or nip projecting shards. For breaking, calculate their accuracy for trims up to 2" wide. The point of application of the pliers is important. The ends of the jaws must be as parallel to the score line as possible and not more than 1/4" away. Locate the glass so that the score is parallel to the table edge and about 1/16" in from it or right above it. To break out the glass trim, grasp the sheet with the pliers and pull out and down, stabilizing the sheet with the other hand. (Courtesy of Fletcher-Terry Co.)

Glass pliers can also be used to break a piece of glass after it has been scored. Once the score is made, providing it is a straight cut, the glass is laid flat on the table surface with the score uppermost. The glass should be extended over the edge of the table until the score is directly above the table edge. With the glass pliers, firmly grasp the glass piece directly at the score line so that the pliers' lower jaw is almost against the table's edge. With your left hand (if you are right-handed) press the main surface of glass against the table to keep the piece from moving. The pull on the pliers should be out and slightly down; this force will allow the two pieces to separate with a musical "ting." Keep your feet out of the way—occasionally the glass will break into more than two pieces.

Because the width of their jaws makes the procedure somewhat chancy, glass pliers shouldn't be used to break sharp curves unless you are skilled in their use. Here it is

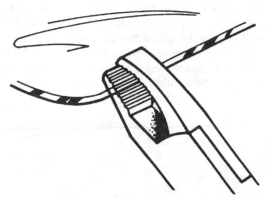

Using grozzing pliers. Narrow trims can be removed and sharp corners rounded by nibbling the edges as shown, using the serrated surfaces of the jaws in a file-like fashion. (Courtesy of Fletcher-Terry Co.)

better to use grozzing pliers. An excellent beginner's pliers is one with either a 6" or 8" handle with a 3/4" or 1" grooved jaw.

Grozzing Pliers

Grozzing pliers have narrow jaws with fine teeth and are used strictly for grozzing or for carving difficult shapes out of glass. They are made of soft metal and any use other than glass grozzing or occasional breaking may damage the teeth. They are also good for nibbling away the fine points and inconsistencies left on the glass from less than perfect cuts. Using these pliers requires more practice than other pliers, but they're worth the effort.

Make sure your grozzers are well oiled so they will open and close with minimal work of the hand. It's easiest if they open from the weight of their bottom handle alone. If you hold grozzing pliers with one handle up, the joint should be so free that the lower handle will drop. Keep all your pliers this spry. It eliminates the tiring motion of constantly having to open them by force even if the force is minimal. Many of the newer pliers have handles that are spring loaded.

Running Pliers

Probably the most difficult cut to score and break out of a glass piece is a thin long strip. This break tends to run off the score line somewhere along its length. Running pliers help such breaks run true.

The jaws of running pliers curve into one another. The top jaw is concave and the lower convex. The lower jaw

Running pliers break more than straight lines as demonstrated with wavy curves.

thus becomes a fulcrum for the two pressure points of the upper jaw. Such an arrangement allows even pressure above and below the score line. To ensure even pressure, a screw gauge is provided on top of the pliers. This screw is turned so the pliers are permitted to grasp only the surfaces of the glass with the smallest amount of pressure—just enough to fracture the score but not enough to crush the glass. You must spend a minute or two arranging the pliers at the score line, since the central mark on the pliers must be matched to the score line. The procedure is as follows:

1) Score the glass in a straight cut.
2) Bring the glass to the table edge so the table edge is at right angles to the cut. Take the running pliers and line up the score on the glass with the guide line shown on the upper jaw of the pliers.
3) Turn the screw gauge so the jaws of the pliers grasp the glass as lightly as possible without slipping. Then loosen the screw perhaps half a turn more. Press firmly on the handles and the cut will travel along the score line.

Another style of running pliers is specially designed with narrow jaws. The handles are spring-loaded for easier handling. This lightweight tool, manufactured by Glastar, is molded of a strong, durable, glass-reinforced Acetel. With the narrower jaws compared to other running pliers, the tool can break much smaller pieces of glass. It works equally well with large pieces.

The spring-loaded handles are a special advantage since they are always open to 3/16"—the perfect spacing for the insertion of an 1/8" piece of glass. Some workers tend to have trouble opening pliers with one hand. Since the bottom jaw of the Glassnapper extends beyond the upper jaw, it is easier to insert the glass in the jaws.

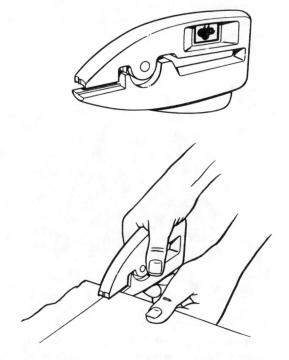

Glastar's Glassnapper running pliers snapping or running the score line.

Round-Barrel Grozzers

These not often seen grozzers will remove a small half moon out of glass rather than a straight line like square jawed pliers will. They are handy when grozzing inside curves and will work well when small concavities must be taken piecemeal out of a pattern. They should not be used as breaking pliers; their grip on the glass, because of the tube shape of the working surfaces, is applicable only to a small glass area. In effect, these are more of a crushing pliers than other types and their use is very specific. Still, when they are necessary, they are very welcome.

Heavy-Duty Grozzers

Heavy-duty grozzers essentially do the same work as small grozzers, but they rest more firmly in a large hand and provide more leverage against the glass edge. It's a matter of individual preference whether to use these or the smaller version. Some workers use the small grozzers exclusively because they don't like the wider grozzing jaws, perhaps feeling that grozzing more surface at a time leads to rougher results. Others feel just the opposite. Which you prefer will depend on the strength and size of your hand. The large grozzer is 7-3/4" long with a jaw width of 7/16". The small grozzer measures 6" in length with a jaw width of 5/16". Although these differences seem small, they make a considerable difference in the amount of leverage obtained, the area encompassed, and the grip and consequent stamina of the hand muscles. The width across the widest point of the large grozzers with the jaws closed is 2-1/4"; that of the small pair is 1-3/4".

Glass Nippers

Glass nippers are not grozzers. Their function is to chew into the glass edge rather than file it. The jaws are two sharp-edged pincers that catch the glass between them and literally bite it away. Some workers use them mainly for rough grozzing of areas that will not sustain a cutting and breaking technique, particularly inside curves. These nippers work well if you avoid taking larger and larger bites. Using this tool unskillfully will inevitably lead to breaking the glass.

Underslung Jaw Breakers

A variation of regular glass pliers, underslung jaw breakers provide a more direct line of pressure under the score line during the breaking process than do regular

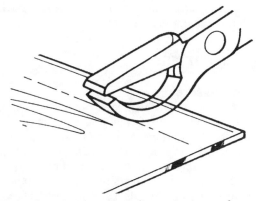

Underslung jaw breaking pliers gripping at the score line. The top jaw holds while the bottom exerts pressure from below.

glass breakers. They also allow you to see more precisely where that lower jaw is. Once the glass breaks, the fragments tend to fall out of the pliers unless a substantial piece is being broken.

Round Jaw Grozzers

The smaller version of the round barrel grozzers can be used where tiny curved areas are to be gnawed out of pieces of glass. However, this process is time consuming. Unless you have the time and patience, forget them and use regular grozzers. The pointed jaws are roughened rather than grooved. Such roughing is essential, given the tiny grasp of these jaws.

Chain Pliers

If you make and wire stained glass lampshades, chain pliers are a must. The application is simple. The action works the opposite of regular pliers. Instead of the jaw opening as you separate the handles, it opens as you squeeze them. The jaws have small ridges that serve to lock a link of chain against them, then as you squeeze the handles the jaws open the link. Our suggestion: if you intend to do any lampshade work and include wiring service, get a substantial pair of chain pliers. It's not impossible to open chain links without them, but it's difficult and frustrating.

Came Cutting Pliers

Some workers use came cutting pliers in addition to their lead knife. (We've discussed these pliers in the chapter on leading.) As an addition to your stock of pliers, you might want to have a pair of these handy. As with a beef steak, you never know when you're going to run into a tough lead came with a dull knife.

PATTERN CUTTERS

Pattern Scissors

Pattern scissors come in at least two sizes—1/16" and 1/8"—the measurement referring to the amount of paper cut away between pattern pieces to make room for the lead came. If you're using lead up to 3/8", you are probably better off with 1/16" scissors. For anything over that, you might want to have both sizes, since you probably will be varying lead sizes within the framework of certain designs.

Pattern scissors consist of three blades, two below and one on top (or vice versa if you're using them that way.)

The bottom two blades are joined to allow a slight space between, which is commensurate with the size of the paper cutout. It is into this space that the top blade falls. Thus the paper is cut precisely and with guillotine sharpness. This sharp edge on the paper pattern is important. A pattern with imprecise edges is a cloudy guide.

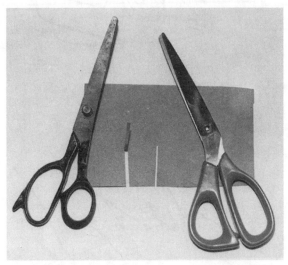

Pattern shears for lead (left) and copper foil (right). The three blade scissors remove the pattern line to allow for the heart in lead came and the space for solder to flow when assembling foiled glass.

Using the scissors for the first time is an experience. Rather than cutting like ordinary scissors—by taking a bite the length of the blade—the best way to use pattern scissors is to take small bites with the back of the blades, inching up on the piece you want to cut out with a crafty maneuverability. Turns and angles can be cut readily after some practice.

Pattern scissors can be used either top blade up or double blade up. If you use the top single blade up, you can sight along the blade against the line being cut. If you want to use the scissors with the double blades on top, sight between the two blades and make sure the line being cut falls between them. Once the pattern is cut, you can't trim frayed edges with regular scissors because you will impinge on the pattern, so cut the pattern correctly the first time. Practice using the scissors on scrap paper before going on to your project.

Electric Pattern Cutters

Two electric pattern cutters that are no longer on store shelves still turn up from time to time in used tool baskets at very reasonable prices. If you are lucky enough to locate either of these they make pattern cutting a lot easier and are fun to use. We won't spend much time on them, just briefly mention them in case. The Carrousel pattern cutter cuts a single-size channel and has a rheostat on the side to speed up or slow down the cutting. There are five speeds to give fast or intricate cutting on papers up to a ten point stock.

The cutter made by Simon Industries has a laminated blade that makes accurately cutting complex patterns easy. It doesn't have a rheostat. However, disregarding these slight differences between the two, it's impossible to decide which does the better job. Each is a tremendous advantage to a hobbyist turning out a reasonable amount of work and therefore cutting a lot of patterns; for an active studio situation, the time saved with one of these devices is incalculable. The heads on both cutters are reversible.

THE LEAD KNIFE

One of the most essential tools in stained glass work is the all-purpose lead knife, which is at once a cutter, fitter, hammer, flange, straight-edge, bender, and straightener of lead came. The leading knife is a basic tool that ranks next to the glass cutter and soldering iron in importance.

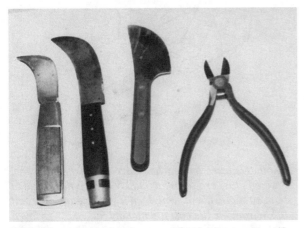

Different style lead knives and lead nipper pliers for cutting came.

Leading knives without weighted handles are cheaper than weighted ones, but we don't recommend them. You can put your own weighted end on a knife by carving down the wood and melting lead into the space. This is what many glassworkers did before weighted knives were made commercially, but it's easier to let the factory do the work. The blade of the leading knife comes either straight or curved and here individual preference takes over. We feel the curved blade can be put to more uses than the straight one. We have several of both in the studio.

The point of either shaped lead knife can be used to hook and position leads within a panel prior to soldering. Cutting the leads with the sharp surface is a technique in itself. With the soft leads, such as 1/8", 1/16", 3/16", either U or H, the danger is that by applying too much force your knife will crush the channel. You then have the additional job of opening the crevice and straightening the lead.

A professional leading knife is made of the best steel and will keep its temper far longer than the operator who is inefficiently wielding it. You don't want to come down with it like a hatchet against the lead nor should you apply body pressure hoping to push the blade through the came. Let the knife edge do its job. The best way to cut lead came is to lay the blade straight on the top surface of the came (not on the channeled side) and with a small amount of pressure, wiggle it from side-to-side, not up-and-down. It will cut through the lead with surprising speed without disturbing the came profile.

Use the same principle for cutting leads 1/4" and up. It's safer to use more pressure on the knife than with the thinner leads. With heavy leads, you may have to use both hands, but wiggling the knife blade from left to right will enable the sharp edge to gain purchase and cut through the came, making neat usable slicings.

A word of caution: A professional leading knife is a precision tool but it occasionally needs to be sharpened. Don't use a kitchen knife sharpener, since it will chip the blade. An Arkansas whetstone will put an edge on your knife with ease, readying it for another year of use. Such a sharpening process involves strapping the knife across the stone, which is oiled with light machine oil. Don't be impatient with this process and try to keep the angle at which you are strapping the knife the same with each stroke.

LATHKINS

Lathkins widen and straighten the lead channels so the glass will seat. No advanced worker in stained glass would consider beginning a leaded project without this convenient item at hand.

Imported metal lathkins come in two sizes—thick and thin—and they can either be pushed or pulled through the came channel. If you want to push the lathkin through the came, hold the instrument with the rounded end within the channel and wiggle it slowly through the came, using the force of your arm to push it along. You must keep the lead straight and braced behind the instrument as you go. If you would rather pull the lathkin through to straighten the channel, dip the point into the channel and pull it toward you. Don't pull it too hard—especially if the piece of came is twisted—or you will tear the lead.

Many workers make their own wooden lathkin to fit their hand. Start with a hard wood such as oak, walnut, or maple, and sand it with a bench sander to the appropriate dimensions. Dipping it in a hot oil will lubricate it and seal the wood. Let the wood stand in oil overnight. The top portion of an old pool cue cut to size is an excellent base for a wood lathkin. It's already almost entirely shaped for your grip. Wood lathkins, no matter how hard the wood, will wear out in time and will begin to chip and fault irregularly along the working surface.

Many lathkins today are made from plastic. This material wears well and is so smooth that it slides readily through the lead channel. Various sizes and shapes are on the market, since no single lathkin design has yet achieved general approval. In an emergency almost anything that will widen or open a lead channel will serve the purpose, even the point of a pencil.

LEAD STRETCHER

The lead stretcher is a specialized vise, calculated to hold lead came securely while it is being stretched. It is composed of a fixed lower and a movable upper jaw. It can be screwed firmly to a shelf or table, which itself must be strong enough to withstand the pull of the worker at the other end of the came.

With the top jaw laid back, one end of the came is placed against the lower "teeth" and the top jaw closed firmly. The lead is not yet snuggled into the vise; this happens as the came is pulled, since the teeth or ridges are so angled that when the came is pulled they automatically lock against it. However, it's wise to hand lock the top jaw against the came with some force because the teeth don't always automatically grab it.

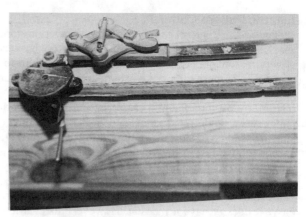

One example of a spring loaded came vise. This swivels to anchor the lead to a pre-measured point on the bench, then moves out of the way.

Glastar Corp. makes a spring-loaded lead stretcher that is probably the best on the market. The jaws can open wide enough to accept the thickest lead while making certain they close with the proper force. To remove the came, simply open the vise. You can use a workshop vise to

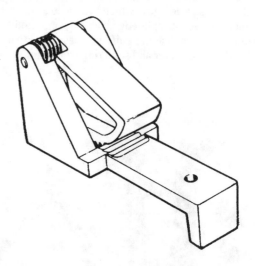

Another spring loaded lead stretcher from Glastar. Stained glass crafters can quickly stretch their lead to both strengthen and straighten it. Your lead can't pull loose from the die cast aluminum lead vise's grooved teeth—a strong spring keeps the arm firmly down at all times.

hold the lead, but more work is involved in opening and closing it and the lead will be crushed and torn and likely tear loose during stretching. Most stained glass workers buy a lead stretcher sooner or later; it's easier than holding the end of a six foot length of came under your foot and pulling up at the other end.

LEADING NAILS

Commercial leading nails (imported from Germany) are an excellent means of stabilizing your project as you work on it. With their tapered sides, they minimize gouges in the lead came and help prevent chips in the glass and they are so finely tapered that they anchor firmly in the wood of the work table when tapped with the end of your weighted lead knife, but allow removal with finger force alone. This is highly desirable since you will be constantly hammering in and removing these nails.

Obviously the project keeps building as you add more and more glass. Such nails seem to never blunt their points. A good leading nail makes leading up not only easier but a lot quicker. A good leading nail: 1) is thin enough so that it won't split or chip the glass edges it is meant to hold, but not so thin it will fail to maintain a proper purchase in the wood of the work board; 2) is tapered to allow removal by finger force alone; 3) has a sharp point, but not one so fragile that it will blunt or skew after the first few uses; 4) should be high enough to stand reasonably above the working area but not so high it will interfere with the worker's hand movements.

Remember that any movement of the glass pieces while you are leading them up can mean redoing a section of the work in progress since if one moves it affects others. You are dependent on leading nails to hold the completed pieces where you have set them. After all, once you take the time and effort to draw a design, cut a pattern, and cut glass to match the pieces, you should feel secure that the pieces will at least stay put as you work.

We all tend to use what is easiest to hand and various kinds of nails are certainly available in most homes. Various kinds will not serve the purpose here. Imported German leading nails are the best; they can be obtained from glasswork supply houses and once you use them, you will find they are practically indestructible.

A second choice nail is the #10 horseshoe nail. These are sold by many stained glass distributors as leading nails. Horseshoe nails are flat and will do the job almost as well as the German ones. However, they may indent lead came if placed too tightly and, in many cases, their

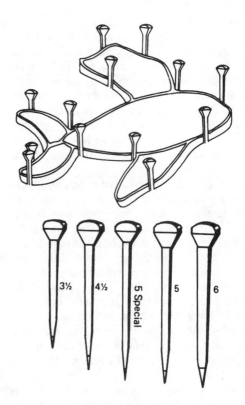

Five diamond horseshoe nails shown actual size. Sizes 3-1/2 and 4-1/2 are packed in one pound boxes, sizes 5 and 6 are packed in five pound boxes. The nails hold a piece of leaded stained glass prior to soldering the lead joints. Note that the widest flat side of the nail is against the leaded surface of the glass.

points are not nearly as impervious to constant use as the German ones. If you're going this route, at least specify top quality horseshoe nails of Swedish steel. These are boxed approximately 150 to 160 a pound for use in stained glass.

You can also use push pins to hold glass pieces, depending on the material you intend to push them into. It's tiring to push them into plywood. They are usually used with Homosote boards. These pins come with aluminum or glass heads, measuring about 5/8". They are usually used only with small projects though if you get a large enough piece of Homosote, you could do a good sized window with push pins.

GLASS DRILLS

Drilling a hole in a piece of glass is not quite as simple as drilling a piece of wood or metal. A special carbide drill bit must be used. Glass drill bits fit into standard hand drills and can be used with water lubricant. However, if too much heat is generated by the procedure, the glass will crack. This usually occurs when the job is almost done and you think you're out of danger. The desire to avoid cracking sometimes leads to overuse of the lubricant, which, if it puddles over the surface, will prevent the drill bit from acquiring purchase on the glass and cause it to slip.

The best indication of successful drilling is sound. If you hear no sound at all from the grinding process and the bit keeps turning in the beginning hole with no perceptible progress, chances are you are using too much water (some workers prefer to use light oil as lubricant). If, on the other hand, you hear the "cry" of the glass as you drill (a grinding sound that increases in intensity) and feel frictional resistance to the drilling, you need more lubricant. You will also see quite a bit of glass dust coming up from the hole. Diminish the sound with lubricating material so it is faint but still audible. If you can maintain it at this volume, you should be able to drill safely through the glass. The average hole should take no longer than a minute or two.

Carbide glass bits are available in different shapes, from spear-headed to triangular. Price varies according to size and shape and they are expensive. Dimensions are from 1/8" to 1/4". The most frequently used size is 3/16". This hole size serves the purpose for most people using it to hang small objects.

Glastar makes a glass drill bit with a specially designed diamond-coated surface for round glass holes. It will cut a 3/4" hole in 1/8" glass in less than 15 seconds. Also available is a 1/4" drill bit.

Diamond-coated bits are far superior to the traditional carbide-tipped spear point bits. They are much easier to use, more convenient, and their life is many times that of the carbide-tipped drill bits.

If you want to use a carbide-tipped bit in an electric drill, as opposed to a hand drill, you have to build a dam of putty on the glass and fill it with kerosene. Then use a slow speed of about 400 rpm to drill through the glass. This is a time consuming tedious process and cracking the glass is likely. With diamond-coated drills, you merely sponge out a teaspoonful of plain water on the glass. Then you quickly and easily make a hole at any speed, depending on your drill. Breakage is minimal. Such a bit can make several hundred holes before it has to be replaced. This is many times more than the spear point drill bit can do and many times more holes than the average hobbyist will require. The diamond bits will fit any standard portable drill. Glastar makes diamond bits for electric drills for almost any size hole.

Another use for holes in glass, incidentally, other than for hanging small objects, is for installing jewels to simulate eyes in types of suncatchers. Inlaying is more professional looking than mere surface gluing.

GLASS GRINDERS

No piece of technology has so changed the aspect of stained glass as a hobby and art form as the glass grinder. It competes with the glass cutter as a revolutionary development. The notion of using a rotating head, lubricated and diamond-coated, to grind pieces of glass into shapes that could be cut only with great difficulty by a glass cutter, was taken from the lapidary industry. The main manufacturers of glass grinders are Inland Corp. and Glastar and each makes an excellent product in a variety of grinder sizes and abilities so they make it easy to find a grinder for your particular budget and purpose. There are diamond grinding bits for every application, from 1/8" to 1" in diameter. The grits vary from the speed bit rough knurled texture to the 220 fine grit for softer glass. See a local retailer for prices and choices.

Basic to the function of the glass grinder (or glass router as it is also called) is the head. Many shapes are offered

A large work surface grinder (Glastar) and one of the Diamond Laser saws.

for grinding various surfaces. The heads are divided into two groups, depending on whether their purpose is grinding or cutting holes. Such heads provide grinding sleeves of a metal/diamond process, allowing for a controlled and consistent grinding surface for the life of the sleeve. Brass and stainless steel have been used for grinding bodies to prevent corrosion and freezing in the motor shaft since silica powder, generated by grinding glass, tends to creep

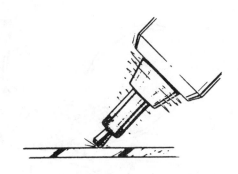

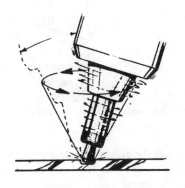

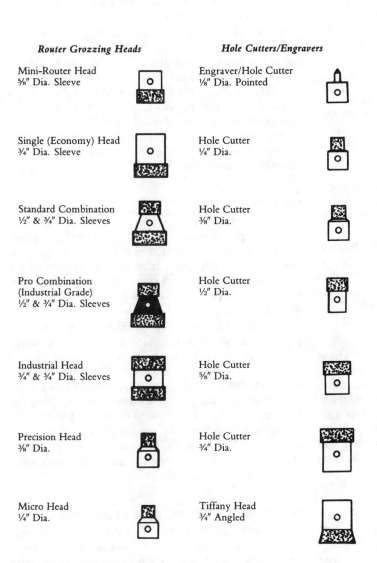

Router Grozzing Heads	Hole Cutters/Engravers
Mini-Router Head 5/8" Dia. Sleeve	Engraver/Hole Cutter 1/8" Dia. Pointed
Single (Economy) Head 3/4" Dia. Sleeve	Hole Cutter 1/4" Dia.
Standard Combination 1/2" & 3/4" Dia. Sleeves	Hole Cutter 3/8" Dia.
Pro Combination (Industrial Grade) 1/2" & 3/4" Dia. Sleeves	Hole Cutter 1/2" Dia.
Industrial Head 3/4" & 3/4" Dia. Sleeves	Hole Cutter 5/8" Dia.
Precision Head 3/8" Dia.	Hole Cutter 3/4" Dia.
Micro Head 1/4" Dia.	Tiffany Head 3/4" Angled

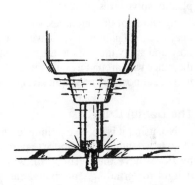

Cutting a hole in glass using Glastar's diamond-coated drill bit in a standard drill. Top: The hole is started by placing the tip at an angle to the glass. Center: The drill is gradually straightened as it gains purchase on the surface. Bottom: The hole is completed with the drill vertical to the glass.

Router grozzing heads from the Glasscrafter Co.

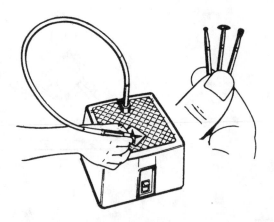

Glastar's flexible shaft attaches to all its glass grinders. This ancillary tool is especially useful for engraving on glass. Three diamond-plated tools for grinding and engraving come in a kit: an inverted cone, a ball, and a disc.

between the grinding body and the motor shaft. These can solidify and freeze the body in the same manner as rust and corrosion will do. Using Delrin, a tough industrial plastic, solves this problem.

Speaking of drilling holes, with a grinder it can be practically second nature. If you have the right head for the purpose and apply the glass to the grinding surface rather than the other way around as with the drill, you can drill a hole to meet almost any need quickly, easily, and safely.

The Dental Drill

No, using it is not like pulling teeth and you don't have to go to a dental supply house to purchase one; many hobby stores have them. This drill, with its hand piece, is a delight for grinding, engraving, and polishing small objects whether they be glass chunks or glass pieces or metal overlays. The advantage of the hand piece is that it's so easy to hold and the long arm-like pulley system will stretch across whatever you have on the table. Various bits are available for different tasks.

WIRE BRUSHES

Wire brushes are not to be confused with flux brushes. They have a stiff copper-bristled, fairly wide scrubbing area and are used to scrub the oxidized surface off lead prior to soldering a joint. Their use is especially advised

where joints have been allowed to sit for some time prior to soldering. The more oxidation formed on the surface of the lead, the more difficult it is to get the solder to "take." Employing this sort of brush with a little elbow grease cuts the frustration factor considerably.

Don't use a brush with tough steel bristles that will scratch the glass and probably tear the lead away from it. An instrument more in the nature of a heavy suede brush will do. A few sweeping back-and-forth motions should produce a nice shiny surface to the lead, which will then take the solder well.

If you have a large window to do with a great number of oxidized lead joints, you could save time by using a round brush with a central axle that fits into an electric hand drill. These brushes should be used with great control since the rotation of the drill against the glass will try to tear the brush out of your hand. A stiff brush used this way could scratch the glass, though if you use a soft enough one it's unlikely. A little cleaning and polishing powder placed over the glass before brushing will clean off oxidation even more speedily.

MARKING PENS

Glass marking pencils, crayon-like markers, have been used in the past to mark areas of glass for cutting or grinding. They are still used in studios to some extent, but most workers prefer felt-tipped markers with permanent ink that, unlike crayons, won't come off the glass when you are using a grinder or a saw which, of necessity, will be wetting the surface.

We recommend ultra-fine tip markers that make lines to match (as closely as possible) the width of the cutting wheel of the glass cutter. The more focused on this line you are, the more accurate your cut will be. With the broad line from a marking crayon, you can't be exactly sure where to place a score. We never use a marking pen to make our cut lines, we always cut from a pattern.

Marking pens come in several colors, among them gold, silver, and white for dark glass. If you are placing any glass in the kiln, be sure to clean such marks off or they will bake right into the glass.

PATTERN, ABRASIVE, AND CRAFT PAPERS

Pattern paper should be heavy-duty, about 80 pound stock. This thickness should be precise. The cartoon is drawn on it, traced from the work drawing and the paper must allow for a certain amount of wear and tear when cut for pattern pieces yet be thin enough so the glass cutter wheel can ride along it without being raised from the glass surface. Use white or a light colored paper to contrast with the glass. Pattern paper, when cut with a pattern scissors, should leave a clean edge.

Craft paper is a rugged brown wrapping paper often used by artists for making sketches. In stained glass we use it to make our work drawing. This work drawing will be with you throughout the course of your project and will be subject to nail holes, spilled flux, and hot solder. Craft paper holds up surprisingly well through it all, whereas a lesser strength paper might disintegrate, leaving you without guide lines.

Abrasive paper is a special type of wet-dry sanding cloth that will take rough edges off glass pieces. Although this cloth won't take the place of a grinder, it can do similar work though with more effort on your part. For glass it is best used wet. Dip it in water and place the glass on the work table, allowing the surface to be sanded to extend over the tabletop. Abrasive paper works fairly rapidly and will last a long time if you let it dry after use and shake out the glass dust. Or rinse it out in running water to get rid of the glass dust. Using abrasive paper dry on glass considerably shortens its lifespan.

PUTTY

Stained glass windows or panels that will be exposed to the weather or that are larger than one square foot should be puttied. This weatherproofs the work and adds strength by supporting the glass within the lead channels. Linseed oil putty is preferred because it is freely workable and tends to harden as the linseed oil evaporates. It is either white or black. The puttying process is messy and no one yet has found an easier way to accomplish it than just pushing the putty beneath the lead cames with your thumb. When all the lead has been so treated, turn down the lead channels with your lead knife or putty knife, sprinkle cleaning and polishing powder over the glass surface to take up the excess putty and, with a floor scrub brush, go over the entire glass surface. Vacuum up the residue, turn the window or panel, and treat the other side in a similar manner.

SLAB GLASS WEDGE AND HAMMER

The specialized tools used for slab glass, or dalles de verre, are described in the Slab Glass chapter. They are used for no other aspect of stained glass and can be purchased if and when you begin working with this interesting material.

PATINAS

The basic patina has been copper sulfate, long used to change a "tinned" came to an antique, coppery color. There are other patinas to color such a soldered line either black or antique brass. The purpose of patina is to give color to the metal and to coat it to prevent the dulling or graying of either the plain leaded line or the tinned one due to oxidation.

A sampling of the many brands of flux and patinas for working in stained glass.

Tinning at first will keep a shiny new look but after enough time passes, this luster will begin to fade to a grayish tone. Some workers don't care for this transformation and want to head it off with patina; others don't like the shiny appearance and want to change it immediately; some are satisfied to allow the tinning to age naturally and never use patina. It's your choice.

Some patinas are best applied with a barely damp sponge which cuts the concentrate just enough to allow it to attach to the underlying metal. As more patina is applied, the color gets darker. When patina is applied shortly after tinning when the metal is still warm, the patina will transform the underlying color almost instantly. Application can be done with cotton, a rag, paper towel, or a flux brush (which should not be used afterwards for flux). Just about any applicator will do, though a damp sponge usually works best.

Color Magic

Color Magic, manufactured by Eastman Corp., is not a patina, though it is used to change the color both of lead came, copper foil, and other metals, and will color the glass itself if you so desire. It is more of a specialized stain or paint that does not need to be heated in a kiln to provide an overlay. The permanence is not completely known because the material has not been around as long as the stains and paints discussed in the painting chapter.

This carousel horse and back of the glass nuggets were painted with Color Magic paints.

To best preserve the color of Color Magic (there are a variety of colors which may be used separately or mixed), use its Ultra Violet sealant as base coat as well as top coat. Color Magic comes in three modalities: opaque, transparent, and glitter (a metallic flake paint). The company also provides a thinner/solvent to make the material flow easier after the bottle has been opened. Each bottle of Color Magic is about the size of a nail polish bottle with a similar cap and brush. The thinner/solvent can be used to clean the brush which, in the case of fine lines, may be too thick. A thinner brush of your own may be substituted in this case; the material will work just as well. You can use the material on clear window glass or as an adjunct of colors to stained glass itself; it will provide some stunning effects in either instance.

ACID BRUSHES

These look like library paste brushes; a box is inexpensive and they are the best way we know to spread flux on a joint. Spread is not the right word for this process which truly involves scrubbing the flux into the lead or copper foil to acquire a neat, tight join. Scrubbing with these brushes means treating the brush prior to use since the bristles come much too long to get enough force behind them to literally scrub the lead or copper surface so the flux can penetrate. We cut down our flux brushes to almost the nub, leaving only about 3/4" bristles which now are really stiff and will do the job. Such a flux brush can be used over and over. They usually get lost before they wear out.

If you use different kinds of flux, you can use the same brush for all but if you are using your brush for patina, don't use the same one for flux or you'll contaminate your flux, making it less than effective.

FLUXES

Fluxes are discussed at length in the chapter on soldering and we mention them here only to emphasize their importance. Flux is a term applied to a chemical which, while itself remaining unchanged by a physical or chemical process, helps that process go forward. An appropriate stained glass flux: 1) will clean the surface of a metal without harming the metal; 2) won't affect or stick to the glass; 3) won't produce harmful fumes; 4) is liquid rather than paste; 5) will leave minimum residue which will be easy to clean; 6) is inexpensive since you will be using a lot of it.

For years, the flux of choice in stained glass was oleic acid but now various fluxes are available. Experiment with samples until you find the right flux for you.

SOLDERING EQUIPMENT

The Solder Pot

Most hobbyists may not require this item which is, as its name implies, a pot that holds molten solder. It's a fantastic time saver if you are foiling a lot of small pieces. Esico-Triton makes a wide range of models for tinning, stripping, or dip soldering from small pieces to dipping printed circuit boards. Obviously they are mainly for continuous production requirements but that is a very elastic term. A solder pot for stained glass requirements need not be large; a small pot going to 200 watts may be all that's required.

After foiling the glass pieces, dip the foiled rim into the molten solder and in seconds you have tinned foil. The process does away with tinning by hand. Then solder the pieces together, bead them, and you're done.

Soldering Irons & Tip Cleaners

The Inland Co. also makes soldering irons. We have used both theirs and those made by Hakko Corp. Despite what you may think, soldering irons are not all alike and we recommend that you purchase a good quality iron either from these companies or others that make irons for the stained glass industry.

The Inland solder station has built-in compartments to hold a solder spool, flux bottle, brushes, iron tips, wet sponge, and the iron which plugs into the temperature control.

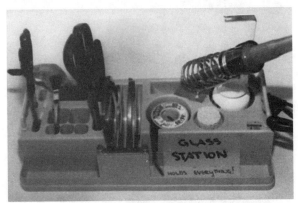

This Inland tool caddy is geared to be portable. It holds pens, scissors, cutter, solder, and flux. The foil rolls can be set up to use the added feature of a dispenser for wrapping.

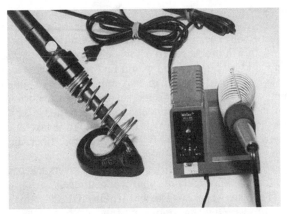

Basic soldering stands for when mobility counts. Inland's heavy weight (left) will hold any iron and the Weller (right) has the temperature control at your fingertips.

We like a 100 watt iron engineered for quick heat production, transfer, and recovery with a stainless steel stem. This stem allows for cooler handles. These should be standard irons that operate on standard 110 line current. All components of the iron, from tip to heating element, should be replaceable without having to spend more than ten minutes at the job.

We recommend pre-tinned tips in various shapes (see the Soldering chapter), depending on the type of work they are calculated to do. Tip cleaners are also available from both companies as are soldering iron control units. Glastar also provides soldering elements such as tip cleaners and soldering control units.

Soldering Iron Control Units

Using a bare iron to solder lead came can lead to burning a hole in the lead as the iron gets hotter and hotter. A soldering iron control unit from Hakko, Glastar, Inland, or Esico allows you to control the amount of heat the iron will reach. It cycles the electricity going to the iron to keep the heat level. Even working with copper foil can become difficult with a too-hot iron. You won't put a hole in the foil the way you can in lead with an overly hot iron, but you'll find the solder won't take, it will tend to roll off the foil or melt solder at the joint. Before these control units, we had to put a line switch on the iron's cord and keep switching it on and off to regulate the heat. And you had to be careful where you put the switch so it didn't catch on the table edge and jerk the iron out of your hand. It's much easier with a control unit.

KILNS

Unless you are firing large pieces of glass for painting or (especially) bending or slumping glass, a tabletop beehive kiln will probably serve you well enough. The Paragon QuikFire 6 is one you would find acceptable. It will go from zero to 1000°F in five minutes (we've timed ours) and it will plug into the standard electric current. You can fire and cool in about 35 minutes. The QuikFire measures 6" by 6" inside and is light enough to take anywhere. It is rated at 2000°F. It has a ceramic fiber shell with an embedded element. The shell rests on a ceramic fiber base. The steel bottom completely covers the base and lifts the kiln safely off your work surface.

The Wale Apparatus Co. and Jenkins Kilns also make several varieties of tabletop kilns. Wale's Dome Kiln/Bead Kiln Converter has an interior space of 6-1/2" x 6-1/2" x 4-1/2" tall and is also a fine firing unit. Larger floor model kilns are also made by these companies should you decide kiln fired glass (fusing, bending, shaping, sagging, molding) is the way to go.

WOOD FRAMES

You may or may not use a frame for your panel or window; many workers use the practical frame that is also the bordering lead or zinc, simply attaching copper loops and hanging it that way. However, if you made something you are particularly proud of, or you've taken on a commission requiring a frame, or if you are entering your piece in a show where wood framing is a must, obviously the bordering zinc or lead won't do. You can either make such a wood frame yourself—not so easy a task, especially if the window is round or oval rather than square or rectangular—which takes time and effort, or you can purchase one.

Available from McNeil Woodworks Inc. are quality oak frames such as clock frames, round, oval, octagon, shelf frames, and frames for specialty shapes. Many of these are stocked by local suppliers or can be ordered. You should decide at the start if you are going to use a frame for your project. It is much more practical to design your pattern for compatibility with the dimensions of a frame that has an inside opening close to your final proportions than the other way round. Differences between your completed project and the size frame available can be minute but may require a certain amount of reworking on your part or an extra expense to custom cut a square or rectangular frame. Northern Hardwoods Framing, through your supplier, will do this and send you the pieces to put together along with any extra stock from which your frame was cut. Frames are mitered, drilled, and supplied with framing screws.

McNeil frames are constructed of red oak and finished in Watco medium Danish oil finish. All frames are supplied with flexible reed and except for clock frames and straight grain frames, all are one inch thick. Your local supplier will have catalogs showing the details of framing more extensively.

MISCELLANEOUS TOOLS

A hacksaw is nice to have around to cut re-bars and even heavy lead came. In a similar vein, have a good all-purpose metal cutting shears available. This will come in handy as tin snips if you want to cut tops for lamps or lanterns or metal overlays. You may want to include a foot switch for such items as saws, grinders, or dental drills.

For wiring lamps you will need a good pair of wire strippers. And there is always a need for screwdrivers (both regular and Phillips), hammer, regular pliers, electric drill and, yes, rags. Rags are not a tool, but forget definition. When you spill something or need to wipe something down, it's usually right now and to go off and start looking for a rag at that time is counter-productive. A handy roll of paper towel may or may not suffice, depending on the extent of the disaster, but keep one around as a backup. The philosophy here is to be prepared for every contingency and then no evil ones will occur.

An example of a wood framed mirror with applied stained glass flowers.

CHAPTER 6
Ancillary Materials: Jewels, Rondels, Nuggets, Filigree, and More

GLASS JEWELS AS SUCH

Glass "jewels" are compact, self-sustaining pieces of glass that cover a wide array of provocative characters and choices. They can be pressed or cast, spun or sculpted, carved or hammered, reflective, faceted, multi- or single colored, and new or old. As elements of varying texture, design, size, and shape, they are used to add an aesthetic wallop to windows or lamps, most often in border arrangements. They can also be used to point up a whimsical creation, or brighten a suncatcher or even, pierced with decorative chain, wear around your neck. They serve as punctuation marks in the grammar of stained glass design. Tiffany used them, as did LaFarge and most of the designers of that era. From those older windows came the old jewels, many of which have been duplicated today so it is sometimes difficult to tell them apart.

Most of the old jewels (and many today) were made from molten glass pressed into three-dimensional form in steel molds. The Heidt Co. of Brooklyn produced most of them and they were known as "Heidt jewels." The fabrication was simple: the end of a solid colored glass rod was heated to molten state in a beehive oven, then quickly placed into a Swedish steel mold press. The glass jewel

Pressed and cast jewels from the Heidt Co.

was pressed out, placed in a lehr, and allowed to cool slowly. Most of these old molds have been lost to us, but if you can find these jewels, they will add a charming antique look to your design.

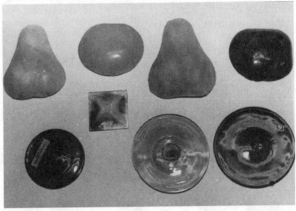

Jewels, rondels, and bent fruit. The bent fruit is often used in lampshades.

Jewels can dramatically emphasize and heighten the effect of a piece, though, they shouldn't overwhelm it. Jewels also may be used in abstract hanging objects as the central portion of a glass arrangement; prisms work well here.

Jewels are much in demand, particularly reds, golds, and yellows. We have found old stained glass windows in antique shops that, even though mistreated over the years, still yield up a handful of old jewels. New jewels, often clearer in color than the older ones and of more modern design, are inexpensive and provide lovely ornamental fillips to a creation.

RONDELS AND "BOTTLE BOTTOMS"

Rondels are circles of glass that have been handspun or pressed by machine. They come in most colors and in sizes from 2" up to 12" or even larger, usually by special order. It is not always easy to tell the difference between a spun and a pressed rondel. Both types are beautiful, and both are equally effective used within panels or freeform mobiles, or even just leaded up as is and hung. A spun rondel usually contains more whirls of color within it than one that is pressed by machine. These whirls give a soft, beguiling appearance that, added to its geometric shape, makes the rondel one of the more emphatically effective stained glass design elements.

Since rondels come with a rounded edge, they are not difficult to lead though too narrow a lead will prevent the rounded flange from being inserted. Designing a window or panel with rondels is a tricky task because it's easy to get carried away and overdo it. These colorful circles may then take over the design of the window, overwhelming rather than intriguing the eye.

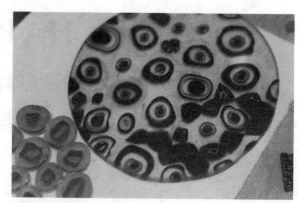

Millefiore shown in slices off the rod and after they have been kiln fired into a plate.

out into dazzling whirls of colors rather like a firecracker going off, though much quieter. Designs vary from stars to fleur-de-lis, to concentric rings of color. When a millefiore is placed on top of a piece of glass and heat is applied, it melts into the glass base and forms a technicolor addition to the underlying surface. But millefiore do not have to be heated to be effective. Used as eyes for small glass animals or grouped in patterns and glued in abstract designs, they form unusual three-dimensional effects. While millefiore are not cheap, a few of them go a long way.

An assortment of spun and machine made rondels.

Rondels are fairly expensive due to the nature of their manufacture. Glass circles that resemble rondels (sort of) are cheaper, and they also may have swirls of color within them. These are bottle bottoms—the bottoms of the glass cylinders that form sheet glass. These bottoms are cut away once the form has been blown and are sold as decorative items. They are usually somewhat irregular in circumference with rough edges that have to be smoothed before use. Bottle bottoms can be opalescent or clear, just as rondels, and are about 8" in diameter.

MILLEFIORE

Millefiore, also known as Venetian beads or tube glass, are short multicolored cylinders. On end they look a little like a pizza pie. When heated in a kiln they spread

GLASS NUGGETS

Glass nuggets, or globs, are exactly what they sound like: small lumps of solid glass in various colors and shapes. They are not individually molded but produced in freeform fashion. They can be foiled, leaded, or glued to an underlying design to give it dimension as a prism-like overlay.

Glass globs usually have one fairly flat surface where they lie best. This surface is where the glob itself rested while it was being formed in the kiln on a flat charcoal plate. Occasionally you will find twinned globs or globs of interesting deformities among a particular batch. Such unusual configurations may be put to imaginative use as ancillary items: the centers of flowers, decoration for glassware, bottles or jars to make candleholders; in stained glass jewelry; or as lamp ornaments. They are cheap and if you have enough different sizes and colors, you can use them to create a mosaic effect. Spaces between may be grouted or filled with liquid lead or glued with special glues that dry to a transparent, rapid finish

Glass nuggets of various colors and sizes. Now also available in iridescent and cat's eye.

and will not shrink. Beware of the general all-purpose hardware store glue here; it will likely lose its holding power as it dries.

METALS: EMBROIDERY AND OTHER USES

Thin brass or copper sheeting can be used to cut leaves, wings, or other overlay items that you can design yourself with scissors or purchase ready made from a local supplier. More than likely, your supplier will have it in brass. While somewhat more difficult to work with than copper as far as cutting your own designs, brass will impart more rigidity. Stencils for multiple painting patterns can also be cut from either material to satisfactory effect.

Sample of brass filigree kits available for night lights to box decoratons.

Some workers use parts of wire hangers for skeletal structures, such as flower stems or backbones of glass animals which must be self-supportive and reach a certain height. Using metal or wire hangers for this purpose involves a certain amount of fuss, since any metal not ordinarily solderable, such as a wire coat hanger, must first be sanded clean of paint, fluxed vigorously with an inorganic acid flux (such as hydrochloric acid in glycerin), and then tinned. Tinning is impossible unless a strong flux is used because the solder will roll off the metal. After tinning and soldering, the hanger becomes a convenient stem, wand, spike, handle, or body in its new incarnation. It's usually not much good for hanging clothes after this treatment.

Galvanized steel bars are used for bracing windows that need more strength than lead and putty can provide. Older windows were braced with ungalvanized steel. Since steel cannot be soldered, copper loops were wound around these bars at juncture areas and these loops were then soldered to the leads.

Completed little angel with clear jewel for head and filigree wings, halo, and robe trim.

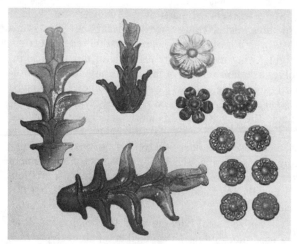

Cast lead flat decorations, floral buttons and corner decorations to solder on intersecting lines for windows and doors.

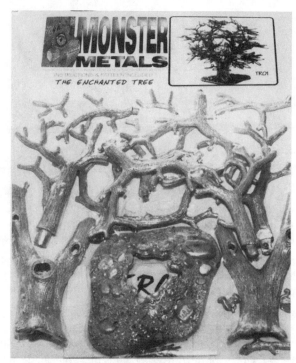

Larger statuary forms are being made. This is a lead tree to assemble where the glass would be the leaves. The lead can be patinaed or painted with Color Magic paints. Casting by Monster Metals.

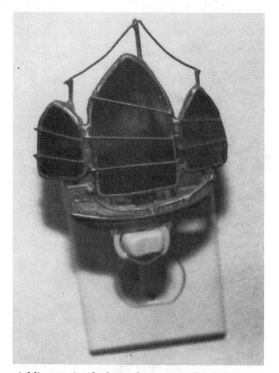

Adding stained glass elements to lead castings has become popular recently. A Chinese junk night light with three glass sails and wire rigging are from Outkast Metals lead kit.

The lead cast figures are based on fantasy type characters such as fairies, mystical nudes, and warriors. Shown here is a dragon that requires glass wings to fly from Monster Metals.

Pieces of galvanized steel scraps cut to size make excellent crossbars for the tops of lanterns to support the underlying socket and the hanging ring above. If you want to try this, be sure to get a wide enough piece of metal to allow for the hole you must drill through it for the socket to be placed. If you don't want to go to the trouble of drilling through one of these metal straps, cut two of them to size, leaving room between them for the socket nipple, and rely on the pressure of the hanging ring to maintain stability.

Lead castings are an old and effective decorative technique. They can be used as overlays or leaded directly into a window as dimensional inserts. You can make your own lead castings from waste came (you'll have plenty—keep all off-cuts in a special waste receptacle). Molds for such castings are available or you can make your own from plaster of Paris. Lead is easily melted with a small torch. It's as much fun making castings as working with glass.

In recent years, lead cast figurines have become popular as a quickly accomplished project due to the simplicity of the work. Basically all you do is add glass flower petals, fish fins, bird feathers, sails and dragon wings to the pre-formed casting. Most cast figures are fairly detailed and factory cleaned, but you should examine it for any sprue (excess lead along the seam resulting from joining a two-part mold casting). Not only is this excess aesthetically improper, you can scrape skin with it. You can use a metal file or carefully carve this away with a craft knife blade.

Depending on the complexity of the item, you may need to assemble it before you can add the glass elements. When you solder the glass elements to the casting, don't melt the casting. Remember, lead has a low melting point. Once the glass elements have been added and cleaned, you may patina or paint the figure to give it more oomph.

GLASS RODS

Glass rods are available in various sizes and thicknesses. They can be cut with a glass cutter by nicking the rod and breaking it or by sawing through a thick rod with a carborundum blade fitted in any hacksaw handle. Glass rods can be melted in the kiln to interesting shapes and designs (the heat must go to 1800°F since you are dealing with a solid glass core), and they may also be used for support, especially for mobiles. Fish line, which is all but invisible, can be purchased in any sporting goods store to hang the mobile, and it can be attached to the proper balancing point on the glass rod by making a deep score around the rod at that area and wrapping the fish line into the groove. To smooth the ends of cut rods, polish with wet abrasive paper.

BOTTLES

Bottle cutting, a craze from some years back, is back to some extent and kits for cutting bottles can be purchased from a stained glass supplier. Instructions for this operation are simple enough and come with the kit. Uncut bottles also have their uses. They do not have to be molded in a kiln to be used in stained glass work, although if you have a kiln you can get some interesting shapes by twisting and collapsing bottles with heat, both with and without molds.

In addition, the bottoms of many wine and beer bottles can gain a secondary life of their own as decorative items when separated from the bottle itself. Not only the bottoms but also the sides of bottles because of their ready curvature, are natural for a boat's sails or any object requiring a bend. Even the tops of bottles can be strung together as effective wind chimes.

Without a bottle cutting kit, bottles can be cut with little difficulty using a hot wire or a carborundum blade in a hacksaw handle. The hot wire technique requires just that: a wire heated red hot is wrapped around the bottle and then removed and the bottle plunged into cold water. It should break apart neatly after you a practiced a bit. Cutting with a carborundum blade takes longer to do the job, with more work on your part, but it is equally effective. *One caution:* Cutting bottles with a blade can be tricky at first because of the curvature of the bottle. Hold the bottle securely. Wear a glove, at least at first in case the blade slips. Once you get used to handling the curved surface, you will find that bottle cutting, like glass cutting, requires nothing more than common sense.

CRUSHED GLASS

You can purchase bags of crushed glass from a local supplier or make it yourself. It's not as easy as it sounds, however, and we recommend that you buy this material rather than waste a lot of time pounding pieces of glass into atoms. The manufactured material will be uniform and you can choose from different colors. Crushed glass is usually glued to other glass bases as a decorative item. Candle holders are especially favored here.

For children just entering the glass world (not under ten years), working with crushed glass may be their first glass experience. One project that has done well for us with children is making crushed glass shapes from cookie cutters. Use the cookie cutter as a mold to wrap a piece of U lead around; remove the cookie cutter and solder the lead seam. Place the lead shape carefully on a piece of waxed paper and fill it with crushed glass. Allow a clear glass glue to trickle into and through the crushed glass so that the space is pretty well taken up with it. Once the glue has dried, you should be able to remove the item from the wax paper and the result will be a glass medallion that will glitter and sparkle in the sunlight. Cookie cutters are great because there are so many shapes, but as you experiment with this technique you can make all sorts of shapes from other objects. And it will serve to keep your child content and involved while you get busy making that large window for your home.

BEVELS: STRAIGHT AND CLUSTERS

Glass bevels are made, in the main, from 3/16" plate glass. (Heavier plate glass can be used to make specific artistic statements, but commercially this is rare.) The glass edge of the thick plate is ground and polished to a 45" angle. The idea is to provide a prism-like border to the glass so that when light strikes it the light is broken up into its individual wave lengths to form a rainbow effect both within the borders of the glass pieces and from there onto walls, floors, ceilings, wherever the light flows. Ad-

ditionally, the edge provides a dimensional look to the glass that brings it a striking individuality, especially when it is combined with flat stained glass or clear window glass. Windows composed only of bevels, even where daylight doesn't reach them, can still be stunning just because of their shapes and combinations.

The bevels available for working with glass can be squares as small as 3/4" to as large as 4" x 4" or larger. Rectangles range from 1" x 2" to 6" x 9". Not only squares, but triangular and circular bevels are available as well as bevels shaped to almost any figuration. Odd-shaped bevels were initially custom produced by hand and were very expensive, but with the growth of interest in them, most bevels now are imported and shaped bevel clusters have come into the marketplace at an affordable price.

Several window pattern books have incorporated specific clusters as part of the design for you to follow the pattern as originally conceived. There is a company that produces a line of shaped bevels (Beveldine) and a template guide for designing your own clusters to fit whatever pattern you want.

Building large windows with many bevels requires support considerations due to the weight thrust forward as well as downwards. With the average small panel, that is not a factor.

Bevel clusters are extensive. There are clusters for flowers, birds, and even angels, arching frames and fancy knots. It's safe to say this is one aspect of glass you'll never take the edge off.

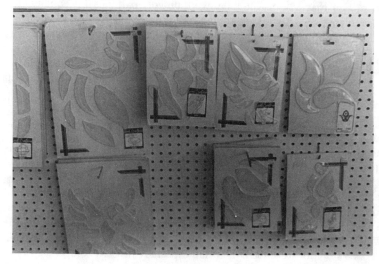

Beveled glass clusters to use in lead or foil work. Some beveled clusters are featured as a necessary component needed to complete a pattern in specialty window books.

CHAPTER 7
Dichroic Glass and Stained Glass Art

by Allen H. Graef

Allen H. Graef is the owner of Allen H. Graef, Dichroic Glass of Long Beach, California. The author is constantly working on new and innovative dichroic coatings for the art glass industry and is currently at work on a book entitled Dichroics.

WHAT IS DICHROIC GLASS?

Glass that has had deposited on its surface dichroic coatings or thin films of dielectric materials (materials that do not conduct electricity) to add unusual colorations is called dichroic glass. Typical materials are silicon, titanium, and magnesium. The materials are evaporated and vacuum-deposited on the glass in such a fine degree of thickness that certain wavelengths of light will pass through while others will be reflected. Up to 20 or more layers of these materials can be deposited. In effect, the dichroic process changes the nature of the glass/light relationship.

Dichroic coatings are not new. The technology was actually developed over 100 years ago in West Germany by Dr. Arthur Pfeiffer. Dichroics eventually found their way into the glass art field in the late 1960s when a handful of sculptors started using dichroic glass in their work. In the late '70s, I saw this new glass as a viable product. After much research and development, I was able to set up my company as a supplier of dichroic glass to the art glass industry.

Dichroic glass is extremely diversified in its effects and applications. The base, or preliminary color of the glass is identified by viewing the glass from the front, looking straight on in transmitted light. When the glass is turned approximately 45°, the glass shifts to its secondary color. When there is no transmitted light, the coating becomes a third color in reflection.

The reason the glass changes color when viewed from different angles has to do with the laws of refraction, the relationship between refractive indexes of air, glass, and the particular materials that have been evaporated onto the glass surface. Occasionally the colors may vary from

run to run. This is because the thin film coating is somewhere around 700 angstroms (ten billionths of a meter) in thickness and is very difficult to control to the eight millionth of an inch the coating takes up. There is about a 98% success rate for the process.

APPLICATIONS

Dichroic coatings have diverse applications that range from diagnosing diseases (tracing fluorescent antibodies) to use in heat-seeking missiles, to doing duty as a principle component in solar cells, to serving as a quantitative measuring device in research photography. This technology is "thin film physics."

THE COATING PROCESS

In the coating process, the glass must be optically cleaned. If this is not done properly, the slightest speck of dust can mar the coating. A clean atmosphere is essential for this operation. The glass is first polished with rouge, then cleaned with several types of solvent alcohol. The glass surface must actually be cleaned down to the molecular level in order for the films to adhere. In the case of textured glass, an alcohol cleaning process is sufficient.

The coating chamber has a planetary rotating system in its upper portion. The glass is clipped to the system and, during the coating process, rotates in the chamber for even coating. The chamber has to be roughed down to a low vacuum by means of a mechanical pump which removes most of the air. When this is complete (approximately 30 minutes) a high-vacuum pump (cyropump) removes all remaining residual gasses from the chamber.

The vacuum creates an environment similar to outer space.

The chamber is then heated to 300°F. This takes another 20 to 30 minutes. Depending on the type of coating, the proper material is placed in a small crucible in the bottom of the chamber before the chamber is closed. At the proper temperature and vacuum, the material is shot with an electron beam gun and evaporated. The end result is that the material, once evaporated, coats everything in the chamber, including the glass. After the proper number of layers are applied (the measurement being monitored electronically) everything is shut down and the glass is allowed to cool sufficiently before the chamber is unloaded. The entire process takes about two hours.

ON THE AESTHETIC LEVEL

Because of the beauty of dichroics, many artists now feature this "new glass" as a major emphasis in their work. People who buy glass art are enthralled by the spectacular end result of the treatment described above. Collectors have begun to add dichroic glass works to their hoards. This is especially true in the jewelry field, though the stained glass area is not being neglected. At the same time, given the small nature of the pieces compared to stained glass, fused and non-fused dichroic jewelry can be fabricated at a relatively low cost. Dichroic glass added to a necklace, pin, or ring made of other material can help sell such an item that might appear high priced without it. The same "added value" can (and does) apply to stained glass.

WORKING WITH DICHROICS

For the glass craftsman, dichroic glass is yet another modality in your armamentarium. It scores and breaks out and leads up (or copper foils) just as any other glass. Used by itself or combined with non-dichroics, its effect is both to set off other glasses and to project its own unique qualities. Fused dichroic jewelry is also an option because the kiln is always another way to go. For the craftsperson seeking that aesthetic perfection that is forever elusive and forever beckoning, dichroic glass can be a major step along the road.

Today you can find glass art utilizing dichroics in many glass art galleries and fine craft shops throughout the country. There is so much fantastic, innovative work being done with dichroics that it is virtually impossible to cover it all, though we can take a look at some of it in the following photographs and descriptions. No matter where you are in your stained glass development (and you may never work with blown glass), just reviewing the techniques and imaginations of these artists can only add to your own appreciation and experimentation.

SOME WORKERS AND THEIR WORKS USING DICHROICS

"Vessel," a blown piece by James Nowak opens up a new realm for dichroics. Using a coating design that withstands higher temperatures, glass blowers and those working in hot glass have a new exciting medium to use in their work. Nowak has his hot glass studio deep in the woods of Oregon, where he uses dichroic glass in almost every piece he creates.

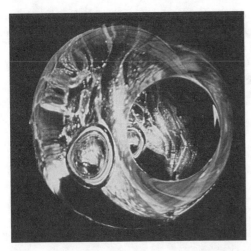

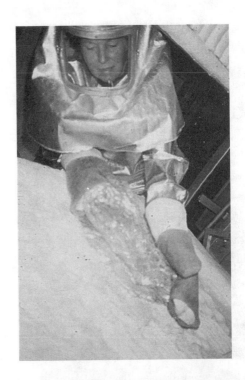

Another hot glass artist using dichroics in her blown pieces is Rebecca Stewart. Her "Nebula World" is made with multicolored dichroic glass. A small window is cut and polished on the piece so that when you look through the polished window, it is like viewing the night sky through the lens of a telescope.

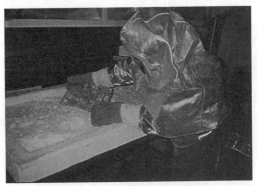

Adorno's "World Colors" was formed in this manner. I know of no one else working this way. From my background in ceramics, I have often thought of how it would be to throw a pot on a pottery wheel using molten glass. I may try it sometime, or teach Zoe to throw so she can try it. Personally, I don't like temperatures above 95°F.

Zoe Adorno uses dichroics in hot-worked sculpture and approaches her work with a very adventurous and somewhat dangerous technique. She first fuses and slumps her pieces and then, with the glass at 1400°F, she dons an asbestos outfit and hand forms the piece to her liking.

Linda Ethier uses cast crystal and dichroics in her work. In her piece, "Preservision," an actual mold was pulled from a boy. After the mold was fired and prepared, she cast the dichroic glass and crystal into it to create a fantastic likeness.

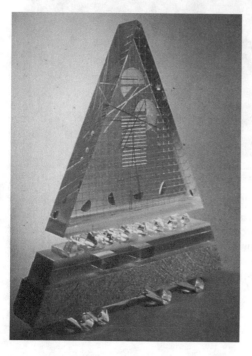

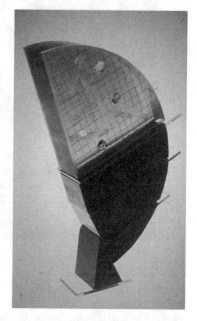

In cold-worked sculpture, Toland Peter Sand, a glass artist living in the woods of New Hampshire, uses UV (Ultra Violet) glue to assemble his dichroic work. He first cuts, grinds, and polishes the many parts to a piece, then aligns the parts with the UV glue. When he is satisfied with the shape, he exposes it to the UV light source. The glue sets up almost instantaneously. In his pieces "Scallop Series" and "Heiroglyphica" he used laminated dichroic glass, Japanese opal, German crystal, glass rods, and granite. Both pieces are fabricated in this manner.

Paul Manners lives and has his studio in the mountains near Santa Cruz, California. He also uses UV glue in his work. He uses optical crystal and dichroic glass. He cuts up and painstakingly grinds and polishes his glass to achieve two very flat surfaces. He then puts them back together in different configurations with the UV glue. His piece, "Kube I" (coo-bay-eye), named after an Amazon rain forest chief, was constructed in this manner. When he finishes a piece, the reflection and refraction within the sculpture produce changing and unexpected color effects when viewed from different angles.

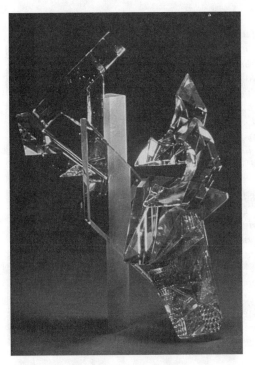

Another glass artist living and working in the mountains near Santa Cruz, California (a mecca for glass artists, it seems) is Grant Miller. Grant casts crystal shapes, then cuts them up and uses UV glue to fabricate the parts back together with dichroic glass. His two pieces were created in this manner.

In flat glass/architectural work, I (Allen H. Graef) created "The Graf Zeppelin". I wanted to use the most unconventional, abstract treatment I could think of. I used lots of 6mm coated German crystal, dalle glass, and dichroic glass in the piece. The parts were all sawn, cut, and beveled. I thought the most unique technique I could use on this piece in keeping with the art deco design was to "soft bevel" or round all the edges of every piece. Note no hard edges as in conventional beveling.

Another flat glass artist using massive amounts of dichroic glass in his work is Jeff Smith of Dallas. Smith's diverse glass palette (including transparent and opaque mouth-blown glass, dichroic glass, and cast lenses) provides a dynamic, ever-changing experience whether viewing the windows from the street, sidewalk, or from the inside. Dichroic glass changes color as it is viewed form various angles, and at night becomes reflective like mirror. The Leviticus and Deuteronomy windows for the Washington Hebrew Congregation, Washington, D.C., are fine examples of how Smith uses dichroic glass in his work.

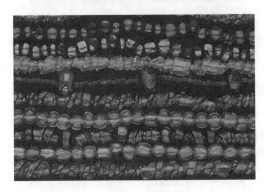

Dichroic glass has not only found its way into the sculptural, flat glass, and architectural glass fields, but dichroics can now be found in giftware and jewelry as well. One of the most recent uses of dichroic glass is in bead making. Paula Radke, a glass artist whose studio overlooks Morro Bay, California, uses dichroics in her beads. In Radke's fused plate, "Quail," she used acid to etch the dichroic coating in addition to using a diamond bit on a Dremel tool to create an intricate design before fusing. She also used dichroic coated stringer glass which she first bent to a desired shape with a torch and then fused into the center portion of the plate.

An example of the more unusual coatings available today is in Teri Sokoloff's wall piece "The Creature Of". The background is a single piece of multicolored dichroic glass called "FX" developed by Allen H. Graef. Another piece of this "FX" dichroic can be seen in Teri's mask pin.

Jan Schrader, a dichroic jewelry artist from Olympia, Washington, used cut and fused separate pieces of dichroic glass in her neck piece and earrings. After the pieces were cut and fused (to get rid of the sharp edges) holes were drilled in each piece for stringing.

Shawn Athari also uses "FX" in her work. It can be seen in her "Aduma Mask" wall piece which was inspired by an African mask of the same name.

DICHROIC GLASS IS HERE TO STAY

Some people believe that dichroic glass is a fad that will die out. From where I stand, this is doubtful. I compare dichroics to precious metals like gold and silver. The use of these materials obviously evolved at one point in time and they have never lost popularity. While dichroic glass is (fortunately) not nearly as expensive as gold, aesthetically it has an effect equal to it for sheer beauty and unique workmanship. It is and remains elemental, durable, and lasting.

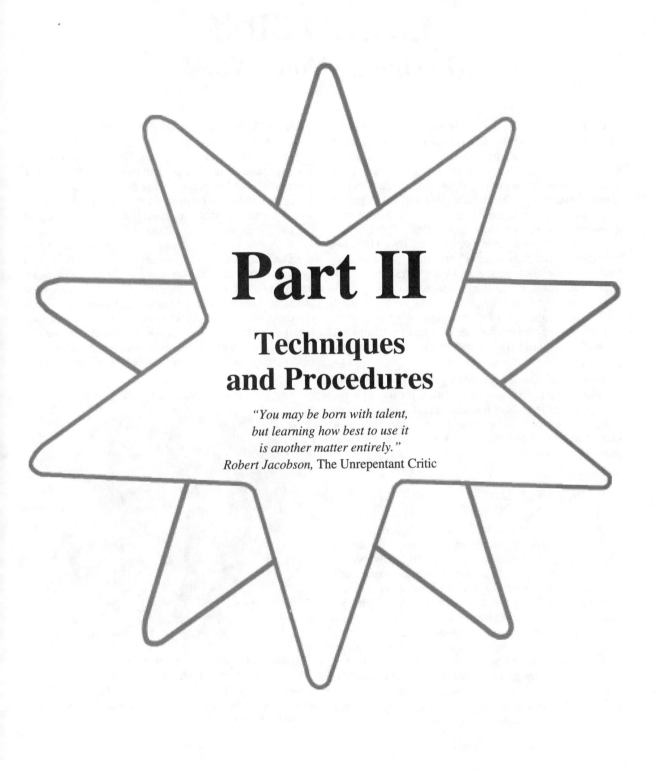

Part II
Techniques and Procedures

*"You may be born with talent,
but learning how best to use it
is another matter entirely."*
Robert Jacobson, The Unrepentant Critic

CHAPTER 8
Designing Your Work

Designing for stained glass is not like designing for any other art form. Often we have students who are adept in watercolor, oil painting, architecture, or graphic design who have to relearn how to approach the design procedure for glass. People coming from other modalities tend to think in terms of reflected rather than diffused light and the structure/form relationship in terms of a balance quite different from such a relationship in glass. This relationship has changed over time. For instance, if you look at a medieval stained glass window you will see the lead lines running every which way, even through the faces, partly because the glass was difficult to make but also because their object was solely the projection of the glass itself. Look at more modern windows, especially those of the German school, and you will see they form a definite linear statement equal to (and sometimes overwhelming) the glass itself.

There are extremes in everything, but we want to point out that stained glass as it exists today for most professional workers is a mix of line and color, the two elements offsetting each other. This is the main factor you should keep in mind from the start when you are designing your stained glass work.

THE LINEAR ELEMENT

The stained glass pieces in a window or panel or even a small suncatcher are held together by metal rims, whether lead or copper foil or brass or zinc. These are not merely background qualities; they should be involved as a composed statement in harmony with the glass itself. The lead lines in stained glass can inject themselves as foreground or background or simply as an adjunctive quality, but they should always be considered as flowing of themselves, not merely static supportive provisioning. Once you understand this you will have a lot more fun designing your work and your work will become bi-level. Students (and often professionals) become so involved in the color statement they end up with a design that is confusing to the eye simply because they are forgetting that the linear quality is equally important.

CAN THIS BE CUT? AND IF SO, WHY?

The other big design problem beginners face is designing pieces that look fine on paper, forgetting that glass is not paper and certain shapes can cause you a lot of grief when transposed to glass, both in the cutting and later. It is true that today, as compared to years ago when we began, equipment is available to cut just about any shape out of glass. Saws are literally at one's fingertips so even the most six-fingered novice can cut picture puzzle formations unimagined by workers previously. But cutting such designs is still begging the issue, since the stresses and strains inherent in the glass, even in its most stable form, are exaggerated now that it has so many convolutions. Often these pieces will crack when you try to solder them and if they don't self destruct on the work table, they are liable to do so weeks or months later when they are part of a completed, and possibly embrasured, window.

This arresting design presents the circular mirror broken not only by the large owl standing within it, but by its wings coming out over the top, forming an adjunct circle. For a feathered look on the wings, a small ripple pattern was used.

Whether your finished product is a large or small piece of glass, it is distressing to find, even as you proudly show it off, that it is remaking your design into one of its own.

It is also wise to remember that every glass piece you cut with the saw because it is impossible to cut it by hand, will have an equally impossible piece that it must fit into. And all these pieces must finally be leaded, or more likely, foiled; a procedure that, considering the literal ins and outs of the things, can drive you to distraction.

We are not negating using the saws for a specific purpose. Like any other good tool, a good glass saw certainly has possibilities to achieve particular statements in glass that can project a totally new dimension. What we see as the problems with glass saws in the designing process is that the uninitiated tend to overuse them in the rush to create something unique. And under such technologic self-hypnosis they forget that glasswork is, at bottom, a hand craft.

Even a sign in stained glass can be designed so as to be creative. Here the borders were requested to be a sort of medieval leaf design, and while repetitive, the repetition was broken by the reversal of the patterns. The lettering was chosen not only for readability, but for design value that would coordinate with the borders. (See color pages)

BALANCING LEAD LINES

We like to think that simple is better. Whether you are working on a pictorial or abstract, don't make the design unnecessarily complicated. That doesn't mean just to control the number of pieces, but also keep in mind how you are running the lead or foil design. These lines are a guide for the eye. They move the eye either across the entire composition or to a certain focal point. These lines should not lead the eye to dead ends or make the work so jumbled that whatever good qualities it possesses are lost. A workable stained glass design should have rhythm, with line and color forming a conclusive entity.

To enhance the design:

1) Avoid having too many lines intersecting at the same point. Although this may look fine on paper, what happens when you solder the area where they all meet? All you will have to show for your efforts is a big glob of solder.

2) Don't stay with the same quality of line. With foil it's not so easy to change the linear width, but with lead you can make statements using thick and thinner lines by changing lead cames to match. This, to our mind, is one of the most efficient design elements you can use in glass, comparable to many parallel painting techniques. Like anything else, it should not be overused or it falls flat.

3) Don't design small glass pieces by themselves in corners, especially if they are the same color as surrounding larger pieces. They will look as though the larger ones simply broke off.

4) Avoid passing lead lines through painted areas or through glass that has a lot of movement of its own, such as antique streakies. This kind of glass is very showy and any line going through it breaks its spell.

5) After you design the drawing and before making the cartoon, sleep on it. Think of it as a rough draft. You will see things in it later that you didn't see initially. Of course, this also can work the other way and you can end up putting so many new touches into it that you end up drowning your original intent.

MIXING LEAD SIZES

We touched on this briefly, but there is more to know here. First, in mixing lead sizes there are no hard and fast rules other than the obvious one of not using very thin lead for very large pieces of glass. This is not only a practical matter, it is also an aesthetic one. As far as juxtaposing lead, you can go to extremes if your design statement warrants it, even to the extent of using a 1/8" lead with a 1/4" or even a 3/16". You can even change leads while circumventing a single piece of glass, though this can end up looking merely peculiar. It is possible to get some magnificent effects while leaping across lead sizes, but this should be designed into the cartoon, not carried out willy-nilly while the work is in progress. Nor should the final product look as though you have changed leads because you ran out of a particular width.

The general rule is that small pieces of glass take thin leads and large ones take larger leads, which also adds strength. But this rule can be broken if there is purpose behind it. However, small pieces of glass surrounded by oversize leads will tend to disappear. That kind of linear statement can be hard to justify.

DESIGNING CORNERS

As we mentioned earlier, a large number of lead (or foil) lines meeting at one point will create an ugly solder joint, though in a pencil sketch it may look fine. That doesn't mean you can't have lead lines coming toward a common focus, just be reasonable about it and stagger them so they meet slightly apart from one another. This is especially true when corners are involved. You don't need lead lines crowding into the corners of a panel to give it additional strength. Usually the two outside leads of the panel or window will provide plenty of oomph to hold the thing together.

Some individuals feel that more strength is added to a corner by mitering these outside leads and spend a lot of time getting the angles just right so the corner will have two absolutely even surfaces of lead butting exactly. Which is very well and good, now you have this seam most artistically accomplished. And then what do you do? You cover it with solder so no one will be able to tell you mitered it in the first place. Of course you know, but is that knowledge worth all the time and effort when a simple butting together of the corner leads will lead to the same end result? It's up to you.

POINTS

Points can be similarly frustrating. Whether you are using foil or lead on glass that comes to a point, remember that both take up room, and the thinner you make the glass points, the more glass surface you are going to lose because the lead and foil will cover them. You will end up with long surfaces of solder with the glass surface starting some ways back as it gets thicker. It's useless to cut the glass to such needle points, even though it demonstrates your cutting ability. Leave room for the lead or foil to grip

the glass and still show glass between. To find the best glass width, cut a piece of glass and measure two pieces of appropriate channeling (foil, lead, brass, or zinc) against it. You will then be able to see how much glass you will lose once the piece is fabricated.

DESIGNING FOR REINFORCED LEADS

Reinforced leads have a hollow center (heart) with a thin metal rod running through it. The purpose of these leads is to avoid having to run a re-bar (reinforcing bar or rod) over the (usually back) surface of a window, thus interfering with the design as seen from the front. This problem only occurs when a window is a certain size, generally over nine square feet. Windows larger than that are apt to buckle (at least to some extent) eventually, even when held in a frame. Of course the larger the window, the more reinforcing rods are called for. In the old days, such rods were made of iron and since iron doesn't solder (though it does rust—another difficulty), they were attached to the window by copper wire wrapped several times around the rod and soldered to convenient joints. These rods usually ran vertically and were scarcely invisible. Believe it or not, however, after a while you didn't see them, the eye disregarded them in favor of the flow and color of the window itself. But try to convince a prospective customer that a bulky piece of metal isn't going to ruin the tracery of a design he cherishes. "No, no," he will cry in anguish, "you can't put that there. You can see it!" Well, the reinforced lead is an attempt to reinforce without you or your customer seeing it.

However, reinforced leads have problems of their own. They have to be cut with a hacksaw, which is not much of a problem unless you don't own one, and they are difficult to work with on anything other than straight lines. The best way to incorporate such leads is to consider them while the window is still in the planning stage and make sure you create straight lines that are design friendly and will serve the function you have in mind.

If your design refuses to allow straight lines, yet the overall size requires reinforcing, such leads can be bent to take curves, even circles if you want to be extreme. It does mean a lot of extra effort. The windows on the cover of this book contain many such leads worked into their fabric to provide extra strength without emphasizing their presence. A special tool is available for this, though the best tools are those attached to your wrists.

We have found the most effective way to bend reinforced leads to take design curves is by trial and error. We cut the lead overlong to take up the curve or curves, then, taking the design curve inch by inch, bend and straighten, bend and straighten the lead to fit. You have to go slowly here and, although it may be tempting, do not modify the design to fit the lead. At this point, the glass pieces will already have been cut and changing the design now can lead to re-cutting most of the window. Just take it easy, go slowly, wipe off the perspiration from time to time, and you will eventually get there. Remember, in order to provide strength, reinforced leads must run the entire length or width of the window.

DESIGNING WITH REINFORCING RODS

This is a similar process to using reinforced lead, although the term "rods" is a carryover from the past. These elements are actually flat zinc-coated strips, too thick to go between the pieces of glass and are used behind the lead line, attached to it by solder and running the entire length of the window. You won't be able to see these reinforcements from the front; from the back they will stand out, of course, but since they fall directly within the leaded line, they don't interfere with the design. Like the reinforced lead, these strips may be curved to follow the lines of the design. They may interfere to an extent when cleaning the back surface of the window, but that is a small price to pay for strength and design.

DESIGNING WITH REINFORCING STRIPS (STRONG LINE AND OTHER AIDS)

These are mainly used to reinforce foiled objects. The strip (whatever it is) is placed between two or more pieces of glass that have been foiled and soldered in place. This helps make the space these strips traverse a lot more stable than the foil alone. Of course, such an addition, unless planned at the first (and it rarely is) will take up room between the pieces. If you overuse it, you may find the window or panel burgeoning out beyond its borders. Copper wire may also be used (16 or 18 gauge wire are the usual sizes) and takes up less room than the Strong Line. Another product called Restrip made by Cascade Metal and Venture Tape is thinner than the Strong Line and more flexible. Restrip can be used to add stability to smaller works such as suncatchers which often have decorative portions hanging from their edges that tend to pull the foil away due to their weight. It doesn't take much weight for a claw or petal to develop a gravitational inclination over time.

Whether or not you use any of these additional strengtheners, you should always design a freeform object so that the foil around the edges is held to the body of the piece by internal lines specifically designed for the purpose. Don't depend on artificial strengtheners to keep the outside foil from coming away. They won't.

DEVELOPING A COLOR SENSE

Color interpretation is such an individual matter that it's hard to compare one appraisal with another. All the same, stained glass with its multitude of hues and tones, must betoken some guidance, some direction toward a use of this vast palette that will not lead to mere slapdash contrivance. We recall the student who made a stained glass lampshade with each panel a different color and texture simply because a) they were available and b) it was prettier that way. The fact that these colors clashed rather than blended didn't matter to this individual because to her, color was a sensation rather than an aesthetic.

Understanding the way colors blend is easy for some people, difficult for others. One way to achieve a beginning understanding of color is through the color wheel. This is by no means a precise guide since the colors that are printed are reflective, not the same as the transparent glass. A better way is to get boxes of sample glass that most glass manufacturers sell. The charge for these samples is usually minimal and always worth more than the price as far as training your eye. It is no exaggeration to say that glass colors are infinite. But their interaction is not the same as with oils, watercolors, or pastels. Probably the closest parallel is stage lighting. The superimposition of colored lights provides a measure of what happens in glass with colors side-by-side: one impinges on or enhances the other. This dramatic effect is modified by the size of the glass pieces. Working with samples of similar size pieces on a light table and then comparing them in daylight is excellent practice for training the eye to color subtleties.

Looking at a variety of works in stained glass can also educate the eye to a good color sense, as well as to a sense of design. Modern stained glass works usually have a wider—and wilder—color spectrum than medieval ones, when the color range was limited by the difficulty of making the stuff. But the matching of medieval colors is certainly spectacular. Go to as many shows, museums, and churches as possible and not only look at the glass, but take color slides (not prints) if permitted. This is the best schooling in stained glass you can get.

Even after you have developed a good sense of color, it still will not be sharp enough for the challenges you will meet every time you take up a new project. We don't mean just the ability to pick and choose colors from the light table, but to know what these colors will be like in bright sunlight, cloudy daylight, and dusk. What color will blur out or be emphasized by the interplay of another tone elsewhere and by the available light? What colors will project best toward the outside when the inside lights are on? Where is the window to be located and how much light will be available? What effect do you want to achieve: muted, jewel like, insidious, or provocative? Most times stained glass is all of these, changing as the light changes. But occasionally it cannot be so mellifluous, color-wise. When Pat did the window for Javier's restaurant she knew precisely where it was to be hung and how to best allow for the illumination it would have by choosing colors that would achieve the maximum brightness in what is essentially a dark area (see color section).

Keeping the glass color sense sharp is a never-ending battle between the ideal and the actual light that will be available to allow for the statement you want to achieve. It's not always easy but it's always a learning process.

COLOR AND THE LIGHT TABLE

Take the finished design drawing and lay it over the light table. The light penetrates the paper fairly readily. Then place the colors of glass over those respective areas of the design without cutting the glass to size, simply to get a rough notion of how the colors will mesh. Keep in mind that looking at colors on the light table is not the same as seeing them by true light (daylight). You should try to lay out as many colors of your choice as possible. Then stand over the design on a chair or small ladder, as far away as possible, and study the color pattern. You may find that what you thought in your mind's eye was a

good balance now appears bland or even clashes. It is easier to change the color scheme now, before cutting the pieces. Don't be afraid to change all the pieces if you think the colors are not working well together. Hold a few up to (preferably) daylight if you're unsure and see what the quality is with this light. This will also give you some idea of the modification between daylight and the light table for all the colors.

A stained glass composition is a relationship of design elements acting alone and in conjunction with one another. The effect of the piece should be one of unity. Subject matter has less to do with design and color than you may imagine. A blue horse, for instance, may be perfectly valid in a particular statement. But the type of blue might be critical. The shape of the horse may likewise be crucial to the overall design of the piece, whether it be realistic or surrealistic, if it can be cut or painted. The fun in working in glass is to explore the unique possibilities that the medium itself proposes. If you are just beginning, don't worry about what is good and bad as long as you develop a *sense* of what is good and bad. Be prepared to make mistakes, and realize they are mistakes no matter how many of your friends compliment you on them. It's all part of the learning process.

On the following pages are a few panels that can be made into interesting stained glass pieces for your practice and enjoyment. We've tried to present both simple and complex designs, basically for the beginner in stained glass, but even those who have been working in the craft for a while can have fun with them. You don't have to follow these designs exactly. Improve on them by all means.

Each panel has its own particular stained glass challenge based in part on some mention in the text of this book. Dotted lines suggest overlays (double glazing). Heavy lines (and some others) should be painted. The colors are your choice.

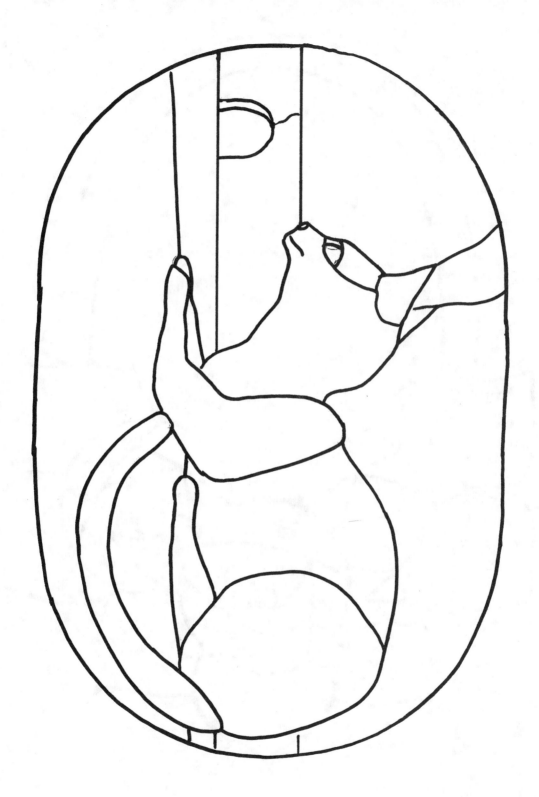

CHAPTER 9
Working with Lead Came

Lead—that stoic, ponderous, and occasionally murderous element—is paradoxically a main element of flights of fancy in stained glass. It is rigid, yielding, forceful, supportive, and, if used correctly, inevitably compliant. Most beginners in our experience shy away from using lead, favoring foil instead because they assume foil is easier to work with and requires less in the way of guidance and involvement. This is only partly true. If you've put lead on your "someday" list, you're missing out on 90% of the fun of working with stained glass. True, lead work does require more of a commitment because the work isn't as easy to pick up and lay down again as foil is. And you can't lead the pieces, like foil, in your lap while watching TV. But once you start working with lead, TV will take a back seat. We've recommended it for individuals who want to diet. When you're working with lead, even food can be a secondary incentive. And you don't have to start with a six foot window. The best way to become acquainted with lead to is begin working on a small panel.

It's also part of the mystique of this endeavor and its use elevates you (rightly or wrongly) into a company of artisans that stretches back for centuries.

SHAPES AND FORMS

The lead cames used in working with stained glass are made by an extrusion process where the molten metal is pressed through a steel die, a process rather like producing spaghetti. Lead came is usually pure lead with nothing added, but some companies add alloys to toughen the came or make it bright, or encase it in a brass "skin" to provide a measure of inflexibility. Inflexibility may also be due to the shape of the came, so some are more difficult to cut and bend than others. Round came (rounded top and bottom) is generally harder to work with than flat came. Other metals may also be used in came form, such as zinc, copper, and brass, but lead is still the paramount material, still the old reliable companion, still the classic partner in this long-standing ballet of line and light.

AVAILABILITY

Lead came is available in six foot lengths of various dimensions and in coiled spools of 25 foot lengths. The spools are convenient because they cut down on waste and store easily. However, you must be careful to uncoil them so they don't twist, especially in the smaller sizes. Most serious lead workers use lead flat out of the case. Twisting is also a problem when purchasing (and storing) lead in these six foot case lengths. As you pull one strand out, others tend to lock onto it and writhe into hysterical holding patterns. The first step in lead technique is learning how to get the lead out so it all stays usable.

The word "came" is Old English for "string" or "length." It is also spelled calme in older books. The word has hung around for a couple of centuries and still sounds more dignified than "length" or "strand" or just about anything else.

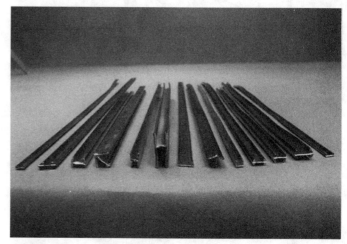

Various sizes, shapes, and styles of lead came.

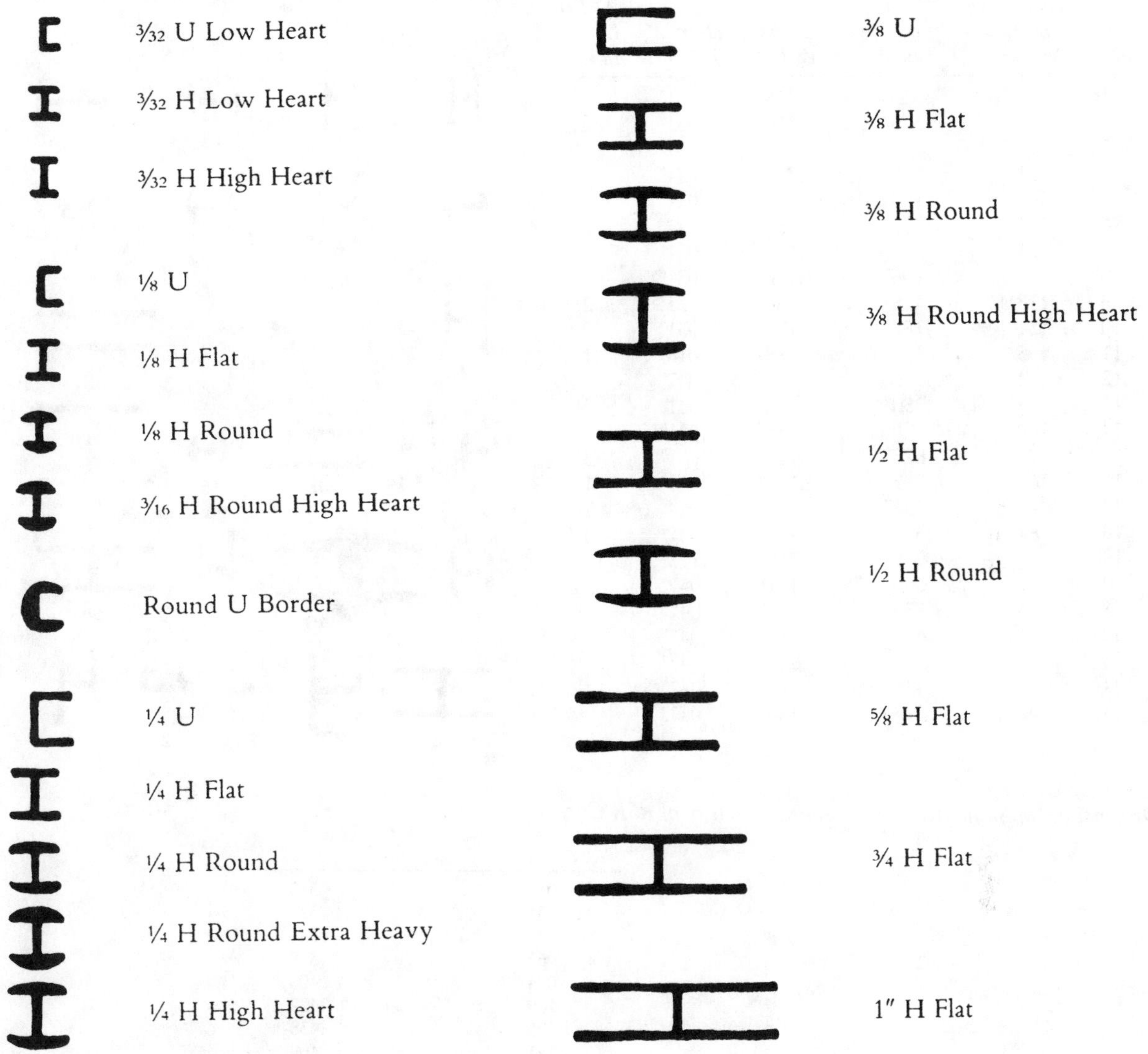

3/32 U Low Heart

3/32 H Low Heart

3/32 H High Heart

1/8 U

1/8 H Flat

1/8 H Round

3/16 H Round High Heart

Round U Border

1/4 U

1/4 H Flat

1/4 H Round

1/4 H Round Extra Heavy

1/4 H High Heart

3/8 U

3/8 H Flat

3/8 H Round

3/8 H Round High Heart

1/2 H Flat

1/2 H Round

5/8 H Flat

3/4 H Flat

1" H Flat

Shapes and forms of lead came.

No.	Approx-imate Strands Per Box	Face Width	Channel Width	Heart Thickness	Wt.Per Lin. Ft. In Ozs.
1	195	.313"	.125"	.031"	1½
2	118	.375"	.156"	.031"	2½
3	195	.156"	.156"	.031"	1½
4	131	.219"	.375"	.031"	2¼
5	148	.188"	.188"	.031"	2
6	107	.438"	.156"	.047"	2¾
7	131	.250"	.188"	.031"	2¼
8	195	.156"	.156"	.031"	1½
9	118	.438"	.188"	.031"	2½
10	131	.188"	.172"	.031"	2¼
11	195	.125"	.188"	.016"	1½
12	74	.750"	.156"	.047"	4
13	118	.250"	.172"	.031"	2½
14	169	.406" (Overall)	.156"	.031"	1¾
15	79	.625"	.156"	.031"	3¾
16	169	.219"	.125"	.031"	1¾
17	40	.734"	.422"	.094"	7¼
18	84	.344"	.188"	.047"	3½
19	19	.969"	.250"	.125"	15½
20	91	.500"	.141"	.047"	3¼
21	53	.750"	.234"	.047"	5½
22	74	.625"	.219"	.047"	4
23	84	.516"	.250"	.047"	3½
24	65	.438"	.188"	.047"	4½
25	91	.313"	.188"	.047"	3¼
26	107	.500"	.156"	.047"	2¾

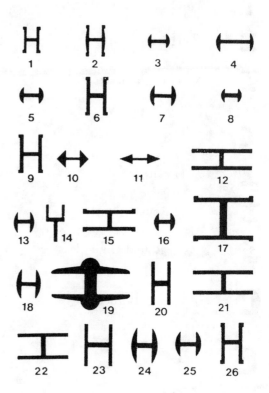

Dimensions of Standard Lead Cames (Courtesy of RSR Corp.)

.016	¹⁄₆₄	.313	⁵⁄₁₆
.031	¹⁄₃₂	.328	²¹⁄₆₄
.047	³⁄₆₄	.344	¹¹⁄₃₂
.063	¹⁄₁₆	.375	³⁄₈
.094	³⁄₃₂	.406	¹³⁄₃₂
.109	⁷⁄₆₄	.422	²⁷⁄₆₄
.125	¹⁄₈	.438	⁷⁄₁₆
.141	⁹⁄₆₄	.469	¹⁵⁄₃₂
.156	⁵⁄₃₂	.484	³¹⁄₆₄
.172	¹¹⁄₆₄	.500	¹⁄₂
.188	³⁄₁₆	.516	³³⁄₆₄
.203	¹³⁄₆₄	.563	⁹⁄₁₆
.219	⁷⁄₃₂	.625	⁵⁄₈
.234	¹⁵⁄₆₄	.734	⁴⁷⁄₆₄
.250	¹⁄₄	.750	³⁄₄
.266	¹⁷⁄₆₄	.875	⁷⁄₈
.281	⁹⁄₃₂	.969	³¹⁄₃₂
.297	¹⁹⁄₆₄	1,000	1

Decimal Equivalents

No.	Approx-imate Strands Per Box	Face Width	Channel Width	Heart Thickness	Wt.Per Lin. Ft. In Ozs.
27	98	.375"	.297"	.047"	3
28	148	.250"	.188"	.031"	2
29	84	.469"	.172"	.031"	3½
30	84	.500"	.188"	.031"	3½
31	53	.625"	.172"	.031"	5½
32	42	.750"	.188"	.031"	7
33	24	1.000"	.234"	.125"	12
34	118	.328"	.172"	.031"	2½
35	195	.156"	.188"	.031"	1½
36	169	.313"	.188"	.031"	1¾
37	84	.500"	.172"	.109"	3½
38	65	.484"	.234"	.125"	4½
39	98	.563"	.188"	.047"	3
40	29	1.000"	.188"	.047"	10
41	43	1.250"	.219"	.031"	6¾
42	19	(.250")(.500")	.125"	.125"	15¼
43	290	.125"	.125"	.016"	1
44	98	.313"	—	.156"	3
45	37	1.500"	.219"	.047"	8
46	118	.375"	.156"	.031"	2½
47	118	.188"	.172"	.063"	2½
48	148	.281"	.156"	.031"	2
49	84	.625"	.172"	.031"	3½
50	230	.125"	.203"	.031"	1¼
51	107	.313"	.219"	.047"	2¾
52	56	.625"	.250"	.031"	5¼
53	195	.188"	.125"	.031"	1½
54	45	.875"	.234"	.047"	6½
55	169	.234"	.156"	.031"	1¾
56	84	.281"	.250"	.031"	3½
57	65	.344"	.266"	.063"	4½
58	79	.750"	.188"	.031"	3¾
59	98	.328"	.234"	.047"	3
60	230	.188"	.156"	.031"	1¼
61	195	.188"	.203"	.031"	1½
62	65	.500"	.188"	.047"	4½
64	118	.234"	.234"	.047"	2½
65	53	1.000"	.156"	.047"	5½
66	118	.375"	.203"	.031"	2½
67	148	.281"	.203"	.031"	2
68	107	.375"	.156"	.047"	2¾
69	70	.500"	.203"	.047"	4¼
70	84	.344"	.125"	.047"	3½
90	295	.104"	.172"	.041"	1
91	165	.172"	.188"	.078"	1.8
94	110	.266"	.203"	.078"	2.6
95	98	.313"DIA.	.188"	—	3
707	195	.188"	.156"	.047"	1½
727	84	.500"@90°	.188"	.035"	3½

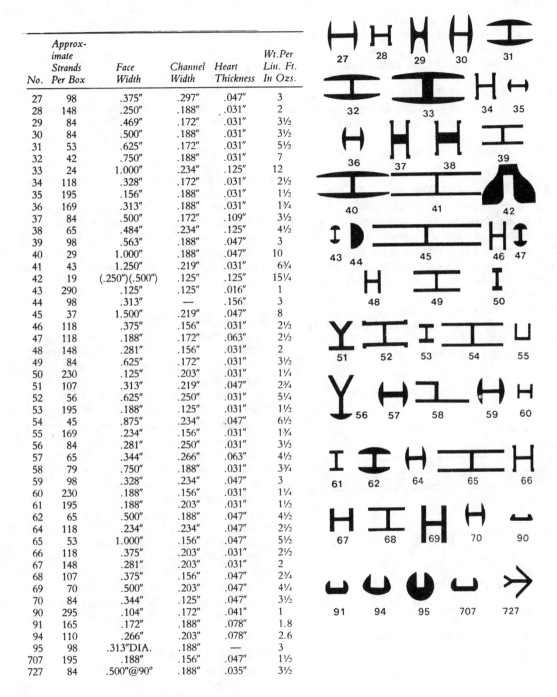

Dimensions of Standard Lead Cames (cont'd) (Courtesy of RSR Corp.)

PURPOSES

Lead came serves an obvious practical purpose: it holds pieces of glass together, forming a framework within which the various colors wink and glow. Perhaps a less obvious purpose is that it has an aesthetic quality, no less important, as a linear focus. The flow of the design can be impeded or emphasized depending on how you use the various sizes and shapes of leads. Knowledge of the idiosyncrasies of came is essential to anyone who wants to work with stained glass. The lead becomes as crucial to the overall statement as the glass itself.

HOW CAME IS MEASURED

Lead came is always measured across the top surface, not across the channeled side. Nor is the depth of the channel a factor. Since the channel may be artificially pinched or widened, such a measurement would be inconstant. The top surface does not change to any degree and it's here that we measure whether the lead is 1/16", 1/8", 3/16", 1/4", or 1/2", to name just a few of the many sizes. Hobbyists generally stay in the range of 1/16" to 1/4", but if you undertake an extensive project of wide dimensions, especially if large pieces of glass are being used, you might want to use larger leads both for strength and design.

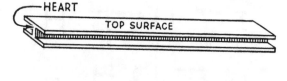

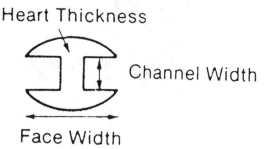

How came is measured.

Whether came is round or flat applies also to a description of the top (and bottom) surface. Most leads come both ways.

H AND U CAMES

H cames have two channels, one on either side with a wall or "heart" in the middle. This lead heart is usually 1/16". H cames are generally "inside" leads, accommodating themselves to pieces of glass in each channel. U cames, or "high heart" cames, are always "outside" leads used for finishing a single surface that will show, such as unframed panels or the skirts of lamps. Their single channel is considerably deeper than an H channel and they give a completed look to the edges of a piece. You may want to use H came on the outside of a work for a specific purpose (see Finishing Techniques) or just because you want to suggest that the piece was initially part of another larger work. Or you may like the unfinished look. It's always your choice.

SPECIALIZED CAMES

In addition to the regular H and U cames, there are a number of other, specialized cames. Among these are cames to hold glass in a three-dimensional position and for right turns and other angles. Many of these cames are used primarily for lamp manufacture; others are used in freeform sculpture and in self-sustaining glass wall pieces. Today there is a came for practically any use. If you don't find the came you are looking for in one of the many catalogs available, no doubt one of the large lead companies, such as Gardiner, is either working on it or only waiting for enough requests to do so.

The amazing number of shapes of lead cames does not mean the old standbys have fallen by the wayside. These standard leads still do most of the work; their ultra-designed brothers only point up certain shortcuts for specific effects. In general, the more involved the design of the lead, the more expensive it becomes. Inevitably there comes the point where you may find it cheaper to take more time and combine the standard leads, especially if you are not producing that many items for resale.

DEGREES OF LEAD CAME

1) The two standards of lead came are **pure** and **mixed**. Pure lead came is exactly that—the lead content is 99%. No alloys have been added to toughen it or give it a bright sheen. Mixed lead

may contain quantities of tin or other alloys to provide a particular advantage, usually to make the lead more hardy or to prevent or slow oxidation.

2) The two silhouettes of lead came are **flat** and **round**. Looking at the came in cross-section, flatness or roundness is determined by the shape of the top and bottom lips. Although rounded came is actually stiffer than flat came of the same dimension (since more metal is used to round the surfaces), the choice of one over the other is generally a function of the design, not a matter of stability.

3) The two dimensions of lead came are **height** and **width**. The cross-section height depends on the came "heart" or central support (in U came, the border). A "high heart" lead is one with a wider channel (or channels) than a comparative "low heart" came because of this taller support. This type of came is used for extra thick pieces of glass, such as English streaky. The cross-section width is the dimension that gives the came its essential identification and it is the same as the linear width.

4) The two qualities of lead came are **length** and **width**. The standard came length is six feet. If you buy the lead in three-foot lengths for the sake of convenience, you are buying half a came. Linear width is the same as cross-section width and generally is measured in multiples of 16ths—1/16", 1/8", 3/16", and 1/4". To determine the "size" of a came, measure the side-to-side diameter. After you have worked with came for a while, you will quickly be able to size it by eye. Came widths extend up to 1". Such leads may be used in large windows with large pieces of glass. Although this may be an architectural necessity, a good stained glass designer will make the lead complement the design even under these circumstances.

5) The two structures of lead came are **U** and **H**. U (bordering) leads have a single channel and may

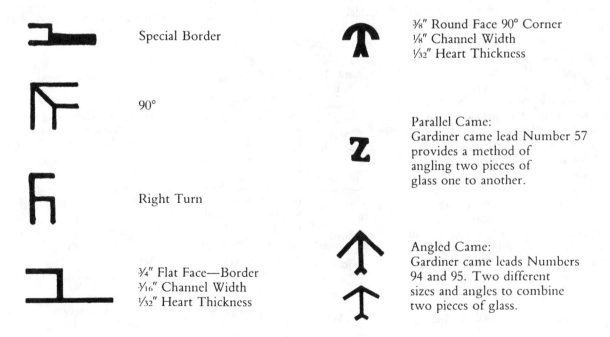

Special Border

90°

Right Turn

¾" Flat Face—Border
³⁄₁₆" Channel Width
¹⁄₃₂" Heart Thickness

⅜" Round Face 90° Corner
⅛" Channel Width
¹⁄₃₂" Heart Thickness

Parallel Came:
Gardiner came lead Number 57 provides a method of angling two pieces of glass one to another.

Angled Came:
Gardiner came leads Numbers 94 and 95. Two different sizes and angles to combine two pieces of glass.

Some specialized lead came silhouettes. Chances are you will rarely order these and in small quantities unless you are mass producing a piece.

be rounded or flat. The one channel allows the lead heart to provide a finished, smooth surface around the object. H cames have two channels, one on either side with a wall or "heart" in the middle.

6) The styles of lead are almost too numerous to count. In addition to all the extra rounds, extra high hearts, and extra thins, there are special bordering styles such as 90° turned came with a 45° heart and a right angle came with a 90° heart—actually a combination of two U leads. Many of these bordering leads are especially useful in lamp making, but they also serve well in stained glass sculpturing, since they offer more support than copper foil and can inveigle themselves over as many surfaces as the glass provides just as foil will.

WIDENING AND NARROWING CHANNELS

The channel width of lead came measures about 1/4" and accommodates the majority of all but the most uneven colored glasses. For hand-blown antique glass, the lead channel may prove either too wide or more often, too narrow. English streaky glass, with its variable thicknesses, is especially difficult to get into the lead channel.

To narrow the channel to accommodate thin glass, pinch it against the glass by pressing with the broad blade of a lead or putty knife. Obviously use caution here. To widen the channel, use a special instrument called a lathkin. If a particularly thick piece of glass is to be placed, a portion of the lead channel may have to be opened so wide that it may gape. This is acceptable if enough of the channel margin still grasps the edge of the glass without the possibility of the glass falling out. However, if the opening of the channel does not allow a sufficient grasp of the glass piece, use a larger lead or a thinner piece of glass even if you slightly compromise the color scheme. Nothing looks more unprofessional than pieces of tortured came, the edges of which seem to be all but nonexistent around the glass. These areas will stand out awkwardly and unprofessionally no matter how hard you try to convince yourself that no one will notice.

TAPPING GLASS INTO CAME

Tapping is not always necessary. If you must tap, use the leaded end of the lead knife. *Carefully.* Most cames will accept their glass borders without any extraneous

urging. However, occasionally you may need to tap the glass to make sure it's in all the way. But beware, tapping can become a habit and it's not a good one. It's all too easy to chip a glass edge or even break a piece by tapping. A slight push of the finger against the glass will correctly seat it within the came in most cases; if it rocks it usually means the glass has been incorrectly cut to fit the space and no amount of tapping will make it fit. In fact, tapping it may rearrange all the pieces that have been set so far by forcing them apart.

Never tap glass into came with a hammer. You will apply far too much force with very little effort and you know what that will do. Even with the knife handle, tap gently. Remember, if you have taken the pains to see that the glass fits correctly, you will need little, if any, tapping to make it seat properly. The idea is to slip the edge of the glass easily into an open channel which you may or may not have widened beforehand. Often the glass you are trying to fit will be stuck against the bottom margin of the piece or pieces of came you are trying to enter. Check to see; otherwise you will mash these lead borders and have to replace them. To offset this, try sliding the blade of the leading knife under the glass, thus raising it from the table surface and allowing it to slide over that lead margin. You'll find it suddenly locking into place in more than one spot with this small amount of effort.

STRETCHING CAME

Lead came below 1/2" (and sometimes even that) is usually stretched. Came should be stretched just prior to use. This process not only straightens the came of all kinks and twists, but it makes it much easier to work with because it firms up and tones the lead. The process of stretching is easily done by placing one end of the came in a lead stretcher or vise and pulling, gently at first, with pliers at the other end. You will actually feel the lead give and elongate. Don't do this with an open window behind you. If the lead breaks from too much pressure (as it may do if it has been badly twisted), a sharp jerk will literally send you flying. Always keep one foot behind you during the stretching process—lead came has a sense of humor.

Another method of stretching the came is to step on one end and pull up on the other. This procedure works only for the thinner leads from 1/16" through 3/16". Working with unstretched lead can be frustrating. The came tends to be flaccid and does not adhere well to the borders of the glass it is supposed to encompass.

STORING LEAD

All sorts of methods have been devised to store came for easy identification and access. Came can be doubled over and hung from padded hooks to avoid kinking. This requires wall space and, depending on the quantity, can involve a lot of hooks secured firmly to the wall. Again, if a great number of cames are involved they will tend to twist together no matter how neatly they are hung.

You can also lay it in individual bundles or place it in long boxes (came comes in long wood or cardboard boxes) with dividers for the different types. This is fine when not more than a dozen of each type of came is involved. If more than that, you will have a problem getting to the bottom layers and the top layers will become a mess.

Another option is to place the came in heavy, color-coded cardboard tubes to avoid mix ups. Again, this only works if a small amount of came is being stored. And you have to purchase these tubes, which are not always easy to find.

Of course, you can store it in the case it comes in and remove it from the end of the case. If you buy in case quantity rather than individual strands, this is obviously the most efficient way. But then, how do you store the cases? They are heavy and awkward to move. One obvious place is under the work table. Lead cases, with their ends removed for access, can be stored on shelves, with each shelf holding a separate style. If you choose this method, don't stack the cases directly on each other. If they are cardboard, they will collapse; if wooden, you will have to move the top ones to remove the bottom ones once they are empty. One idea is to build supports under a work table to hold individual cases. You can do this with the same long metal brackets used for steel shelving. The nesting area they form can support your work table-top as well. The disadvantage here is that you still have to remove the came from the side of the case and it can readily tangle with other pieces as you pull it out, pulling them out as well. These secondary strands can be stored on top of the case and used next time you want that style, but chances are, as the strands tangle within a case it will be more and more difficult to pull one out that hasn't mated. The whipping motion used to get out a strand will help and as the case gradually empties it gets easier to remove the various came. But it can be more trouble to get the lead out than it is to apply it, and that's no fun.

We recommend storing the cases flat in a case rack and removing the came from the top. A case rack resembles a step ladder frame with arms stretching forward. Each arm holds a single lead case so each case has its own space and

Lead storage came rack made of sturdy metal posts. This design takes up little room, but it will hold 14 boxes of 100-pound lead came. The dimensions are 5" x 72" x 57" high. (Courtesy of CAC Co.)

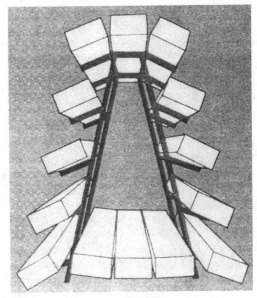

Side view of the came storage rack.

each case is open from the top. In this way, you can remove a single came by grasping it on the two ends, making it almost impossible to twist around its case mates. All the same, if you are selling lead in your studio, don't allow your customers to remove came on their own. Invariably they will make a mess of any storage system, even this one. Customers seldom make up their minds without touching, holding, scanning, comparing, measuring, projecting (and, one almost expects, tasting) things they haven't intended to buy in the first place. And they don't care how they pull came out of a case. *You* should be the only one to remove came from the storage system.

PHYSICAL CHARACTERISTICS OF LEAD

Lead has a tendency to form an oxidative coating on its surface when exposed to air. The process is gradual, but even the thinnest coating will diminish the ability of the surface of the came to accept solder, and a heavy coat of oxidation will stop the soldering process altogether. This thickening barrier cannot be removed even by the strongest flux. If the lead isn't absolutely shiny, it has oxidized to some degree. If it has a dull finish, the oxidation is extensive.

There is no problem removing this coating once you understand what has occurred. It is best removed by scrubbing the surface with a stiff wire brush, either brass or copper bristled. Steel bristles are likely to scratch the surface rather than buff it. Brass or copper bristle brushes can be purchased in most hardware stores. The oxidative coating doesn't have to be removed until you're ready to solder. The coating has no effect on the malleability or the firmness of the came. When you are ready to solder, scrub each joint with the wire brush. You will see the shiny, newly minted surface of the lead appear fairly rapidly. Some workers make it a habit to scrub each joint even if the surface still looks shiny, claiming that the solder spreads more evenly over the joint.

While there is no way to prevent the oxidative process, it can be slowed down. Dampness and humidity will quickly dull the shiniest lead, so store the came in a dry area. You can further protect the came by storing it in plastic wrap. Keep all storage boxes tightly covered. Separate layers of came in a single box with paper to avoid dampness seeping from one layer to the next. This will also help keep the came from tangling. Most factories ship came this way, so try to maintain it. Keep the lead away from any chemicals you are working with. The fumes from inorganic acids such as hydrochloride, sulfuric, and nitric can affect the surface of the lead even if they don't come in direct contact with it.

CUTTING AND MITERING

Came can be cut straight across or mitered at an angle to fit against its neighboring leads as snugly as possible. The close butting of the cames allows for smooth soldered joints, which will enhance the linear quality you are trying to achieve. This provides a neat professional-looking result.

Several items on the market can be used for cutting lead, the best of which is a professional leading knife. Mitering, however, is not always so easily accomplished.

Don't use scissors or tin snips to cut came, the blades tend to crush the channels or deform the cut end which must be restructured before it can be used. This takes time and effort. Cutting came with scissors will also dull and eventually ruin the scissors. A very dangerous lead-cutting tool is the hand-held razor blade. Even thin cames are tougher than they look and razor blades are too thin to withstand the stress of cutting through them. A corner can chip off and hit you in the eye or the brittle blade may twist and shatter, mitering your fingers instead of the lead.

A utility knife can be used to cut came because it has a more rugged blade than a razor blade, but it's awkward. A heavy-duty linoleum knife can be used as a lead knife if one edge is ground sharp onto the back (convex) surface. Treated thus, it resembles a professional leading knife and is at least a step in the right direction, if a faltering one. You need a bench grinder to put the edge on the blade, as well as a good quality steel to maintain the edge. In the long run, it is far more efficient to buy a professional leading knife.

USING THE LEADING KNIFE

For a description of this item see the chapter on tools.

To miter or cut with the leading knife, make the cut across the top surface of the came regardless of the size came being used. Never make the cut across the channeled surface or you will crush the channels. Mitering is more easily done when calculating from one surface to another. Place the came to be mitered across the top of the one it is to butt against and angle the blade of the knife to match the angle of the came you want to seat against. Once you've made the mark, put the lead on the table and cut according to the guide line you established. The lead knife works best with a side-to-side rocking motion and gradually increased pressure. Don't hack with the knife or try slicing with it—it doesn't work that way. Unless you develop this technique, the knife will not work for you.

A came cutter does a similar job as far as cutting is concerned. This is a specific tool for the purpose, not one adapted for the procedure. A good came cutter can also be used for cutting items other than lead, such as copper foil, zinc came, and wire. The sharp nose and the keen edges of this tool enable you to cut and miter came without distorting the channels. Although we find the lead knife an indispensable item (in many ways an extension of the hand), the came cutter is a possible addition to your hand tools, though not an alternative.

We recommend learning to use a lead knife regardless of any subsidiary items you add later since it is all but indispensable for this process. Our experience has been that the leading knife, regardless of what other tools come on the market, remains the basic precision instrument for the leading operation.

ANCILLARY ITEMS

In addition to the leading knife and came cutter are lead came choppers, lead saws, lead slicers, and who knows what new method of cutting lead will appear on the horizon. Many items of this nature have come and gone fairly rapidly, and many workers who purchased them, thinking they would make cutting lead came easier, leave them on the shelf gathering dust and return to using the lead knife.

WIDENING THE CAME CHANNEL

A number of tools can be used to widen the channel—in a pinch even a pencil will suffice. Usually widening the channel is only necessary to fit an especially thick piece of glass or to re-expand a channel that has been pinched in the rough and tumble of storage. Special instruments called "lathkins" come in various shapes and are made of various materials (Mylar, wood, metal).

When using any item to widen a channel, it is important not to snag the came. A good lathkin will slide easily along the length of the channel, widening as it goes. The shape of the lathkin you use is up to you. We prefer the wood-handled model with an angled metal tubular point that can be used in a pushing fashion. Push the point of the metal to plow through the channel with one hand and hold the came firmly on the work table with the other hand. Lathkins can also be used point down, scraping against the channel wall or heart. A lathkin can also be pulled toward you with the point down against the channel surface.

If the came is positioned channel up, the pressure from the lathkin is down against the table. If the channel is positioned sideways, the balancing pressure of your other hand must hold the lead firmly against the table while you work. The best position usually depends on the length of the came. As long as you are comfortable and the job is being done efficiently, the positioning of the came is up to you.

CORNERING

Whenever you work on corners, such as where the outside edges of a window or panel meet, you will encounter some special leading problems. You may prefer to use U leads on outside borders because they provide a neat finished appearance.

Simply butting the corner leads against each other is the simplest way to lock them together. However, for better strength and a more trim look, you can interlock the cames at the corners. We like to splice the corners, one into the other, in a sort of lock-and-key process. This is not a procedure universally adhered to, and we do not always follow it ourselves, but it does allow for good tight corners that hold up well.

LEAD POISONING

Many professional workers in the craft are not well versed on this subject, and indeed, it is only fairly recently that it has surfaced as a problem. There are obvious ways to avoid lead poisoning—wash your hands after working with the stuff, work in an area with plenty of space for soldering fumes to dissipate, don't work so close to the soldering that the fumes surround you, and don't have food or drink in the work space. Some safety advocates even advise you to wash your work clothes separately.

Because this subject has become a matter of concern, we have included as wide-ranging a discussion of the situation in the Appendix as we found to date. We recommend everyone working with stained glass read it. While this is certainly not the last word on so prolix a subject, being forearmed can save you a lot of grief. Needless to say (so we'll say it), all lead products should be kept out of the reach of children.

DESIGNING WITH LEAD

We have covered a good portion of this topic elsewhere in the book, but some of it bears repeating. Always keep in mind what can and cannot be cut in glass, and what the leading procedure will do to the cut lines. Points, as we have noted, tend to disappear, swallowed up by the came. The idea is to let the lead work with you in the design. If you need a long thin line, don't try to cut it out of glass—use a wide piece of lead instead (mustaches, for instance). If you want the eye to follow along a certain path, let the lead lines carry the flow to that area.

Remember, lead came is an integral part of the design; it is not there simply to hold the glass pieces together. Lead lines that wander erratically over the surface of a work to no ostensible purpose detract from what otherwise might be a very pleasing prospect. The type of lead you use depends on the effect you want to produce and the amount of strength you need. Don't fall into the trap of designing with small pieces of glass, then allowing them to be swallowed up with large pieces of lead.

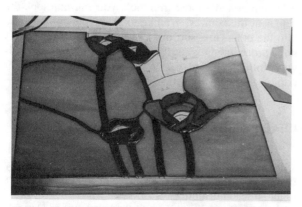

Tulip panel being leaded. The glass pieces are being matched to the underlying drawing and leaded.

In this regard, consider mixing various sizes of lead within the same panel, as a painter would mix different brush strokes depending on what he wanted to emphasize or subdue. It is not essential or artistic to stick to one type of lead throughout a window or a panel. All of this must be noted in the original design or blueprint, and only when this is completed to your complete satisfaction should the actual glass cutting and leading operation begin.

This fireplace screen is a good example of designing with lead. (Courtesy of Brum Studio)

H CAMES

As previously noted, these are inside leads used within a work to accommodate a piece of glass to either side. While there are almost infinite styles and variations, six major H leads are in common use. We list these in order of size:

1) 1/8"—No room for rough cutting. The smallest H came, this is very thin lead indeed. In rounded form, it appears even thinner than it does in flat, since the edges are foreshortened. There is no room for glass not accurately cut when using this lead. Your glass cutting must be precise because there is very little channel to cover mistakes. In fact, this lead is not advised for beginners unless the glass edges are ground, and even then, if the grinding is not done correctly the glass edges will show. This lead is used for its delicate statement and where small pieces of glass are to be leaded, though if used only for this in a window where the majority of glass pieces overpower it, it can stand out as a poor design element. It is used a lot in small suncatchers as an internal lead and, because it is so thin, it takes bends readily.

2) 3/16"—A good beginner's lead. This size is wider than the 1/8" but not as bulky to inexperienced fingers as the 1/4", the next size up. As is true of all these leads, 3/16" comes in both round and flat silhouettes, with the flat being somewhat easier to manipulate. Glass cutting need not be

as specifically precise as with 1/8" came, though it is a good habit always to cut the glass as precisely as possible. Because of the small channel in this lead, it will not accept thick pieces of antique glass and if you use such glass in your design, don't use the 3/16" lead in those areas. With this one exception, you will find that this basic lead is good for intermediate panels, mobiles, and windows since it furnishes a feeling of delicacy without fragility and adapts well to inner and outer curves.

3) 1/4"—All-purpose. This is possibly the most popular lead for panels and lamps, especially in rounded form and especially for beginners. In its flat shape, it comes in handy for large windows because the channel width is quite user friendly. Glass edges that are not altogether smooth will have minor defects hidden. In its rounded form, it allows enough room for lamp panels to angle within it without showing the edge of the glass. It is strong without appearing bulky. The rounded edge serves to intensify the three-dimensional effect of a lamp and gives the surface a finished appearance. In windows or panels, it provides a more definite line to the work than either of the two smaller leads we have discussed.

4) 3/8"—A more professional heavy lead. With this size we usually leave the hobbyist and move to leads used mainly by professional studios. A stiff heavy lead, 3/8" came firmly clutches the glass on either side and gives a definitive linear quality to the window. It will not conform well to sharp curves, though with care it can be used at such points usually by V-nicking the channel surfaces above and below to allow bending to occur more easily. Its rounded form is strictly for a design element and in such use this lead can make a most effective statement. This is a heavier lead than we have so far discussed, and it is also more expensive, since lead is priced according to weight.

5) 1/2", 3/4", and 1"—Strength and little flexibility. These professional leads are rarely used by the hobbyist, if at all. When we say they have more strength than flexibility we don't mean they don't bend at all. Any came will bend to a greater or lesser circumference; these take fairly wide turns grudgingly and smaller ones only with a great deal of persuasion. Rugged and difficult to work around curves, they are mainly used in large windows where they provide an emphatic, if not a stark linear flow to the design around large pieces of glass.

Although these leads are more massive than hobbyist leads, they are worked in the same way. They need not be stretched; above 1/2" they cannot be. Occasionally a section of one of these wide leads is used in a small work with a thinner and more delicate line complementing it. Here the larger lead can form a quirky break in the pattern rather than the graphic jump one hoped for, so its use calls for the utmost discretion on the part of the designer. There is the possibility of unbalancing the entire work for this one novel effect.

U OR END CAMES

As previously noted, these are used as bordering leads in windows or on glass surfaces where no other piece of glass abuts, as in suncatchers. Popular with hobbyists, these leads are seldom used by professional studios. This is because studios mainly create large windows designed for an existing framework. They use H leads as bordering leads both to furnish more strength to the borders and allow leeway in fitting the window in its space. That extra empty channel can be shaved to allow more room for a proper fit because it will eventually be covered by molding.

1) 1/16"—Back-to-back leads. These leads are mobile and accommodating. They are available in at least two widths of channel: 1/4" and 1/8" for different thicknesses of glass. The 1/16" U width is popular with hobbyists because its flexibility approaches foil with the sturdiness of a leaded line. Actually, it is used like foil, with each piece of glass leaded in a wraparound technique. These leaded borders are then soldered together at the ends. The line of solder is "beaded," meaning that it is laid down to an extent that the leaded line becomes convex. This lead is dear to the heart of freeform designers, since it can take angles up to 60° and more and still cling to the glass, provided it is pressed firmly around a smoothed edge. Its flat outer surface is perfectly suited to the application of a sister lead against it. This is the "back-to-back" technique.

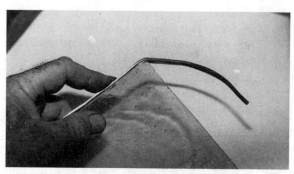

A demonstration of back to back U lead being wrapped around a piece of glass. In a way, this is similar to foiling. The channel is extremely narrow and must be pressed tightly against the glass. Over long spans, the lead will tend to come away from the glass so short areas are covered and strutted with ancillary lead lines. Otherwise, on long spans this lead can be glued to the glass edge.

After each piece of glass is cut it is wrapped with the came, similar to foiling except the lead edges automatically grip the glass. The ends are soldered together and the wrapped pieces are placed back on the pattern and solder flowed along the surfaces where they meet. This is a rapid technique for putting together freeform objects such as hanging mobiles, small animals, shade pulls, and pendants. The main problem is running the came over long surfaces of glass. Unless the design is calculated to hold the lead in place (with other leads forming internal struts to support it) the lead on a hanging piece may eventually pull away from the glass. This is annoying to say the least. You can glue the channel to the glass but this is extra work and messy because the glue will squeeze over the glass and must be cleaned away. The best way to use this lead is to calculate in advance how best to design what you have in mind so this border lead will be firmly affixed.

2) 3/16"—Finish for small panels. This is the first of the truly "high heart" cames. It is used along flat surfaces as a finishing lead for a panel that is to be hung in a window with no frame other than lead. This came will take curves if they are not too abrupt; otherwise it will tend to kink. To prevent this, smooth it gently as you progress along each glass surface. If the curve is still too extreme, you can cut small triangles out of the sides of the came to take the bend and solder the

lead at these areas after they accordion together. The process is like sewing a dart in a dress.

There is no rounded version of this lead that we are aware of. It is a popular lead for the bottom of the skirt of paneled lamp shades and is also used where three-dimensional objects must be soldered together at angles, where use of an H lead would involve too much channel bending. This lead is amenable to a number of shapes and designs if it is worked carefully and with patience. Again, it can prove balky if it is tugged or pushed into awkward curves. Because of its flat surface, it will fit against a sister lead with little trouble, providing the glass has been cut accurately.

A secondary use for this lead is as a "belt" on a panel lamp to overlay the juncture of the lamp body and the lamp skirt made separately. When 3/16" U is flattened out it has just the proper width to cover the seam between body and skirt so that solder need not be used to fill in the area. It's a lot quicker and neater (and less expensive) to apply this belt which is tack soldered to the individual lamp struts, than to use half a pound of solder to accomplish the same purpose. Once this belt is applied you may tin it with a thin coating of solder to stiffen it, though this is not necessary.

3) 1/4" Round—Three-dimensional. This lead is especially designed for curves of three-dimensional objects, usually the skirts of straight panel lamps or the bottom curved portion of lamps with bent panels. It may also be used to wrap rondels—spun glass circles—within a flat panel, providing you press the lead firmly enough against the rondel's surface to make sure it grips. This lead does its job superbly where it is called for, although it is not called for often. It is also used in stained glass jewelry and stained glass freeform items such as belt buckles where peculiar curves are manifest. It's a heavy lead and comes only in rounded form, having more a C than a U shape. It's not a lead one sees too often and we mention it here just to exemplify some of the varied shapes and styles of came.

4) 3/8"—For large panels and windows. This is the largest size U lead in general use. It complements 1/4" H leads. Keep in mind the deep channel—a space almost 3/8" deep—when you plan your design since this lead will swallow up some of the border glass. You want to allow for this. This lead will also cover up errors in measurement.

A common problem when beginners make a panel is that they cut the inside H leads too long, impinging on the border leads, or too short so the consequent gaps must be filled with solder. If the gaps aren't extensive, 3/8" U will cover them and overlap leads that are too long, provided they don't extend beyond the borders of the work. If overlapping occurs, you will see bumps in the bordering lead where it runs over the H leads; this may bother you aesthetically and practically since the extra thickness may disallow the window from fitting in its projected space. In this case, the inside leads must be pulled out and trimmed back to proper lengths and then resoldered to the bordering lead. Better to get it right in the first place.

SPECIALIZED CAMES

Specialized cames have some particularly distinctive feature that marks them for specific use. They are not general all-purpose leads and they are more expensive than the leads so far described.

Reinforced Cames: These are leads with a hollow heart. Through this portion runs a flat steel rod that provides a stiff support for the came. Although these leads may conform to gentle curves without too much trouble and to moderate curves with some effort, their main purpose is to add strength to the window. Because they run side-to-side within a window, an outside reinforcing bar is unnecessary. They may be worked into a design and still furnish needed support. They may also be used as border leads, although here they are much less difficult to use, since they would run straight from side-to-side. Because of the inner bar, reinforced cames cannot be cut with a leading knife or hand came cutter. Instead, you must use a hacksaw. If you intend to use this lead in a design, you must allow for its wider heart and calculate the pattern accordingly.

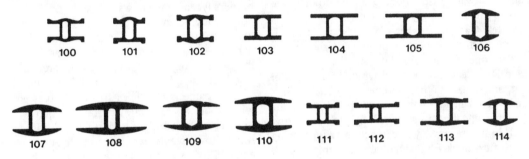

Came No.	Approximate Strands Per Box	Face Width	Channel Width (Inside)	Heart Thickness (Overall)	Steel Bar Size	Wt. Per Lin. Ft. In Ozs.
100	84	.500"	.172"	.125"	³⁄₁₆" × ¹⁄₁₆"	3½
101	84	.438"	.188"	.188"	¼" × ³⁄₃₂"	3½
102	74	.500"	(.219")(.250")	.203"	¼" × ⅛"	4
103	91	.500"	.234"	.203"	¼" × ⅛"	3¼
104	74	.625"	.250"	.203"	¼" × ⅛"	4
105	65	.750"	.250"	.219"	¼" × ⅛"	4½
106	49	.500"	.250"	.219"	¼" × ⅛"	6
107	53	.625"	.234"	.219"	¼" × ⅛"	5½
108	37	1.000"	.250"	.219"	¼" × ⅛"	8
109	42	.750"	.234"	.219"	¼" × ⅛"	7
110	26	.750"	.313"	.250"	¼" × ⅛"	11¼
111	98	.438"	.156"	.125"	³⁄₁₆" × ¹⁄₁₆"	3
112	74	.625"	.156"	.141"	³⁄₁₆" × ¹⁄₁₆"	4
113	53	.625"	.250"	.219"	¼" × ⅛"	5½
114	74	.500"	.188"	.188"	¼" × ⅛"	4

Dimensions of reinforced lead cames (Courtesy of RSR Corp.)

Reinforced cames are usually reserved for large windows or glass sculpture involving heavy areas that require firm support. Using these cames within a window, whether in one area or several, does not mean you can discount the outside reinforcing bars automatically. Depending on the design and dimensions of the window involved, you may need outside support bars anyway. However, you should need fewer of them and you can probably place them away from the parts of the design where the reinforced came supports so as to impinge on as little of the window as possible. This whole question of support must be individually applied to particular windows and occasions.

Colonial and High-Heart Cames: These rather ornate leads are applicable to special types of windows, usually "leaded windows" where clear glass is cut into shapes of recurring patterns such as diamonds, squares, and rectangles, rather than in windows of colored glass in a pictorial or freeform pattern. Use of these cames is an adventure in discretion, since they can be overpowering. You should be aware of them because they do offer another modality in designing your window.

Off-Center Cames: In these H leads, the heart is placed away from the center, impinging on the second channel. Thus one channel is shallow and the other channel is deep. This lead can be used where two pieces of glass abut, one thin, the other extremely thick. The thick piece can be given a wider flap of lead to fit into using the deeper channel, and the thin piece will fit into the narrower channel. In this manner, you can get away with using 3/8" lead to fit a thick English streaky to a thin French reamy rather than going into a standard 1/2", 3/4", or even 1" lead, which might satisfy the thick glass but may overpower the thin one.

Extra Wide Cames: These widths may be purchased with a channel that is almost double the width of usual sized channels. This is to allow the placing of either very thick pieces of antique glass or for the process of "double glazing" where one piece of glass is placed on top of another and the two pieces are embedded into a wide channel of lead. Interesting and novel effects can be obtained in this fashion and two and even three tiers of glass can be placed together, depending on the colors being used and the effect you are after. Obviously you don't want them to cancel each other out. Tiffany used this technique to obtain special drapery effects as well as deeper tones for flesh, though in many instances he used foil instead.

Brass-Crowned Lead Came: The coating, or crowning, of brass that covers the top and bottom surfaces of these leads (the channeled areas remain uncoated) serves practical and aesthetic purposes. On the practical side, strength is a decided factor, and on the aesthetic, there is the finished quality immediately provided.

Brass-crowned lead came is of special value for its effectiveness in beveled windows where the weight of the plate glass elements is a factor and there is no color to the glass itself. This came provides the necessary rigidity and the brass color stands out beautifully against the clear bevels. This came is best cut with a hacksaw, with the cuts made firmly from the start. If the saw slips, you will end up with scratches in the brass which cannot be fixed.

Similarly, soldered joints with this type of came must be as unobtrusive and neat as possible because the slightest awkwardly soldered joint will stand out and the more you try to fix it (unlike uncrowned came) the more of an eyesore it will become. We suggest that until your soldering is exact, don't try using brass came.

Zinc Came: No one ever called zinc came beautiful, but for strength it is unsurpassed. It is generally used as borders for large windows where the borders may or may not already be enclosed by H or U lead came. Since the channels in zinc came are fairly wide, these existing borders can be inserted into the zinc just as they are, making things very convenient. Zinc came is rarely used as an inside lead, though, this is not a rule of thumb.

Zinc came is also used frequently between sectional windows as a structural material. It requires little solder to make a smooth tight bond; if the surface is clean the solder flows evenly over it with little effort. Oleic acid is a good flux for zinc soldering; solder may be either 60/40 or 50/50 as with lead came. Zinc cames come in standard six and eight foot lengths.

THE REINFORCING BAR (RE-BAR)

The reinforcing bar was, in the past, nothing more than a steel rod the width of the window, cut into the wooden framework and attached (since steel doesn't solder) by copper wire soldered to those internal joints of the window bypassed by the bar. Such bars were placed approximately three feet apart and were very visible, at least at first. Oddly enough they did manage to fade eventually into the background so that the window itself did not appear imposed on.

Today it's unlikely anyone would consider such an arrangement. No matter how you assure a prospective customer that these bars would eventually be sight unseen, he would object strongly to having them slap bang in the middle of the stained glass window they wanted to show off.

Instead, today we have a different kind of re-bar—a thin strip about 1/8" thick, either galvanized or electroplated to permit accepting solder directly and bendable to conform to an existing lead line so as to be completely obscured. They solder directly to the joints they bypass and, unless you look in back of the window, you won't know they are there. Even from behind, they form no objectionable interference. It might be said that as stained glass came out of its ecclesiastical confinement and into the realm of the homeowner, demands for such aesthetic modifications as the re-bar were to be expected.

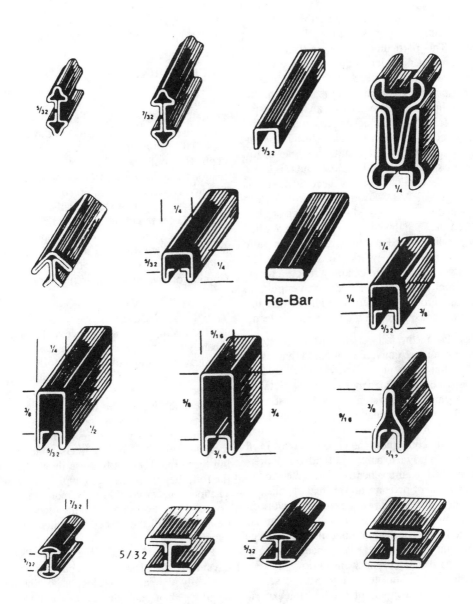

Some shapes and dimensions of zinc came.

CHAPTER 10
Working with Copper Foil

There are a number of misconceptions about this process. First is the notion that it is "easier" than working with lead came. This particular view is partly based on technique. Certainly it is easier to do a sloppy job with foil than a precise one with came. Second is the image of foil as a more rapid process than using lead. Again, this depends on skill. In a race between two craftspeople, specialists in either technique, it is questionable which would complete the project in the shortest time. Third is the image of foil as a more delicate end result, with lines of foil producing a more spidery, lace-like effect. But this effect is based more on the size of the glass piece than what is holding them together. A 1/8" lead, used correctly, can provide the same thin line and hold small pieces of glass just as firmly as foil. Then there is the proviso that a foiled piece is stronger than a leaded one because it has more substance in its metallic framework. To our knowledge, no one has really tested this. We can only report a newspaper account from years ago of a burglar attempting to break into a house through a leaded sidelight. He was unable to get into the house through the interstices of lead.

More or less last in the foil versus lead debate is the idea that foiling is a more convenient method than using came—you can foil glass pieces individually, holding them in your lap or on a table, away from the work table, perhaps in the evening while watching TV. This, at least, is true; you can't do this with lead and if this is the basis of your choice, then foiling is your baby. But other than this, as far as we are concerned, the choice between foil or lead usually comes down to a matter of individual preference based on which your teacher uses best. We want to stress that a good deal of patience and critical appraisal is required for either process. If you are going to work in stained glass to any great extent, you should be familiar with both methods because they are not mutually exclusive. If all you want to do is make a lampshade, foiling is probably your best bet. If all you want to do is make a panel for your home, then stick to lead. In either case, using just one process will rob you of much of the experience of working with stained glass. By all means, learn

the foiling process, first if you must, but learn to use lead came as well. You'll never regret it.

BACKGROUND

Use of copper foil with stained glass came about in the Tiffany era, probably in the 1920s, but whether Tiffany himself invented the technique is not really known. La-Farge used the same process, as did other artists of the time. Tiffany was a great borrower of other people's concepts. He would then add his own ideas to take them to ingenious lengths. Using foil, he produced intricate works that involved the juxtaposition of thousands of small, faceted glass pieces that went together in a mass production facility faster than lead came would have allowed. These mosaic-like creations needed a supportive metal that was at once delicate, flexible, inexpensive, adhesive, readily solderable, and which could become rigid on demand. Copper foil met these requirements.

THE TECHNIQUE

It's a simple enough process if done right. Foiling means wrapping the edges of the glass pieces with copper foil, leaving enough overlapping foil to be pressed *evenly* against the surface of the glass to either side. The operative word here is evenly. If the foil is uneven (too much on one side), it provides too thin a line aesthetically and will not support the glass properly. You must choose the foil width (several widths are available) to allow for a reasonable overlap. Many beginners come to grief when foiling their initial pieces because they do not evenly place the foil; they think they can apply it in slapdash fashion. The more pieces you have, the more time you must spend foiling them. Foil and place the pieces back on the cartoon. When all the pieces are foiled, they are then soldered together.

For your final foiled piece to be accomplished to best advantage, the glass must be cut and ground to the size originally planned (or as close as possible). Foil is far less forgiving than lead, though this is partly dependent on your critical sense. We have seen foiled objects with gaps

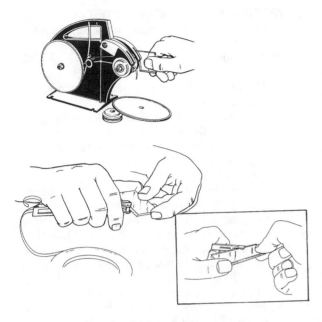

Foiling a piece of glass is simple—you might think. All you have to do is wrap a thin piece of foil around the edges of a piece of glass. Yes, but you have to get these edges even, otherwise when you go to solder the piece to other pieces, you may have plenty of foil on one edge and none on the other. And glass by itself doesn't solder very well. In fact, not at all. So while many individuals will hand foil while watching TV or the sunset, when they go to solder their pieces together, they may find the foil not exactly precise. The tools shown (stained glass foiler, hand foiler, and foil crimper) help make foiling exact, especially if you're foiling a great many pieces of glass. (Courtesy of Glastar Co.)

FOIL SIZE AND THICKNESS

Several foil thicknesses are available for use in stained glass work. For convenience, we may consider them as hard, medium, and soft. The degree of the metal's rigidity will depend on the thickness of the foil and the amount of solder used in the final "tinning" process. Hard foil is .002" thick, twice the dimension of soft foil at .001". Medium foil has a thickness of .015". The weight of the foil determines the price, since most foil runs the same length.

Your choice of thickness depends on the type of work you're doing and the effect you want. Small pieces of glass require only a thin foil to hold them together. However, you might want the bulky rough effect of a heavier thickness even with small glass pieces. Not so much choice is possible when large foiled panels of glass are to go in a lampshade. Here heavy foil is essential for support.

In the past, foil came in 6"-wide rolls from which the worker cut strands of variable widths depending on his needs. We used petroleum jelly to hold the foil to the glass. It was a messy process. The introduction and perfection of individual rolls from 5/32" to 1/2" with a pressure-sensitive glue backing to adhere the metal firmly to the glass made foiling the comparatively simple process it is today. But it took a long time to convince manufacturers that foiling was more than a passing fancy.

between pieces that did not seem to bother their creators. With foil, there is no channel to hide defects in the glass cutting. Because they are creating their own channel with foil to hold the glass, some beginners (and advanced workers) don't take the time to make sure the pieces fit precisely with the initial pattern. "Oh, well," their attitude seems to indicate, "close enough is good enough." It isn't, and if you think that way, your end results will be shoddy.

Carefully cut and grind the pieces to fit to the pattern before foiling. Notice on the right bottom of the wing how wide the line becomes with the foil wrapping.

There are a variety of widths and backings available in adhesive copper foil rolls. Sizes range from 5/32" for thin antiques to 1/2" for thick textured glass. Plain copper backed is used primarily, black works well on transparent and mirror glass, and silver on bevels and other clear glasses. The color should be coordinated with the patina finish you choose if the inside foil will be visible, but don't use black foil on opalescent—it gives a gray halo to the glass around the foil. Some of the foil shown is manufactured by Edco Co. and some by Venture Co.

Ideally, the thinner the foil the better, since the effect produced will be more delicate with the least amount of metal visible. However, there is a point of no return. You don't want to use foil that is so thin it fails to fulfill its bracing function. The width you choose should be roughly three times the thickness of the glass edge. This allows a delicate tracery of foil on the front and back with a substantive 2/3 unseen glued to the glass edge and contributing to stability.

The mistake many beginners make in choosing too-wide foil is forgetting that while a single piece of glass may show only 1/16" of edging, when that piece is placed in the design it will juxtapose a similarly foiled piece, combining two edges to show a line double the size. The amount of visible foil—the amount overlapping the glass—will thus enlarge when the pieces marry. Add solder, which may thicken the line even more depending on how many gaps you fill, and your delicate tracery can look obese. The solution? Cut the glass pieces precisely to the pattern, choose foil to match their size and your aesthetic intent, and solder very carefully so that even if you have no gaps to fill, the solder doesn't thicken the line by running over the foil onto the glass surface.

COPPER FOILING STEP-BY-STEP

1) Draw a design for a freeform hanging such as a suncatcher.
2) Cut the design out of glass and grozz or grind the glass edges until they are absolutely smooth. The smoother the glass edge, the better the foil will adhere to it.
3) Choose the width of foil that will accommodate the edge of the glass and overlap just enough to show a delicate line when combined with another piece. As a beginner, you may want to arbitrarily select 1/4" foil.
4) Anchor the end of the foil against the starting area of the glass edge with your fingertip. As you wrap the foil round the glass edge, remove the paper backing. Press the foil firmly and evenly against the glass edge as you go and at the same time over the edge to either side. If you are foiling a square piece, check the corners. You do not have to cut the excess foil at the corners, though some foilers do. We generally just fold it down and burnish it later. If the piece is circular, just follow the shape. You should always spot check as you foil before pressing the material on either side. You must have an absolutely even amount of foil showing front and back; it's easy to lose this measurement as you go along. Should you look back and find the foil is thicker on one side than another, pull the foil

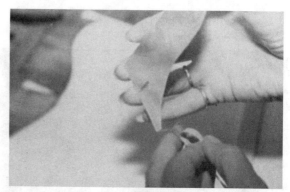

Start the foil on an edge of the glass that will be joined to another foiled piece and soldered. This will prevent the overlap on the foil from being lifted while handling or cleaning the project in progress.

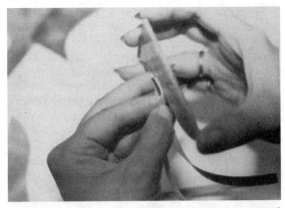

The easiest way to hold the glass is by the ground edges so you can see left and right of the sides to center the foil. Anchor and guide the foil with your middle finger and use your thumb and forefinger to pull the paper backing off the foil.

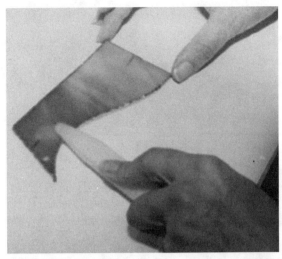

Burnishing the foil with a book binder's bone or flat fid onto the glass puts the adhesive to work. Stroke it once or twice to smooth the wrinkles and seat the foil into the ground edge. Over rubbing will stretch the foil, break down the adhesive, and allow flux and water to seep underneath to loosen the foil.

off the glass (hopefully without tearing it) and try again. Should the foil tear, don't be concerned. Just match the ends as best you can and keep going. The solder will take care of the break in material.

5) The pressing motion should be toward the center, not around the circumference, as this may off center the foil. Once the foil has been hand-pressed, you can iron out any wrinkles with a bone or similar tool. This process is called burnishing. Corners especially may need this treatment. If you are working with textured glass, you may need to spend extra time burnishing the foil against the uneven surface.

6) When the foil is even and flat, tack solder the ends together and match the glass to the pattern and against its neighbor pieces.

7) Some workers like to run solder around each foiled piece of glass prior to soldering them together including the inside edge. If you do this, be sure the solder you lay down here is absolutely smooth. Whether this pre-soldering makes the finished piece stronger or not is open to debate. It's your option. If you do pre-solder and you are working with small glass pieces, use pliers or a similar tool to hold the glass to keep the solder heat from your fingers. If you have trouble soldering, the foil has probably become oxidized to an extent. This is why foil should always be kept

The pieces to be foiled are checked against one another (top right). The red cathedral (bottom left) is marked for cutting by outlining a cardboard pattern shape with a silver ultra-fine marker. The thin line is nearly the width of the cutting wheel and easy to follow.

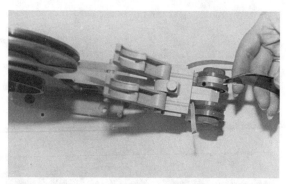

Using the Inland foil machine loaded with 7/32" silver foil applied to red cathedral glass. The foil is positioned by hand and the glass pushed into the grooved wheel to lay the foil on the piece. It can be drawn on using the top of the foil wheel. Curved pieces use the more forward point of the roller. Longer glass will require the foiling machine to be screwed to the bench with the rollers extending beyond the bench to manipulate the glass around on the roller.

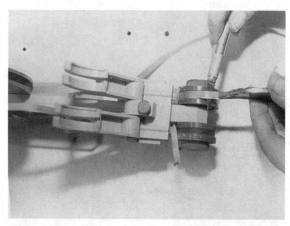

The glass is wrapped and the cut foil end will lap evenly on the glass. You will have to finish crimping the foil over and burnish as in hand foiling. This piece took about 30 seconds to wrap compared to the usual minute or more to hand foil. It will take getting used to, but it can be quite a time-saver.

in the packages it comes in. Scrub the foil gently with Triple O/extra fine steel wool to clean and re-flux it.

8) After all the pieces are properly foiled and placed in position, hold them with leading nails around the outside so they are bound according to the lines of your design. Check for fit before soldering any of the individual glass pieces together. Very often, the pieces don't come together because the foil on one or more is not pressed tightly enough. This will take up room. More likely, pre-soldering the inside edge may have left a small mound of solder that is holding the pieces apart. Investigate and smooth away the offending portion with your iron.

9) If, after checking all the above, your pieces still don't match precisely, one or more may have to be re-cut. Don't try to justify the new relationship among the pieces no matter how tempting it might be.

10) On a happier note, if the pieces fit snugly, solder them together. If there are many pieces in a sculptural arrangement (three-dimensional) you may want to tack solder them before doing the more extensive soldering. Tack soldering means placing a small amount of solder in a few critical areas to hold the pieces together to obtain a perspective. If the pieces are all in one plane, you may completely solder them two pieces at a time. If one or two pieces are arranged in a three-dimensional format, tack solder those first, since all other pieces must relate to them. The advantage of tack soldering is the ease with which these few spots can be unsoldered if necessary. It is possible but hardly worth the time and effort to unsolder two foiled pieces that have been fully soldered. It's easier to strip away the foil, solder and all, with the iron, and re-foil and re-solder the pieces.

11) Once all the pieces are foiled and arranged back on the pattern, we tack solder them at the corners or anyplace that will hold them together effectively. After these portions are tacked, you can take out the nails and more easily solder up the entire panel. Don't let the iron get too hot or the solder will flow through the joints to the other side. It may do this in any event, but it's best to keep this to a minimum. When you get to the other side, you must fix all these spots (they usu-

ally resemble mushrooms and that's what they're called). Flux all visible copper to make it solder readily. When your panel is finished, there should be no foil showing to the sides of the solder line. If there are, use a lead knife to press these areas against the solder line. Then carefully add a little solder to the bottom edge of the solder line, enough to cover the foil but not enough to thicken the line. This problem occurs because a) the foil hasn't been cleaned properly along this edge and oxidation or dirt hasn't allowed the solder to flow properly, or b) the flux you used wasn't scrubbed into the edges of the foil and the solder didn't cover it all. It's easy to miss this in the excitement of your first foiled creation. Chances are you won't miss it again.

12) When you've soldered all the exposed foil on one side of your work, turn the piece over and solder the foil on the other side. Do this not only for looks, but for strength. It's sometimes more difficult to solder the back surface than the front since the back may have picked up dirt from the tabletop or dirt and flux residues that have percolated from the front. Clean the back surface with Triple O/extra fine steel wool before attempting to solder it. This should remove most of the problem. As for the mushrooms mentioned above, the best way to handle this excess solder is to melt it and sweep it away with the iron. This takes practice and it's best not to wear sandals when doing it. A less athletic process is to use some form of solder removal—either Solder Off mesh or a rubber bulb that will suck up molten solder if you act quickly. However you remove the mushrooms, make sure the underlying foil is uninjured and soldered properly.

SOLDERING TIPS AND IRONS

Any soldering tip can be used for foil. Some craftspeople prefer a thin tip for more control of the thin foil edging, but it's really up to you and what you get used to. The same iron you use for leading is used for foiling. Don't let anyone con you into buying a separate iron for the foiling process. Although foil won't melt from the heat of the iron as lead came will, the solder will tend to flow between foiled pieces rather than over them if the iron is too hot. The effect most workers want to achieve in soldering foil is "beading" and to get a really nice bead you should use a rheostat control to maintain a proper iron heat. One rheostat control is all you need for working in any phase of stained glass. The ideal temperature is not a constant, it's based on the type of soldering iron you're using, the kind of solder, and the amount of solder you want to lay down. These things you find out through trial and error.

BEADING

Beading is the final step in the copper foil process. It occurs after all the pieces have been firmly soldered together and prior to the cleanup. It establishes a rounded curve of solder over the foil line, giving depth to the pieces of glass. Through beading, the glass pieces become aesthetically discrete, allowing each more of an emphasis. Beading is done with a moderately heated iron (moderate meaning whatever heat works for you).

Beading can be frustrating for the inexperienced worker who may find the bead of solder flattening out and running onto the table as you try to work it. If you are especially inept, you may loosen some of the foiled glass pieces at the same time. Don't think of beading as a simple, last minute icing on the cake. It is an integral part of the work. Keeping a cool head, together with a warm iron, is imperative. Our rheostat control reading when we bead is about 1/2 to 3/4 line voltage. Try to keep the solder plastic rather than liquid to allow it to build up on the previous layer. It is this buildup that shapes the bead.

COMMON PROBLEMS WITH FOIL

1) If tinning the foiled pieces is not done smoothly, the edge surfaces will be irregular and the glass pieces won't meet each other. Over-tinning also gives an additional thickness to the copper which may interfere with the glass pieces joining.

2) Unclean foil. Copper will not take solder if it has an oxide coat or is dirty.

3) Not enough flux or the wrong type of flux, which may be too strong to bond the solder. This can also create a foul odor and dangerous fumes.

4) Watch your iron temperature. If you're having trouble flowing solder, your iron may be too cold. If the solder runs, the iron may be too hot.

5) If you're having trouble soldering into the glass concavities, you are probably using the wrong shape or size tip. Your best bet here is a flat, thin, chisel shape, such as a 3/16" or a flat 1/4".

6) Poorly cut glass presents problems. If the glass doesn't conform to the pattern to begin with, the foil will follow this ad libbing and you'll end up with a design that has no relationship to your pattern. If the glass is cut to the correct shape but has splintery edges, the foil will not adhere smoothly and a chipped edge of glass may be visible alongside the foil's edge. This is unprofessional and sloppy. We cannot repeat enough that glass cutting must be precise and the glass grozzed, sanded, or ground so that it shows no discrepancies in the edges.

7) Make sure the foil is pressed tightly around the glass pieces. No matter how well the glass is cut, if the foil is not crimped to the edges, it will loosen.

COMBINING COPPER AND LEAD

Copper foiling and lead caming are not mutually exclusive. Copper is usually used with small pieces of glass (in a lampshade, for instance, the curve is produced by foiling small glass pieces over a form). The smaller the pieces of glass, the greater the bend or curvature that may be achieved. To shape large pieces of glass, the glass must be fired over a form in a kiln. In general, while leading gives a bold, emphatic look to a piece, copper foil provides a delicate, lacy effect. Foil is not ordinarily used for the long spans of glass that lead can handle with ease; nevertheless, provided a panel is given proper support with brace bars and the design is well planned, foil can be used throughout an entire window.

Lead and copper foil can be combined in a window where small and large pieces of glass are used together or where the design involves "foiling in" jewels, chunks, stones, seashells, or perhaps your graduation picture. There are no rules here but be cautioned: you can easily overdo a good thing. Just because the materials are available and the technique is understood doesn't mean either should be used to excess. Adhesive-backed copper foil, pre-cut in rolls, allows even the most inexperienced worker to achieve a finished, professional look. The inclusion of the copper foil technique into classic stained glass opens up great new possibilities. Its use provides effects that would be awkward with lead.

FOILING MACHINES

If hand foiling doesn't suit you, there are machines available that will more or less do the job for you. Foilers run the gamut from the simplicity of a bare wheel attached by screws to the work table as a mere holding unit for a roll of copper foil, to electric ones that apply the foil, strip away the paper backing, and even crimp the edges around the glass. These more sophisticated units will hold several different sizes of foil for different glass thicknesses. Thus the multiplicity of hand operations is transformed into a single machine procedure. Since hand foiling could not be made easier, the object of the foiling machine is to make it more productive and the end result more professional looking. The carelessness of many workers in keeping their foiled overlap even is eliminated by the machine. This alone, for a worker who does only a minimum of foiling, would make the purchase of even a cheap foiler worthwhile. If you do a lot of foiling (and some workers do almost all of their stained glass this way) and if you find it tedious, any of these machines is a dream purchase.

Essentially all foiling machines work alike. The roll of copper foil is held by the unit and fed into a smaller wheel against which the glass edges are hand (or machine) turned. The advantage of an electrically driven wheel is the lessening of finger fatigue. Electric foilers are run by foot pedals guided by the operator. Tiffany's workers would undoubtedly have appreciated a dozen or so.

CHAPTER 11
Finishing Techniques

Cleanup is something most of us don't like to think about, whether it's the dishes, the floor, or the laundry. Cleaning up the finished stained glass may strike you the same way, but you may as well know it now, it's just as much a part of the creative process as designing and developing your technique. We're not only talking about cleaning up at the end of a project—cleanup should be ongoing so the work table is neat and clear of glass chips, the tools should be put back in their places, and your hands certainly should be washed. But above all, the glass project should be cleaned of flux, the grime of soldering, and all other conglomerations that have accumulated during its fabrication.

To skimp on the final touches that must be applied to any stained glass project, partly because you don't want to take the time and think it won't make much difference, is a compromise of all the work you've done beforehand. Stained glass that is not thoroughly cleaned, whether puttied or not, remains forever unfinished and can come back to haunt you.

CLEANING THE GLASS

Once all the soldering has been done, clean the piece as soon as possible. The longer you wait, the more difficult it will be to clean. Flux residues and grime that have accumulated during the fluxing and soldering operation, along with dirt from your hands and, yes, even your fingerprints, will form a filmy surface over both lead or foil and glass. No matter how tired you feel after completing the work, start cleaning! It's a good idea to allow a specific amount of time for cleanup prior to closing up shop.

First rinse the project in soapy water. It may appear clean while wet (glass is notorious for this), but when the water is wiped off, it can appear smudgy, tacky, and probably still weeping flux from the joints. This is frustrating but you still have several steps to go.

If the object is a panel, lay it flat on the table and sprinkle it with cleaning and polishing powder—a mix of calcium carbonate and diatomaceous earth (about 75% to

25%) available in hardware stores. We have found this acts as a twofold cleaning agent. It is absorbent so will dry any liquids left on the glass, and is just abrasive enough to clean glass, leads, solder joints, and foil at one stroke. Sift the cleaning and polishing powder over the glass with a small strainer to get rid of any lumps or other debris that may scratch the glass. Cover the glass surface with sifted powder. With a flexible bristle floor scrubbing brush (flexible enough to ride over the leads without tearing them loose), brush the powder all over the glass. You can use a great deal of force pressing straight down, providing the object is lying flat. If you work in an enclosed area, wear a mask or keep a handkerchief over your nose; the powder can fly about and you may find yourself sneezing it onto the work. For difficult areas you may want to use steel wool with cleaning and polishing powder on it. Steel wool should not scratch the glass.

Once the surface is clean, turn the panel over and apply powder to the other side (first clean the surface of the work table so you won't have to clean the first side all over again). Scrub in the powder then remove it from both sides with a vacuum cleaner or rag. Don't reuse this powder—it's pretty thoroughly contaminated. Tap the panel against the table to remove the remaining powder from under the cames and hold it up to the light. You might still have a few places that look smudgy or feel tacky. Repeat the process. Once the panel is clean and the leads are uniformly shiny, use soapy water or window cleaner to clean the surfaces further (window cleaner can leave a film so don't overuse it).

PUTTYING

Usually putty is used prior to an extensive cleaning, but students sometimes use the fact that they are going to putty as an excuse to leave their panel or window pretty dirty. They assume they can clean at one stroke after they putty. This is not a good idea because the time spent puttying, together with the mix of putty and grime, will make the window much harder to clean. At least a moderate cleaning should be done prior to applying putty, and the cleaner the window the better.

Putty is used to weatherproof windows and provide support. For stained glass, putty with a linseed oil base is best. Linseed oil putty hardens after a time and provides a stiff lining between the lead came and the glass in the channels.

When getting ready to putty, use an old pair of kid gloves or coat your hands with a protective glove coating such as Pro-Tek. This DuPont product guards the skin against oils, grease, and oxides and washes off with water. It prevents the putty from sticking to your fingers, which makes it easier to work. Pro-Tek is greaseless and within a few moments after applying it to your skin, you won't even know it's there.

Start puttying by rubbing a handful of putty into a ball between your palms. If it's too sticky and moist, add a little cleaning and polishing compound to stiffen it up. If it's too adherent, it will come away from the came as fast as you push it under, preferring to stick to your fingers. Putty comes in black or white. Black putty will leave a black line under the lead; white putty will leave a white one. It is especially important to protect your hands if you are using black putty. The carbon that furnishes the color is difficult to remove from skin.

After getting the putty to the right consistency, snip off a bit with your fingers and start pushing it under the cames with your thumb. Each piece of lead should have putty under it. This is not as painstaking a procedure as it may sound. In fact, many workers find it relaxing, but be careful not to crack any pieces of glass by getting too relaxed. The border leads should also be puttied. Be careful when pushing the putty under them so you don't push them away from the glass, especially when they cover long unstrutted edges (which, being a good designer, you have not allowed).

When you are done slapping on putty you will find a really sloppy object in front of you covered with gobs of putty. Take a bent putty knife or even a lead knife and turn down the came edges against the glass surface. (If you have used foil this will not be necessary.) Putty will ooze out from beneath the came. With a pointed object such as a sharpened chopstick or an ice pick, go around each border of lead. The putty will easily cut loose from the came. Scoop up any excess putty with your hand, roll it into a ball, and pop it back into the can. Seal the can tightly. If you leave the lid even slightly ajar, the putty will harden. After puttying, clean and polish the piece again. Then go ahead with the final cleaning.

If puttying has been done within the last several days, warn your customers that the work will continue to ooze putty for at least another week. Ask them not to clean the glass until the putty has thoroughly set. After that, they can go around the leads to clean away the excess, and then clean the panel with window cleaner.

ANTIQUING

This is somewhat of a misnomer since you can't really turn a new object into an antique by applying a liquid. But copper sulfate, the chemical most commonly employed, does give a rich coppery look to any soldered area, making it appear aged. Chemicals are available to change soldered areas from bright silver to black. For this to occur over a length of came, the lead came must be tinned; that is, solder must be run along whatever length you want to antique. This procedure is not only time consuming but also somewhat costly. If you are making a commissioned object and antiquing was requested, include the extra materials and labor in the price.

Clean the entire panel before antiquing the leads. If they are covered with oxides and flux residues, you may have to use a wire brush to clean them. Leads can be cleaned again after the antiquing patina is applied, but not with steel wool and cleaning and polishing powder. This would strip away the copper coat provided by the copper sulfate solution and once again make them shiny. When you tin the leads, use flux sparingly and if any should spill on the glass wipe it off immediately.

TINNING THE LEADS

First flux the leads. They shouldn't need much since you have already cleaned them. Keep the soldering rheostat on medium so as not to burn through a lead in your enthusiasm. After fluxing the length of lead, run solder along the length in one stroke. Go slowly enough to flow the solder but not so slowly that it puddles and runs onto the glass. After a bit, if you learn not to chase it with the iron, you'll see the solder flow nicely over the lead surface. Try to get all the tinning even over the surfaces. This takes practice, but that's all part of the fun of getting your work done right.

FILING SOLDER JOINTS

You're not supposed to have to do this and don't say we recommend it, but the occasion may arise when you look at the window or panel and notice that some of the joints look a little mountainous. You try fixing them with the iron and the solder runs all over the place and you end up with the same bulky joint you started with and a lot more frustration. Don't despair—you can smooth them to a certain extent by filing, either by hand or with a Dremel or Foredom hand drill using a moderate rasp bit or a carborundum disk. This is rather tricky and you should practice on some scrap before tackling the good project. These disks and rasps can slip and scratch the glass or dig right through the lead. You need good eyesight (behind protective lenses) and a good steady hand to make the thing look better rather than worse than before. However, the end result, if done right, can make a world of difference to the completed piece. Remember that solder contains lead and lead is toxic, so you don't want to be right on top of the drilling and filing which will send up a spray of metal you don't want to breathe.

Ideally the initial soldering shouldn't evolve in this fashion and filing won't be necessary. But nobody's perfect and, especially if you're a beginner, you're supposed to make mistakes. What's nice (or perhaps distressing) about stained glass is that even poor technique can be overcome by the interplay of light and color. The ideal is to be critical about your work. True, filing solder joints can make poor soldering look better, but you could have saved a lot of time and effort by learning to do the process right to begin with.

APPLYING HANGING LOOPS

Copper loops used for hanging stained glass objects should be tinned before being affixed. This makes it a lot easier to join them to whatever it is you want hung. Use a pair of needle nose pliers to dip the loop into muriatic (hydrochloric) acid to remove the oxide coat instantly; if you leave the loop in too long it will remove the loop as well. Muriatic is a strong inorganic acid that should be treated with caution. Please keep it away from children and if any gets on your hands, immediately wash with water.

Once the loop has been dipped in this acid bath, it should be dried, fluxed, and tinned immediately. Do not attempt to tin it without using flux (it won't accept solder) or without drying it off, since the acid will pit soldering tips, may spit, and will cause dangerous fumes.

A copper loop ready for tinning will allow solder to run full circle with one application. Keep holding the loop with needle nose pliers, since copper transmits heat readily to unwary fingers. Occasionally the loop may adhere to the pliers, but is easily removed by tapping it against the

work table. Apply the loop at the balancing point of the piece or use two or more loops at either corner for balance. One may have to be placed behind the panel in order to support it from the bottom or the middle. By pre-tinning the loops, you will find it simple to solder them to the piece, which can be an awkward one-handed process. You may even find yourself holding the panel with your chin during this activity. This is not the time to find solder rolling off an untinned loop.

REPAIRING CRACKS

You finish the panel and stand back to admire it and...heavens, what's that? Is that a crack in the glass? You look away and back again and the thing stands out worse than before. How did it happen? What do you do about it?

Most cracks during the finishing process are heat cracks, stresses that come about from too hot a soldering iron held too long in one place. You may hear a ping as the crack occurs or you may not. It may not occur until later, when the stressed area is further pressured by puttying or by being moved. Cracks can also occur from the pressures of scoring or cleaning, perhaps because the glass was weak to begin with, or the crack may have been there from the first but was not noticed, or a host of other reasons. The question remains, what are you going to do about it?

If it's not too obtrusive you might try ignoring it. Some individuals can get away with this mind set, others simply can't. If you fall in the latter category, you will have to take action—as drastic as replacing the offending piece of glass or as simple as gluing the crack. Unfortunately, gluing can make it worse if the glue doesn't dry clear, and many don't despite what it says on the label. If you decide to replace the glass and it happens to be foiled, you can knock out the bad piece, remove the inside piece of foil and just refoil another piece to fit. (If it's leaded, see the chapter on repairs.)

If you aren't keen on removing the glass and it's leaded, you can "dutchman" the piece. Take a piece of lead similar to what is already being used and cut it in half lengthwise. Cut away the remains of the heart so you have only the top and bottom strips of the came. Glue each of these strips to the front and back of the crack, being careful they match and follow the crack line exactly. You should end up with a cover of lead over the crack that looks like all the other lead lines. Of course, you know it wasn't a part of the design as planned, but no one else will. And we won't tell if you don't.

FITTING THE WINDOW TO AN EXISTING EMBRASURE

This involves the border leads of any window or panel to be fitted to an existing space. We suggest you plan initially to use H leads here. The empty outside channel of an H lead is a kind of insurance. If the window is a trifle too large for the space, you can cut away the empty chan-nel. If the window itself is a trifle too small, the H lead channel can take up space. Of course we assume you have measured accurately to begin with so that you won't be dealing with incompatabilities that are so far out that nothing will help. In most instances, embrasures, especially in older homes or restaurants (and sometimes new ones as well), are offline somewhere in their measurements. This can be made up for by cutting away the H empty channel wherever necessary to allow for a proper fit.

Iris Vase lead panel. (Brum Studio, Sarasota, Florida)

Door panel with leaded bevels. (Brum residence, Bay Island, Sarasota, Florida)

Bevels, clusters, and Pilkington Taffeta glass door panels. (Brum Studio)

Abstract doors using a variety of bevels and textured glass. (Brum Studio)

Wizard. Sandblasted flash glass, custom bevel, and stain. (Brum Studio)

*Mermaid. Bevel,
nuggets, and
individually
painted scales.
(Brum Studio)*

Flying Egret. Installed bathroom window. (Margaret Heap, Casey Key, Florida)

Green Man stepping stone (see Mosaics chapter). (Kaleidoscope Studio, Sarasota, Florida)

Egrets and Flowers. Installed bathroom window. (Margaret Heap)

Floral panel as part of a room divider. (Brum Studio)

Formal Flowers and Vase. Double stepping stones. (Brum residence)

Glass Galleon. Slumped glass, glass rods with copper wire rigging. (Seymour Isenberg)

Enameled and slumped nightlights. (see Nightlights chapter) (Kaleidoscope Studio)

Detail of a wall mosaic. (Brum residence)

Business card holder. Black iridised Baroque and bevel. (Paul Barsalou, Bradenton, Florida)

Exterior wall sconce. Cathedral glass and brass channel. (Paul Barsalou)

Airplane and Pilot. Single and layered glass with shaped prop. (Seymour Isenberg)

Two Dolphins. Sculpture with rondel glass. (Kaleidoscope Studio)

Si and Champ. Hand painted fired stain.
(Patricia Daley, Sarasota, Florida)

Grant me the strength
to be the kind of person
my dog thinks I am.

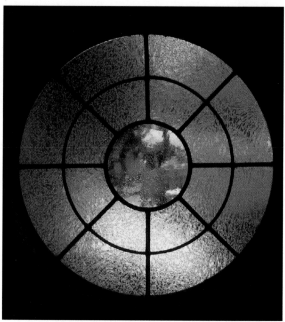

Leaded circle window. Glue chip and seedy antique.
J. Peterson residence Sarasota, Florida
(Kaleidoscope Studio)

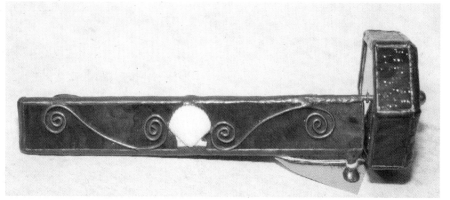

Kaleidoscope. Shell and wire
decorated. (Kaleidoscope Studio)

DUCK CREEK
BOOKS
antiquarian gallery

Sign panel from
Duck Creek
Books, Sarasota,
Florida (see
Design chapter).
(Kaleidoscope
Studio)

Macchu-Picchu. Copper foil with details of fired enameled walls and shadings at Javier's Restaurant, Siesta Key, Florida. (Kaleidoscope Studio)

Flying Angel. Enameled drapery and stars detailing. (Kaleidoscope Studio)

Sign panel from Third Floor Used Books, Sarasota, Florida. (Kaleidoscope Studio)

Small rose panel lamp on ceramic base from the Paquette residence, Brunswick, Maine. (J & P Stained Glass)

Water Lily mini four panel shade. (Harold and Shirley Wyman, Freedom, New Hampshire)

Woven basket of green and red apples from the Paquette residence. (J & P Stained Glass)

Antique bent panel lampshade with brass filigree. (Stained Glass Connection, Sarasota, Florida)

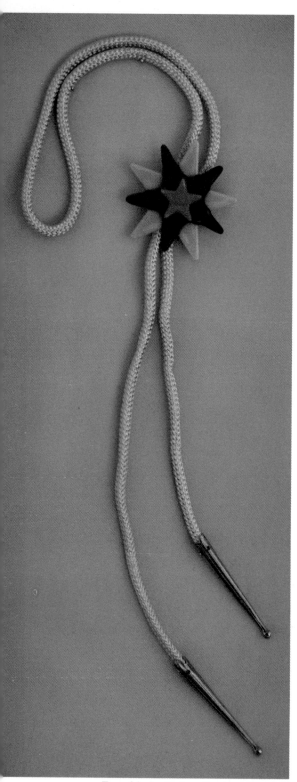

Fused bolo tie (see Fusing chapter).
(Johnson and Lee)

Fan decorated photo frame (see Fusing chapter). (Johnson and Lee)

Glass crafts-man Pat Daley with Champ visiting at Stained Glass Connection.

Fused black and white clock (see Fusing chapter). (Johnson and Lee)

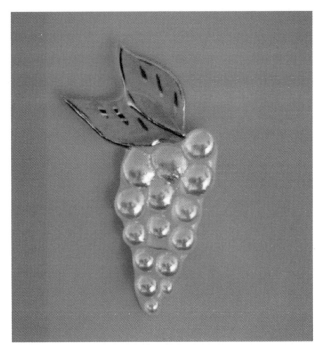

Dichroic glass grape cluster pin (see Fusing chapter). (Johnson and Lee)

Color Magic paints on a lead cast carousel horse and clear nuggets. (Glass Crafters, Sarasota, Florida)

Necklace made with black beads (see Fusing chapter). (Johnson and Lee)

Oriental landscape side-lights from the L. Carter residence, Sarasota. (Kaleidoscope Studio)

*Assortment of glass beads showing
different color combinations and
variety of shapes (see Bead chapter).*

*Examples of decorated larger beads strung
with smaller coordinating colored beads.*

*Christmas Star tree topper.
(Patricia Daley)*

Sunset and Bette's sailboat. Two windows from Miguel's Restaurant, Siesta Key, Florida. (Kaleidoscope Studio)

CHAPTER 12
Traditional Leading: Making a Window or Panel

The stained glass window is fabricated like a stained glass panel. It may be larger and more complicated in design, but the same techniques (in the main) are used for both. These techniques vary with the worker. Someone who has practiced the craft for years may have developed shortcuts, special tools, and idiosyncrasies that work well but are not standard.

The same applies to our case. The information we supply is necessarily flavored with our own experience from teaching and making windows on a commercial basis and is not written in stone (or glass). These techniques have served us well over the years and we pass them on in the hope they will serve you as well. If you modify or compress what we describe, that is your privilege but don't blame us if your end result doesn't match your expectations.

THE DESIGN

Let's assume we are building a stained glass window for your home. We start with a simple geometric design such as diamonds. At first glance, diamonds may seem too bland or simple for what you have in mind (perhaps Venus rising from the waves), but you will be surprised how complexities can suddenly arise in just attempting to get two square glass pieces together with came.

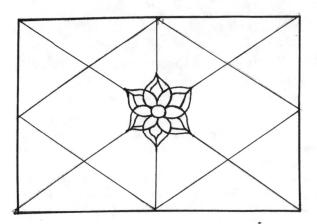

If you have cut glass before or have done some work in stained glass (probably foiling) but want to know more about correct leading procedures, draw your own design and follow along (see below). The process we describe will be the same for repetitive as well as more involved windows. We present the process as it is done in professional studios. Beginners should follow the diamond pattern we provide. Once you acquire the basic techniques, you may apply them to your own designs.

Designing for stained glass involves submitting to the regulations of the material. No matter how beautiful a design may be, if it can't be cut out of glass, it's useless. Even a design for a square panel, divided into quarters, thirds, or halves, involves difficulties. Suppose you can't draw. Where should you go for design ideas? There are innumerable pattern books on the market—good, bad, indifferent, and (in some cases) inane. Also artists in other fields—Mondrian, for example—are worth studying. There are many books with pictures of stained glass, old and new, that will give you ideas of line flow. Geometric configurations in themselves can be balanced in a beginning panel. Triangles, diamonds, squares, rectangles, rhomboids, and trapezoids all qualify as grist for your mill (see Designing Your Work). Pattern books are available for beginners and advanced students alike, though as you progress you will find yourself depending less on these and more on your own imagination.

Sketch, draw, erase, sketch again, tear up, re-invent until you have something on paper that looks good to you. Don't be afraid to detail your sketch, but keep in mind that such details may have to be summarized in the cartoon by two or three lead lines. Exact and precise detailing on glass can be done only by painting or etching. These techniques are used to complement the basically leaded end result, not to supplant it.

The design should be sketched in charcoal so that extraneous lines may be easily rubbed out. It need not be drawn to scale or size. Once you have a notion that looks as though it might do, concentrate on developing it. When you think it is satisfactory, ink it in with a magic marker. Don't worry about too small pieces or avoiding curves that look especially difficult to cut and fit. The idea is to get down on paper some informal statement you can build on. A design starts as a preliminary survey and becomes specific as it progresses. Once the design is set on paper in its entirety, you will have realized a beginning, middle, and end to the progression as you conceived it.

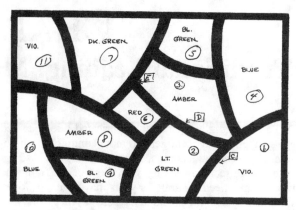

A typical cartoon for a stained glass panel.

A studio drawing for a church window. This has been pencil shaded to show lead lines and the painted segments.

Color choice is going to affect your design strongly. Think in terms of color as well as linear quality. Study pictures of stained glass windows to get a feel for the color choices of professionals. Don't be afraid to change your design until it's exactly what you want (at least for the moment).

THE CARTOON

The cartoon is the stained glass blueprint drawn precisely to size. Every line in it is either a paint line or a lead line and every space between lead lines is a piece of glass that must be cut. Some designers make it a point to draw lead lines in one color and paint lines in another, so the two may be easily distinguished. Only the lead lines are to be cut. All extraneous lines from the original design are removed or condensed, while contiguous spaces are divided into individual cuts of glass. Lead lines are indicated as being wide or narrow and joints are clearly marked.

The original sketch may suffer some radical changes during this procedure. The extent to which it doesn't depends on the craftsman's ability to design for glass. As you practice cartooning, the more obvious facets will soon become second nature to you. All pieces from the original design involving impossible cuts must be redesigned when applied to the cartoon. Balance your lead lines foreground and background so they flow.

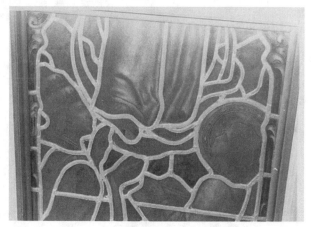

The detail of a leaded panel shows how the lead lines flow around the shapes of the glass in reflected light.

Once the cartoon is inked in, you can begin laying it out to make a work drawing and patterns. Number each piece in the cartoon, even though it may have only a few easily recognizable pieces. It's good practice to do this. The work habits you learn at the start will stand you in good stead throughout more complicated projects in stained glass. Be patient and follow directions.

THE LAYOUT

The layout involves the cartoon, the work drawing, and the pattern pieces themselves. The work drawing, which is made on brown craft paper, will be used as a guide to lead up the panel. It should be an exact replica of the cartoon. Once you've transferred your cartoon to the work drawing via carbon paper, keep the cartoon in front of you for reference. The work drawing will show where each piece of glass goes.

HOLD IT RIGHT THERE

Let's review the process so far. First comes the design which can be drawn to scale or not. It can be a pencil sketch, a watercolor, whatever suits your creative processes best. The design is an embodiment of the end result you are striving for.

Having worked hard at the design and embellishing it with shadowing, perspective, color, and what not, you transform it into a cartoon. This must be done to scale on stiff paper. All the embellishments go by the wayside. What you have left is basically a skeleton—only the outlines of forms, which are the lead lines. At this point, you are not painting so there are no paint lines.

Once you make the cartoon, make a sandwich with a piece of craft paper of similar size as follows: on top is the cartoon, under that some heavy reusable carbon paper, below that craft paper or work drawing, below that another piece of carbon paper, and finally a piece of oak tag for patterns.

The layout.

Heavily trace all the lines from the cartoon so they go through all the layers (check this before you take the sandwich apart). Also number all the pieces to correspond with your glass, then pin the cartoon up somewhere so you can consult it as you go. The cartoon will be your only guide to the entire work because the pattern paper will be cut up into patterns and the work drawing will be covered with glass pieces on the table and not able to give the necessary overview.

LET'S TALK ABOUT PATTERNS

To cut glass accurately for a predetermined space such as a window, you should cut directly from patterns; patterns placed on top of the glass, not below it on a light table, not from lines drawn with a grease pencil on the glass surface itself, not freehand in any way. Yes, we know there are teachers who tell you differently but we can only advise you from our own experience.

Once you learn to cut patterns precisely and then cut your glass using them as guides, it is practically impossible to end up with a piece of work that overrides its borders. We are, of course, speaking of making a window which must fit into a predetermined space. All right, you say, but suppose what I'm making is a freeform piece with no real borders? Why is it necessary to cut from patterns in this way? To which we can only say that any planned object in stained glass is an exercise in precision and the work habits you establish carry over into every project you undertake. This doesn't mean you can't cut glass for a window or a suncatcher using other techniques. It means that we have found a method we consider the most all-around efficient, especially if you begin doing commercial work. There are exceptions to any technique and if you can cut it (literally) your own unique way, then you are free to do it your way, not our way. Harpo Marx plays the harp all wrong—but it certainly sounds all right when you hear it. We've seen workers in stained glass cutting all sorts of ways that end up being absolutely accurate. But if you are starting out in glass and want to learn the way most commercial studios work, our way is probably the best guide.

DESIGNING THE PATTERN

Every stained glass piece begins as a drawing. When you make the initial sketch, draw in everything as you see it in your mind's eye. Put it all on paper: perspective, shadowing, linear qualities, and even the colors if you wish. Use pastels to match the colors you have in mind to see how they will blend. If the colors are too extreme, find out right away.

Once you have the sketch on paper, it must be transformed into a cartoon—the overall blueprint for the work. The cartoon shows all cut lines and may show color as long as the color doesn't interfere with the linear structure. These lines are transferred as described above to pattern paper and these patterns are then cut.

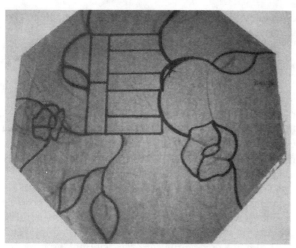

The sketch for a window. The lines were drawn in charcoal and reworked. They were then inked in.

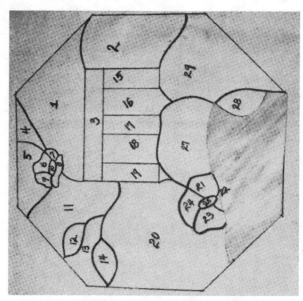

Checking a piece of glass against the work drawing.

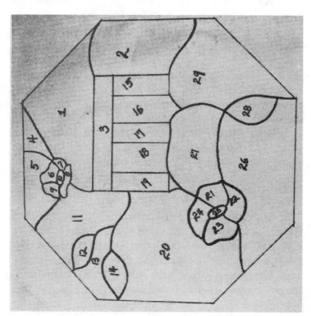

The cartoon of the sketch with every piece numbered.

The main objective in cutting patterns for leaded work is to make sure you leave space between patterns for the heart of the lead came. There are various tools for this, the most popular and probably the best being a pair of pattern scissors. These have a three-bladed cutting arrangement which automatically leaves space for the leading. Pattern scissors can be a little difficult to use at first; it takes practice to feel comfortable with them. It's best to make small cuts around the pattern using mainly the back portion of the scissors. If you make large cuts with the entire length of the blades you will get tangled up in the disposal portion of the pattern, that part the scissors are cutting away to leave room for the lead. We like to use the scissors with the two-bladed portion at the bottom so the excess paper comes out away from us. Others prefer to use the device with the double blades up, sighting through them to the line they are cutting away. It's up to you how to best learn to work with this new tool; however you do it you will get used to them. It's easy to make a mistake with the scissors, certainly while learning to use them. You can cut away too much of a pattern, especially if you are in a rush. Some beginners feel if they make a mistake in cutting the pattern they can fix it later when cutting the glass. This is the wrong approach and will always lead to sloppy work. If you make a mistake cutting a pattern, substitute a new piece or everything will be thrown off.

If you don't want to invest in scissors, there are other ways to cut patterns almost as accurately. The pattern knife is another tool, although we find that unless the knife is absolutely sharp, using a knife to cut patterns leaves ragged edges on the pattern. It's really easier to use scissors than the knife, but you are welcome to try. The least expensive method is to go over your cartoon lines with a magic marker and then, with an ordinary scissors, cut to either side of this line (you can also use a craft knife). This will leave an empty space where the black line was, which will be the approximate space the lead will take up. But for the production of a large commercial window, this is not recommended. Obviously not all magic markers are the same width and even if they were, they wear down with use. You may well find, when you go to lead up, that you have a variable space between glass pieces, in some cases too wide, in others too narrow. In an extreme case, you may end up having to re-cut all the glass. There is also the problem of having to cut this line out twice—to either side. The mechanics here allow additional possibilities for error, especially if you're tired or in a hurry.

USING THE PATTERN

When the pattern pieces are cut to size, it's crucial to number them and put each numbered piece back on the cartoon to check that the spaces between them are accurate. Much to your dismay, you may find that a few pattern pieces have developed a propensity to shrink away from the borders and others may overlap. You have not cut accurately. These errors will go undetected unless you match the pattern against the cartoon. Now is the time to fix such problems, not when you are cutting glass. Each pattern should fit within its predetermined space so you can see the inked line directly around it. If you can't see any part of this line, re-cut the pattern so the line shows. If you think the pattern is accurate and yet a portion of the cartoon line does not show, check your original design. The pattern must fit exactly. If you don't check, when you cut the glass you'll find that the piece will be either oversized or undersized in this area, which will cause either butting against neighbors to the extent of pushing them right over the border of the panel, or will leave so much room between pieces, you couldn't fill the excess space with a steel girder, let alone lead.

CUTTING THE GLASS PIECES

Here we reiterate the basic rules of glass cutting:
1) Hold the glass cutter properly.
2) Work on a flat and steady surface.
3) Don't tilt the cutter to the left or the right, but hold it as vertical as you can.
4) Cut standing up whenever possible and remember that the pressure you put on the glass should be pressure from the weight of your body, not from the muscle of your arm. The pattern paper should be thick enough to withstand the pressure of the cutting wheel riding against its borders, but thin enough not to hoist the cutting wheel in any way off the glass surface so you don't get a good score. Make each cut individually and break it out before going to the next.
5) Cut the glass so it matches the pattern exactly. If the glass breaks improperly and leaves a space where the pattern shows no space, re-cut the glass, not the pattern. Beginners (and others) sometimes forget that cutting seven facets on one piece of glass accurately does not make up for cutting the eighth badly.

Once more, before leaving the subject, let us stress that you place the pattern *on top* of the glass, not below it. We feel that cutting with the pattern below is imprecise by its very nature. Opalescent glasses and some antiques may be too dark to see through accurately, but other than that, you can only approximate the pattern in this way no matter how good you are. If you are that good, our blessings go with you.

FITTING THE GLASS

Once you have a glass piece cut, resize it against the individual pattern. It may surprise you how much off measurement a piece of glass can be, even though it looked good when you cut it. It's easier to be objective about a cut piece after you've let it sit for a while. We are all human and try to make the best of our mistakes. If the pieces are to be critically close (as with copper foil), grind off all pinhead edges and small chips. All pains taken at this point will achieve better end results and make your job easier as you progress. Grozz the pieces first, but if the fit is still not good, sand them or, in extreme cases, re-cut them.

Once the pieces are smooth and accurate to the pattern, place each one on the work drawing one more time to check their relationship. If you have large spaces where small leads will go, you may have to revise your leading design or re-cut the pieces. The mistake was probably made cutting the initial pattern. No matter how well the pattern pieces seem to fit, the thicker glass pieces add a discrepancy. For one thing, they may have slanted edges, which provide deceptive space between them for the leading. You may have chipped glass edges or small indentations. These can seem unimportant when you consider each individual piece, but they become emphatic when the pieces are matched up, fault to fault. The lead may not cover both flaws. Avoid this mess by going back to the work drawing and either cutting the pieces over again, or in an extreme case, taking apart the entire panel and re-working the design. It is much less frustrating to find out if your glass is going to fit before you get begin leading it.

LEADING THE PANEL

If all your glass matches and all the spaces seem adequate for the lead, and if you have planned the leading according to the thicknesses of glass, remove all pieces of glass from the work drawing and place them within easy reach. You are now ready for the leading up process.

If the lead cames are bent, straighten them by placing one end in a vise or lead stretcher and pulling with gradually increasing pressure at the other end with a pair of pliers. This will stretch the lead slightly. All unstretched lead, even if it is straight, should be stretched. Once stretched, it can't be re-stretched. Open the lead cames

with a lathkin to allow the glass to fit into the groove easily. Use a lathkin before fitting any strip of came, even if the grooves look adequate.

The correct way to cut came is to place the leading knife on top of it and rock it with a side-to-side motion, exerting only minimum downward pressure to cut through it. The came should be scratch marked to show the angle of miter. Measure it directly over the drawing space, then cut accordingly.

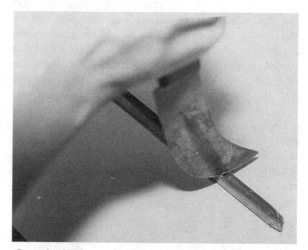

Seat the knife on the flanges to begin rocking downwards to make a straight cut.

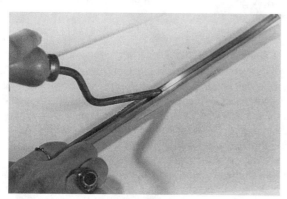

Open the came after stretching it with a lathkin. Be careful of twisting or bulging the side of the came by forcing the lathkin directly into the channel. Slide the lathkin into the channel down to the heart and push along or pull the lead against it.

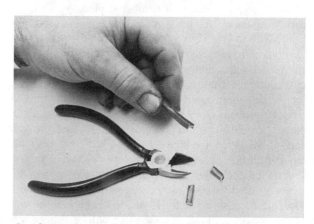

Lead nippers or dykes are useful as an alternate tool for straight cuts and accurate mitered points. Due to the slight offset of the jaws, always hold the tool on a slight angle to make a vertical cut on the lead. A knife is still necessary for long tapering cuts to the came.

Begin leading up by laying your finished work drawing flat on a board or table. Nail two wooden strips, about 2" wide and somewhat longer than your work drawing, at right angles to each other along the lower right corner of the drawing so you can just see the outside margin line. You must have enough excess on your drawing paper to allow the boards to grip the edges.

Cut a piece of 3/16" U lead to size so it is slightly longer than the border line of the work drawing and place it along one edge of the wood strip with the groove toward the drawing. Put a leading nail through the excess end to hold it in place. Cut another strip of this same lead slightly longer than the border line and fit it at a right angle to the first, along the other strip of wood. Place a nail through the end. The corners where these two pieces of lead meet can be mitered to fit at an angle or one may fit inside the other. You can also cut the top away from one of the lead cames and the bottom away from the other so the two interlock in the corner. This last is the method that gives the most strength.

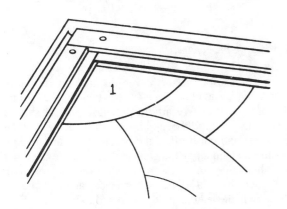

Interlocking the corner leads. They are flush against the bordering strips of wood.

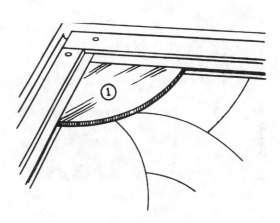

The first piece of glass fitted into the corner leads. A few taps should seat it properly.

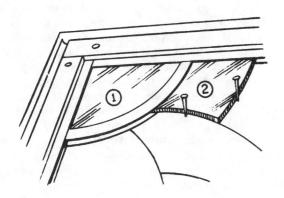

The first inside piece of lead cut and placed and the second piece of glass placed and held with leading nails.

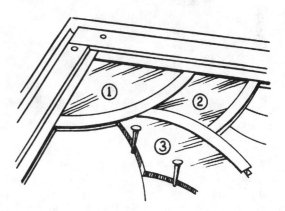

The pieces of glass and lead fit together like the pieces of a picture puzzle.

Pick up your first piece of glass, the right-hand corner piece, and place it in the groove of the leads at their corner juncture and along the sides. Tap it gently with the leaded end of the leading knife to be certain it is seated properly within the channel. The line on the work drawing should be visible around the edge of the glass. If it isn't, either the glass is not seated in the lead groove correctly or there is an inadequate cut somewhere on the glass surfaces. Try to correct this immediately rather than trying to make up the difference in the next piece.

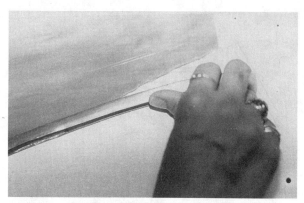

Place the lead against the glass as tightly as possible.

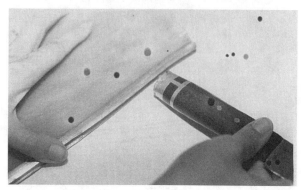

Tap the lead with the end of the knife to seat it.

Measure, mark, and cut each piece of lead came to fit exactly in its proper space as you go along. Each piece should be slightly shorter than its glass border. Cutting it slightly shorter allows room for the next lead came to meet it. If your leads are too long, they will interfere with each other. If they are too short, you will have a gap between them. *Do not* bridge any such gap with solder, in-

stead re-cut the lead. Even one of these soldered gaps will make your panel look sloppy.

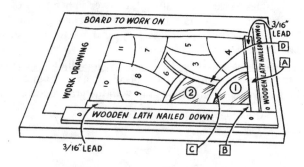

The leading procedure.

Let us describe the method in detail. You've placed leads A and B and glass piece #1. Next comes the first inside piece of lead. We arbitrarily chose 1/4" H shaped lead for this. Carefully bend the lead to shape against the glass edge and cut it off at the proper miter at one end. Measure it again along the glass and cut it off at the other end. The proper miter means making the cuts on both sides to correspond to the border leads running up each side. Again, the leads should be mitered to fit as snugly as possible against the opposing surfaces. If not, you will have a gap. Place the cut and mitered lead around the exposed edge of glass and fit it into place.

Put glass piece #2 into the lead groove. If you can see the lines of the work drawing around it, it is in proper position. If you can't see the lines around it, check the glass to make sure it was cut properly. Usually the most difficult point of entry to the came is at either end where the lead has been cut. Even slight crimping of these ends prevents the glass from properly seating. After cutting came, it's a good idea to reopen the ends to allow the glass to seat without fighting the lead. It's easier to do this with the lead in your hand prior to placing it. Once the lead is seated, hammer two nails to hold it in place.

A word about nails. All glass pieces should be held in place with special leading nails, not ordinary finishing nails (the usual beginner's choice) which are difficult to use, hard to remove, and may crack the glass. Leading nails are tapered for ease of inserting as well as (very important) removing, and will not press too forcefully against the glass. Horseshoe nails work pretty well but tend to go blunt or (worse) bend at the points. Don't use carpet tacks, which are notorious for bent points. A bent carpet tack will probably crack the glass. Don't use a hammer to place your leading nails. The force of the blow can be dangerous, especially if you miss. Use the back (leaded) end of your leading knife to tap rather than smack your nails. By the way, don't use oak or any hard wood for your work board as this will require a jackhammer to nail into.

Measure and cut lead D, remembering to cut the one end short at the proper angle at point E. Notice that this lead goes past the piece of glass just placed, piece #2. It may do this because it is continuing the line of the design directly to the line of piece #7. Of course, you could cut the lead between pieces #3 and #6 and put a new lead in, but that would give you three separate pieces of lead and more labor than if you used the single lead to sweep by this particular joint directly to piece #7.

Glass piece #3 goes into the groove next, again with a nail at each end to hold it in place tightly against piece #2. Fit and form the piece of lead going between #3 and #4, then place piece #4, tapping it into place from above with the handle of your leading knife, being certain that all other pieces are secured with leading nails so they don't move. It's now a matter of building up the rest of the pieces in their proper places, cutting the leads to fit as you go.

PLACING THE REMAINING PIECES

Pieces are placed consecutively and in a manner that allows maximum pressure—one against the other—to hold them in place. Obviously, you would not place piece #6 or #8 before placing #3 and #4. As you continue to fit the glass pieces in position, remove the leading nails that

secured them one at a time. To insure that the lead came lower channel edge is allowing the glass to enter the channel (glass will sometimes mash against this border even if the channel is sufficiently open because both lead and glass are flat against the table), slightly lift the glass you are placing with your leading knife. This will allow it to slide over that lower lip of lead rather than find it a barrier. Remember to use the lathkin often to insure that the cames are open to receive the glass.

When all the pieces are in place, check the border lines to make sure they just show. If they don't, the glass pieces may not be seated. Pieces should be individually tapped into place with the weighted end of the leading knife. However, don't get carried away and tap them too hard or you will chip the edges or break the glass.

Once all the glass is seated properly and the borders are even, fit two pieces of wood similar to the two you have already used securely against the other two sides, first applying U leads as before. Cut all U leads to size. Tap these new boards into position so they are at 90° angles with the two already in place. Make sure everything is square and that the U lead borders of the panels are flush against the pieces of wood. If not, you can back the U leads slightly against them with the leading knife. This process may now leave some pieces of bordering glass a little less than perfectly seated within the U lead border, but it's better to have an even border with a few pieces of glass not seated all the way to the edge of the lead than to have glass seated well with an uneven border. Best is to

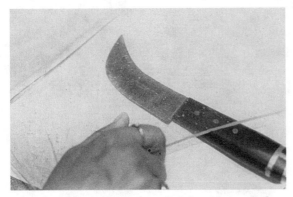

Use the knife to lever the adjoining piece of glass into the H lead.

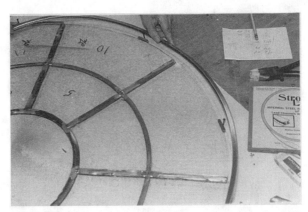

Adding 1/2" zinc U channel to frame the edge of a 36" round window. The nails are placed against a shim of scrap came to hold the glass and prevent chipping the glass edge. The joints have been roughly soldered.

have the border glass cut so accurately that they seat perfectly and the border lead is perfectly even. However, it's an imperfect world.

When the boards are securely fastened and all four sides of the window are even, you are ready to solder. If the window is to fit into a predetermined space, before soldering recheck all measurements to make certain you are within them. If not, rework to the requisite dimensions. If you made the window or panel marginally smaller than will fit, hopefully you can build up by changing to a wider bordering lead—even to a wide H if necessary. If it is too large, you may be able to trim down the bordering lead or, failing that, take off the bordering lead and trim the border glass edges. Again we stress: find this out *before* you solder. If your dimensions are totally off, so much that no trimming will suffice, you will have to re-cut and rebuild. There is no reason to be off to any extent, however. If you've followed the lines of the work drawing and if the drawing was correctly measured to begin with, you should have no trouble with final dimensions.

SOLDERING THE JOINTS

Recheck all lead joints; make sure they are neatly cut and fit well. It may be necessary to clean the joints with a fine wire brush, such as a suede brush, or with steel wool. Lead that is not clean will not solder. If you are not using an iron clad tip, be sure your copper tip is well tinned so it will pick up solder.

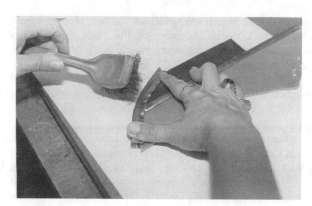

Wire brush the joint to clean the leads.

Flux each joint well with the stiff flux brush. Lay about 1/8" of solder directly on the joint and apply the iron to it. If your iron is the proper temperature the solder should immediately melt and form a puddle at the joint. You can cut the solder into working lengths or roll it in your hand with the end resting on the joint and melt it directly as it sits. Don't hold the iron to the joint any longer than is necessary to flow solder or you may melt the lead away from the glass, leaving an ugly hole to fill. Don't lift the iron too quickly either, or the solder won't have time to flow properly and you will have just a dab of solder and a weak joint.

Solder the joints when the glass is in position and look for missed spots before turning. (Lynn Palmer class project.) (Courtesy of J&P Stained Glass)

Flux the joint.

Place solder in one spot next to the joint.

Add more solder to flow left and right of the joint about the width of the iron tip in both directions. This will cover the joint and feather the solder onto the came.

If your iron is not hot enough, you can drag the solder and make a rough joint; you want a nice even, smooth one. As you progress in the craft, you will learn how much time to give the soldering iron to get the solder to whisk over the area. It's not necessary to exert pressure with the iron. Its own weight is pressure enough. Some students think the more pressure they apply, the better the solder will flow. That isn't so. Solder all joints and check the panel for missed joints before removing the pieces of bordering wood. Then, turn the panel over and do the same to all the joints on the other side. Both sides must be soldered securely.

PUTTYING

Once you have soldered all the joints on both sides of the panel, putty the panel with either black or white putty,

depending on the color you want to show beneath the lead came (see Finishing Techniques).

If you apply too much pressure while applying putty, the glass may crack. If the panel has thick and thin glass and your pressure against one is the same as the other, the thin piece may snap. Beware. If a piece of glass cracks, it must be replaced, and that's another technique (see Repairing).

Once you've cleaned the putty from the panel and turned down the leads, it's time for the final step, cleaning the panel as described in the chapter on Finishing Techniques.

If you've made a panel rather than a window you may want to hang it in a window to brighten up a corner of the room. To do so, tin two loops of moderately heavy copper wire with solder. Then solder one to each corner of the panel and string fishing line through the loops. The fishing line will not be seen from any distance. It's strong and will support the stained glass panel nicely. Fishing line comes in different tensile strengths and if your work is exceptionally heavy, check the amount of weight the line can bear before using it.

If you made a panel, your work is finished. If you're making a window, your work is not yet done.

TURNING THE WINDOW

Let's say you've made a 300 piece window which is now leaded and soldered on one side but not puttied. You don't want to putty the one side until you solder the leads on the other side in case some putty leaks through and makes portions of the back side unsuitable for soldering. Of course, you may take the chance and solder and putty one side before going on to the back portion. Generally we like to solder all joints on both sides before puttying. The next step then is turning the window. We have postulated a large window with 300 pieces, so the exercise will be somewhat awkward, but that's what you will run into.

Turning a large window is not the same as turning a small panel. Attempting to raise the window by two corners may fracture it, since it won't be able to take its own weight without bending. A good rule is never to attempt to turn any good-sized window by yourself. The best method is to sandwich the window between two pieces of plywood slightly larger than the window itself.

To begin, wriggle the first piece of plywood under the window as it lies flat on the table with your partner gently raising those portions of it that are being so supported. The piece of plywood should be thick enough to allow for the weight of the window without bending. A 1/2" piece of plywood should be sufficient. The thicker the plywood, the more you have to raise the window to get the wood beneath it. The process sounds more awkward than it actually is. Once the wood is situated beneath half the window, it should easily slide under the rest.

With the window now resting completely on the plywood, put a similar board over the window so that your project now is sandwiched between them. For very large heavy windows, put several screws through the plywood at its bottom portion and let the window rest on these. In this way it won't slip through the sandwich as you raise it from the table.

With the window thus secured you can move it safely. Raise it from the table onto the floor, turn it around and put it back on the table, remove the screws (if any) take off the plywood and your window's second side is ready for soldering. Some workers leave it resting on the bottom piece of plywood since you will have to eventually move it off the work table to its final residence and the two pieces of plywood will thus once more come into play. With the second side soldered and puttied, your window will achieve a far greater measure of solidity but it will still require special handling to move it safely. Large windows, no matter how protected with lead, solder, and barring are still vulnerable in their unembrasured state.

BARRING THE WINDOW

Rule of thumb: if a stained glass window is larger than three feet by three feet (nine square feet), it should be barred. Bars of some nature should be installed approximately every two feet. In the old days (back in the 1920s and before), these bars were made of steel and stretched across the window from one side to the other. Notches were cut into the wood framework of the embrasure to allow for them. Steel doesn't solder so copper wire was wrapped around these bars to allow for their attachment to the solder joints they happened to pass by. Of course, the bars interfered with the design of the window since their placement coincided not with the aesthetic intent but with practicality.

Today barring is done within the leaded design of the window in several ways. First of all, "bar" is a misnomer since what is often used are zinc-coated steel or brass flat strips about 1/8" thick. These can be cut to length with a hacksaw and are placed behind a lead line so they will be invisible; they are flexible so they can follow shallow curves of the lead and are soldered to it at the joints. To

provide strength they must stretch the entire length or width of the window to attach to the border zinc cames. While these strips can be bent by hand, this can be something of a trial of strength and special bending tools are available. One design addition is that these re-bars form right angles along the leaded line they follow, which is noticeable from the side they are on. Though few customers are apt to complain, this should be called to their attention at the time the window is being discussed.

Reinforced lead came is another way to add strength to a window. Here the reinforcing is truly invisible because it' produced by a steel strip traveling through the heart of the came that has been hollowed out to allow for it. This came is usually 1/2" or larger, though smaller dimensions may be available. Once again, the came is stiffer by far than ordinary lead and must be cut with a hacksaw and molded to follow the curves of the design.

Another option, strongline, is a heavy copper stripping that may be applied to either or both sides of a regular lead came within its channels to stiffen it up. The advantage is that it can be used with smaller dimensions of came that don't come reinforced of themselves. It may also be used for copper foiled windows. It's the heaviest supporting device placed between the foiled pieces and then soldered in place. It can be run to any length but it's difficult to make it take extreme bends and it must be guided along literally by inches.

Restrip is similar to strongline though not as heavy and is used to strengthen areas of copper foil where not so much support is necessary. It's easier to work than strongline.

Copper braid is the least difficult to work of the supporting materials; it is a type of mesh that can be run between foiled pieces to add strength to an area.

INSTALLATION

It's not necessary to install your window yourself; you may prefer to have a carpenter or glazer do it. However, you should inform your client at the start whether you or someone else will do the installation. Doing it yourself is sometimes preferable, you will be able to address any difficulties that arise at the site. Improvisations by someone unfamiliar with stained glass could make a simple problem worse. On the other hand, we've both installed our own windows and had others do it and, provided the window's dimensions are adequate, you should find no difficulty in either case.

One of the main problems with installation is transporting the window. A special glass truck might be necessary for large windows. There is also the risk of cracking a piece of glass on the way. Nothing in the installation process should be taken for granted. The window should be transported, crated, and blanketed even if this crating and uncrating takes up valuable time. Obviously if you have made the proper arrangements at the start, you will be paid for your time. Many customers like the artist on the job, if only for security. You certainly can be there to oversee the installation if someone else is doing it. In many cases, this can be your best bet.

The finished lead panel by Lynn Palmer, Portland, Maine. (Courtesy of J&P Stained Glass)

CHAPTER 13
Stained Glass in Artificial Light: Lampshades

There are as many types, styles, sizes, designs, forms, considerations, and conditions of stained glass lampshades as there are lamp makers with original notions. While not all these ideas are aesthetically sound (at least not for an observer; they all seem to work for the creators) they offer interesting sidelights, if we may use the word, as to how many extraneous items can be incorporated with glass. Some make a statement, others a murmur, still others a groan.

For some reason the fact that the light in a lampshade can be controlled—that it is dependent only on the size and intensity of the bulb—prompts imaginations to run wild on how to use this illumination to show off a melding of glass and whatever. Here are only a few of the items we have seen combined (foiled, glued, fused, soldered, leaded, etched) with stained glass in lampshades: geodes, agates, tile, glass chunks, copper or other metal stampings, color slides, fabric swatches, photographic negatives, preserved insects and butterflies, newspaper clippings, cameos, filigree, beads, rope, postage stamps, bevels, fingerprints, and, in one instance, dollar bills. In other words, you pays your money and you takes your choice!

In this chapter we have no intention of going into such oddities; space allows only a description of the basics of lamp making. The rest we leave to your imagination.

MULTI-PANELED LAMPS

The multi-paneled lamp may be made in a number of different dimensions by varying the number of panels or making them individually smaller or larger. Multi-paneled lamps consist of long panels radiating from a central role and terminating in a skirt. The simplest type is a basic two-piece unit—a single panel and single skirt. This design can be varied in any number of ways. The panel can be broken up into a design of its own, or the skirt can be broken, or both. The basic principles here apply to any type of paneled lamp.

Outfit yourself with the following supplies: a large 3/4" plywood board approximately four feet square, a sharp knife, leading nails, a good soldering iron, flux and solder, lead came in size 1/4" H rounded and 3/16" U. You should have at least three six-foot lengths of the former and about four six-foot lengths of the latter. You should also have at least five square feet of stained glass.

Preparing the Pattern

The basic pattern here is for a lamp 16" in diameter: panel A is 8" tall with a width at the top of 1-3/8" and a bottom width of 4"; panel B (the skirt) measures the same 4" at the top to meet the bottom of panel A and measures 2-1/4" at its widest diameter from the top to the center of the curved bottom. Panel B measures 1-3/4" at either end, from top to bottom. Twelve of these panels will produce a lamp 11" high. For larger or smaller lamps adjust the measurements accordingly. Cut the panels out of cardboard first to make sure you will be able to close the circle to the proper dimensions.

Be sure the pattern is drawn exactly on graph paper before tracing it out on heavier pattern paper. You will be cutting 12 exact pieces from this pattern and it's imperative that the material stand up to it. If you are careless with the glass cutter and the pattern starts to fray, the pieces will begin to change shape and you will have problems later on. Better to cut another pattern if you are in doubt. The panel B, or skirt, must match the bottom of panel A exactly for the two pieces to fit later on. Even l/16" difference here will multiply drastically as the pieces are being cut and in the end, the top and bottom of the lamp won't fit together. You can make the initial pattern out of a thin piece of sheet metal, but it must be cut exactly with tin snips. Be sure you get a thin enough piece if you're going to do this to allow your glass cutter to ride freely along its rim.

Cutting the Glass

Cut the sheet of stained glass in 12 exact duplicates of panel A and 12 of panel B. It's best to cut a long strip from your piece of glass, measuring from top to bottom of the panel, with the lines running the way you want them. Then lay the pattern on this long strip and cut out the panels one at a time. Since you are cutting on a bias, running pliers are the best tool to break out these score lines. You can cut panels quickly with little waste by laying the pattern first one way and then the other. The glass edges should be as smooth as possible. Very slight irregularities may be covered by the lead, but anything more should be sanded away with abrasive paper or the piece re-cut.

Cut the skirts out of the glass in the same fashion, by cutting one long strip and then laying the pattern along it and cutting out the pieces for the skirt. Use running pliers to cut the straight edge and glass pliers to pull away the curved edge. Remember, the pull of the glass pliers is out and down; use the edge of the table as your guide. Sand the panels smooth and lay them aside. Many workers alternate colors from one panel to another or from one piece of skirt to another. We recommend opalescent glass for all lamps because it keeps the bulb from showing and it allows for an even diffusion of light throughout the surface of the lamp. Antique glass or any clear glass does not treat a bulb quite so courteously.

Preparing the Lead

Cut the 1/4" H lead into 12 8" strips. Cut 12 pieces of H lead, each measuring 1-1/4" long. The smaller pieces will be the ribs for the skirt. Make sure the channels are not crimped at the edges from the cutting. If they are, pry them open with your lead knife so the channel runs completely free along the entire length.

Measuring the Circle

Lay the panels side-by-side to see how much room they take on the table. Then you'll know exactly where to place the first panel as a starting point. When laying them out, you'll notice that they form an almost complete circle.

Remove all the panels except the first one, which is the starting point. To the left of the panel, hammer in two nails. These will serve to support the side of the panel and keep it from moving. To the right of the panel place a strip of 1/4" H lead. Make sure it fits the side of the panel exactly within the slot of the came. Push the lead firmly up against the panel to make sure there is no extra room for motion and that the lead is seated properly. The lead came shouldn't cover the entire length of glass; a small amount should show above and below. The piece of lead should not be quite as long as the glass.

Cut approximately 20" off one of the 3/16" U leads and fit it over the top of the glass panel, making sure the glass fits into the slot of the U lead. Start the U lead almost at the end, but leave a little overlap to the left of the panel.

Following this procedure, cut a 60" strip of U lead and drape it as best you can in a circle so that none hangs over the table. If any does, it will be a drag on the portion you're working on and will tangle and twist. Drape it in a rough circle and keep it on the table in its entire length. Fit the end portion of the lead into the bottom straight edge of the first panel. This should fit exactly.

You now have in front of you the basic building block of your lamp. Each strip and each panel will follow successively from this one, and the same procedure will be employed.

Building Your Lamp

Fit the left side of the second panel into the right open slot of the first long H came. Continue the U lead on the top and bottom, making sure to hold the top and bottom of the first panel as well as the second panel with leading nails. It is imperative that these panels be held securely so they don't move and throw off your entire effort. The third panel should be treated exactly as the second. Remember that you are going to continue the top and bottom U leads concurrently.

By this time the glass is starting to bend into the same circle that it took previously and it is necessary to form the top and bottom U leads to fit into this circle. Make sure they are tightly pressed against the glass and that they are butting against the ribs formed by the H lead cames. They don't have to butt exactly, since a small space between the two leads can be filled later with solder (make sure it's a *small* space). If the H leads are too long, cut them down to fit. If they overlap the top and bottom U leads, they will create unsightly bulges. Submit all your remaining panels to the same procedure; when you are done you will have an incomplete circle composed of 12 panels, ribbed with H came and circled top and bottom with U came, all pressed tightly against the glass and all held in place with leading nails.

Note that the last panel has on its right only an H lead, while the first panel has on its left no lead at all. It is essential during the next soldering step not to allow any solder to flow into the free channel of the H lead on the right. To prevent this, place a scrap piece of glass in the channel and hold it with a leading nail. A small piece of glass top and bottom will do, since it's those areas that will be soldered. You will have trouble otherwise melting solder out or digging it out, and you might even have to substitute another lead.

Soldering the Panel

Brush flux vigorously on all the joints and run a small amount of solder over each joint, making certain that each is securely tacked. Be careful not to burn a lead rib. If you do, you will have to replace it because it's impossible to repair with solder and have it look right. If you have to replace a lead, you must detach all your leads to that point and remove the offending rib. The further you progress, the more you will have to take apart later on. So try not to burn any cames, but if you do, replace them then and there.

Solder only the side facing you. Don't turn the panel over and solder the other side. Once you have soldered the proper joints, trim the excess lead on the top and bottom of the lamp and remove all the nails.

Bending the Lamp into Shape

Care must be taken here or your work to this point can be made useless in one easy step. With one hand, grasp the middle of the top circle of the lamp and bring it away from the board toward you. You should be standing with the open circle facing away from you. Be careful while raising the lamp that the left-hand panel, which has no outer lead rib, does not come away from the rest of the lamp. If it does, push it into position again. It will slide easily into its groove. Very slowly fold the lamp around away from you, a little at a time, being careful not to crack any of the panels. Try to give each panel a little bit of fold. Each should take the same amount of strain. Should the lamp not fold smoothly, check the non-soldered side to see if the lead is crimping. This is a critical stage where confidence, not exuberance, is required. Continue to fold the lamp until the free edge of the left-hand panel inserts into the free flange of the H lead of the right-hand panel. Manipulate the top, then the bottom, into position. Once you get the top seated, solder the two sides together while holding them tightly with one hand. Then fit the bottom to meet and solder that in the same fashion. This way, you will be dealing with one joint at a time instead of trying to fit top and bottom at once. If the top fits snugly and smoothly, the bottom will too.

The upper part of the lamp is now completed. Don't solder the inside at this time. Place the lamp on the work table and press to make sure the bottom of each panel touches the table. This will automatically bring the lamp into proper shape. If a panel or two is not resting on the table, manipulate it gently by pressing around the surface of the lamp. It should settle in. If it still doesn't, check the inside; a piece of lead may be folded in the way.

Making the Skirt

Fasten a piece of wood approximately 4" long and at least 2" wide securely to the edge of the work table. You can either nail it down or clamp it down with C-clamps.

Stretch a piece of 3/16" U lead, open it with a lathkin, and lay it against the straight piece of wood with the channel facing away from you so the flat end of the came lies directly against the wood. Insert the first piece of skirt with the flat side toward you into the U lead, making sure it seats all the way into the channel. This is a deep channel and may fool you, so be sure the piece of glass is well in place. Hold the left end of this first piece of skirt with a leading nail. Take one of the 1-14" pieces of H lead you previously cut and insert the right-hand channel of this first piece of glass into a channel of this piece of lead. Repeat with each piece of the skirt so that you have a straight line of skirt pieces—the first one held at the left edge with a nail and the last one having a lead rib on its right with an empty channel, also held by a nail or by another piece of glass in the channel.

Starting at the left, press another strip of 3/16" U lead firmly against the half moon edges of each piece of skirt, making sure it dips down far enough to meet each lead rib between the skirt pieces. This lead is quite malleable and can be pushed into shape with your fingers or a lathkin. Don't be concerned if there is a slight space between the lead rib and the bordering U lead. If a gap occurs, you've probably cut your lead rib too short. It must be re-cut. Work one piece of skirt at a time, securing each with nails before going on to the next. When finished, trim the lead margins on either end and solder all the joints, making sure to solder only those joints that are facing you. Don't solder the side facing the table.

Bending the Skirt

Remove all the nails and the strip of wood from the work table. Stand the skirt line on edge so the straight edge is uppermost and the curved edge rests on the table. Bend the line inward against the unsoldered side so the free edge of the left side of the skirt inserts into the empty channel of the lead on the right. Solder these two joints, again being careful not to let solder get inside the channel itself. You now have the two parts of the lamp completed.

Putting the Lamp Together

Place the top part of the lamp on top of the skirt, making certain that the panel you are going to solder exactly meets the margins of the underlying skirt. If this is off, all the other panels will be off. Don't worry if all the panels don't seem to meet the underlying skirt at the same time. Work one at a time and if you are accurate on your first one, all the others must fall in line. If you are making a shade of alternating colors, you should decide now if you want the color of the skirt to match the color of the corresponding panel or if you want it to match the alternating panel.

The Finishing Touch

Tack solder all the joints, working one panel at a time. Once you are satisfied that the skirt panels meet as accurately as possible, solder each joint firmly. Turn the lamp on its side, solder all the other joints, and run solder in the area between the skirt and upper panel, both inside and out. For a smooth finished look, flatten a piece of 3/16" U lead and wrap it around the lamp so it covers the seam between the top and bottom parts. This belt is soldered in place at the joints. Do the same with the inside seam.

Clean the lamp as soon as possible to prevent the glass from clouding; it may already be tacky from the flux. A vinegar and water mixture is a good cleansing agent used with a piece of steel wool. We also use cleaning and polishing powder. Follow this with an ordinary glass cleaner. The leads and soldered joints will darken slowly over time. If you want to antique the leads, they must be tinned (solder flowed over them), then antiquing patina applied with a stiff brush.

Another Method

Another way to make this lamp is to lay out the panel in a straight line along the table edge, using a long piece of wood as a bottom guide, and place the strips of lead between them. Then lift the panels carefully, sliding a yardstick underneath, and wrap around and fold down at the same time into the lead channels. This is difficult, however, and can involve a number of broken panels if you are not careful.

THE MOLD METHOD (MULTIPLE PIECED OR TIFFANY TYPE LAMPS)

This is a very different type of shade and it is much more time consuming. It uses copper foil instead of lead and involves a mold to shape the project. When designing for copper foil, keep a thin margin between the pieces. You may even cut the pattern without the use of pattern scissors, since the copper foil takes up very little room. Your glass cutting must be absolutely precise.

As a guide for the lamp, you can use a pre-formed Worden Styrofoam mold, a clear plastic shape, or even a turned-up wooden salad bowl. The Worden Co. has made

Lamp forms from Odyssey Co. arranged on a wall. (Glass Crafters, Sarasota, Florida)

A Tiffany reproduction, Flowering Lotus, on a reproduction lily pad base.

making this type of shade a lot easier than it was formerly. If you buy a kit you will still need to use this portion of the chapter as a guide. If you are working from your own design, the best advice we can give you is to keep your initial design simple, especially if this is your first attempt. Don't try to design a pictorial Tiffany-type shade at the outset.

On the surface of the mold, draw the pattern from your cartoon. (If you use a Worden mold, this is done for you.) You need not make the pattern to cover the entire surface of the mold since your design will be in a repeating pattern around the shade. Once you have traced the design on the mold, transfer the pattern to pattern paper and cut it out. Then cut the glass to match the pattern. As you cut each piece, place it on the mold, starting at the top. Hold the pieces in place with push pins or pieces of plasticene clay. The plasticene will anchor the glass pieces to the mold but still allow you to remove them to check the colors and lineup. Work around the top of the mold as though you were knitting a hat. If you work down one column at a time, the pieces will likely start to slip off the mold as the combination gets heavier. However, there is no rule of thumb here.

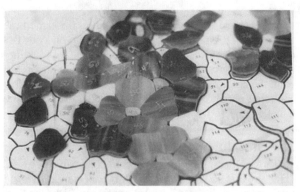

Detail on the Odyssey Dogwood pattern sheet. The cut and ground glass is being checked against a flat copy of the pattern before foiling and attached with tacky wax to the mold. (Denise Younk class project) (Courtesy of Kaleidoscope Stained Glass Studio)

The first row is completed with an installed tinned vase cap. The next row of glass will be fitted and spot tacked into position before soldering. (Lea Ferris class project) (Courtesy of Kaleidoscope Stained Glass Studio)

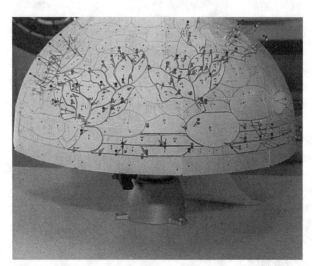

The Waterlily pattern from Worden on the 16" full form. The mold is mounted on the lampshade holder and the pattern strips and cut pattern pieces are pinned in place. (Glass Crafters)

Once you've covered the top surface of the mold, remove the pieces, check them under the light, and solder them together. Then remove the holding clay. The next line around the mold can be tack soldered to the previous section as you go. Thus you will build up bit by bit. The glass pieces must be small enough to conform to the bend of the mold. Don't solder the pieces together firmly, but continue to tack solder as you go along so they can conform to the mold shape. Leave a hole in the top of the lamp for the socket and electrical wiring. Don't get so carried away that you foil the lampshade directly over the top of the mold. Then you'll have a stained glass hat, not a shade.

Once the work is completed, lift it off the mold, solder all the joints together, and bead all the seams. Solder the shade on the inside. The lamp will get stronger and stronger as it is soldered together.

The Odyssey Dogwood now being soldered on the inside using our homemade lamp holder to balance the shade. The outside is completed but the Odyssey vase cap set has to be added.

More decorative effects are possible once you master this technique. The designing must first be done flat, then measured to conform to the turn of the mold. If you want to make a swan, for instance, you must measure the size of the swan against the circumference of the mold. Using graph paper will help give you an idea how many swans you can fit into the space available. Remember to allow some space for the copper foil.

Dimensions

We check our dimensions by cutting designs out of pattern paper and scotch taping them directly to the form. Another way to compare space to design is to square off all odd-shaped pieces and take the measurement of this square around the form. The square then may be broken internally into any number of configurations.

For a finished edge, you can line the border of your lamp with a piece of came, such as a 3/16" U or apply an extra heavy coat of solder to the ends of the copper foil that form the lamp borders. Finally, clean the lamp as before.

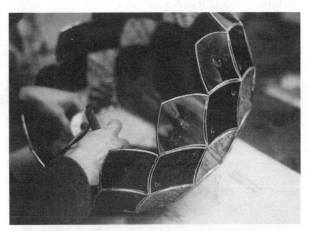

The bottom row of glass already has an edge bead completed and has been tacked in position on this cone with skirt shade. Final soldering is being done to the inside of the shade before using a bar lamp holder to complete the outside. (Danielle Burnett class project) (Courtesy of Kaleidoscope Stained Glass Studio)

Some Don'ts

Originally, multiple pieced lamps were made from molds of rock maple or aluminum but today such molds are difficult to obtain, are very expensive, and are really not needed. Don't get one unless you are making your own for a special oddball shape. We recommend Worden molds for their variety of design and proven sturdiness. Try not to draw your own modifications directly on a Worden or plastic mold since this will ruin the design already impressed on the mold.

Above all, don't try to make a multiple pieced lamp without using a mold, as in the previous method described. It is likely the small pieces will begin to tear through the foil as you apply pressure to bend to the requisite shape.

Don't immediately apply large amounts of solder to the glass pieces; only tack them in a few places. It is frustrating to find that a piece must come out for whatever reason and that you have soldered it firmly into place and now need to use so much heat and force to unsolder it that you waste a lot of time and energy. If you tack only here and there, you can easily melt away the small bridgings of solder that hold the pieces together, remove the offending piece, and replace it.

Watch Those Curves

Test each piece of glass for its ability to allow for the curve of the mold. Don't assume the glass will fit simply because the pattern paper does. The paper will bend against the mold surface, the glass will not. Simple as it may seem, many beginners overlook this and cut glass pieces too large to conform to the mold.

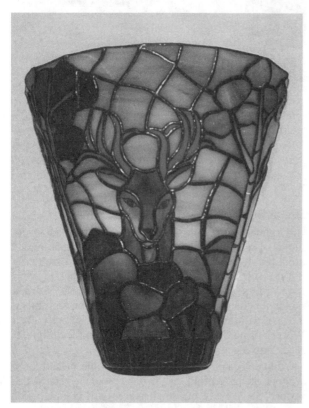

A wall sconce built on the Bradley lampshade mold. Note the random breaks to insure the glass conforms to the tapered round form. (Original design by John Daley)

Combinations

You can combine the multiple pieced lamp with the paneled lamp using small glass pieces as the skirt rather than the larger formed pieces. If you do, make a form out of cardboard or heavy paper and tack the small pieces to this rather than laying them flat and trying to bend them around to form a circle as you would ordinarily do with this type of lamp. As previously noted, multiple pieced anythings don't bend as well as single pieces. Of course you can modify any straight panel lamp in this fashion, breaking up both panels and skirt with multiple linear arrangements and filling these with small pieces of stained glass. It's up to you what effect you are after.

Antiquing

Multiple pieced lamps look shiny because of the amount of tinning required. They are generally antiqued with patina eliminate this effect. This should be done soon after the lamp is finished and before any oxidation has started to form on the soldered surfaces. The more oxidation, the more difficult the antiquing process will be. For quicker action, heat the antiquing solution, but be careful not to inhale the fumes.

Small pieced lamps are wired and hung exactly the same as any other type of lamp. They are quite strong and if you have soldered the pieces correctly front and back, you should have no trouble with them coming apart in midair. Use plenty of solder to keep the pieces together and get a nice rolled (beaded) edge, but keep the copper foil border edges thin. Solder dripping onto the glass as you work is usually not in sufficient amounts to crack the glass and is easily scraped away. When you bead, turn the lamp on its side so that soldering is easier.

Always maintain your lamp in a position best suited for you to work and to see what you are working on. It will not collapse, whereas you may if you are twisted into contortions while trying to do the best job you can. Keep in mind that once the joints are tacked sufficiently, the lamp should maintain its shape, even when it is no longer supported by the mold. Multiple pieced lamps, more than any other type, require some support, if only to allow their pieces to be soldered readily and comfortably. There are manufactured supports on the market (shade holders) or you can make one yourself using a basic wooden cross beam that will support almost any type of lamp. (See photos on pages 163, 170, 172).

DOUBLE TIERED LAMPS

These are essentially straight panel lamps with panels broken into two pieces (or more depending on the size of the project) and angled toward the upper opening at their joints. The tiers may be composed of multiple glass pieces rather than single, giving the lamp a shape similar to but more angular than the multiple pieced Tiffany type lamp. A skirt is usually an element of such a lamp and this, also, may be pieced out or have decorative elements imposed on it such as curved apples or pears or hanging berries or cherries made of globs or a beaded curtain, though this latter effect seems to have gone out of style.

BENT PANEL LAMPS

Bent panel lamps are single pieces of glass that take a single or double S-shaped curve. These lamps describe a circle that is dependent on the widest portion of each individual panel regardless of the number of bends in it. Plan your circle from this measurement. If you want a certain diameter, you must divide this by the number of panels you want in your lamp (usually an even number.) Bent panel lamps usually have eight or more panels of similar or alternating colors. The panels are held in place by decorative brass stripping or white metal or lead came. In these latter instances, the panels are held to the decorative stripping by small strips of metal. Whatever metal you decide on, make sure it is easily solderable.

Once you determine the diameter of the lamp and calculate the circle, design the panel. Your design can be of any style but must taper upward from the widest part of the circle.

Making The Panel

Transfer the original panel design from graph paper via carbon paper to pattern paper. As usual, you may want to make more than one pattern to prevent a single repeat pattern from fraying due to excessive cutting pressure. Cut the glass exactly to the pattern and lay the panels flat, making sure the measurements are exact.

The Mold

True bent panel lamps can only be made in a kiln. Such panels are first measured and cut to size, then a mold must be made, usually from plaster of Paris or from a mold mixture we prepare ourselves that we will tell you about in a moment. Plaster of Paris will allow you to make changes while it is wet, but once it is set it should be allowed to cure overnight undisturbed.

Molds are of two varieties: drapes and saggers. A drape mold is a "positive" mold upon (or over) which the glass is balanced and heated to temperature so that it drapes. A sagger (or negative) mold allows the glass to sag into it. Plaster of Paris can be used in the kiln as a drape mold, but we have had little success using it as a sagger. Before using it to bend glass, it must be heated in the kiln to approximately 1200°F and then allowed to cool for 24 hours. After it has cooled, you may find tiny cracks developing through its surface. If great chunks of the mold crumble away, the plaster mixture was bad. The mixture should be thick and creamy and free of air pockets; we like to place our mix on a jogger to get as much air out of it as possible.

Still another type of mold is made of terra cotta, a clay which hardens as it bakes. Whether you use terra cotta or plaster of Paris, you must apply a mold release to the mold so that the glass will not stick to the surface. Mold releases are available at ceramic supply stores.

Our own mold preference allows for multiple use practically forever and requires no setting whatsoever nor any mold release. We use a mixture of kiln wash and diatomaceous earth (found at swimming pool supply stores). We mix the two in a proportion of two parts kiln wash to one part diatomaceous earth (add more diatomaceous earth to make the mix more firm, if desired). Once the mix has been stirred together completely we pile it in the kiln, dry, with no water added, and impress upon it the sample panel we want to make. This is pressed firmly into the pile and excess earth/wash mix is wiped away from the borders. The sample panel is then removed, leaving a perfect impression on the pile. We place our glass blanks on top of this drape mold, heat them, and get perfect bent panels every time. If we don't have a sample panel, we make one out of sheet copper, bend it to match our dimensions, and use it as a sample panel in the same way. The mixture can be used over and over for similar or different panels. It's a cheap and efficient mold.

Bending the Glass

If using a drape mold, once the mold is ready and the glass cut, place the mold in the kiln with the hump uppermost, and balance the glass on top so it drapes over the mold. If you are using a sagger mold, place the glass over the declivity so will sag into it. Check for undercuts in the sagger mold. These will cause the glass to break when you release it from the mold. Each mold should be well coated with mold coat and the kiln gradually heated. Most stained glass bends between 1150°F and 1300°F, depending on color, thickness, and manufacturer. You really have to test bend a piece of glass to obtain its individuality to heat. We bend our glass by eye using a top loading kiln. Not all colors of stained glass, even of the same manufacturer, bend at the same temperature. The cone firing method is of little use here since each piece must be individually watched. The molds described (except for the kiln wash/earth mix) may last for five to eight bends before they begin to crumble.

Assembling the Panels

Bent panel lamps should be assembled vertically. A small block of clay makes a good stand for each panel. You should (usually) have an even number of panels, generally eight or more, and they should be upright at the angle at which they are to be joined. Use only enough clay to keep the panels upright. Move the panels so they meet at their juncture points and tack them together with solder after either foiling or leading each one. You may have to maneuver them to get them to meet exactly. Make sure they are all at the same angle or your circle will either not close or be deformed if it does.

With the panels tacked together, you can fill in with solder along the remainder of the lead lines. The panels at the bottom may splay out from one another according to their design.. Here they must hang free, supported by the juncture lines above. They will be close to the angle point. You can use brass banding as decorative strips over the portion of the lead that holds the panels together. If the curved panels follow each other closely all the way down, you can extend your brass or copper decorative banding this far as well. This banding should be soldered to the lead from inside the shade so no solder shows from the outside. When bending brass strips to fit, make a Styrofoam mold as a guide.

Most brass strips are a little whippy and may have to be over-bent at first to take a proper shape. Don't be too concerned about this—the solder will hold them in place. When soldering these strips, hold the brass with a protective mitten so the heat doesn't burn your fingers (brass conducts heat very readily). It takes only one or two solder points to tack these strips firmly to the came. You can solder them as well through existing areas of solder which are holding the came skeleton together, being careful not to loosen these leaded areas. The solder will puddle against the brass band from the heat of the iron and will tend to strengthen the lampshade as a whole.

THE LANTERN

Compared to multi-paneled, small pieced, and bent panel stained glass lampshades, the lantern is a piece of cake. Most lanterns consist of four-sided rectangular panels with a long bulb that effectively lights up all the corners and angles. The panels can be the same design or alternating designs.

Start by designing the panels. Don't use too many small pieces or you will detract from the effect. The pieces should be fairly large since there is no angle or bend to climb. An old jewel or two or a few chunks can be incorporated into the design. Whether you design a simple piece with four straight panels, a more complex flaring design, or a top/bottom combination that must be fitted together, make a mockup in heavy cardboard before cutting the glass (good cardboard comes from sides of corrugated boxes). The mockup should be as neat and precise as possible. If the mockup is incorrect or ungainly, the final product will look the same. The mockup should show the shape of each panel. Tape the cardboard sides together and keep this form in front of you as you work. The mockup should be slightly smaller than your finished product to allow the glass edges to meet at the proper angles.

Cutting the Panels

Cut the glass panels and place them on the form. Lead (or foil) and tack them with solder. Remove the mockup and thoroughly solder the panels. Using the mockup as a guide gives less chance of error in forming the angles between the panels. Ninety degree angles are difficult to get precisely right and if you attempt to form them without a mold, the lantern will be off in contour.

These right angles may show solder between them. Once the lantern is well soldered, flatten a strip of 3/16" U lead into a belt, as was done with the multi-paneled lamp. This belt may be run over the sides of the lantern and tacked top and bottom to form a covering for the seams of any glass sides that were not precisely cut.

UNUSUAL SHAPES

Some stained glass shades are neither square nor circular. Consider the star lamp, shaped with rectangles of glass built up to form a three-dimensional star effect. Although such a lamp looks complicated, as you take it apart panel by panel and see how it is put together, it devolves into nothing more than multiple rows of glass angled together to form the final shape. The mechanics follow closely the making of the lantern, except that the star is an extended and more ornate form. Professional shops that mass produce non-circular lamps make their molds out of metal so they are more durable and exact than cardboard. These molds are difficult and time consuming to make—in some instances, more difficult and more time consuming than the lamp itself. But they last indefinitely.

THE COPPER FOILED MULTI-PIECE PANEL SHADE

Copper foiled multi-pieced panel lamps have panels that are broken into design elements with a few or a great many pieces. They can include not only glass but geodes, shells, metallic inlays—in short, any ornament. They can be designed to repeat the design in each panel or use each panel as a portion of an overall design. If these pieced panels are to work, they must all be of the same dimension. The easiest way to do this is to build each within a specific size frame using wood strips or layout blocks affixed to the work board. This will insure that each panel matches for accurate joining when soldered into final shape.

The wood frame set up on a small board to hold a copper foil shade panel. (Lisa Inkhen class project) (Courtesy of Kaleidoscope Stained Glass Studio)

Whether you design your own lamp or use a book pattern, you should measure to make sure the outline is true. Book patterns can also be off and if one side is too long or off center, this will show up only when you are ready to solder everything together. Measurements being off can lead to glass edges not aligning correctly and twisting the panels to make them fit will only risk breakage.

To check proper measurements, fold the pattern in half and hold the paper to a light source. The lines must overlap exactly. Or measure the width of the top and bottom of the pattern and divide each in half. Lightly draw a straight line down the center and again measure left and right of the line to the edge of the pattern. The most important measurements are the length of the two sides—they must be equal. Two copies of the pattern are needed, one for cutting and one to build on. Place one copy of the pattern on the work board, position the frame guides on the outer edge of the printed line, and secure them with leading nails. The second pattern should be marked with directional lines and numbered with color shadings as needed. Cut the glass and grind it to fit exactly within the frame, especially up to the sides, to create a straight edge.

Foiling

When the glass is correctly fitted to the pattern, begin foiling the pieces. Pieces on the edge of the panel need the foiling started on an edge that will adjoin interior pieces to protect the foil seam as the panels are being put together. Using the frame as a guide, foil and spot tack each piece, then finish soldering the top and remove the panel from the frame. If you used any foil less than 7/32" on the sides, clean and dry the panel and apply 7/32" around the left, top, and right edges. If this bottom edge doesn't need additional glass added, it should always have 1/4" foil for soldering an edge bead. This can be done at this time.

Soldering

Finish soldering the back panel and do the edge bead to the bottom. You will find it easier to do this to each panel separately rather than trying to balance a completed shade to place the solder correctly. Don't solder down the side edges because this and extra solder here will prevent the panels from fitting together and will throw off the circumference. If you must stiffen the foil on the sides to keep it on the glass, lightly tin coat with solder but keep it smooth. Complete the required number of panels for the shade and carefully clean and dry them for the next step.

Remove the frame from the work board so you have a flat surface. You will need a second work board for turning the shade over. Lay the panels on the board in a semicircle face down. Check the bottoms and tops for fit next to each other. If you built within the frame, all areas should join evenly to a smooth continuous line. If there are slight discrepancies in the sizes of the panels, place them next to the nearest matching one. Mismatched top edges may be concealed under a vase cap to an extent, but the bottom edges should be matched evenly around.

Taping

Place strips of masking tape down the panel seams leaving about 1" to 2" exposed at the bottom and top for inside soldering. Add extra tape across the panels to help hold the tape in position. Be sure the tape sticks to the glass as this will hold it in shape while you form it. Tape that doesn't stick will cause your lampshade to collapse as you try to position the panels for spot tacking and you will have to clean the glass and start again.

An eight-panel cone for a shade with a flared skirt. The tape has been applied to face down glass. If you try to pick it up to make the cone shape, the tape will not bend and could tear the foil away from the glass.

With the panels taped together in a semicircle face down on the first work board, place the second board on

top of the glass. Draw the two boards together off the table and turn them over quickly. Put the boards on the table and remove the top one. Your shade is now right-side-up, with tape on the bottom surface, and ready to pull up into shape. Since the tape is on the inside it will bend with the glass as you pull up.

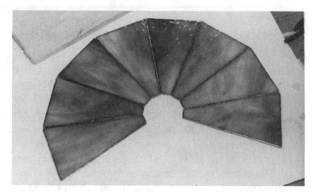

The taped panels have been turned over and are laying face up on the bench.

Use two hands to grasp the center of the shade. Support and lift as many of the pieces as you can at one time to raise the glass straight up and allow it to come together into the cone shape of the shade. The inside tape will bend with the panels, holding them together as they come up to sit on their bottom edge.

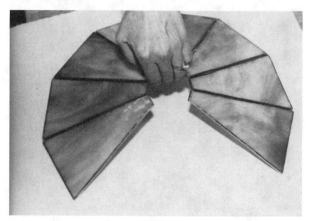

Now you can lift the shade by the vase cap area and the tape underneath supports all the panels as it moves.

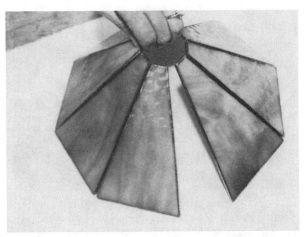

The taped panels are moving together to make the complete circle as it is raised into the cone shape.

The panel bottoms should now all be resting on the work board and the cone should be fairly even in round. Lightly flux the side of the panels and join them by spot tacking. The weight of the glass is now pushing inward but each panel is supported by touching the inside edge of the adjoining panel; that and the masking tape will make the shade stand on its own.

If the shade has an uneven border that prevents it from standing on its bottom edge, don't turn the panels over with the two work boards. If you do so and lift from the center, the tape—now on the outside surface—will tear and probably tear foil loose as well. Instead carefully

If the bottom is uneven, lift the face down taped panels from the outside edges to pull into a vase shape.

When joining the open panels of the vase shape, be prepared to either add pieces of masking tape inside and outside or spot tack the top and bottom of the seam to complete the drawing up of the shade.

Placing a multi-panel dragon fly into a round container for support for soldering. The panels couldn't be turned and drawn up to the cone shape because of the delicate eyes on the dragon fly on the bottom edge. (Carol Hodges class project) (Courtesy of Kaleidoscope Stained Glass Studio)

bring the taped panels up as a whole, raising the bottom edge up into a vase shape and use a round bowl, bucket, or wastebasket to support the sides while soldering. This can place the shade at an uncomfortable height to work on but it will do until you can spot tack, remove the tape, and fill some of the inside seams (which will not be facing you) one at a time.

Soldering

Lightly flux and spot tack about 1/4" down from the top and 1" up from the bottom of each panel. When spot tacking has been done, check the panels to be sure the shape is correct and begin adding solder into the seams from the top down. At this point the solder will be dripping and running down the seams and over the glass and

A close-up of the dragon fly shade with filigree wings being placed back on the table after tacking for the outside seam soldering. The gap in the seam allowance shows masking tape which will keep the solder from flowing through.

Spot tacking the inside of the shade about 1" down and if necessary peeling the masking tape back for more coverage.

Another student's lampshade in level position for soldering the seams.

not looking too terrific, but this is just a base coat to stabilize the shade. The finished soldering will occur later.

The masking tape inside will help keep the solder from flowing through any gaps in the seams while allowing it to build up on the outside. When this has been completed all the way around, the shade will become rigid but still slightly flexible and will remain so until the inside is soldered. Either tip and support the shade on its side to continue soldering or use a lamp positioner to hold it level to finishing soldering the outside seams (the wooden cross arm supports pictured can be made at home). The last step is to add the vase cap or spider—a thick brass or steel ring about 1/2" round with three or four spokes radiating from it. The spokes are cut to fit just inside and underneath the opening below the crown of the lampshade and allow heat to pass out of the shade. The addition of the vase cap or spider will firm the shade up substantially.

Soldering the Vase Cap

If you have a spun or unfinished brass vase cap and want it to match the patina, you must tin the whole outside of the cap. Rub the cap with steel wool to clean it, then flux it. Hold the flat portion of the iron tip on the cap and slowly add solder (60/40 will melt and flow rapidly). Stroke the solder as thin as you can around the cap. If the solder stops flowing, it is because the flux has evaporated and needs to be replenished. A thin coat is all that is needed. If you have marks to get out, hold the iron underneath the cap and heat the area. The solder will reheat and can be coaxed around the surface of the cap. If you have heavy buildup, heat the area from the top and pull the excess solder off by shaking or stroking it off the edge.

To help you attach the vase cap to the inside of the shade, add a ring of solder to the inside lip of the vase cap about 1" around the rim. This "priming" will prevent you from having to heat the vase cap enough to flow solder onto it while you are in position inside the shade and risking a heat crack. The solid polished brass caps do not get soldered on the outside! They are more difficult to work with because you may need to file or steel wool the inside rim to make it accept solder, which you must do prior to soldering it to the shade. The mass will take longer to heat and you will have to add extra solder to the inside to get it to adhere.

Use pliers to position the vase cap evenly on the shade. The lip of the vase cap should either meet the edge or extend slightly over the glass. A cap that extends out beyond

1/8 of the glass is not usable because there will be no way to bring solder up onto it to secure it to the shade at the seams. Heat the edge of the vase cap using the corner of the iron tip and then flow a small amount of solder onto the cap and join to the seam below it. Spot opposite seams to tack the cap on, then tip the shade to allow you to join all the lines to the cap. This will solidify the shape and you can continue to the inside.

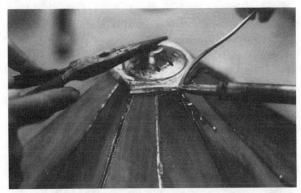

Attaching the tinned hexagon vented vase cap to the top of the shade at the corners of the seams.

Rest the shade on its side and slowly peel the masking tape from the inside seams. You may need to lightly steel wool to remove the tape adhesive from the foil. Flux and solder all the seams with a small bead. You don't want an excessive buildup of solder in the seams so be cautious how much solder you place. At the top of the shade, add solder around the top to fill and join to the vase cap from underneath. Touch up any spots inside the shade and outside at this point and carefully join the edge bead across the seams to each other. Now you are ready to clean the shade and patina.

Choose a lamp base that will complement the style of the shade and properly fit. You don't want to see the socket, but you should be able to reach under the shade to turn it on. The height can be adjusted by changing the harp or using shade risers. Also make sure the base is wide enough to support the weight and is stable when turning on the light. We recommend bringing the completed shade to the shop when selecting the base.

A collection of commercially produced lamp bases of different heights with a standard 6" harp. (Stained Glass Connection, Sarasota, Florida)

Odyssey Tiffany reproduction bases to finish the Odyssey lamp projects. (Glass Crafters, Sarasota, Florida)

One of the various lampshade mold holders. This intricate design allows you to rotate the form around the axis and tilt back and forward. The shade was soldered from a sitting position on a low chair.

LAMP AIDS

The Worden Co. manufactures a lamp form holder that every lampshade maker must appreciate. Shade positioners have made brief appearances on the market over the years, but most were either too cumbersome to fight or so ingenious that no one could figure out how to use them. When you make your first lampshade you will find yourself going through many contortions to keep the panels lined up and the solder from dropping on the table. Burned fingers can result if you let your impatience take hold. Of course you can design your own holder to your own specifications.

WIRING THE LAMP

The canopy is a decorative plate that fits directly to the ceiling and through which the electric wiring passes. Its purpose is to cover the hole in the ceiling made for the electric box and to allow the chain to hold the lampshade. Canopies come in all styles, from simple brass bowls to ornately carved highly polished or antiqued designs in metal.

Select a canopy that won't detract from your lamp. This doesn't necessarily mean simple. An extensively foiled Tiffany shade might have an ornate canopy, not a bare metal cap and a plain geometric lamp might have a plain canopy.

Canopies come with two types of center holes and with or without small side holes meant for screwing into the underlying electric box. In the latter instance, the center hole runs 7/16" and the two side holes are spaced 4-1/4" center to center. We prefer the single large center hole, which is 1-1/16" and supports the lamp directly to the electric box by means of a decorative hanger unit. Some popular canopy finishes are brushed brass, black, bright brass, polished copper, weathered copper, chrome, and weathered antique brass.

SWAG KITS

If you are not going to place your lamp in a pre-existing fixture box, swagging allows decorative and functional placement. A swag is nothing more than a loop of chain attached from one spot on the ceiling to another. Two swags are enough for most lamps, but three can be used for a large lamp, with equal or diminishing loops of chain. Both the lamp and the chain loops are held by ceiling hooks with "molly" screws. If your lamp is heavy, try to place the ceiling hook directly into a beam. When swagging, run the chain all the way down the wall to the baseboard socket. It will look unfinished if the chain runs only halfway down the wall.

You can make your own swag kit by purchasing the items separately or you can purchase a kit with the correct amount of chain (providing you know what that is).

DIE-CAST LOOPS

Die-cast loops connect the chain to the lamp and hold together the two vase caps that stabilize the lamp either for hanging or on a base. The wiring passes through its center hole. Loops, like canopies, should match the lamp in style.

CHAIN AND CHAIN PLIERS

Chain is sold in three foot lengths and usually each loop is notched so it can be opened with a pair of chain pliers. Anyone who has struggled to open decorative chain by gripping the loop on either side and pulling like mad with regular pliers will appreciate the ease of working with chain pliers. Even if you make only an occasional lamp, you may find that you can't do without chain pliers. For anyone producing numbers of lampshades that must be wired, they are a necessity. When passing the electric wire through the chain, it is not necessary to weave it through every loop. Every other one or every third one will do.

SOCKETS

There are a various kinds of sockets, but we find it best to use those with a set screw in the neck. The set screw al-

lows a definitive measurement to be made along the length of the nipple and holds it firmly in place. We try to avoid sockets with either a chain or a push-pull switch, as we find them awkward. If it's a light that will be hung from the ceiling, electrical code requires a porcelain socket. Any lamp where the socket is above the bulb requires the same. A brass (brass or nickel coated) or bakelite socket can be used for table lamps where the bulb is above the socket. The bakelite socket has an advantage because it's shorter than the brass, although it's a little more difficult to wire. Be sure to get one with a standard base. The base is held by a small screw in the socket, and it's best to take this off before you begin to wire the socket. The keyless brass socket also has a standard base, which is held in place by pressure locking to the cap. This also must come off before wiring.

VASE CAPS

Vase caps are molded disks of brass that rise tent-like from a flat plane to a shallow center peak where the nipple hole is located. One way to use them is to place one inside the neck of the lamp and another outside. When the two are compressed by the outside lamp ring and the inside socket with a nipple acting as a lever between them, they neatly sandwich the neck of the glass and grip the lampshade securely all around. Such caps can be used only with lamps with round necks. They change size approximately every 1/8", so it's better to first make your lamp and then fit your vase caps to the existing hole rather than having a specific center hole and trying to force your measurements to conform to it.

Vase caps come in unfinished brass, lacquered brass, and polished brass but it's difficult to get them in any oth-

A sampling of flat and coned solid vented vase caps and the two sizes of spiders for assembling the lamps.

The top two caps are authentic Tiffany reproductions by Odyssey. Flat vented and solid spun brass caps are below. The small 3" on the far left is one of the styles available for the solid cast brass polished cap. (Glass Crafters)

er color. The brass coloring can be changed chemically to an antique copper or a pewter or you can paint the caps. If you paint them, first remove the lacquer coat from the cap with alcohol or acetone. It is always easier and cheaper to paint an unfinished than a finished vase cap. Use a good quality paint to avoid chipping.

The Odyssey Co. produces vase cap three-part assemblies that are among the most complicated and the most unique of their type. There is the cap itself, the shade ring (which solders to the shade inside the neck), and the inner ring. The inner ring screws to the vase cap through the attached shade ring. Odyssey claims their vase caps are "true to Tiffany." They are arguably the best designed and you are not limited here to polished brass. Odyssey also produces antique verdigris vase caps which are quite handsome, quite heavy, and a quite pricey. But if you have made yourself a lamp you are proud of and wish to give it the ultimate finishing touch, see your local retailer for an Odyssey combination vase cap.

The company also makes lamp bases and lamp forms. Unlike the Worden lamp forms, each Odyssey form is specific to a single style lamp. Whereas the Worden form provides a shape for any style lamp that can use that shape, the Odyssey form has the design imprinted on the form. This makes it easier to build on but, unless you are producing a single style, rather limiting. Of course you can always buy more styles.

There are those who argue that it is a waste to use two vase caps in a lamp and that the decorative cap should be used only on the outside. For such individuals, check plates—brass-spun round flat plates with an 1/8" lip—are available. And if you want to stick to a single vase cap for your lamp, you can always solder one to the top, first tinning it so it will not have solder spots around its edge.

Also available from local suppliers are decorative vase caps with soft fencing in the form of an edge filigree, as well as an additional 1/2" edge that tucks in the top portion of the lamp. This is particularly effective if you want to hide a poor leading/soldering job. Remember when calculating vase caps to allow in your measurements for the top rim of lead covering the top rim of your lamp. The vase cap should fit neatly over it, not look half-cocked on top of it.

GLOBES

Duralite bulbs are fat and sassy looking and give an air of importance to the inside of the lamp. However, if your lamp's inside dimensions are such that even this bulb will be lost in it, you would do better with a globe.

Globes have their own problems. They not only require a different fitting operation, but they require a hanger to support them. Hangers are essentially cast brass holders with three thumb screws that grip the lip of the globe. Make certain these set screws turn easily because they will have to be opened again to remove the globe to change the bulb. If you have to use pliers to turn them shut, it will be difficult to open them again without cracking the lamp. When you buy a hanger, check the set screws and make sure they fit. They usually are packaged separately and they don't always screw in properly. You would be wise to test them before buying.

NON-CIRCULAR LAMP FITTINGS

If you have made a lamp with a square or hexagonal top, there is no reason you can't wire and hang it. Of course, you can't use vase caps, which come only in circular form. Two bars of galvanized steel should be measured across the top of the lamp at the strongest points, usually at two solder joints. Leave enough room between the bars for an 1/8" nipple. This can then be caught from below by a brass check ring and led into the socket. Another check ring and nut will hold it from above and fix it to the bars. You can then apply the lamp ring and chain. If you don't want to see the ceiling through your lamp, cut a piece of thin sheet metal to fit the top. Drill a hole for the nipple and solder the sheet metal all around the top surfaces of the lamp. This will provide a holding plate and finishing plate at the same time. It is usually not necessary to solder the inside of the plate to the lamp. If the lamp is unusually heavy, consider placing a few galvanized steel supporting rods across the plate at requisite intervals and soldering them to the top surfaces of the lamp.

For lanterns, a flat plate leaves a somewhat unfinished look. Try your hand at bending your own decorative top for such pieces. A sheet of copper and an instrument called a "bending brake" will help you do the job. The bending brake provides a means of bending metal into requisite angles that leave only one seam to solder. It can allow you to make the typical tent-like top one feels a lantern should have. We like to make ours out of heavy copper sheeting.

Wiring

Once you have the measurement of the top hole, fit the vase caps top and bottom (the bottom one will be smaller) and measure the size nipple you will need. This nipple will run through the two holes of the vase caps from bottom to top. Enough should protrude so that it can be caught by a lamp ring above and below so it can screw into the top of the socket. We usually start from below, screwing the nipple into the top of the socket and then tightening the socket set screw. We then place the nipple through the inner vase cap and upper vase cap. The top of

the nipple is caught with the lamp ring and tightened so the vase caps are held securely in place. Once this is done, you can move the lamp in any direction without fear of the vase caps falling off. Measure the amount of lamp wire you will need. Lamp chain comes in three foot lengths. Measure the wire slightly more than three feet. Pass the end of the wire from the top through the hole in the lamp rings, through the vase caps, and through the top portion of the socket below. Split the wire, take the insulation off the split ends, and wire the copper directly against the two screws in the socket. Then tighten the screws, pull the socket up against the top, place the bottom of the socket holder in place, and press it closed so that it snaps into the top of the socket.

With chain pliers, open one of the links of chain, hook it to the lamp ring, and close it. Weave the lamp wire through the chain at every second or third link. Be careful not to stretch the chain away from the lamp as it sits on the work bench. The weight of chain can easily pull the lamp to the floor. This is especially true if you are using extra chain to make a swag. You may unconsciously back away from the table as you weave the wire through the chain. Your lamp can then challenge your ability to sprint..

Once you have the lamp wire through the chain, split the end of the wire as before, taking the insulation off, and wire on a small lamp plug. Your wiring job is now complete.

At this point wait until dark, get into a comfortable chair, put your feet up and turn on your lamp.

A multi-piece Tiffany style bell shape. This shade has molded fruit, nuggets for grapes, and birds resting on a vine in the skirt design. It also has a decorative band as a collar under the crown. (By Anita Isenberg)

Scalloped copper foil on a simple cone and skirt table shade.

CHAPTER 14
Sandblasting

by Kathy Bradford

Kathy Bradford's cut, sandblasted, airbrushed, and etched glass pieces are a unique blend of art media. She has a long-standing tradition of breaking with tradition, using things that others consider taboo. Bradford treats glass like a transparent canvas and much of the strength of her work rests in her talent and background in graphic arts and watercolor painting.

A sandblasted piece by Kathy Bradford.

Sandblasting on glass creates an etched surface. The technique is the same as any sandblasting activity. A compressor is used to blow compressed air and sand (or some other grit) onto the glass. The grit etches away an outer layer and makes the glass appear frosted. The artist can control the frosted design by setting up different kinds of resists on the glass surface. A variety of exquisite results are unique to the technique and cannot be duplicated by any similar technique, including chemical etching.

There are no rules or regulations that should dampen your natural curiosity as to what effects you can produce with sandblasting. Whatever works the best for you is the best way to work. Many craftspeople shy away because of the cost of the equipment. Don't let that stop you from at least exploring the technique, even if you do this just by renting time on someone else's equipment. By no means should you think that you must invest a lot of money in equipment in order to sandblast. The fanciest and most expensive equipment does not produce good art. Only you can do that.

UNDERSTANDING POSITIVES AND NEGATIVES

Sandblasting is really a graphic technique. Setting up a resist for a sandblasted panel is similar to setting up resists for airbrushing and silkscreen or stencil printing. The object is to block out what you do not want the sand to etch.

It is important to develop a habit of thinking along the lines of positives and negatives just as you would if you were printing photographs. On sandblasted clear glass, the frosted glass, or positive, will read the whitest. The clear, or clearer areas of glass, will read as dark or negative. When you shade a particular form, you must remember that the white areas will advance and the darker values will recede. The idea is the same as in a rendered pencil drawing, except on clear glass the frosted areas advance and the clear areas recede. Before sandblasting anything, you take the time to render—that is, shade—the pencil drawing accurately. As you shade the various forms, your mind should be thinking through the process you will repeat in the sandblast booth. Mistakes are sometimes very difficult to correct. Instead, make your mistakes in pencil and correct them then. Remember that the values on the drawing will be reversed on the glass. The shaded areas of a form would appear in heavier pencil on white paper, whereas on the glass they would be the clear areas. The possibilities of rendering on glass are no more limited than with pencil on paper.

FROSTING

If you include light frosting as well as deeper cut details, the details should be cut or blasted first. Then the rest of the resist can be peeled away and a light sandblasting done. The sand will continue to frost the surface on a flat plane, so the detail (as long as it is cut deeply enough) will not disappear because of the frosting. Only the edges of it may smooth out. However, this makes them blend in better within the pattern.

SUBTLE GLASS EFFECTS

Even when glass is lightly frosted, it will react to light but this effect depends to a great extent on which side of the glass is blasted. For instance, if you want an object to appear to be coming forward, blast on the front of the glass—the surface facing you. If you want the object to appear to recede, blast on the back surface. A fish swimming underwater will be more emphatic if it is under the front surface and blasted onto the back. Sometimes the true effect is achieved by blasting on both sides of the glass. Clouds done on both sides of the glass, even on 1/8" clear glass, will give the illusion of space. The thicker the glass, the more distance will appear between the two surfaces. Usually the smooth side of the glass—the unblasted surface—gives the piece a more finished look. The light is enhanced as it passes through the sandblasted areas and out through the smooth surface facing the viewer.

DEEP CUTTING

Sandblasting can be carried to many extremes. If an area is blasted for a long time using several layers of resist, the result is a deep cut, almost a carving. It's possible to carve a bas relief figure into glass. The direction here is sculptural and it is particularly beautiful when it is viewed from the smooth side of the glass. When deep cutting is desired, usually several layers of adhesive paper will suffice as a resist. A thicker opaque, rubber-like material called Buttercut is also often used as a resist for deep cutting. Buttercut has a peel-away backing and will stick on glass like adhesive paper. A surprising amount of detail can be cut into Buttercut, and sometimes the stencil can be used over and over, depending on the design. The only problem with it, other than not being able to see through it, is that it is fairly expensive.

SPATIAL ILLUSION

The thickness of the glass can have an important effect on a piece of sandblasted art. Spatial illusion can be heightened by using several layers of glass together within one frame. The sandblasted surface also can serve as a ground for other media such as paint, ink, or shoe polish. Sandblasting mirror differs in two ways from sandblasting clear glass. It makes even more of a difference which side is blasted than when clear glass is used. If the blasting is done on the mirrored surface, a double image will result. If it is done on the back, where the mastic is, the mirroring effect is removed and the blasting shows white from the front of the mirror.

COMBINING SANDBLASTING AND STAINED GLASS

The combination of sandblasted glass and constructed stained glass is something that must be done with extreme caution and finesse. Even beautiful sandblasting combined with beautiful stained glass can sometimes cancel one another, making the end result chaotic. Sandblasting should never be used as a gimmick or shortcut or as an excuse to camouflage poor workmanship. To be effective, it should be compatible with all the other glass in the panel. Sandblasting at its best is lightweight, ghostlike, clear on clear. The glass you choose to go with it in a stained glass panel should not overwhelm it.

USING THE RESIST

One of the most common resists is adhesive paper, such as Contact paper. Clear adhesive paper is heavier than the plain opaque type and a fairly detailed design can be created with a craft knife, similar to cutting a silkscreen stencil. It also allows you to see through to the rendered drawing. If an even more detailed design is desired, then perhaps another technique such as photographic etching should be employed. You should develop a skill for stencil cutting or resist cutting because you will be imparting your most perfect drawing directly onto the adhesive paper with the knife. The drawing should eventually serve only as a guide, with your focus of attention jumping from pencil drawing to the surface of the resist material to the surface of the glass. The pencil drawing should be followed as accurately as possible and it's a good idea to take it into the sandblast booth with you.

If you want a deep cut, you will need two or three layers of adhesive paper. The number of layers will depend on how deep you want to cut into the glass. You can usually tell if you do not have enough layers of resist, since the first layer will blow off before the second. If you pay attention, you will have plenty of notice in order to repair the resist. Make sure the resist is firm against the glass before you start to sandblast. Small air bubbles in the adhesive paper will enable the sand to blast through the resist.

Blasting on mirror requires that you transfer the original drawing, since the mirror, being opaque, will not permit you to see the guide. Transfer the design with carbon paper onto solid light-colored adhesive paper. Remember to reverse the original drawing, especially letters and numbers, when working on the back surface.

Another good resist material is white glue, such as Elmer's, which is easily painted on the glass directly from the container. A little experimentation will prove how thick it should be to be effective, but even a thin bead will resist the sand if no especially deep cutting is required. White glue allows you more "painted" effects. Sometimes a particular effect may be obtained by first applying the glue, letting it dry, and then going over it with an adhesive paper resist. At the completion of the project, the glue can easily be washed off with warm water. Greasy fingerprints and greasy dirt are also excellent resist materials, so be sure to keep the glass clean.

Other materials such as fabric, lace, wire mesh, or coarse screens can serve as a resist when glued lightly to the glass. A piece of fabric, even one as fine and delicate as lace, will resist the sand nicely if it is first immersed in a watered-down solution of glue, pressed down, and allowed to dry against the glass. Interesting patterns can be achieved by stretching and pulling the lace before the glue dries. A whole world of things can function as resist media. Be inventive and experiment.

SANDBLASTING EQUIPMENT

The compressor: Probably the most expensive or difficult to find piece of equipment for sandblasting is the compressor. The compressor releases a continuous stream of air under pressure. A sandblasted surface will result with a small amount of pressure, but it's better to have a large amount of pressure, say 90 pounds, over a long period of time to ensure full control of the work process. To obtain that much pressure for even several minutes, you will need a fairly large compressor, hence a fairly expensive one.

The key to having a large quantity of pressure is to have a compressor with a large tank. A compressor with a two horsepower engine but with a large tank, say 100 gallons, will produce an adequate amount of pressure for several minutes. A compressor with a three horsepower engine but with a smaller tank will produce the same amount of pressure for about the same amount of time. There are several ways to get around the cost of a compressor. Many places will rent compressors or let you rent time on their compressor. There are numerous sources for picking up used compressors, such as gas stations going out of business, farm or ranch auctions, companies who are selling their equipment, as well as air equipment dealers. You may find a situation where you could rent a corner of a shop and quick connect into their compressor when it is not in use. Perhaps you could find an old compressor with a burned out engine. If it's in good condition otherwise—and most tanks last practically forever—you could have a rebuilt engine installed. An old compressor, if it has been taken care of, will probably work just as well as a new one.

One hidden cost to be aware of is that any compressor must be properly wired in. To save on electrical costs, look for single phase wiring. Most large compressors run on 220 current which can be expensive to wire. Also, a safety feature that all compressors have is a drain valve. Moisture builds up inside the tank and must be periodically drained off. Otherwise the moisture can rust the tank and the compressed air could blow up the tank—not to mention you.

The pressure pot: One piece of equipment that provides a larger amount of pressure from a comparatively smaller compressor is a pressure pot. This is a second piece of machinery that is hooked onto the compressor. Sand and pressure go in it together and are released together. A pressure pot can be very effective for deep cutting. However, the pots do not hold much sand and the pressure is released with so much force that it can blow off the resist with frustrating ease. It offers little control over shaded and softened areas, but it may suit your particular needs.

The sandblasting gun: The sandblasting gun resembles a small pistol. One hose supplies air and another supplies the sand. Air and sand are mixed in the gun and released together. The air hose must be a pressurized one, similar to those in gas stations. Most hardware stores carry these air guns. The gun has a trigger and with a minimum of practice you will be able to modify the pressure to whatever degree you want. Eventually the tip of the gun wears out, but it is easily replaced.

The sand hopper: A container for the sand, or hopper, is a must. An adequate size hopper will hold approximately five gallons of sand. It is best to situate the hopper above the working area, since the sand will feed by gravity into the gun.

The respirator and safety glasses: A respirator is an absolute essential in sandblasting. Breathing sand and powdered glass can be deadly, so be certain that the respirator you buy is a good one. Pinching pennies here is not common sense. The same rule applies to safety glasses. Use them whenever you sandblast.

The sandblasting booth: Where is the best area to sandblast? It is nice, but not necessary, to have a completely enclosed sandblasting booth with a viewing window and arm holes to work through. These booths can be expensive to buy, although you could build one yourself readily enough. For more than a year I sandblasted inside a large cardboard refrigerator box. It worked just fine. Naturally I used respirator and safety glasses. When working within the confines of a studio, however, perhaps an enclosed booth would be the best idea because little sand will escape. Unfortunately, an enclosed booth tends to be limiting and inhibiting. It is difficult to see the work up close or to remove small pieces of resist in the middle of the sandblasting procedure. This is especially true if you are wearing those heavy rubber gloves that generally go in the arm holes.

I prefer to be inside a booth with my piece of work. The propinquity is comforting—I can see close up exactly what I am doing, feel the glass, check it out from both sides, remove tiny bits of resist as I work from one side of the glass to the other. I remove bits of resist to enable shading to occur during the sandblasting process. The only problem with this cozy arrangement is that you get sand all over yourself. As long as I have respirator and glasses, I am quite at home inside this sand box. I follow up a sandblasting session with a long relaxing hot shower. If you use too much white glue as a resist, you may take the piece of glass to the shower with you.

My sandblasting "booth" is very freeform and consists of a corner of my garage. This area is draped on two walls and the floor with one large piece of black plastic. Black plastic offers a good contrast to the glass as I hold and sandblast it. The two outside walls are draped with clear shower curtain liners, which allow in natural light. I also have one fluorescent light suspended from the ceiling, but I often bring a secondary light with me for extra illumination. A fair amount of sand does manage to escape into the garage, and about once a year I sweep it all up, run it through an 80-grit sieve, and pour it back into my sand supply. I have found that a 100 pound sack of sand will last at least a year, maybe two. Since the entire booth is made out of draped plastic, it is easy to expand it for a large project or shrink it for something small. The whole thing couldn't cost more than $10, unless you use an extra expensive fluorescent light.

Sand: A number of different types of sand can be used in sandblasting. Even playground sand will cut glass. Look in the Yellow Pages under Sandblasting Supplies or Abrasive Equipment. Some lumberyards also carry sand for sandblasting. Most monument dealers sandblast their headstones and they can also be a source of sand. Silica sand is inexpensive and may be the best sand to try at first. It will work well for a time; the trouble is it eventually wears out because the individual grains become rounded with reuse. Many people who sandblast outdoors use silica sand.

For most sandblasting, an 80-grit sand will work just fine. The higher the number, the finer the sand, hence the smoother and whiter the sandblasted surface will be. However, the finer the sand, the less cutting force it will have. For deep cutting, use a coarse sand. Experiment with different grits to see which works best for what you have in mind. Some particularly sharp sands will do a great job on the glass, but they will also tear the resist to pieces.

A fairly expensive sand, but one that is long lasting, is aluminum oxide sand, a reddish sand that comes in several grits. Aluminum oxide has a good cutting edge and the grains of sand actually become sharper with use instead of duller. Because of its price, try to recover as much of it as possible. It will last forever if you recover it.

Different types of sand will give different textures to the glass surface. However, be careful not to mix sands in the sandblasting booth. It is horribly time consuming to sift them apart. An 80-grit sieve, found in a ceramic supply house, can be a fairly expensive item to add to your sandblasting equipment. However, a spatter lid made to cover a frying pan has a screen of about 80 grit and works just fine.

TECHNIQUE

One technique that I use in sandblasting is what I call progressive shading. In this method, a contrast is made between different areas by lightly blasting against heavily blasted areas. Imagine a group of shapes, such as clouds, one overlapping another. If the resist of the first cloud is pulled, but only that one section, then you can blast heavily along the edge that will contrast with the next cloud. The area can be shaded from a heavy blast at the top edge, to lighter blasting as the edge goes down to the bottom. Then the next cloud section's resist above is removed. Heavier blasting is done at the edge tip and gradually shaded down the bottom of the section, leaving a contrast between the lightly shaded area and the former heavily blasted edge of the first section. Each section can be done in such a progression, the contiguous edges being treated as you go. Small sections can be blasted in contrast to create fine detail. The progression may be done from side-to-side, top-to-bottom, or bottom-to-top, depending on what you want to achieve. The same method can be used with deep cuts in glass, only be sure to use several layers of resist here. Occasionally I deep cut detail lines that will not be affected by soft blasting. Then I do some progressive shading over the detail lines to give them a softer value. With experimentation, you will soon realize that a very slight hand can create stunning effects on glass, whereas deep cutting can be almost violently dramatic.

Don't be afraid of sandblasting. Try out different sands, different resists, and different techniques until you discover your own way of working. Then you will find that sandblasting is a kind of magic—like glass itself.

CHAPTER 15
Painting on Glass

WHY PAINT?

Since stained glass is already colored, why color it with paint?

If you ask that question you don't really understand that glass painting is not like painting on canvas. It's a way of working the light coming through the glass to achieve a special artistic statement in addition to the colorations in the glass itself. There are various techniques for accomplishing this modification.

Glass painting has little if anything to do with reflected light. It deals with transmitted light, light transitions, and taking away light. Paint should not be used arbitrarily over a surface. If paint obliterates the character and quality of the glass, it is being misused.

SHADING

Shading can be abrupt as in a direct transition between matt paint and unaffected glass, or gradual as in blending from a thick to a thin matt within the same piece of leaded glass. The range of effects is inexhaustible.

To belabor the obvious, stained glass, though colored, is not the same as glass colored by paint. Stained glass has been colored in the factory by the addition of various metallic oxides. Painted glass is stained glass that has been painted to enhance shadowing, details, or highlights to produce a totally different effect than that generated by the glass alone. The paint may or may not be fired, though in this chapter we deal exclusively with fired results.

WHAT ARE GLASS PAINTS?

The paints described here are used only in the stained glass craft. They have been, up til now, leaded paints and are mixtures of powdered glass along with other substances. Unleaded paints are now being produced and you should check with a supplier if you are worried about using leaded paints. However, if you use routine safety precautions you should have no difficulty with the standard paints on the market. We have been using them for years.

There is a difference between glass painter's paints and enamels. Enamels are low-fire, less wear-resistant colored paints that alter the underlying color of the glass and use the glass surface more or less as a canvas. One instance where enamels are used in glasswork is in the painting of Tiffany figures, especially Tiffany flesh (head, hands, feet, etc.). Tiffany painters generally employed an obscuring white paint for backgrounds. This is

---

PAINT ON COLORED GLASS:

* Blocks out or shades areas, thus enhancing others (matting).

* Directs light through specific detailed portions of the glass (highlighting).

* Saves a lead line by the use of a paint line or lines (tracing).

* Allows fine detailing of features, drapery, hair, etc. (stick lighting).

* Adds color on white or tinted glass for effect or detail (enameling).

* Provides intricate designs to a border (diapering).

* Changes color within a single piece of glass (staining).

* Facilitates mass production of glass items (silk screening).

* Provides additional depth to a subject (reverse glass painting).

* Allows blending over the glass surface that almost serves to slow down the light passing through it (double glazed painting).

* Produces texturing of the glass surface (stippling).

a basic ground for the Tiffany head style, as the obscuring white diffuses or obscures the light coming through the glass, forming a translucent backdrop. Other enamel colors are then added over the white to get the true Tiffany effect. Tiffany artists often double glazed the glass behind their semitransparent foreground glass to give depth and perspective to their work. However, enamels are vulnerable to weather and, if used in windows faced to the outside, must be protected against the elements. Even protected, many Tiffany painted details are faded because of the impermanent nature of the enamels.

Glass paints, as we employ the term, are high-fire permanent paints that have maintained their color for centuries despite exposure to heat, cold, snow, and rain.

COMPOSITION

Glass paint is composed of two substances—the vehicle and the coloring agent. The vehicle is glass. It is made the same way that glass is made, but with certain modifications. It is composed of red or white lead oxide, sand, boric acid, clay, alumina, sodium, and potassium, all in powder form. Some vehicles have a higher lead content, which makes for a softer (lower firing) glass, others a lower lead content which makes the vehicle higher firing.

These powders are first mixed and then, in a clay crucible, heated in a furnace to about 1800°F. The amount of heat is dependent on the type of color added to the vehicle. At 1800°F this mass of powder melts, fuses, and becomes a glass. This molten glob of glass is poured into water where it explodes. The amount of water used depends on how much glass you intend to pour in. Enough water must be used to allow the glass to cool instantly and crack and fragment to as great a degree as possible. This broken-up material is called a frit.

MAKING THE PAINT

The frit is placed in a ball mill, essentially a large jar half filled with a very dense porcelain material called barundum, and tumbled. Ball mills are very effective in reducing particle size. It can take from 48 to 72 hours to make a powder out of the frit, depending on the size of the mill.

The particle size must be watched carefully so the resulting powder is not too fine. Too fine a powder leads to a very poor grade of paint that cracks after firing. While such fine powder is not good for glass paints, it is some-

times used in china painting in the formation of raised ledges.

Once the particle size is correct, the wet powder is dried by evaporating the water. The result is a white substance resembling talcum powder (it may be yellowish if very high amounts of lead were used). This powder is called flux, a word that means different things to different craftspeople. We use it to mean something that causes something else to fire at a lower temperature than it ordinarily would.

This flux is the base of the paint. We must now add a color to it, since at this point the powder will form a sort of milky film. What is this color and where does it come from? In the Middle Ages and the Renaissance, glass painters made their colored glass a bit differently than we do today. They started by making a very soft (low firing) glass and added specific coloring agents directly to it in the molten state. Any metallic oxide would serve: cobalt for blue, copper for green, manganese and iron and antimony—all would color the molten glass according to its disposition. Gold from gold coins was used to make a deep ruby color. Some of these coloring methods are still used today, though gold coins are used for other purposes these days.

If you want to try to make ruby glass, try throwing some gold coins into melted down glassware. You will find, to your financial embarrassment, that the glass will stay clear. However, if you then take this glass down to a somewhat lower temperature, throw in the gold coin and hold the temperature constant, you will be rewarded by seeing the glass turn ruby. This process is called "striking the color" and it was well known in the Middle Ages. The molten glass begins to grow a colloid of gold. A colloid is a suspension of particles in a liquid that never settle out, such as milk. These particles are infinitesimally small. In fact, the smaller the particle size the redder the color. As the particle size gets larger—if too much gold is added for the amount of glass available—the color begins to move from red to maroon to blue.

This was how the old "pot metal" glass was made, but when it came to making a colored paint, early painters found they needed a medium that would hold the color to the already existing glass. They were looking for colors to block out the light. They weren't interested in transparent colors because they already had transparent color in the glass. They used umber (an iron oxide), oxides of manganese, or any of the earthy metallic oxides available to them. These they ground and mixed with a frit (glass), and mulled the whole thing into a fine powder. When this was mixed with water it would flow over the glass surface and when fired, the frit would melt onto the surface and hold the color in place.

Paint manufacturers today mix substances such as cobalt, chrome, clay, and alumina together with sand and fire it to 2600°F. At this point, all these elements fuse (they do not melt) and form a "clinker." This is almost like an ash. The clinker is formed through a solid state reaction during which the cobalt and chrome join together with the silica and form a spinner, a chrome alumina silicate. This is a black pigment which is insoluble in glass. The manufacturer grinds the clinker into a powder. The two ingredients for paint are now side-by-side—black powder and flux powder from the frit. When these are mixed, you have a black opaque trace paint that is estimable for use on glass.

Two heads painted, as often is the case, against black (painted) backgrounds so the background light will be blocked and forced through the foreground faces, adding a very dramatic quality to extremely visual painted details.

THE REUSCHE CATALOG

The Reusche Co. in Newark, New Jersey, is the great paint supplier to the stained glass trade. Their catalog is important to anyone doing stained glass or china painting. It lists a great number and variety of paints. This can be confusing to the novice who must differentiate glass paints from china paints. The glass stainer's paints fall into two main categories: those manufactured by Hancock and those by Drakenfeld. There are subtle differences between the two. The Hancock paints seem to have better resistance to weather. However, Hancock colors are not as uniform from firing to firing and can be more difficult to work with than Drakenfeld colors, tending to be gritty and to require grinding with muller and palette to get them to flow smoothly. You should use both and decide for yourself which you prefer.

Throughout much of the history of painting on stained glass, clear glass was another alternative. This technique, called grisaille (gray), is splendidly shown on the famous "5 Sisters" windows of York Cathedral. There is no reason why you cannot paint on window glass since many subtle effects can be achieved that might be missed because of underlying color. As a practical matter, you should practice your painting strokes on clear glass because it's less expensive than stained glass. Also, more light is available through clear glass to show your mistakes.

WORK AREA AND MATERIALS

You should have enough space to not be cramped and enough atmosphere to avoid breathing in dust and fumes. This applies to any work in stained glass, which can have noxious byproducts. You will use vinegar and certain oils and alcohols, to say nothing of the powdered paints which contain lead. Allowance should be made for these odors to dissipate. Glass painting requires a light table which can be hard on the eyes if you're using it constantly. Some painters mask out portions of their light table that are not directly needed for the work at hand to take the strain off their eyes.

An ideal setting allows for natural light through a window equipped with a shade so the light may be controlled. Below the window might be the tracing table/easel. Behind the work surface, perhaps a curtain to keep extraneous lighting from penetrating the area. An artificial light behind the worker is convenient. A source of water should be available near the work area. If you are using the kitchen sink to wash out brushes etc., you should wash away all traces of paint before putting any food in the basin.

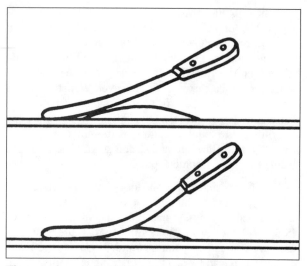

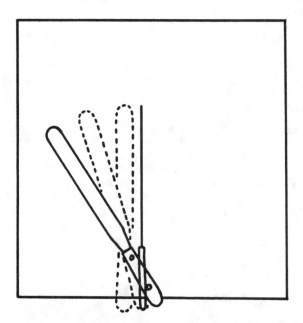

The spatula must be held at an angle so it will stir as much paint as possible per stroke. Incorrect position (top): The spatula is barely touching the pile of paint, and mixing, no matter how energetic, will be inefficient. Correct position (bottom): The spatula is directly contacting the paint and can move around large portions of it.

Positions of the spatula in mixing, from flat to the palette to an angle of approximately 90°. During the mixing process, the spatula keeps rising and flattening, guided by the wrist, so as to constantly gather fresh paint under the survace of the blade.

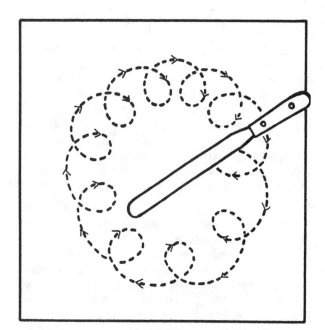

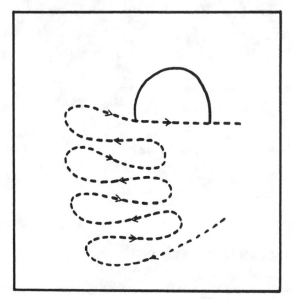

In addition to the spatula blade lifting up and down, it travels around the palette to mix all the paint that is there.

Alternate mixing pattern. This one goes from side to side.

STORAGE

The more tools and supplies you have on hand, the more effectively you will work if they aren't all over the place. A small cabinet with drawers is inexpensive and ideally suited. Allow for storage niches and shelves. Baby food jars are good for storing paint. The paper packets that paint comes in are awkward to store. They develop holes, get paint dust all over them, are difficult to find, and difficult to measure from. Make a hole in the center of the lid of a baby food jar and attach the lid with a screw to the bottom of a shelf.

Brushes are best stored lying flat in a cigar box or any small toolbox. Don't store brushes upside down in a jar since this will splay the hair and make them unusable.

A glass painter's carryall. Note the palette knife alongside the brushes in the bottom.

Paint palettes can be stored in a palette box. It's easy to make your own. Allow room for the palette box when designing the work space. A storage area should be reserved for drawings and cartoons, which can be stored rolled up both to save room and for their protection.

Clear glass squares for testing color and consistency are also good to have on hand. These can be stored in those wire separators used for storing phonograph records or dishes.

The work area should not be too damp, cold, or humid. Any or all of these will affect the paint. Vinegar trace paint is especially susceptible to changes in humidity. Air conditioning in the summer and a humidifier or dehumidifier in the winter can make for an effective work space. You don't need a hood or a fan going when you paint nor do you have to keep the windows open, but proper ventilation is very important when working with any chemicals.

Keep your materials in good working order. Brushes caked with last week's paint on their bristles or carelessly put down in puddles of sticky gum or oil will not do the best job for you. Clutter is self defeating in any craft; when working with pieces of glass it can also be dangerous.

Be careful with food and drink in the workplace. Make certain your hands are clean before nibbling on that sandwich or piece of fruit. Glass paint is not particularly digestible. It's best never to mix food and your work. Needless to say, keep all paints away from children.

If you leave paint on the palette overnight, you may find some dust has settled into it. Just blow it off. Paint costs money and a little dust won't hurt it. Grease or grime is something else. In such a case, you have to clean the entire palette.

MAKING A GLASS PALETTE

Painting on glass requires palettes where you can mix and blend colors. You will mix the paint with several materials as well as other paints. Each color of matt, trace, or stain should have its own palette for convenience; that way you don't have to keep cleaning off and washing up.

Palettes can be 1/4" clear plate glass, approximately 12" x 12". Sand the edges and round the corners. Roughen the surface in the center so you have a 4" textured circle by grinding carborundum (silicon carbide) grit into the glass with a glass muller. The muller is essential and should be purchased with the paints and brushes. Mullers are available from glass paint suppliers and come in different sizes. Carborundum grit is available at hardware stores.

Roughen the palette by placing a small amount of carborundum (mixed with water to make it pasty) in the center of the glass and grinding with the muller. Use a small circular motion and moderate pressure. The palette should be on an even surface on a layer of newspaper. As you progress, the glass will become cloudy and then more and more translucent. Feel the surface from time to time to get an idea of the roughness. The process shouldn't take more than 15 minutes. The rough surface will make mixing more effective.

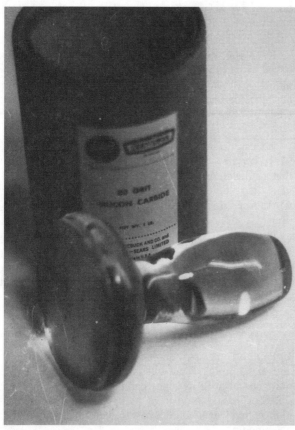

A glass muller and a can of carborundum to grind a palette.

A typical palette box showing several palettes.

MAKING A PALETTE BOX

This is a closed container with runners on either side to hold palettes. All the palettes should be made the same size to fit in the box. Allow for accumulating a number of palettes. The cabinet of an old hi-fi speaker or any wooden box will serve. We use a palette box made from two small speaker cabinets put together to allow for depth. Ours is 19" high, 12" deep, and 11" wide. Wooden strips support the individual palettes inside. Allow enough room between palettes to remove and replace them. Put a back on the box for stability. The type of paint on each palette can be scratched with a fine point into the dried paint on the palette itself. That way you won't have to guess at the color.

THE EASEL

This piece of equipment is used for waxing up, a process we will discuss later. It can be as simple as a piece of clear plate glass raised to a 45° angle. An easel can be two long angle irons joined top and bottom with supports for the clear glass. This may be leaned against a window since natural light is best for glass painting. If you are painting small pieces of glass a few at a time, you can make a table easel or a self-supporting self-lighting easel from a small light box on end. An x-ray view box is perfect for this. We purchased a used one from a surgical supply house and replaced its plastic surface with a piece of white opalescent glass. It is portable and the angle can be almost vertical—a great help in getting perspective correct.

THE LIGHT TABLE

The light table is used for tracing, stick lighting, and diapering as well as checking colors. You'll need one for any kind of stained glass work. The light comes from below and is spread over the surface as evenly as possible. Fluorescent lighting is most frequently used, because incandescent bulbs tend to create hot spots which will give false value readings. Incandescent bulbs are much warmer than fluorescent and will dry the tracing color too quickly.

Place the lights as far from the surface as possible. This helps spread light on the surface and diminishes clustering of light from the individual fluorescent tubes. Our light table is a combination light table and easel. The top portion is hinged so that it can swing up and be braced during the matting process. This eliminates the need for a separate easel, and can also be used with natural light. It is a very convenient space saver.

A light table showing a portion of it raised and supported to make an easel. Such a double use saves a lot of space.

THE MAHL

The mahl stick is basically a hand rest used for support when working on the easel. Since one end of it rests directly on the glass of the easel, it must be padded to avoid breaking the glass or slipping over its surface. The mahl stick is held at the unpadded end with the non-painting hand to support the working hand. Sign painters use mahl sticks to help make large sweeping strokes, as a guide as much as a support. In glass painting it is used primarily as a support.

You can make a mahl from a 1/2" wooden dowel about 26" long. If it is much shorter, it will inhibit your arm motions; much longer and it becomes awkward to manage. Pad the end of the mahl stick with a dry piece of thick kitchen sponge, cut in a 1-1/2" circle. Cut a hole in the center the size of the dowel and glue the sponge to the end of the stick. The porous sponge won't slip on the glass. You can also wrap one end of the stick with cotton and tie or tape a piece of rag over it to make a bulbous end. There should be between 1/2" to 3/4" of soft material around the end of the stick.

Using the mahl. The artist is supporting the painting hand on the mahl as she works on the easel on a waxed up portrait. The soft end of the easel is against the glass of the easel.

THE BRIDGE

Like the mahl stick, the bridge is easy to make. The bridge is used both for support and for technical aid. It's merely pieces of wood nailed together to form a raised surface with enough room for the hand to slide on. We use a bridge 20" to 22" in length and about 1-1/2" to 2-1/2" high. Get a feel for the proper height of the bridge before nailing or gluing the elements together. Make sure the top is sanded smooth so you don't get splinters.

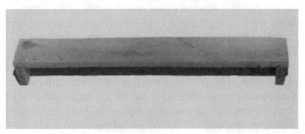

The bridge, a necessary tool in glass painting, is a focal point for keeping the painting hand off the glass while giving it a place to rest while making trace strokes. You can make your own bridge from three pieces of wood.

Students practicing painting strokes on a light table using the bridge.

THE MULLER

The muller is similar to a pestle. It is made of glass, not porcelain, with a thick stem attached to a flat grinding surface. Mullers are used to grind all gritty paints, though some workers routinely grind all paints; a process we have found unnecessary.

GUM ARABIC

Often referred to simply as 0gum, this is an essential ingredient for painting. It comes in both powder and liquid form and is available at most art supply stores. Either form works well. Purchase a minimal amount since you will only use a little at a time and a small amount goes a long way. It's hard to dictate how much gum arabic to use, since it depends on individual preference, but the classic instruction is to make it appear on the paint pile as snow on a mountain top. In reality, it will be trial and error. The more gum you use, the less flow you will have from the paint. If you use too little gum, the paint may not stick to the glass or may flake when fired.

PALETTE KNIVES

You'll need several. Use different palette knives for trace, matt, stain, and oil so you don't contaminate the different mixes. Palette knives are used to mix the color on the glass palette to get the right consistency and to blend the ingredients. The technique of mixing paint is not as easy as it may seem.

Because these knives are constantly being honed through their use, they can develop edges as sharp as a razor. Don't run your finger over the edge of the palette knife to see how sharp it is; but do round the edges with carborundum paper occasionally.

WAX

There are as many mixes of wax as there are painters. Beeswax can be used by itself or with resin to make it stiffer. Wax is used to hold pieces of glass to the easel during the painting process. You can purchase resin and chunks of beeswax from paint suppliers.

To mix the two, heat the beeswax in a regular pot (a double boiler is not necessary), making sure the wax doesn't catch fire (have a cover ready), and add the resin a little at a time. Glass medicine droppers are fine for putting melted beeswax mix on the corners of the glass to hold it on the easel. We drill a hole in the pot handle to store our medicine dropper in; it's easier to find that way.

Check the wax mix; if it is too soft and tends to be runny, add more resin. The glass painted pieces should be easy to remove from the easel by prying with a spatula; therefore the wax has to grip and release instantly. Too much resin makes the wax less adherent; too little makes it gummy.

Wax is reusable. Don't worry if it has some paint in it—wax isn't really any good until it has become mixed with a lot of color and has a professional "employed" look.

·"Thumb wax" is a ball of wax you hold in one hand so you can pinch off pieces with the other. It is used for quick temporary stickups on the easel, either for pieces of glass or pattern to check color or shape. Placing glass on the easel in this manner is called "stopping in." You can put a number of pieces of glass on the easel with thumb wax, take them down and substitute others, then lock them in with beeswax.

Formula for thumb wax:

1 lb. beeswax (453 grams)

1 lb. cornstarch (453 grams)

4 ounces resin (113 grams)

7 ounces Venice turpentine (198 grams)

1-3/4 ounces sweet oil
 (olive oil, measure 35 cc)

Melt the wax in a double boiler. Add cornstarch one tablespoon at a time, stirring the mixture thoroughly after each spoonful. Add the resin, turpentine, and oil. When thoroughly mixed, pour into a muffin or cookie tin and allow to cool. Don't put it where someone will try to eat it.

NEEDLES, QUILLS, AND STICKS

These are all used for taking out the lights (scraping away paint to allow a measured amount of light to come through) stick lighting, or highlighting of one form or another. Each may produce certain effects and can also be used to clean up the edges of a spotty trace line. They are useful for diapering, outlining, highlighting hairlines, among other things.

Demonstrating the varying quantities of paint a needle can remove.

With sticks, make one end pointed, the other chisel shaped. Chopsticks serve well if they are made from bamboo, a hardwood which won't lose its point. Metal pointed objects do not work as well as wood, tending to slide on the glass during use.

BRUSHES

Brushes come in different shapes and are made from varied materials. You only need a few to paint, at least initially. Don't be confused by the names in the Reusche catalog, which shows brushes dealing with techniques from scrolling to shading, from grounding to tinting. These brushes are meant for china painting. Others are special glass painting brushes you won't need as a beginner, such as deerfoot stipplers and certain of the tinting brushes. These are used for the specialized oil and alcohol techniques of glass painting which you may want to experiment with at a future time.

Each brush will give you a different result, since each is meant for a specific job. Brushes usually come with some sort of protection for their bristles—either a cardboard or plastic sleeve. Use these and don't lose them. They will help maintain the shape. Always store brushes flat. Storing them handle down in a glass will make the bristles flair out and ruin the brush, though some painters like their blender bristles with this outward curvature and purposely keep them upside-down. New brushes are stiff, the bristles protected with gum arabic. Dip any new brush in water before using and give it a good soaking to let the bristles splay out to their natural shape.

THE BADGER BLENDER

Badger hair is used to make one of the most important of all glass painting brushes, the badger blender. This brush is used in the matting process and is the most expensive brush you will buy. It is used to distribute matt paint, first over the glass then to gather the matt into specific areas and, finally, to blend these areas together. Matt can be spread uniformly or irregularly, thick or thin, patterned, smooth, or crosshatched. This brush will do all these jobs and more.

A typical badger blender is about 11" from handle tip to the end of the bristle and about 4" wide. They come in at least two price ranges: cheaper and expensive. Other brushes have been substituted for the badger (most popular are old-fashioned round shaving brushes). While they may be worthwhile for individual effects, they lack the sweep of the flat badger for even blending. No round brush is the same as a flat one because the bristles tend push the matt rather than spread it in a wide homogeneous plane.

If you are going to do any serious painting, a good badger blender should be among your first purchases. The cheaper blenders have thinner tufts of hair and may shed hairs that get into the matt and must be picked out. You may not notice these hairs until the matt has dried, in which case, after picking out the hair, you will have to re-blend the area to remove the marks. You may be ready to tear out your own hair at this point.

Cleaning the Blender

Since only the tips of the blender hairs get wet, cleaning them is not a big job but it is a constant one. These hair tips dry rather quickly and as matt paint dries on the tips, the hairs will chip into the matt. Excessive moisture on the hairs will make the blending effect just about impossible, so one is constantly cleaning this brush.

There are a couple of quick ways to clean the blender. You can twirl it bristles down (so the wet paint that comes flying off doesn't get you in the face); after the paint has dried you can dust it against a stiff surface such as a table

leg or your leg if you're wearing old clothes. Whatever you do, don't dust the blender against sharp edges or you'll cut the hairs. If you are using stain (we'll get into this later) have a cheap blender available since silver nitrate (which is what stain is composed of) dries out the hairs and will eventually ruin the brush.

TRACERS

The other basic glass painting brush is the tracer. Tracers are long-haired brushes that come to a point. Learning to use a tracer is not easy, partly because their hair is so long they tend to bend and flex on their own. They are used to produce straight, curved, circular, or wiggly lines that follow an underlying pattern. Although they come in various sizes and are made from various types of hairs, their basic shape is pretty much the same.

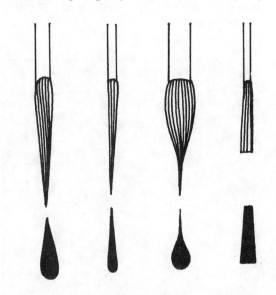

Four tracing brushes showing the basic shape of different strokes. These strokes are the same whether the brush is oxhair, camel, or sable.

Some of the finest tracing brushes are the French oxhair series 30 (in the Reusche catalog) sizes 3, 7, and 9. They will do to start you off. The camel hair tracer series 3 are also excellent, although they tend to be very responsive to subtle variations of pressure which can be disconcerting for beginners. This is due more to the configuration of the brush than the hair.

The red sable brush is also a fine tool, though some consider it better suited to oil tracing than vinegar and water, which is what you start off with. Red sable hair seems to be less porous than either oxhair or camel hair so this type of brush does not hold as much paint per stroke as they do. While a camel or oxhair brush will provide a longer, more flowing line in a single stroke, a sable tracer is excellent for producing thin lines of equal consistency.

Use a sable hair brush for very fine line detail; a camel or oxhair for a more flowing stroke with thick and thin variations. As a beginner if you want only one tracer, get the oxhair. (Incidentally, camel brushes are made from the hair of a Russian squirrel; camel is the name of the man who discovered it.)

All the above brushes are handmade. That's one of the reasons they are priced as they are.

Sizes

Whichever tracer you buy, we recommend you purchase three different sizes—small, medium, and large (or thin, medium, and thick, sizes 3, 7, and 9) from series 30 in the Reusche catalog. This will allow you to practice with each size.

A tracer should give a continuous flow of paint along the line of a single stroke. That's why tracers have such long hairs in proportion to their width; these long hairs act as paint reservoirs. A tracing brush, unlike a watercolor brush, is not meant to dab. The idea is to keep the brush down, keep it moving, keep it steady, and outline whatever you are tracing with bold continuous strokes. This takes practice (we cannot emphasize this enough).

STIPPLERS

Stippling is a form of shading in which a myriad of tiny dots is formed in the matt. The matt can be laid on with a stippling brush or applied with a blender and then stippled. Sometimes the blender hairs themselves are used to stipple, and often a pig bristle or other bristle brush is used to provide the proper texture.

A good stippling brush is next in importance to tracers and blender, and we recommend the English glass stainer's stippler series 32-A in the Reusche catalog.

MATT BRUSHES

Never use the badger blender to apply matt. If you do, you will spend a lot of time cleaning it. For applying matt, we recommend the 1-1/2" camel brush, series 18 in the

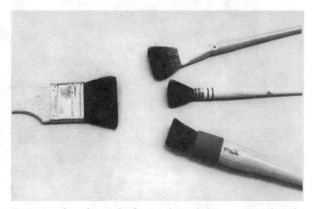

Oxhair tracers in size 9, 7, and 3. Note how each size brush paints a totally different line in width and character.

Painting brushes (clockwise from left): matting brush, tinting brush, deerfoot stippler, and hard stippler. A matting brush not only puts matt on the work, it can also stipple. It is a wide soft hair brush and is sort of all-purpose. The tinting brush is for delicate shading, almost like a cosmetic brush. The deerfoot stippler is for just a touch of stippling, while the hard stippler hammers the stippling into the paint.

Reusche catalog, which coats a very even matt. This brush can also be used as a small blender or shadower for applying shadow under eyes or along the nose or cheek. The 3/4" or 1/2" tinting brushes will also do this job nicely.

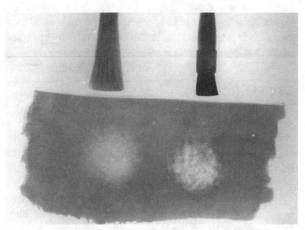

Quantitative stippling. On the left, a soft stipple as from a deerfoot stippler. On the right, a hard stipple from the rather inflexible bristles of the hard stippler.

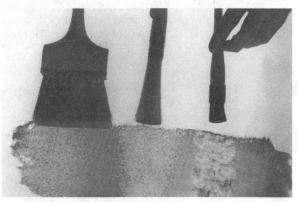

More stippling. Here are the effects in dry matt paint of 1) the hard bristle brush, 2) the pig bristle brush, and 3) the badger blender used as a stippler. Stippling is not only a measure of the type and rigidity of the bristles, but also of the length of time involved in the procedure. It is possible to completely wear away the matt with a deerfoot stippler, given enough time. The idea is to accomplish the proper shading with the proper brush in the least amount of time. It is not necessary to have every brush in your toolbox. You can use one stippler for all stippling until you learn the way other brushes handle this procedure.

TINTING BRUSHES

While tinting brushes are generally for ceramic rather than glass painting, they do cross the line. They are very soft fluffy wide brushes, useful in matting and blending small areas. We use them a lot for facial features where a small expanse is being worked. Among others, the 1/2" Reusche series 16 tinting brush is a fine worker.

LETTERING BRUSHES

This is usually a sable brush cut in chisel fashion straight across the end to make the square-shaped strokes that are particularly important when doing lettering. The hair setting is parallel to enable an even line width. These brushes are available in art supply stores in a variety of widths from 1/16" to 1-1/2". The wider brushes, which have a flat rather than round ferrule, also make very appropriate matting brushes.

MISCELLANEOUS BRUSHES

In addition to the above, you will want a number of cheap brushes available at any art supply store. You can cut and sear the hairs to make all sorts of shapes for very specific purposes. One major use is taking out the lights, or removing matt paint during the highlighting process. A firm non-absorbent ball-shaped brush is best for this. Plastic hairs will do nicely, so you can form a nice ball by searing them. Other cheap brushes can be used for special effects, especially shading and shadowing trace lines. As you progress in the painting field you will learn the types of brushes you work with most comfortably and, when you can't find them, you'll learn to create them.

FIRING PROCEDURES

A small inexpensive ceramic kiln will serve your purposes for firing painted glass; at least at the beginning when you'll fire small pieces. Make sure you have a pyrometer to register the temperature of the kiln. Since kiln information is found in another section of this book, we will merely note some special firing information that applies strictly to painted glass.

Before firing, the kiln shelves should be coated with kiln wash to prevent the fired pieces from sticking to the shelves, especially if you are firing a silver-stained piece which is fired stained side down, or if you are firing pieces that are painted on both sides. If you are firing only a single painted side up (facing you) the wash can be dispensed with. Washing shelves with separator such as kiln wash is more essential when firing ceramic pieces or doing stained glass fusing where the temperatures go much higher.

We prefer electric top loading kilns to front loaders because we like to look in and see how our pieces are doing. We never go strictly by the pyrometer to tell when our pieces are done or look through the peephole. We prefer to crack the kiln. We may provoke a brief drop in temperature doing this but we've never had a piece of glass crack unless we've gotten careless and looked too long. Then you may well hear the distinctive ping of glass that has not made it.

Normal peak firing of most painted glass occurs at about 1100°F. Tack firing (used when firing the same piece of glass more than once to get the paint to adhere before adding another layer) generally runs from 950°F to 1050°F. Once the proper firing temperature is reached, the kiln is turned off and allowed to cool. Because these temperatures vary with the type of glass and paint used, it is very difficult to know when painted glass is precisely fired to completion. You have to fire and observe a great number of different glasses to know when one is done. That's why we like to look. When the glass has a moderate red glow, it has usually fired properly, regardless of what the temperature may read.

It's tricky. Leave the glass in too long and the edges will round and shrink back, reducing the size of the piece. If you don't fire long enough, the paint won't fire in properly and will look dull instead of shiny and may even flake off in spots.

Whatever type of kiln you use, acquaint yourself with its particular characteristics as well as those of the glass you are firing before you trying to determine when the glass has fired properly. One thing seems certain: we have found no difference in the way painted glass reacts to heat from a gas or electric kiln. The difference is a matter of convenience.

One classic type of kiln for large window fabrication is the flash kiln, where the glass and flame are in the same chamber. The flash kiln is very fast firing, which is most advantageous if you are doing a large amount of work. You can fire some flash kilns in eight to 12 minutes, then move the glass out of the firing chamber to cool slowly in an adjacent area of the kiln. These kilns are expensive and not many are made these days, since many major studios have gone out of existence, but those that are still around last a long time.

Either bottled or regular gas may be used in a flash kiln. The gas jets are on the side of the firing chamber, tilted up toward the dome of the kiln. The glass pieces ride in an asbestos tray below them. The burners sweep the fire up to the crown of the kiln, instantly permeating the chamber with a high heat or flash. The glass fires very readily, so flash kilns don't require a pyrometer. The worker goes by eye to determine when the glass is done.

The reason the heat can be brought up so swiftly without cracking the glass is that the glass is very evenly heated. Cooling is another matter. Many flash kilns have trays on racks which are then moved out to a slow cooling device called a lehr.

Cooling

It's best to let the glass cool overnight with the kiln closed. By morning you can safely remove the pieces. If you want to push this process a bit you can open the top of the kiln directly after firing and watch the pyrometer very carefully. You can cool the glass fairly rapidly down to a crucial point, around 520°F. Most painted glass fires at around 1100°F. At 520°F the silicate in the glass inverts to either an alpha or beta quartz. It is an area of expansion and if the cooling is too rapid, the glass will fragment. At this point you must close the kiln and leave it closed until this point is passed. Then you can cool the glass quickly by reopening the kiln.

Workers in full production have no time to wait out a long cooling process or take the chance with fast cooling. This is a bit risky, and if you don't want to take chances we recommend slow cooling in a closed kiln.

We have been purposely vague about the critical cooling point because you must experiment with your own kiln to find out exactly where it is. It should be near 520°F but this varies. You may find the glass will start to ping somewhere above or below this temperature. You may find that the glass has no critical range but cools rapidly right down to a point where you can remove it from the kiln with no problems. The smaller the piece of glass, the more likely it is that this will happen. Larger pieces (over 6" x 8") may break when you try this.

On the other hand, you may be lucky. We have rapidly cooled pieces larger than 8" x 10" with no breakage. We just open the top of the kiln and walk away. However, this could get you in trouble. It is much safer to watch for the critical zone and safer still to allow the glass to slowly cool for the requisite length of time.

Multiple Firings

It is possible to fire a piece of painted glass seven times or more, each for a different color, value, or stain. Occasionally the stain itself is multiple fired to vary its values.

Naturally you want each firing to do as much as possible, to combine many different values or shadings per piece. It's cheaper that way and saves time. One way to do this is to use vehicles (media that carry the color) that do not mix, which will allow you to paint over another vehicle's color or matt without spoiling it and thus fire two or more layers of paint at a time.

In multiple firings, the glass must be cooled more slowly than a single firing. The stresses and strains that occur from a single firing are multiplied by additional firings and coolings. These stresses take effect mostly during the cooling period when the coefficient of expansion of the glass is strained to its utmost.

Tack Firing

As we mentioned earlier, not all multiple firings need go to the maximum firing temperature. A piece of glass can be tack fired—partly fired, perhaps 60% to 70% of the maximum, so while the paint does not totally imbed, it will adhere enough (once the glass has cooled) for you to apply other color or stain. Once all the colors are applied and each has been tack fired, you can give the glass a final firing up to the proper firing temperature to make sure all the paint imbeds. In this way you save time and alleviate many of the potential stresses of repeatedly firing the glass to the maximum.

TRACE PAINTING

Trace lines are done with a tracing brush and are usually opaque. They can be any color but are most commonly black. In fact, we use the phrase "black trace" almost as a generic term. Trace lines generally follow a cartoon or pattern placed under the glass. If the trace lines are translucent, they are called halftones and for our exercises here are considered poor technique.

Trace lines can be purposefully translucent, as in some realistic flesh painting such as Tiffany figures. In these instances, the lines will be put on almost as a matt, though with greater density. There are no strict rules; trace paint can be used as a matt paint or a matt paint as a tracing paint. Nothing in the composition of either rules out its use in either fashion. The difficulty lies in nomenclature, not physical properties. Still it is just as well that beginners differentiate the two paints. It makes things less confusing at this early learning stage.

Tracing Procedure

Start the tracing exercise with a *clean* piece of window glass. Dirt or any foreign matter on its surface will interfere with the paint flowing properly. Commercial window cleaners tend to leave a residue over the glass which can prevent the paint from adhering and cloud it so you cannot see the underlying trace lines, or worse, add impurities that will show up after the glass has been fired. The easiest and best way to clean a piece of glass is to smear a little wet paint on its surfaces and rub it around. The grittiness of the paint will make the glass bright and shiny. The amount of paint you waste doing this is inconsequential. Wet kiln wash will also do a good job. Wipe the glass with newspaper or a clean rag.

If you are dealing with scrap glass that has putty on it, clean it with a handful of sodium phosphate in a pail of water. Be sure to use rubber gloves when doing this. Put the glass in the pail and let it stand for an hour to soften the putty, then scrape it clean.

Once the glass is clean, lay out the tracing brushes you intend to use. Three different sizes will be enough to begin with and you may never need or want more. You will practice tracing without a cartoon line to follow just to get used to the feel of the brush.

First grind the paint, not because it needs it but for the practice and because it's a ritual. Use a spatula to put a small amount of paint on the ground glass center of a palette. Make concentric circles with a muller, catching the paint between the muller bottom and the rough glass. A few moments of this should suffice to let you know how it used to be done. You have now entered the realm of the glass painter.

Now mix the paint with gum arabic and either water or vinegar as a vehicle. The gum is a bonding agent to bond paint, vehicle, and glass. Without it the paint will not have enough body, the traced line may smudge rather than flow, and the matted area won't blend well.

Some painters add a little sugar or glycerin to the paint to retard the vehicle's drying time and help the paint preserve a more even depth in the traced line. These ingredients do not take the place of gum but they may give a more uniform look to the color. Such additions are especially effective when you want a deep dark color over a fairly large area of glass.

The ratio of gum to paint is a matter of personal preference based on experience. A ratio of one part gum to 32 parts paint has been mentioned in the literature, but who's going to take time to measure it out? Most painters go by eye. However, without experience your eye is liable to add too much or too little. Let's try another method. Sprinkle gum over the pile of paint so that it resembles a very light snowfall or, as one student put it, dandruff on a dark suit. With this picture in mind, you can see that not a lot of gum is necessary. If you are using liquid gum, one tablespoon of paint would take 1/4 teaspoon of 14 Baum strength liquid gum. This mixture comes out of the kiln with a smooth uniform paint line.

For the paint, let's say you will use Drakenfeld tracing black #E-458. There are a number of good tracing blacks; this is one of our favorites. Others with equally good consistency are Drakenfeld #401 and #2877. Pile a moderate amount of paint in the center of the palette, add gum as indicated above, mix dry, then re-pile the mix and, with the tip of a spatula, make a small hole in the middle of the pile. Into this hole pour water or vinegar. Let's try water first.

Water Trace

Pour a little water into the hole you've scooped in the pile of paint; no more than a couple teaspoons. Fold the sides of the hole into this center well of water so that as much of the paint as possible is exposed to moisture at the same time. Start the mixing process using a spatula. Keep raising the left side of the spatula (if you are right-handed) as you go to catch more paint. Use a circular motion to mix and keep scraping the pile together in the center of the palette so that you are not just pushing around the same portion of mix. Add water as needed to mix adequately.

The water will keep evaporating and the tendency is to add too much. Then you have to add more paint to compensate for the water and more gum arabic to compensate for the paint. This leads to starting over. The consistency of the final mix should resemble sour cream. Once you have it at this stage, dip the brush in it and try a few practice lines on the palette to check paint flow. When these lines are dry, run the back of the brush handle over them at right angles to see if there is any chipping. Gum tends to flow to the sides of the lines. If flakes chip away there is too much gum arabic and you must add more water and paint. If the cross lines are clean, the mix is probably fine.

Vinegar Trace

White vinegar may be used instead of water. Fresh, undiluted vinegar is best. Do not mix it with water, use it straight from the bottle. Vinegar gives a different flow to the paint than water; there is more of a "bite" from brush to glass surface and some painters say the paint flows more smoothly with vinegar. Another reason for using vinegar is to save a firing. Unfired vinegar trace will stick to the glass when it is matted over with a water matt, whereas water trace will smudge. When water trace is used, the glass must be fired (tack fired, perhaps) and then a matt applied over the partially fired trace lines. The piece must then be fired again.

The Bridge

You cannot do any substantial tracing without knowing how to use the bridge. This tool can make the difference between a professional result and a frustrated series of attempts. The bridge is not a glorified hand rest. Its use involves a precise technique which, while it may seem awkward at first, will pay off later.

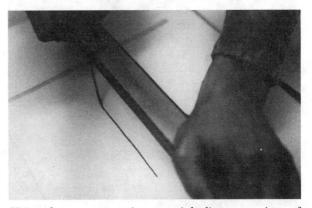

Using the tracer to paint a straight line on a piece of glass. In this instance, the bridge is used as a straight edge. The tracing brush is first loaded with paint, then simply follows the edge of the bridge which is held firmly in place with the non-working hand.

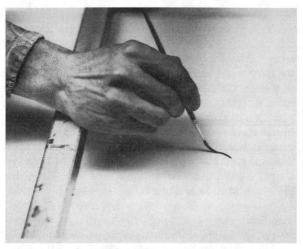

Tracing an arc. The beginning stroke being pulled with finger motion back toward the bridge.

The complete arc showing the resting position of the hand on the bridge. The brush is at the center of the arc and can swing using finger and palm motion from one side of the arc to the other. This is a good practice exercise.

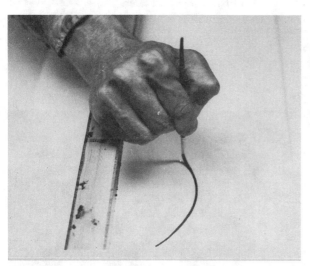

Concluding the arc stroke. Note the tucked under position of the brush. This arc has been done in a single stroke, which is the purpose of the excercise.

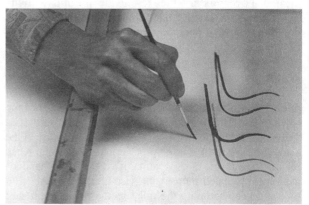

Combination of curves and straight lines. Start at the bottom, trace the curved line, then bring it up straight. A good exercise for wrist motion. Practice using various widths of tracers.

1) Hold the bridge approximately parallel to the line you are tracing. As you follow the line down, your hand should move on its heel along the bridge. It is the heel of the hand that provides the fulcrum for most of the tracing done from the bridge. The fingers and wrist revolve around this area.

2) Try not to lift the heel of your hand off the bridge. Initially you may have to fight this tendency. If you must lift your hand to follow a particular line, lift the front part of your hand up or down (if a curve is to be accomplished or more pressure on the brush is required), but keep the heel stable on the bridge.

3) Hold the bridge from the bottom with the working hand above the holding hand. The tendency of many students is to hold the bridge from the top. This puts one hand in the other's way and the upper hand will limit the type of strokes you can do. It will also limit your ability to see what is going on.

4) You can use the bridge as a straight edge for the tracer.

5) Where you place the bridge can have an effect on your work. Get comfortable with it.

6) Try to make the best use of the natural arch of your hand which is poised on the bridge some distance above the work. This allows a greater range of movement than if your hand were resting directly on the glass.

7) You may have to move the bridge to complete a stroke. Where possible, try to accomplish every stroke within the range of a single bridge position.

8) The bridge should be held close enough to a trace line so you don't have to stretch awkwardly.

To sum up: The bridge is held parallel to the line of work. The hand rests on the heel, angled to get maximum wrist and finger mobility. The tracer is held securely but not in a pinched fashion, the bridge positioned so the tracer is at almost right angles to the glass. With a slight motion of the wrist, the pressure on the brush can be increased or decreased to accomplish thick or thin strokes or a combination within the same line. And yes, it takes lots of practice.

Loading the Tracer Brush

Twirl the full length of the brush hairs in color so all hairs pick up paint. Tracers are long-haired brushes so they can hold a reservoir of paint that allows the completion of lines in a single stroke. The idea is to get a *brush* full of paint, not a *tip* full. Load paint into the back portion of the brush. If this area stays dry, you will run out of paint. Once it is loaded, draw the brush across the palette to restore the proper placement of hairs which have splayed from being swirled. The hairs will fall into a rounded surface for the bottom of the brush and a flatter surface for the top. Turn the brush slowly in front of you to determine this "set." Deciding which is top and which is bottom for a particular brush will give you the optimal working surface.

The tracing stroke can use the potential of your entire arm. It can begin with the fingers, move to the wrist, and then bring in the forearm, or act in just the opposite manner depending on the character of the line. Not all trace strokes will utilize all your arm. Some will call only for fingers, and long flowing lines may employ only forearm strokes.

Concentrate on moving the tracer around, loading it, and reloading it with paint. Hold the tracing brush with about the same pressure as you hold a pencil.

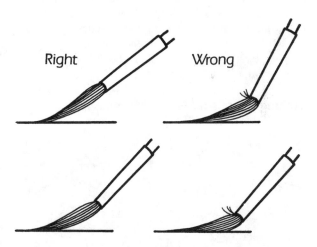

Right and wrong tracing brush angles. In the wrong angles, the angle between the handle and hairs is so great that hairs are broken by the ferrule. In the right angles, the angle between the ferrule and the hairs is not extreme.

Halftones and Pinholes

After you've traced for a while, hold the glass up to the light and see what the lines look like. You might be dismayed to find they are mostly halftones instead of the beautifully opaque lines seen from the top. This means that you may not have enough color on the brush, the paint might not have been mixed adequately, or there is too much liquid. Track down the reason, scrape off the bad lines with a razor blade, and start again. Never fix halftones by painting over them after they are dry. Such "fixed" lines will fry in the kiln—bubble up and char or flake. If the halftone is still wet, you can try painting over it. This is not especially good technique though painting "wet in wet" is acceptable. But since this is practice, the best way is to start afresh.

Other misalignments you may find in the traced lines are specks in the line where the paint has not taken. These could be due to a faulty brush stroke, poor filling of the brush with paint, paint that is too dry to flow properly, or dirt on the glass. Again, don't try to fix these, just begin again.

Of course, if you are painting something as a final step and pinholes occur, you will have to fill them in. Try to do this while the paint is still wet or at least damp. The larger the area you have to touch up, the more important it becomes not to let the paint dry before touching up. You only need a dot of paint to touch up a pinhole. If you need more than a dot here and there, it is no longer a touching up job—it is a restoration. And that is another thing entirely.

Rule: Every trace line should be traced as if there was no way to fix it.

Tracing Exercises: Finger Movements

Some tracing brush exercises for finger movements.

Finger movements should be tight small strokes. To introduce you to this motion, we have provided some specific exercises. Practice all the finger movements, not just the easiest ones.

Don't use a thin brush to trace the main outline and then switch to a thicker brush to put in the center portion of paint. The idea is to use each brush to see if you can complete a particular exercise with it alone. To paint wide lines, use a thick brush which will be able to produce most of the line width in one stroke. Then, while it's still wet, make another stroke with the same brush to fill in the rest of the line even though it is a lesser area. Switch brushes only if it's absolutely necessary.

Tracing Shapes

An exercise in tracing and matting. Trace the lines of the head and hair and let dry. Then matt the foreground hair and add trace paint lines over the matt, then fire. Tracing over unfired matt can save a firing. But you must be careful not to smear the underlying paint or you will have to do the whole job over. This is also a good exercise for silver staining. You can put down your trace lines, then turn the glass over and apply the silver stain for the hair to the back of the glass. This will also save a second firing. When fired, the silver stain will show up as yellow once you wipe off the excess carrier portion.

An application of matt has been added. Apply your matt in this fashion and have fun deciding where the highlights should be—usually the area alongside the nose, under the eye, and along the forehead.

The same figure (A) broken into lead lines with a few indications of painted lines to come, and (B) fully painted with features, drapery flow, hair, and other incidentals, none of which could be accomplished without paint.

Exercise in trace painting and matting. Practice applying the matt and highlights. To add highlights, consider the source of light and then shadow in that portion of the face where the light doesn't strike as readily. In glass painting, since the matt is already applied, instead of shadowing in, we take out matt to add highlights.

Exercise in trace painting: finger and wrist movements.

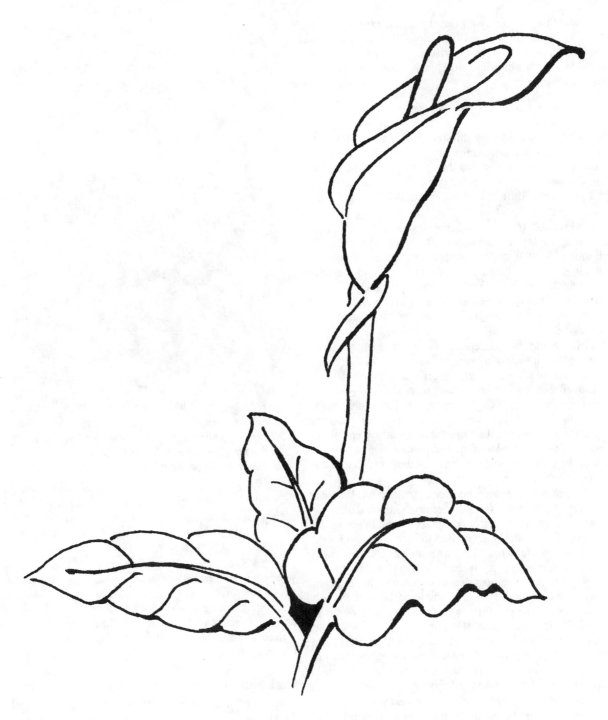

Exercise in trace painting: finger and wrist movements.

Now that you have your finger movements under control, move ahead to actual figurations. These may prove more interesting than the exercises because each will provide you with a finished work, rather than just isolated bits and pieces.

MATTING

Matt paint is not any different from trace paint—the two may be used interchangeably. While most matt paints tend to have finer particles than trace paints, the difference is between processes not paints. Each process is employed for a different effect; each involves different techniques.

While the tracing procedure involves linear detail, matting employs a wash of paint for shadowing and highlighting. Matt is used to emphasize, enhance, subdue, modify, or vary the character of the glass and the light coming through it. The matt may vary from piece to piece or even within the same piece of glass. It should be used selectively and meaningfully rather than mechanically or excessively.

Matt comes in different colors. We frequently use an umber brown matt or a bistre brown matt. There are also flesh reds, black/greens, gray/greens, and other matt colors available. The different matt colors are readily apparent on clear glass. Though many artists use colored matts on stained glass to get a just-so effect, it is debatable if the effect is not more in their minds. In actuality, you'll depend more on the color of the glass rather than on the color of the matt to make the essential statement. The matt is used to round it off.

Mix matt in the same manner as trace paint. Water is the vehicle of choice for matt because vinegar makes the matt harder to remove from the glass when highlights are added. (Trace paint is never used to highlight, so vinegar is fine as a medium for it.) A hard matt will also chip more easily and may also fry when fired. Gum arabic may or may not be added to matt depending on whether a soft or hard matt is desired. The softer you want the matt, the less gum you add. Be careful you don't make matt too soft or it won't stick to the glass. If you trace over very soft matt in its unfired state you are liable to get a halation around the trace lines due to more gum in the trace paint than in the matt. Consequently the matt will "suck up" this gum from around the trace line and cling to it.

As always, experimentation is the best way to decide how much gum you like in the matt for a specific purpose. Start by using about the same amount as the trace paint

Note the highlights, subtle as they are, in this head. Check the difference in the eyes, cheeks, ears, beard, and hair. It's all done with matt.

and either decrease or increase from that level. Make blends and test consistency as you did with the trace paint. Glass painting, as you no doubt realize at this point, is an individualized process.

Keep a separate palette for the matt. If you intend to work in more than one color, maintain a separate palette for each color. You can use the same brushes for matt and trace paint as long as you stick to a similar vehicle. When and if you go to an oil matt rather than water (to provide different effects) you will have to keep oil and water brushes separate.

Matt Brushes

Try the 1-1/2" series 18 (series A-1738) from Reusche for laying down matt. If you use clear-cut strokes, it puts the matt on the glass rapidly and evenly. It's a rather expensive brush, but if you get the best to begin with, you will learn twice as much twice as fast and you won't have to unlearn some of the bad habits inferior tools may saddle you with.

The most efficient brush to use in blending matt is the badger blender. No really fine matting can be accomplished without it. Other brushes can help, particularly in small areas where the wider badger might prove awkward. However, over a wide area there is really nothing like the badger for accomplishing the job efficiently and getting the most precise result.

The Matting Process

The matting process requires waxing the pieces of glass on the easel, however large or small the easel may be. Rarely is matting done down on the light table. In this regard, matting is the opposite of tracing, which is rarely done up on the easel.

Hobbyists do not require the large heavy easels used in studios, but if you are going to matt correctly, you should have some sort of easel as previously described and use wax as previously mentioned. It's not only the proper way to go about the process, it's fun.

If you are doing a large window and don't have an easel large enough to take all the pieces, as you complete painting a particular section, wax up what are called "connection pieces." These are pieces from the bottom of the

Applying matt with the matting brush. These are flat strokes from right to left or left to right. If small areas appear within the brush stroke where the paint doesn't take on the glass (you can see some of these areas in the photo), it means the glass is dirty.

section you have just finished (assuming you start at the top) so you can continue highlights and matt consistency.

There are three processes involved in matting: applying matt with the matting brush; distributing it with the blender; and texturing.

Once the matt is applied it must be blended so it's uniform. This is where the badger blender come in. The fine hairs sweep the matt in its wet state into a uniform coating by strokes at right angles to each other. This is tricky as the matt begins to dry. If it dries too fast the badger hairs will pick it off the glass. One reason we don't use gum arabic in the matt is that it makes the matt too thick to work. It takes a lot of practice to blend matt properly and there's a lot of variation. A lot depends on the mix, whether thick or thin, the medium (water or oil or whatever), the type of badger blender, the wrist motion and speed of blending, the atmospheric pressure, the cleanliness of the glass, and so on. But in the end, it's worth it to get it right.

Matting is not supposed to be a sloppy procedure though it may look that way. The matt shouldn't run all over the glass and drip on the floor. Nor should it leave bare spots. If it doesn't "take" in areas, the glass is probably dirty. Rub the area with your finger, using some of the matt as an abrasive. This should clean the glass and allow the matt to be applied.

How you blend the matt after applying it is not easy. Most effective blending strokes run at right angles to each other. If the strokes only run up and down, the matt may run down the path of the brush stroke. It's easiest to blend

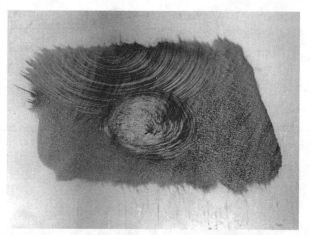

Various texturing of matt. The matt has purposely been laid down quite heavily so as to show some of the ways it can be worked. Matt can be stippled, swirled, twisted, patted, impressed. In addition to the brushes to add texture, wet newspaper patted on matt will leave an interesting design. Almost anything from feathers to fingers will form magical textures.

the matt over large surfaces when it goes first in one direction, then another. Overlying strokes going at right angles to the previous ones usually work best. If you want to have certain areas darker than others, apply more matt in these places to begin with.

Once the matt is applied to the glass, spread it evenly on the glass with a blender. That does not mean the matt need be homogeneous. Certain shadowed elements may need to stand out, some other areas be withdrawn. You may want some portions highlighted, others merely hinted at. Push the matt in position within these design boundaries.

Blending the matt is a direct continuation of distributing it; the two processes actually occur simultaneously since you don't want the matt to dry before it is blended. As the matt is distributed, it is simultaneously being homogenized or blended by the bristles of the brush. This is where most beginners have a hard time. The only way out of it is practice. Blending is not the same as just spreading matt on glass. When you consider that your time is limited (matt dries fast) you will have some idea of the art necessary to accomplish this procedure.

When you blend the matt it may spread to areas where it doesn't belong. You can remove this excess with your

finger or with a highlight brush. Some students work very hard to keep their matt exactly within a specific area. Don't waste time on this. Create with splashes of matt. Put it on, blend it in, and then direct your attention to those areas that you want matted. When you are involved with getting the basic shading values, you can't restrict your approach.

If you are matting while holding a small piece of glass, the heat from your fingers can lift away the matt in those areas so that when you finish blending you will have three or four clear spots in the glass where your fingers supported it. Always hold glass being matted by its edges.

You can apply matt to either side of the glass and many artists matt on both sides to strengthen the values without taking the extra time for multiple firing of the piece. It makes no difference whether you fire matt up (toward the heat) or matt down (toward the shelf).

For certain effects of light and shadow, succeeding coats of matt may be applied, either on the front or the back side of the glass. Matting overlays can be done with oil and alcohol vehicles on top of unfired water matt since the vehicles won't mix. You can also use different colors of matt. It's up to you and the effect you want to produce based on such densities and values you wish to employ. As we have found, the effects are endless, the process endlessly fascinating.

HIGHLIGHTING

Highlighting, also called "taking out the lights," is a technique of matt removal to provide areas of emphasis. Matting can be an end in itself without a single highlight being added if this is the effect you want. But highlighting makes the painting stand out; it is the coalescence of whatever statement you want to make.

Highlighting involves the questions of where to place the highlights, how intense to make the individual lights, and whether to grade them in intensity or have them in abrupt transition. However you determine the aesthetics of the highlights, the process is more than just removing matt. Matt is removed with highlight brushes that are specific to the type of highlight required. If you intend to place highlights, the matt should be laid down with this in mind. It should have enough intensity to allow for both primary and secondary highlights. Also, for a matt to take highlights well it should be fairly thick or the highlights will have little effect. A soft watery matt is practically all highlights to begin with.

Primary and Secondary Highlights

Primary highlights are the areas of greatest matt removal. The transition from intense light to shade is accomplished by taking out secondary lights, areas where only some of the matt is removed. Completely shadowed areas are portions where the matt is left untouched. The best way to understand the difference between primary and secondary highlights is to study various stained glass windows and then compare the technique to oil painting. The effects are similar, while the technique is just the opposite. In painting highlights are put in; in glass painting they are taken out.

Highlight Brushes

Also called scrub brushes, these can be any cheap bristle brushes picked up on sale at an art supply store. Don't pay a great deal of money for these, since you will cut them down to particular shapes. Almost no highlight brush is used in its original form unless it has developed an interesting shape from use. You will eventually want

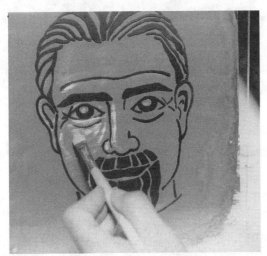

Using a scrub brush to take out the lights. The artist is working on the easel on a waxed up head and is removing matt paint beneath one of the eyes to highlight the area. He is using a mahl to lean on while working. Note how the matt has been brushed over the borders of the glass containing the head onto the surface of the easel. This can later be wiped away. The matt forming a background to the head may or may not be taken away once the head has been finalized.

an entire series of shapes from which to choose because each brush will create a different effect in the matt.

To prepare a highlight brush, first cut the bristles to the shape you want with a razor blade, sharp knife, or scissors. Leave the length a little more than you want to allow for wear during further refining of the shape. Hold and turn the brush against a flat piece of metal on an electric burner to impart whatever roundness or irregularity you wish. When the shape gets close to what you have in mind, run the bristles over fine sandpaper to get rid of the brownish seared areas and refine the shape. Alternate between the plate and the sandpaper to get the brush just right.

INSCRIPTIONS

"Positive" inscribing is just like tracing, only the lines are used to create letters. "Negative" inscribing requires laying down and blending an opaque matt, where the letters are cut (inscribed). Inscribing is normally done down on a light table.

More is demanded of the tracer when positively inscribing letters than in any other form of tracing since the preciseness of the script allows for little deviation from the underlying cartoon. Don't practice just English lettering. Foreign alphabets furnish some interesting twists and turns.

Negative inscribing is a form of stick lighting. You take out paint.

An example of negative inscribing.

Plan the lettering on paper before you begin any inscribing. Show the exact arrangement, size, and spacing of the letters. Then cover the glass with a thick matt. If you have a large area to cover, drying may take longer than usual. You can use the blender as a fan, but make sure the it's clean when you do this. Any dirt landing in the matt may not show up until after the piece is fired.

Next take a very soft white marking pencil (use a white china marking pencil or a Mongol white pencil) and make very faint guidelines for the inscription on the black matt. The first pair of guidelines should provide for the height of the letters. The second pair should mark the distance between the edges of the glass. The letters should fit between these two lines at the height calculated. Also mark the center of the inscription area.

Refer to the drawn lettering of the inscription. Obviously you can't use it as a cartoon because of the opacity of the matt, but you can plan indirectly from this blueprint. Determine the center of the inscription. This will correspond to the center you have marked on the matt. To figure out the center of each line of lettering, simply measure each line in the blueprint and divide the length in half. Once you have established the center letter (or space), work forward and backward from that point. Before you do any inscribing, lay a piece of paper over the bottom portion of the matted glass so that the palm of your hand won't smudge it as you begin to inscribe.

Indicate the middle letter with a dotted line with the marking pencil on the surface of the matt. Do not push so hard with the pencil that the point goes through the matt. Once this letter is outlined as you wish it to appear, do the letters to either side of it in the same manner. If there is a space to one side of this middle letter, leave room for it. Once you have all the letters outlined in this fashion, step back and make sure that the letters are as even as you can get them, the spaces between words are approximately the same, and you have spelled all the words correctly. Have someone proofread what you have done before going on to the next step. A misspelling in an inscription, once it has been fired, can only be erased by redoing the entire work.

With a sharp dependable stylus (stick light) take out the matt along the dotted guidelines. Allow pointed letters such as A, V, N, W, to peak above and below the guidelines. This is particularly allowable when there is no serif involved. With curved letters such as O and U, the top and bottom of the O and bottom curve of the U can overhang the guideline at the point where it meets it. This prevents the letters from appearing shorter when compared with other letters in the word. All serifs should go directly on the line. From a distance, the lettering should look jewel-like.

DIAPERING

This has nothing to do with a baby. The term is defined as "an all over pattern consisting of one or more small repeated units of design or geometric figures connecting with one another or growing out of one another with a continuous flowing or straight line pattern." Diapering, as applied to stained glass painting, involves a repetitive sort of design, almost an embroidery. Looking at some of the old diapers one is reminded curiously of wallpaper. The figurations can be spare or ornate, depending on how this would fit in with other portions of the window. In positive diapering, the pattern is painted on the glass like tracing, while in negative diapering, the paint is taken out of the matt as a form of inscribing.

An example of diapering.

Diapering is usually done along the borders of the glass as ornamentation. It should look like delicate tracery. Make yourself different styluses to remove the matt in different areas.

STICK LIGHTING

We reserve this term to refer specifically to taking out small portions of matt to create small individual effects rather than an overall pattern. Stick lighting need not use a stick. You can use a quill (with feather attached), a needle, a pin point—anything that will give the effect you want. Sometimes we stick light on one side of a trace line to emphasize it. But stick lighting is so intimate a part of so many other techniques already discussed, such as diapering, taking out the lights, etc. that it seems repetitive to give it a category of its own. Nevertheless, it is good to think of it as such if only for the learning process.

TEXTURING

All sorts of methods have been utilized for texturing, either in wet or dry matt, from the blender or stipple brush to rubbing with your palm to patting the area with crumpled newspaper.

One interesting effect can be achieved by splashing small amounts of water on dry matt. (Don't go overboard here.) The problem with texturing is the same as with other dramatic effects such as stick lighting—it can be readily overused. Be careful in this regard. Texturing that is overly unique, ornamental, and provocative may look great but may overpower the basic statement.

TRACING OVER MATT

This specialized technique can be a great time saver, especially if you are doing many pieces and want to get all the tracing and matting done at the same time. The process involves applying and blending a light matt, putting the matted glass over the cartoon, and using vinegar trace directly over the unfired matt. There is no room for error here. If you make a mistake in the tracing, you will have to remove everything right down to the bare glass and start over.

You will notice a slight resistance to the trace brush strokes on the matt surface, so you must adapt your hand to this different feel. Be very careful not to smear the matt underlying paint with your hand while concentrating on the tracing. Don't overload the tracing brush or it will blot, and make sure the tracer is in the right position to do the best job. A few suggestions:

1) Don't matt the glass so heavily you won't see the cartoon when you trace.
2) Don't use a deep-colored glass for the same reason.
3) The matt should be well blended with as few irregularities in its surface as possible to make it easier to move the tracer.
4) Don't trace until the matt is completely dry.
5) Keep practicing.

ACIDING (ETCHING)

Aciding glass is the process of eating away portions, leaving other areas in bas relief and, if you wish, in a different color. Hydrofluoric acid attacks the silica in the glass mixture. (Sandblasting glass, which gives a similar effect, is a different process entirely.) In the aciding procedure a "flashed glass" is often used for a color change:

as the top color is eaten away, the bottom one shows through. Aciding is a simple enough procedure, providing you take a few precautions. Hydrofluoric acid is dangerous to body parts and it is possible to get badly burned. Never handle glass during the aciding process without rubber gloves or tongs (you can buy them in a photographic supply store). Do not inhale the fumes from the acid. Wear a rubber apron. If you don't have a hood in your studio, acid the pieces out of doors. At the very least, be in a very well-ventilated room. Don't use more of the acid than you need for the job and pour it carefully from the storage container into the aciding tray.

You can dilute the acid to slow down the reaction or use it full strength (it comes full strength from chemical supply houses). It dilutes with water; always add acid to water, never the other way around, as the acid has a greater density than water and may splash up if you add water to it. It's usually diluted 1/3 to 2/3 water, but half and half is also a satisfactory mix. With full strength acid the process is faster but cruder and tends to pit the glass.

To prepare glass for aciding, wrap a piece of flashed (two color) glass completely with clear adhesive-backed paper or some other resist material. Remember to cover the edges. Make sure you know which is the flashed and which the "white" side of the glass. Aciding the wrong side can have you waiting a long time for the underlying color to show. Either side will etch but only the flashed side will give the color you want. With a sharp knife or razor blade, cut out the design you wish to have etched. Place the glass in the acid bath using tongs. You can actually see the process begin. The length of time it takes depends on the color, the thickness of the glass, and the strength of the acid. When you are satisfied, remove the glass from the bath with the tongs and place it in a water bath which should be close at hand. Rotate the glass in the water, wash off the tips of the tongs, lift the glass from the water bath with the tongs, and hold it under running water for several minutes before handling it with your fingers. Peel away the paper and the etching process is completed. To rapidly neutralize the acid, dip the piece in ammonia.

You don't have to use hydrofluoric acid if you are nervous about the stuff, as you well may be. There are various etching creams on the market which are safer. They also take a lot longer to do the job. It depends on how many pieces you intend to do. For a busy studio etching a lot of glass, nothing can take the place of pure hydrofluoric acid. And, by the way, you don't ever want to store hydrofluoric acid in a glass container. Guess why.

SILVER STAINING

This is truly a magical process. After firing, silver stain firing turns glass yellow. All shades of yellow are possible, from a faint straw tinge to a deep golden color, depending on the amount of stain and the firing temperature. Silver stain may be used on clear glass to obtain a variety of rich and subtle effects. But glass need not be clear to show a stain effect well. You can get very interesting variations of hue by combining silver stain with colored glass. The halos on saints in religious windows were done with silver stain.

A triple-hue effect would be to acid out (etch) portions of a flashed glass to the underlying color and apply stain to some of these etched areas. With a flashed blue on clear, you can have a blue color, a blue/white from the etched but unstained portions, plus green from the stain over pale blue all in the same piece of glass.

One effect of stain is to save a lead line, to color in a section of the work that otherwise would require a separate piece of yellow glass (as a halo). Such a piece might add awkward lead lines. Staining, therefore, is practical as well as aesthetic.

How Does It Work?

The silver in silver stain is in the form of silver nitrate, itself colorless. However, what you buy comes as a brownish-red powder. This powder is a non-firing pigment which has several purposes: it allows you to know how thick the stain is being applied; it helps stabilize the silver nitrate, providing it with an even, effective firing range; and it contains chemicals that pull certain elements out of the glass, allowing the silver to take their place. Silver nitrate, by itself, is not a good stain since it tends to melt erratically. This makes it next to impossible to predict what kind of stain intensity it will produce. Other silver salts added to the silver nitrate help alleviate this problem.

Silver is classified as a stain and not as a paint because it does not merely melt into the glass surface as heated paint does, it actually becomes part of the glass structure. When you paint the silver stain on the surface of a piece of glass and heat it, you put into motion a complex process. Glass is composed of an irregular network of silica and boric oxide and this network has empty spaces within which other elements fit, depending on the type of glass. In the kind of glass we're considering, one of those elements is sodium. The silver in the stain is also the right atomic size to fit into one of these network "holes." In order to do so, it has to push out whatever element happens

to be occupying that space—namely the sodium. Sodium comes out, silver comes in. What happens to this displaced sodium? Certain chemical reactions occurring in the brown mixture hold onto it. The more sodium in the glass, the easier it comes out, the better the glass takes the stain.

As the silver replaces the sodium in the glass network, the silver changes the light transmission of the glass. It now allows yellow light to pass through it but absorbs the rest of the spectrum, so what you see when you look at this glass is the expected yellow color.

It's always hard to predict the way the stain will look after firing since this depends on several factors: the amount of stain you apply, length of firing time, and type of glass. The intensity tends to become more pronounced as the firing time is increased or as the temperature is raised. And then, some glasses take stain badly, others (Pyrex) not at all. Last, the quality of the stain mixture that you are using certainly plays its part. All these factors contribute to a strong sense of anxiety when the kiln is finally opened.

Test fire various stain dilutions on different glasses at various temperatures. Keep a record of the tests to re-create the effects you want. Because one type of glass takes stain well, that doesn't mean other types will even though they may be from the same company.

The best staining glass is window glass, which gives a deep lovely yellow. But if the window glass has a slight tint, the glass can reject the stain or give it a blotchy irregular appearance. The same is true of stained glass; even more so since stained glass has a great many chemicals added to it, any one of which can dislocate its staining properties. Selenium is one such material, used as a decolorizer in the glass staining process at the factory. Selenium will prevent a piece of glass from taking stain to any degree.

Often glass will take stain better on one side than the other, as in flashed glass where it is debatable whether the white side or the flashed side will stain best. Again, doing samples of various dilutions is the only answer.

Stain that has gotten too hot in the kiln will acquire a light bluish-white halo. This may not be objectionable or even noticeable when you are looking through the glass, but when you gaze from an angle, this reflected halo as a bluish milky film can be annoying.

There are several stains in the Reusche catalog: 1382 Silver Stain Orange 1, 1383 Silver Stain Orange 2, 1384 Silver Stain Yellow 3, and 1388 Silver Stain Orange Intense. Oranges 1 and 2 are basically the same. Number 3 is a deep yellow. The fourth, the intense orange stain, is probably the best for the money since you can dilute it to make most of the other stain values.

Stain does not expire nor does silver stain have to be kept in dark bottles. Nor is there a problem in leaving the stain on the stain palette as long as you like. Don't rinse off the stain palette and flush this expensive chemical down the sink. We have reused stain left on a palette for as long as eight months. The stain was still good. All you need do to reuse the stain is pour some vinegar over it and use the spatula to bring it back to the proper consistency.

Mixing Stain

Keep a special palette for the stains, as you have done with the various tracers and matts. The brown powder is mixed pretty much in the same fashion as is trace or matt. A pile of stain is poured on the palette, a small hole is made in the center, and the vehicle is poured in. In the case of stain, the preferred vehicle is white vinegar because it allows the stain to distribute better in the mix so that the result is a smoother, more even flow over the glass.

Vinegar tends to go "flat" after a while, at least as a vehicle for trace or stain. You can tell when this happens by the difficulty in getting a smooth blend while mixing. Fresh vinegar should solve this problem. It is not necessary or even a good idea to use any gum arabic with stain because it has all the "bite" it needs to take hold on the glass. If you use gum arabic, you will make the stain practically unremovable from the glass, unable to be worked to the desired effect.

Mixing stain is just like mixing trace or matt. Keep a special clean spatula for the purpose. Any dirt will be picked up readily by the stain. After a while, the palette knife will become discolored from the stain but this will not affect its use.

Applying Stain

It's very easy to apply stain. Unlike trace or matt, it does not flow well. That's okay, just spread the brownish mud-like material over the area of the glass you wish to affect. No special brushes are involved. Stain can be blended or worked with a variety of brushes, but a soft brush is best. Use cheap brushes and use them for nothing else. Stain will eventually attack the brush hairs and they will stiffen and drop out after a while. You can extend their life by washing them thoroughly after use in soap and water, especially at the ferrule because stain, like trace and matt, tends to accumulate there. Stain can be used either on the back or front surface of the glass; it is equally effective from either side. Using it on the back is a matter of convenience since the painted elements are usually on the front and since you want to fire these "up," the stained surface will of necessity be "down."

Firing

Stain fires on window glass at about 1025°F to 1050°F, whereas paint can fire as much as 100°F higher. You can fire separately for stain or you can use one firing for paint and stain, compensating for the higher temperature by putting on a slightly more diluted stain. A lot depends on the effect you are after. If you are putting on a very heavy amount of stain, you might be better off to fire the stain after everything else so that you can fire at a lower temperature. If you want to use a single firing, always fire the stain side of the glass down against the kiln shelf so that the paint will be fired up. It is not that stain fires best in the down position, it's because stain will not stick to the kiln wash or the shelf, and the paint just might. In point of fact, stain fires equally well up or down.

Firing paint and stain together usually presents no basic problems provided you don't go too high with the kiln temperature. Up to 1175°F or even a bit over 1200°F is still safe. Above that, the stain will start to develop a dark rusty color and may even go blotchy. Once the temperature has reached the proper level, the kiln must be shut off and allowed to cool. When you remove the stained piece from the kiln you still won't be able to tell how the stain has fired because the brownish pigment will cover the area. Once you wipe this away with a moist rag, like magic, you will find the glorious yellow color you hoped for. With luck, of course. As we all know, it's a malignant universe.

Troubleshooting

Occasionally there are problems with the brown pigment. It sometimes sticks to the glass after firing and can't be removed. If you get these ugly brown blotches, chances are that you fired too high for the type of glass you used.

At the same time, you may go through all sorts of contortions to make absolutely certain each step is precise and still end up with stain that doesn't take or "non-firing" pigment that does. In this case, it could be the fault of the stain itself. The non-firing pigment (iron oxide) that is mixed in with the silver stain is a bit quixotic. For instance, sometimes Venetian Red, a type of iron oxide, is mixed with a certain quantity of lime to make it work better. Unfortunately, if too much lime gets into the mix it can poison the stain and prevent the reaction from occurring. So, if all else fails and the stain is still not working, you might call the manufacturer. They might have already solved the problem, or at least will replace the bad batch with a fresh one. You've nothing to lose by calling; most manufacturers of stained glass supplies are nice people and are interested in any problems that might develop with their products.

FINALE

Of course there's a lot more to painting on glass than we described here. A lot of information can be acquired just by working in the medium. Various short cuts and incidental aids and comforts are acquired on the fly. There are now on the market non-leaded paints which purport to do the job as well as the leaded ones, though we haven't really found that to be the case. But that was yesterday. Things move so fast, who knows what tomorrow will bring. What we have attempted to show is that painting is fun and certainly anyone can do it. Enjoy.

CHAPTER 16
Working with Slab Glass

Slab glass, or dalles de verre or simply dalles (pronounced dallies at least on one coast), is a fascinating medium that not enough glass hobbyists have worked with to any extent. However, once you start working with dalles you'll wonder why you dallied so long to explore this adventurous aspect of stained glass. As it happens, the slab glass technique lends itself well to contemporary designs, not only in massive architectural works but also alone or combined with stained glass in small panels where this "chunk glass" is to stained glass as the palette knife is to painting. As produced by the Blenko Glass Co. of Milton, West Virginia, uncut slabs weigh about eight pounds, are about 7/8" thick, and are made in more than 200 colors.

SHAPING SLAB GLASS

There are several ways to shape slab glass. You will need some special tools: an anvil, a wedge and a slab glass hammer; however. you can use them practically forever.

Breaking on the Anvil

The slab glass anvil is a triangular steel saddle with a rounded edge. Usually larger pieces of dalle, perhaps an entire one, are broken out on the anvil. The dalle is first scored with a straight line using a standard glass cutter. With the score line uppermost, the slab is held directly above the anvil (usually with both hands) and rapped smartly against the rounded edge. The dalle will break precisely along the score. This process can be continued to make medium size pieces; for smaller ones the slab glass hammer (which looks something like a bricklayer's hammer) is brought into play. While the anvil can still be used to create shaped chunks from a dalle, it's easier to facet such pieces using the slab glass wedge. We recommend that you start out with the wedge if you are only going to purchase a few introductory items. The wedge can do pretty much anything the anvil can, though the anvil is best for breaking pieces from individual dalles.

Breaking by Wedge

Breaking the dalle on the slab glass wedge. Not a lot of force is required. The hammer edge is placed directly over the edge of the wedge and a sharp tap breaks the glass. For faceting, a dalle and the anvil are used. This has a rounded surface against which the dalle is held for the hammer to chip the surface.

Tools for working with slab glass: the slab glass wedge and three sizes of hammers. Slab glass, or dalles de vere, is shown in pieces at the bottom of the photograph.

The wedge comes to a much sharper presenting edge than the anvil. Glass is shaped by holding the bottom surface of the dalle against the pointed wedge and tapping from above with the hammer. It is a more controlled process than using the anvil, though you must be careful how hard you tap since the small pieces of glass can fly out with some force. Wedges come with a short stem, the whole rather like the end of a spear. To use one you must first stabilize it so it stands upright. We imbedded ours in a circle of melted lead to keep it firm and steady, though the combination is heavy and not exactly portable. Other workers have made wood frames to support their wedges. Calculating how to support your wedge is another challenge for your creative juices.

The pieces of dalle after being broken on the wedge.

Scoring with Cutter and Chipping Hammer

Curves are broken out in this manner. Take a rectangle of glass that you have broken out of a larger piece, score your curve with a glass cutter, and use your chipping hammer to follow it around, chipping a bit at a time and feeling like Michelangelo. If you have an anvil, you can support your piece of dalle against it. If you don't, the work table will do (though not really well). You need two hands to work with dalles whether you use the anvil or the wedge—one for the hammer, the other to hold the piece of dalle. We've tried supporting a small piece of dalle against the anvil with heavy-duty clay, but the force of the chipping blows tends to make it a moving target. You can chip curves out against the wedge, but it takes a lot of practice. If you don't have an anvil, you might want to forgo curves until you get one.

Faceting

This process involves chipping small pieces off the glass surface, allowing more light to pass through these additional surfaces and reflect from them diamond-like. The smooth side of the glass is usually the interior surface of the panel or window, the rough or chipped side is the exterior. The unofficial rule is to place 1/8" facets over about 30% of the glass in a window, leaving 70% of it untouched for contrast. Faceting is generally done with hand held pieces, with the glass supported against the anvil or wedge and the force of the chipping hammer being minimal. It isn't necessary to whack the glass, the hammer blows must be more controlled than forceful.

Shaping with Just the Hammer

As the pieces get small enough, they can be shaped on the anvil with taps of the slab glass hammer without the benefit of an underlying score line. The hammer must have carbide tips to be effective. Steel will not last. Obviously you must be careful of your fingers. Don't be afraid to experiment in this freehand exercise. Once you start working with slab glass, you will have plenty of chunks at your disposal.

Using the Band Saw

Diamond band saws made for all-purpose glass cutting can be used to shape slab glass. A saw can be used here to break out difficult shapes and to minimize waste. The results are smooth and very satisfactory, though the time involved in cutting out these pieces can be extensive. A lot depends on the type of saw; the best (in our opinion) is the ring saw which allows maximum flexibility in cutting and cuts fairly rapidly. Whether you are using a saw or cutting by hand, it's probably a good idea to wear some sort of protective eyepiece when working with slab glass.

Whether you are shaping slab glass by hand or by saw, once the glass has been shaped, what do you do with it?

THE CARTOON

The cartoon, usually drawn on craft paper, is worked from a design. The process is similar to that used in making a stained glass window and it can be complicated or straightforward. Patterns may be taken from the cartoon and used as guides to shape the glass. These shapes should be rough hewn and fairly large. Don't try to produce a delicate effect with slab glass—the material doesn't respond well to this kind of statement.

The holding material here, corresponding to foil or lead in stained glass, will be epoxy or cement. If you plan deeply cut facets in certain glass pieces, block them with bits of clay so the epoxy doesn't flow into and abolish them. This clay is removed after the epoxy has set, leav-

A wooden frame (two corners of which are seen) is placed over craft paper with the cartoon.

Pieces of dalle being fitted to the underlying cartoon.

Rubber cement is applied to the bottom surface of each piece of chunk glass to insure that it won't move from its place when the epoxy is poured. It takes very little time for rubber cement to secure the glass to the paper.

ing the original facet. If your cartoon calls for a long narrow piece of dalle, say 1" x 8", cut four pieces to that dimension and place them in the design about 1/2" apart so the epoxy will flow between. After you pour the epoxy, even though they are interrupted, you will see the individual pieces as a single line of color.

Where dimension is required, it is not possible to stand one piece of dalle atop another because the holding material will seep between them. For a three-dimensional surface, stand some of the dalle pieces on end. This will raise them above their neighbors and give an emphatic contrast.

If you use a cement mix, place reinforcing wire on top of your cartoon before laying the glass chunks on it. The wire doesn't have to be thick. Match the wire to where the glass will be and cut holes in it to allow the glass to fit within. The epoxy technique needs no such reinforcing. Using cement with dalles has not proved satisfactory as an architectural holding material because of the stresses of cold weather outside the building wall and heated air within. Between an outside temperature of zero degrees and an inside one of 80 degrees, the inch or so of cement separation soon develops hairline cracks that begin to leak air. This problem does not occur with epoxy. When making small panels, either holding material will work well.

The main consideration with epoxy is that it must be mixed well. It comes in two separate cans—one a monomer, the other a polymer; or one the epoxy itself, the other the hardener. Once the two are mixed, hardening begins. Premix the epoxy for about five minutes before adding the hardener. Without a good premix, the panel will not set up properly and soft spots will develop. After premixing the epoxy, pour in the hardener and mix for another five minutes. This is not a 50:50 ratio—it's actually one gallon epoxy resin to 1/2 pint hardener. If you use less than a full gallon at a time, use the ratio of 100 resin (the heavy, thick epoxy) to 2-1/2 of the clear, yellow hardener. That is 100:2-1/2 by weight. If you use the entire unit once, which is generally the case, simply pour the entire contents of the hardener into the can of epoxy. One gallon of the epoxy-hardener mix will cover four square feet, figuring half epoxy and half glass.

MAKING AN EPOXY/SLAB GLASS PANEL

Framing

Frames for an epoxy panel can be made from wood pieces nailed together or from Styrofoam sides attached by nails through pre-punched holes to a flat Styrofoam bottom. The sides can be used over and over to form squares or rectangles. The edges of the frame should correspond to the borders of your cartoon. You must leave a good inch between the frame and where the glass chunks begin; otherwise you won't have room to pour the epoxy. You don't want the epoxy crowded between the frame and glass chunks or it won't level out.

If the frame is made of wood, treat the sides with a mold release to keep them from adhering to the epoxy. Wrapping them with waxed paper, as some workers do, is a nuisance. Nor should you use waxed paper over the cartoon, since the rubber cement that holds the chunks in place sticks better to craft paper than to waxed paper. Just rip the paper away after the epoxy has hardened.

The frame, whether of wood or Styrofoam, should be smooth. Every indentation or defect will appear in the border of the finished epoxy panel. Such panels are heavy, so don't overdo here; we suggest you make a panel no larger than 2-1/2 x 3 feet. For your beginning panel, even smaller dimensions would be advisable.

Place the frame over the cartoon, remembering to leave room at the perimeter and making sure that the craft paper is flat and unwrinkled under the frame. Panels are usually cast approximately 1" in thickness, so judge the width of your frame accordingly. With the frame in place, you are ready to place your shaped chunks in it.

Placing the Glass Chunks

If pouring directly onto craft paper (if you want to save your cartoon, make a duplicate), use rubber cement to hold the glass chunks in place and to prevent the epoxy from running under the glass and smearing the surface. Each piece of glass should be clean (use alcohol or acetone) so the epoxy will adhere. The chunks should be large enough to allow light to penetrate the panel. Pieces that are too small may get lost in the epoxy.

Another method—the one we favor—is to pour roofing sand between the glass pieces to a depth of 1/4". Maintain this level throughout the framed area; if it becomes too deep, the epoxy poured on top of it will be overly thin. The sand is easy to pour from a plastic cup and prevents the epoxy from sticking to the paper (this can be difficult to tear away later). It also keeps the pieces of glass from moving during the pouring process and gives an interesting texture to the finished surface.

Pouring the Epoxy

Epoxy poured from a plastic cup will allow you more control than pouring it from the gallon container. It's best to pour the entire panel at one time. If you don't have enough epoxy and need to pour half today and half tomorrow, a demarcation line will show between the two pourings. If you must pour on separate days, roughen the surface of the old area with a file or chisel before pouring fresh epoxy. This will make the bonding more effective. It will also make the pouring process more work than necessary.

Pouring is not really the right word for this process. It is more a trickling of the epoxy between the glass pieces. If any epoxy gets on the glass, don't wipe it off. Wiping leaves a smear, which is much more difficult to remove than hardened epoxy that can be chipped off later.

Epoxy sets up in about 20 to 30 minutes, so don't dawdle during the pouring process. On the other hand, you needn't rush unduly and make a mess. Once the epoxy is the proper thickness, seed the top surface with coarse or fine sand or leave it smooth, depending on the effect you want to achieve.

Caution: When pouring epoxy, the more ventilation in the room the better and anything that will help get rid of the odor is good. Epoxy contains no solvents, but the smell can be quite overpowering to some people. Epoxy can also irritate the skin if you have a sensitivity to it, so wash off any splashes with soap and water as soon as you can. Avoid using solvents, since these remove fats from the skin and can themselves be a source of irritation.

Double Casting

The completed epoxied panel set in a window with daylight behind it.

Double casting permits the glass to protrude from the epoxy on both sides of the panel. Once you lay the glass in the frame, pour 1/2" roofing sand (instead of 1/4" as suggested above) around the pieces. Pour 1/4" epoxy and let it sit overnight. The next day, turn the panel over, frame and all, and let the sand fall out. If the panel comes out of the frame, replace it. With the panel turned, pour on a second 1/4" epoxy. When this dries you will have a central core of epoxy with glass chunks in bas relief. This makes for an emphatic, clean-looking effect. The problem is that it ties up a work table for two days rather than one if you have a commercial studio. But then, if you have a commercial studio, you should have more than one work table.

The Hardened Panel

Epoxy takes approximately a day to harden (or cure). It may then be handled and cleaned up, clay dams removed, and craft paper torn away (if you didn't use sand). Rubber cement comes easily away from the glass. Acetone may be used to clean any surfaces that remain tacky. Your initial panel may have a defect or two that you will want to improve with your next attempt. Chief among these is the "bleed-through spot" where the epoxy, for whatever reason, has come out to be quite thin. A hole may even have developed here, caused by using too much sand in the area. This problem usually doesn't occur if you pour onto craft paper without using sand. However, by the time you finish tearing away the craft paper, you may decide to take your chances with the sand after all.

Thinner Pours for Decorative Objects

We have poured epoxy less than 1/8" thick for suncatchers and have had it hold small chunks with no difficulty. Such freeform objects are not very heavy and may be hung in windows easily. Cement cannot be poured this thin without developing stresses that will first crack, then crumble away. Epoxy, on the other hand, can be poured thin enough to accommodate stained glass instead of chunk pieces. Fine or coarse sand may be used to seed the surfaces.

SLAB GLASS SCULPTURE

Because of their irregular shapes and faceted edges, chunks of slab glass work well as sculpture pieces held together with epoxy. The resulting freeform airy appearance provides an interestingly rugged look that embodies the granite-like force of stone with the softening colorants of glass. These pieces are often foiled together rather than epoxied, which allows even freer forms to be designed.

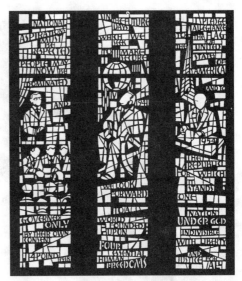

A completed slab glass window. Note the emphatic statement this glass makes.

Where several pieces are used in overlays, the refracted light is all but blocked out, but reflected light remains. Arrangements of slab glass in such formats can capture the wildest imaginations.

OTHER SLAB GLASS EFFECTS

Glass chunks from an original slab can be used as decorative breaks, interspersed between pieces of stained glass. They can be glued to an underlying piece of plate glass to add dimension. They can be polished on a wet belt so all the surfaces are smooth. In this condition, they are gemlike and can be used as jewels. Foiled chunks can be readily incorporated into a stained glass window for contrast.

Many hobbyists don't purchase slab glass as full slabs but as irregularly sized chunks from studios that use slabs. Even these pieces may have to be broken down further for a project. If you don't have a slab glass wedge, you can make do with a cold chisel in a vise. The edge should be directly uppermost and the chisel held securely. With the edge of the chunk glass on top of the chisel, tap the surface with a hammer. The chunk will fracture. This is by no means a foolproof method, but it usually works well enough. The fact is, working with chunk glass is not the same precision work as stained glass. There's more ad lib quality to it. Perhaps that's part of its charm.

Part III
Projects

*"The simplest of ideas sometimes are the
most difficult to bring to fruition."*
Sam Rosen, Art and Politics

CHAPTER 17
Silkscreening and Glue Chipping

by Dorothy L. Maddy

The late Dorothy Maddy was an artist of considerable renown who developed primary interests in the glass surface techniques of painting, silkscreening, and glue chipping. In addition to turning out commissioned pieces and teaching, she also lectured and wrote articles about glass.

SILKSCREENING

Silkscreening is a printing process that can also be used on glass to create unusual design elements. For instance, a pattern that is extremely complex for hand painting can be applied to a screen photographically, then transferred to glass. And all with one pull of a squeegee. You can reproduce such delicate tracery as lace, ferns, and leaves, and the screen can be used once or many times to re-create impressions that stay crisp and precise. Understanding the basic nature of silkscreening opens up unlimited possibilities for creative expression. To add to the joy of the work, the materials and supplies are readily available and are inexpensive.

Materials

The frame: You will need at least one silkscreen frame and may need more depending on how many designs or colors you want to print. You can either make a screen or purchase one. If you make your own, buy choice grade white pine lumber. This will resist warping and have the fewest knots. For a maximum screen size of 18" x 24", use 1" x 2" boards. Larger screens will require 2" x 2" boards. Cut the boards to the proper lengths, bearing in mind that the fabric area should have a 2" border all around the design to accommodate the paint and squeegee. Butt the corners firmly and glue them, fastening one or two screws at each corner. The frame must be absolutely flat and straight. If you're careful with the placement of the screws, you can run the top of the assembled frame through a router, making a 3/8" deep channel with a 1/8" router tip. This channel will be used for fastening the fabric with cord. You can also purchase pre-routed boards in various lengths, but they are more expensive. If you staple the fabric to the frame, the channel isn't necessary.

The master board: The master board is used for fastening the silkscreens when printing. You could use the work table as the board, but it's better to use a specific master board so you can store it when not in use. The board should be made from at least l/2" plywood or particle board that will not warp and should be made larger than the largest screen. For example, if the screen has an 18" x 24" opening, the outside dimension of the screen would be 22" x 28". This would require a master board of about 24" x 28". The 24" width gives you 2" over the screen width to mount a strip of wood the same size as the framing of the screen. On this piece of wood you fasten the two opposite parts of a 1" loose-pin hinge. Another pair is used on each screen in alternate positions to attach the screen to the master board. By removing the pins, the screens are made interchangeable. A small "leg" screwed on the side of each screen is necessary to hold the screen in a raised position when you're not printing.

The squeegee: A 6" and 12" squeegee should take care of most designs. The squeegee must cover the width of the design with some additional leeway. Of course, it must fit inside the screen frame. The smaller size is better for a small design because it requires less paint.

The fabric: Silk is seldom used today, since synthetics are cheaper and more durable. Of these, polyester is more stable than nylon over an average work range. Both polyester and nylon are available with a weave of either multi- or monofilament threads. For fine detail work and easier cleanup, monofilament is better. Fabric also comes in various thread counts. The higher the number, the finer the mesh. The finer the mesh, the better the detail and the less paint printed on the glass. I use 200-mesh polyester monofilament fabric. If your design has broad areas and you want more paint on the glass, use fabric with a smaller mesh number. However, too small a mesh number will produce a checkered effect on the edges of the screen from the weave.

Fastening Fabric to the Frame

There are two ways to fasten fabric to the wood frame. I use both, depending on the availability of a routed frame. If the screen frame has the channel routed into it or if you intend to replace the fabric often, you can use the cord method. Here you will need a roll of cotton silk-screening cord. Measure a piece of fabric so it overhangs the outer edges of the screen frame by about 1". Tearing the fabric to the size is best because it keeps the mesh lines straight on the frame. Wet the fabric to help keep it in place. Partially insert a thumbtack in each corner to help hold the fabric at this stage.

Begin laying the cord in the groove, working it down lightly with a hammer so it will attach firmly. Move around the screen, keeping the fabric tight but not taut. Cut the cord at the end. With a 3" flat-angle iron or any other tool that will fit the groove, hammer the edge against the cord so it depresses fully into the groove. This will stretch the fabric tight. Work slowly and carefully here, alternating sides so the fabric doesn't pull out of any areas before all the cord is fully depressed. When you are finished, the fabric should be evenly firm and tightly stretched like a drum.

The second of the two methods for fastening fabric to the wood frame is to use a staple gun rather than a routed groove and cord. The problem with this method is that although it may seem simpler to lay the fabric, it is difficult to replace it when necessary. This problem can be overcome by using a special tape under the staples. To start, tear the fabric to size, wet it, and anchor the corners with thumbtacks. Start stapling in the center of each side, working toward the corners. Keep alternating from top to bottom and left to right, pulling the fabric tight as you go. The staples will hold best if they are fastened diagonally to the frame. They should be spaced closely enough to provide a good tight flat surface to the fabric without any ripples. Once the fabric is in place, wash it with vinegar to remove any traces of sizing. After it has been rinsed and dried, the raw edges of the fabric should be fastened with wide masking tape. Be sure there are no loose threads that might get in the way of the stencil. If you expect to use the same screen for a long time, you will want to tape it on the inside as well as the outside and then cover it all with two or three coats of white shellac.

Making a Stencil

The screen is now ready to receive a stencil of your design. Although there are many ways to make a stencil, two methods fill most needs and produce dependable results. One is the direct-photo stencil, which is excellent for details and very versatile. The other is a lacquer film, which is good for large designs or for geometric shapes such as circles. It is also possible to cut detail with this method, although it is more tedious than with the direct-photo method.

The Direct-Photo Stencil

If you use a direct-photo stencil, the finished design must be a positive. This is the opposite of the usual negative film, so the image will be black (no gray tones, please) on a clear or translucent background. You can have the design made into a negative, then a positive on Mylar at a blueprinting shop. You can use the negative design as well if you want the painted areas reversed. Shops charge by the square foot, so get as much as possible on each square foot of film. Later you can cut the film for specific areas and reposition them for the silk-screening process. It is somewhat cheaper to have two acetate copies run off on a duplicating machine. A single copy is not dark enough, but with two copies overlapped carefully, a good impression will appear on the screen.

Designing on Translucent Paper

Instead of using a Mylar positive, you can make a design directly on translucent paper. Clear acetate does not have enough "tooth" for most drawing materials, but there are many translucent drafting papers that are excellent for both the drawing and the exposure. Various drawing tools can be used as long as they are opaque. Among these are drawing ink, red photo-opaque felt markers, and lithograph crayons. For good detail work, Rapid-o-Graph pens are excellent. Make sure all the marks are completely opaque by checking them over a light box or holding the design up to the light. Any halftones should be darkened to solids because they do not print well. Used with discretion, transparent graphic aids such as Formatt, Chartpak, or Lettraset are also useful. Strips of opaque tape will make lines and borders.

Applying Emulsion to the Screen

Once the positive is ready, you are now ready for the next step, which is applying the emulsion to the screen for the photo stencil. I use a Diazo-type emulsion with a liquid sensitizer. It is available at local silkscreen suppliers or crafts supply stores. Follow the manufacturer's instructions for mixing. Once mixed, the emulsion should be kept in an opaque plastic or glass container in the refrigerator where it will last for several months.

Once painted on the screen, until the screen is exposed to light, the emulsion must be kept from sunlight or even from fluorescent lights. A low-wattage incandescent light or low daylight will not expose it while you are mixing or working with it. So it is in this low-light situation that you apply the emulsion to the fabric. With the screen held almost upright, we run a bead of emulsion along one end of the screen. With a squeegee or a stiff piece of cardboard the width of the screen opening, we pull the emulsion tight across the fabric, going in opposite directions on both sides of the fabric. We cover the entire screen, carefully but quickly, laying on a very thin coating. You will find that you have to go over each side a few times, since you want to push the emulsion not only over but *through* the fabric each time. When the emulsion is thin and even, put the screen in a dark area to dry overnight. The screen should be in a horizontal position with the fabric side up. If the area is humid, allow more drying time. Drying can be speeded up with a fan. You can also use a blow dryer set on cool if you don't hold it too close to the screen. Once the screen is dry, use it within a day or two; otherwise the emulsion will continue to harden and diminish the degree of exposure.

Time Out for a "Sandwich"

It is now time to build up a "sandwich." Start with a flat sturdy support board larger than the screen. On the board, place a piece of 3" thick foam the size of the interior of the screen. Cover the foam with a piece of black paper cut to the same size (to prevent light from entering under the screen and causing overexposure). Place the screen over the black paper with the smooth side (top side) of the screen facing you. Place the positive design face down on the screen. This is important and in the heat of getting on with the job, you may forget to do it. If you do, the design will be printed in reverse. If the design has letters on it or if you are doing several stencils of one design with various colors, the design will be ruined.

It is helpful when assembling several separate pieces for one design to tape them with transparent tape on a piece of single strength window glass cut to the size of the fabric opening. The edges of the glass should be smoothed to protect the fabric and your fingers. Tape them to the glass as you want them to appear when printed. Lay the glass face down so the positive design is next to the prepared screen. On top of the glass place a piece of 1/4" plate glass larger than the whole screen. The purpose of this is to ensure a tight fit of the design on the screen so that light will not enter around the edges of the design. When exposing, push down on the plate glass to depress the foam, keeping it as tight to the screen as possible. To protect the screen, place a large piece of black paper over the sandwich until you are ready to expose the screen.

The Exposure

I live in an area where the sun is very bright and dependable, so I use it to expose my screens. If you want to use the sun, simply place the sandwich on a table outdoors and remove the black paper. Hold the glass down against the screen for the calculated exposure time, keeping your hands away from the area you want exposed. Then replace the black paper and bring it all inside.

Exposure times vary. If the design has a great deal of fine detail, expose it for about eight seconds. If there are large areas, try 12 seconds. However, no matter what the light source, definitely test a screen before you do the regular screen. This will save you a lot of frustration and once you know the exposure time, you can reclaim the test screen by washing it with bleach and reapplying the emulsion. It's a good time saving idea to make a test screen. Once you have established the proper developing time, you should not have to retest unless you change the design, materials, or procedure.

For the test, assemble the sandwich and expose it in steps. Don't pull the black paper completely away; pull it away in portions, perhaps in five or six steps of gradually longer time periods. This should create strips on the design of the varied exposures, say 4, 8, 10, 12, 14, and 16 seconds. If you use an indoor light source for exposure, these time intervals will be in minutes. That's how great the variable is from sun to artificial light.

When I expose screens indoors, I use a #2 photo flood bulb hung about 18" above the top of the screen. Then I expose the screen for five minutes. To expose the screen evenly, hang the bulb at a distance from the screen equal to the diameter of the screen, but never closer than 12".

Developing the Screen

As soon as the screen is exposed, wash out the design. The transparent or translucent areas that have been exposed to the light source are now chemically changed and no longer water-soluble. However, the opaque design areas are still water-soluble. In a low-light area, rinse the screen with warm, not hot, water. A gentle spraying for half a minute will soften the emulsion. Increase the pressure of the spray on the design areas and you will see the emulsion begin to wash away. This is the exciting part because the design starts to appear. Keep turning the screen from one side to the other. When you think the design areas are clear, hold the screen up to a light source for a few seconds to check the design. Rewash any areas that are not clear. If any areas are stubborn, wipe them carefully with a chamois. Don't rub too hard or you may rub away the background emulsion and ruin the screen. If the background areas wash away readily, you can assume the screen was not exposed to light long enough. If the design areas do not wash away easily, the screen has been exposed too long. These are the incidentals you should look for on the test screen.

When all the design areas are clear, blot the screen carefully with clean newsprint, first on one side then the other. This will prevent any wet background emulsion from running onto the design areas. Let the screen air dry horizontally, fabric-side-up. When the screen is completely dry, use masking tape to seal any areas along the edges of the screen that weren't completely covered with the emulsion. This will keep the paint from overflowing and causing a mess when you print. If any areas of the design are scratched or if there are any pinpoint holes in the emulsion, block them out with a screen block-out material. This is a liquid that you apply with a small brush. If you don't plan to use any water-soluble materials such as Screen Etch, you can block out such areas with white glue. Do this also on the inner side of the screen and let all materials dry thoroughly.

Using Lacquer Film

Another stencil method involves lacquer film, which can be bought by the foot in varying widths. This is a thin green film applied to a heavy Mylar base. The design is cut into the green film without going through the Mylar base. A craft knife or loop cutters are good here. Loop cutters come in three sizes and have a sharp edge at the end of a metal loop. They cut lines of different widths, are easy to use, and are available at most art supply stores. For taking out larger areas from the film, the outside borders are cut with a craft knife and the inside film area is lifted out and away.

To attach the film to the screen, place the cut lacquer film with the green film up on a firm flat surface. Then place a clean screen with the smooth fabric side down over the green film. Lightly dampen a cotton ball with lacquer thinner and wipe it gently and quickly over the inside of the fabric. A clean cloth is used to blot this same area. Remember to blot, never rub. Do no more than a 6" area at a time. The goal is to soften the green film enough so that it will adhere to the fabric but not completely dissolve it. If you use too much lacquer thinner or rub too hard, the film will dissolve. If you wipe too lightly, the film will not adhere to the fabric. As you blot, you should begin to see a difference in the appearance of the film; use these changes as a guide. Once the film adheres to the screen, let it dry for ten to 12 minutes. Then turn the screen over and gently peel the Mylar backing from the film. If the green film pulls off the fabric, stop and reapply lacquer thinner to this area. Once this step is completed and you have taped any open areas at the outside edges of the film, the stencil is ready to use.

Preparation for Printing

Attach the screen to its master board with the pins inserted in the hinges. Tape the original drawing to the master board. Move it around very carefully while looking through the design in the screen until you have it perfectly lined up, then tape it down securely. This will act as a guide for glass placement. If you are screening on square or rectangular pieces of glass, it helps to tape the original drawing to a piece of graph paper. This can then be marked where you want the pieces of glass to be in relation to the design. Then line it up under the screen.

Paints for Silkscreening

The paint for silkscreening should have an oil base. I use L. Reusche & Co. glass paints mixed with the #175 Squeegee Oil. Both opaque and transparent colors are available. A beginning palette might include transparent blue 2867, transparent green V-554, and transparent yellow 2865. The transparent reds are a bit expensive for silkscreening. The opaques might include 7882 MB blood red, 7870 MB dark green, 7872 MB yellow, 2877 black, and 20-511 white. These colors are listed as having a firing range of 1050°F to 1100°F. However, if you use any tracing blacks or matting browns for glass painting, you can use these and fire them all to 1200°F. The higher temperature paints should be printed first, with the lower fire paints on top. Remember that the colors generally do not mix or overlap well. Results are far more satisfactory if you use them singly. Always make test strips of all the paints before using them in a finished work.

Each color must be mixed on a ground glass palette using three parts of powdered color to one part of oil by weight. It is best to weigh for proportion, but if you use half an ounce of color to half an ounce of oil (about three level tablespoons of powdered color to three teaspoons of oil), you should come out all right. This mix should be creamy thick. If you weigh the first batch you mix, it will give you a good idea of the workable consistency. This will guide you later when you mix by eye. Mix only the amount that is easy to handle with a spatula on a 14" square palette. Don't stint on the mixing. Mix paint powder and oil until you have saturated all the powder with the oil and the end result is smooth. Then put the mix in a small jar with a tight lid. This will keep almost indefinitely. If you need more, mix this same amount again. Clean up with turpentine.

Keep in mind that a small amount of paint will screen a great many items. If you need large quantities, you can use an old mixer. I also use Amaco's Versa-Color, which comes already mixed but the color palette is limited and, except for the blue, the paints are all opaque. L. Reusche also carries premixed paints for silkscreening.

Preparing the Glass

The glass should be as flat as possible to get a good screening. Single or double strength window glass works best. Antique and especially semi-antique glasses also work well if they are even in thickness. Some cathedral glasses that are textured only on one side are also good for printing. Watch the temperature on the reds though—many will change color at 1200°F. Opalescent glass will also work well, but some opalescents tend to lose their gloss at 1200°. Always run tests before printing on any glass that is new to you.

The edges of whatever glass you use must be stoned smooth so as not to tear the screen fabric. The glass should be absolutely clean, and once cleaned it should be handled only by the edges. One cleaner that works well is Glass Plus. For a large run of glass, don't overlook the dishwasher. It is a real time saver.

Printing

Before you start printing, make sure you have everything lined up and ready to go. If you spend too much time searching for things between printings, the paint will dry

in the screen. If this happens, you will have to wash it carefully on both sides with a cloth dampened with turpentine. The glass pieces should be cut, cleaned, the edges stoned, and within easy reach. Lay the first piece of glass carefully in place on the graph paper or design outline. Lower the screen over the glass. Run a bead of paint along one edge. (You can pour directly from the jar or use a spoon.) The amount of paint you need will be determined by the design. If there are large areas of open screen, you will need more paint, but don't use so much that it runs all over the edges of the screen. At the same time, be sure to use enough to get a few complete screenings each time. It's a good idea to lay a short piece of a yardstick along the front edge under the screen. This will help the screen to pull away from the glass after it has been squeegeed.

Using a Squeegee

As you learn to squeegee, you will develop a natural rhythm as you go along, although it may seem awkward at first. Holding the squeegee at an angle, not straight up, pull the paint firmly across the design. You should cover it with the single stroke. Raise the screen off the glass, remove the printed piece of glass, and replace it with a clean one. Lower the screen and print in the opposite direction. Continue this procedure until you have finished all the glass pieces.

Cleaning

Clean the screen as soon as you finish printing. The best way is to place several sheets of newspaper under the screen on a workbench or on the master board. With the squeegee, remove as much excess paint as possible and put it back in the paint jar. Saturate paper towels in turpentine (mineral spirits are cheaper but slower) and start cleaning the screen. After you have worked most of the paint off the inside, turn the screen and do the underside. Don't forget this part. Keep changing the paper towels and the newspaper. It's a good idea to protect your hands with rubber gloves. Hold the screen up to the light to make sure it's absolutely clean. Any paint left on the screen will affect the next screening or the reclaiming of the screen. Rinse, dry, and store the screen if you intend to use that design again. If you don't intend to reuse the design, wash the photographic stencil clean with bleach. It may take a few soakings to remove all the emulsion. If the emulsion is hard, you may have to replace the fabric.

Lacquer stencil film can be removed with lacquer thinner and the screen rinsed and air dried.

The Firing Process

The printed glass must be dry before you fire it. In an area of average humidity this will take at least overnight. The drying process can be shortened (especially necessary where more than one color screening is involved) by setting the printed glass in the sun or in a vented kiln at a low temperature. You may find it unnecessary to fire each and every color, particularly if each color is dried completely and the high-fire paints are applied first to the glass. The paints are all put on one side of the glass. Once the paint is dry, you may hand stipple the design. This is easy to do with a fairly stiff bristled brush. Be careful that you don't remove too much paint in the process.

As far as the kiln is concerned, everyone must discover the idiosyncrasies of their own through experimentation. As a guide, I fire my pieces on medium for half an hour at 600°F with the door vented. By this time the oils are burned off. You can tell this by the odor and watching that no further fumes are being produced. This effect must take place before you close the kiln. If the process is not over in half an hour, fire for five or ten minutes more or to 800°F with the kiln door vented as before. You should also vent the room with an exhaust fan.

Once the oils are burned out, close the kiln door and fire on high until the proper temperature is reached for the specific paints. Turn off the kiln, vent it for about a minute, making sure the pyrometer doesn't go below 1000°F and close the door until the kiln is cold.

Leading Up

When leading the finished printed glass pieces, it's a good idea to use flux sparingly when you solder. Acids will dull the paint. You don't want to come this far only to diminish the glory of the end result. Chemicals such as copper sulfate used to antique copper foil or soldered joints will also dull the paint. If necessary, protect the painted area with masking tape and clean it carefully before removing the tape.

GLUE CHIPPING

Although glue chipping is done on a commercial scale, it is fun to chip your own glass. The process is simple and inexpensive. You can achieve consistent results if you control the variables rather strictly. Humidity and temperature should not be extreme, but even without controlling these conditions precisely, you can usually come up with exciting results.

Glass chipping results from a chemical action between the glue and the glass. After the glue is applied, two drying procedures are necessary. One dries the top surface and the other the interior of the glue. At this stage the glass is literally pulled apart and chipped patterns formed on its surface. By adjusting the amounts of glue and water, you can achieve many patterns.

Almost any glass can be glue chipped. Since the objective is to catch the transmitted light, opalescent glasses are not effective. Window glass is exceptional and is a good one to start with.

Materials

The most important, and sometimes most difficult item to obtain is animal hide glue, sometimes called "rabbit-skin" glue. It is the only type of glue that will bond securely with the glass. It comes in flakes or granules. You can find it in some art supply stores, since it is used by many artists to prime canvas and it can be ordered from glass suppliers. One pound of glue goes a long way, so don't over order.

If you are frustrated in the quest for glue, try unflavored gelatin. This is a similar though more refined product. The results are not as effective, but you can use it on small pieces of glass when you can't get glue. The procedures for glue and gelatin are the same.

You will need a small scale to weigh the glue and water, a candy or wax thermometer, an inexpensive 1" natural bristle brush (synthetic bristles will melt in the hot glue), a double boiler for heating the glue, and the glass pieces.

Preparing the Glass

The area of the glass you intend to chip first must be abraded by sandblasting. Hand methods are tedious, but the abrading can be done on a wet belt sander or similar grinding machine. Some glass will chip after being abraded with three coats of Screen-Etch. Brush this on heavily, alternating directions with each coat (don't worry about brush marks). The results of the chipping are not as predictable as with sandblasting, but they are usually more brilliant.

Designing the Chip Area

If you plan to use a design and to glue chip only certain areas of one piece of glass, you must protect the negative areas before you sandblast. Attach a piece of adhesive paper to the front and back of the glass. Cut out the design with a craft knife or a loop cutter. Remove those areas of shelf paper that cover the glass to be abraded. Only a light blast is necessary. If you are using flashed glass, make sure the blast is light enough so that you retain the flashed color. Leave the shelf paper in place during the chipping process and wash the glass.

Chipping

Cover the work surface with newspaper. Elevate the glass and make sure it's level. You can rest it on an inverted paper cup if it's a small piece or on a tin can for firmer support. If you don't elevate the glass, any glue on its edges could bond the glass to the working surface. If the glass is not level, the glue won't maintain an even depth and will chip erratically. A good ratio for the glue mixture is one part glue to two parts water by weight. For one square foot of glass, a mixture of two ounces of glue to four ounces of water will give you a surface thickness of about 1/16" on the glass. This will usually produce a chip with a fern pattern. As the glue dries, this thickness will slump down to half that. If you want to change the type of chip, you must either reduce or increase the 1/16" thickness. However, if you use too thin a coat of glue, by the time it slumps there will not be enough thickness to allow for the two drying stages. It will be completely dry from a single drying, and this is not what you want.

A tighter chip than the fern pattern is called a "snail" chip which can be achieved with a mixture of 2-1/2 ounces of dry glue per square foot of glass. This means 2-1/2 ounces of glue to five ounces of water per square foot. These proportions will put about a 1/8" thick coat on the glass. If you use more than this, you will create an "iceberg" chip. Such a chip cuts deeply into the glass and can be very dramatic.

The ratio of glue to water stays the same for the different chip effects, but the amount of dry glue used varies, as does the thickness of the mixture on the glass. The proportions given here are only a guide.

If you work in a very humid area, you may want to try a 50/50 glue/water mixture. This will be very thick to work with but can be dabbed on the glass with a brush. If the humidity is below 30%, you will have to add more water to the mixture to help slow down the first drying

time. If the glue mixture dries out too fast, it will start to pull away from the glass before it has a chance to chip it. If you increase the amount of water, you will have to build a dam around the glass to contain the glue. Tape the outside edges of the glass with masking tape and make sure the tape is snug so the glue doesn't leak. Remove the tape as soon as the glue jells so the glass edges can dry as well.

After you weigh the glue, soak it with the weighed amount of cool water. Cover it to prevent the water from evaporating and leave it for at least an hour. If you don't soak it, the glue won't dissolve properly when heated. It should look very fluffy after it's absorbed the water. Heat the glue in the top of a double boiler. It will begin to melt as you stir it. Use the thermometer and watch the temperature carefully because the glue rises to 145°F rapidly. You want the glue to be between 140°F to 150°F. If it is not hot enough, it won't bond with the glass. If it's too hot, the properties in the glue will become inactive. Remove the pot from the burner to stop the rise in temperature; the hot water in the bottom will still maintain the temperature where you want it. Let the bubbles settle, then apply the glue to the glass. It helps to warm the glass before you do this. Set the glass in the sun or on top of a warm kiln before you apply glue.

The glue can either be poured or dabbed on with a bristle brush. The size of the area to be chipped and the thickness of the mixture should determine which method you use. Sometimes a little of both—pouring and dabbing—works well too. The important thing is to pour or dab while the glass and the glue are warm. Once the glue starts to jell on the glass, you will do more harm than good if you add more glue or disturb it with the brush.

Any leftover glue can be poured on a sheet of plastic and allowed to dry or can be left in the covered pot for a day or two. After that it will become moldy and smelly. Don't leave the glue in an uncovered pot, since it could harm it. Soak the pot and brushes before they dry.

The First Drying Stage

The glue should dry at least overnight. You can slow the drying by putting the glass in a closed cupboard and adjusting the door opening. In a humid area, it could take several days to dry completely. When it is dry, the glue will no longer look cloudy and you will not be able to cut it with your fingernail. At this stage, the glass is under a great deal of tension so handle it carefully. Don't attempt to chip pieces much larger than one square foot.

The Second Drying Stage

The easiest way to accomplish the second drying stage is with the sun. If this is possible, choose an area where no one will walk barefooted. The glass and glue chips will fly in all directions during the chipping process and these fragments are extremely sharp. Set the glass on newspaper on a table since the humidity from the ground will re-melt the glue. The sun will dry out the inner area of glue. As this dries, it tears the surface of the glass and reveals distinctive patterns. The surface of the glass will get hotter than the outside air, but make sure it doesn't reach a temperature above 120°F. In about an hour, depending on temperature and humidity, you will begin to hear the glue chipping. The process can take two hours or the whole day. The thickness of the glue will also affect the drying time. Let the glass sit in the sun, checking it every so often.

When the process is complete, pry off any loose chips with a small stick. Never use your fingers. Most of these loose chips will fall off when you tip the glass onto the newspaper. If any chips remain, they can be removed easily by soaking the glass in water. Gather up the loose chips in newspaper and carefully dispose of them. The glue from these chips can be recovered by re-melting, but this is not advisable unless you are working with large quantities. It is more work than it is worth and you no longer have control over the glue/water ratio.

Instead of drying the glass outside, you can place it in a sunny window. Set it on the newspapers on a shelf or tray and proceed as above. If this is not practical, you can use a drying chamber. That is easily done using silica gel—a desiccant commonly used for drying flowers. The gel changes color as it absorbs moisture from the air. When the crystals are blue they are very dry and as they absorb moisture they turn pink. They can be reconstituted by setting them in a pan in a 400°F oven or kiln for about 20 minutes or until the crystals become blue again. The gel must be used immediately or kept in an airtight container. The amount of silica gel you use depends on the size of the glass to be chipped and the air space in the chamber. A good rule of thumb is three cubic inches of silica gel for each square foot of glass surface. Spread the silica gel in a flat pan and cover it with cheesecloth to keep the glue chips from mixing with the gel. Set a rack over the pan or put the glass right on the cheesecloth. Slip this arrangement inside a heavy, airtight plastic bag. Fasten it tightly, removing any excess air as you go. Set it aside and you will begin to hear the characteristic snap, crackle, and pop. That means everything is going just fine. Let it happen!

CHAPTER 18
Making a Stained Glass Box

by Patricia Daley

Originally from Massachusetts, Pat has also lived in Maryland, Vermont, New Hampshire, and Maine. Currently in Sarasota, Florida, she is teaching stained glass and producing commissioned work in her studio called Kaleidoscope.

Pat and her ex-husband John became the directors of the League of Maine Craftsmen, an invitational annual Portland craft fair, when her parents decided to retire from producing the event. In 1977 John and Pat began teaching themselves stained glass using the first edition of this book, and in 1989, opened J&P Stained Glass in Scarborough, Maine.

Boxes are among the most popular stand-alone items in glass, not only for beginners but for those who have been working in the field for years. There is something very satisfying about fabricating an item that not only has so many design possibilities but that is also functional. Glass boxes come in all shapes and sizes, with stands and without, and you can exercise your design capabilities on lids, false bottoms, decorative sides and hinges, clasps, and even on multiple Siamese twin boxes—boxes joined together to provide unusual openings.

We aren't going to go into these more arcane projects, suffice it to say that in this category, imagination reigns supreme. We want to give you a general idea of how the "usual" stained glass box is put together. You may think

Letter S with Lady. Reverse painted fired enamel on clear antique. (P. Daley)

Two large compartment-type glass boxes displayed on wrought iron stands. (Brum Studio, Sarasota, Florida)

Round Star Box. Kiln shaped glass highlights this 3" diameter box. (P. Daley)

Materials

6" x 12" opalescent glass for body and lid

6" " x 6" clear or textured glass for box bottom

12" length of 1/8" copper or brass tube for hinge

12" length of 3/32" copper or brass rod for hinge

1/4" and 3/8" copper foil

50/50 solder

masking tape

hack saw (jeweler's coping saw or miniature table saw and K&S mini tube cutter are best)

small flat metal file or round rattail file

right angle setup on work board (or small roofer's square)

wooden clothespins (spring pinch type)

2 wide rubber bands

there is nothing to it, that it's just a three-dimensional rectangle. Not so. It may be as complex or as simple as you make it. We'll make it simple, but simplicity still means accurate planning, cutting, and foiling if you want the sides to match.

Planning How to Cut the Glass

Examine the 6" x 12" piece of glass and see if there are any unusual markings or coloring you want on the front of the box body. Measure four strips across the 6" width—two 1-3/4" x 3-1/2" for the front and back, and two 1-3/4" x 2-1/2" for the sides. Labeling the panels is helpful. Cut the glass strips to save the remaining 6" x 8-1/2" piece for the box lid and set that aside.

1) Cut the glass on the 3-1/2" line to save the rest of the sheet.

2) Use running pliers for the long and short straight cuts to break out the panels.

Foiling and How Not to Be Foiled by the Hinge

Select one of the 1-3/4" x 3-1/2" strips to be the back of the box and mark with an arrow the straighter long edge where the hinge will be attached. Start the 1/4" foil just in on the marked edge and wrap the short side, long bottom, and the short side, ending the foil about 1/8" up on the hinge edge. Use 3/8" foil on the hinge edge, extending down over the short sides about 1/4", and trim the overlap on the 1/4" foil on the sides.

Completely foil the remaining three pieces with 1/4", starting and ending the foil on the 1-3/4" ends to hide the foil seams. Trim any overhang as needed. Burnish the foil onto the glass by stroking it once or twice.

3) Trim all uneven foil overlaps with a hobby knife.

Two Ways to Get a Corner Boxed In

First method: Lay the four side pieces face down on the table in the following sequence: side, front, side, back. The edge of the glass that will be the base of the box is to be the furthest away from you; the open part of the box or box lip will be nearest you. Align them straight against a ruler (be sure the piece foiled for the hinge is against the ruler) and place masking tape across the four pieces. The reason you put the box body together "head down" is to turn any pieces that may not be cut completely straight to the bottom of the box. The lip around the body edge needs to be as even as possible for the lid to fit flat. Tip up the pieces carefully and, still head down, arrange them into a rectangle. The masking tape helps hold all the pieces upright together while you position the glass for soldering. Take special care that the glass edges on the inside corners are touching, not overlapping, and spot tack across the top of each corner outside groove. Turn the body right end up and spot tack the corners again.

Second method: Use the 90° inside corner of a roofer's square or a right angle made of wood strips or lay out blocks on your work board as guides. Stand a side and front piece of glass head down into the corner firmly flush against the guides. Carefully position the glass edges on the inside corner so they are touching, not overlapping, and spot solder across the groove. Set the pair aside and do the same to the remaining two pieces—be sure the hinge edge is down on the work board when positioned for spot tacking. Then place the side and front against the 90° angle and add the back and side to it and join the two sections together at the corners.

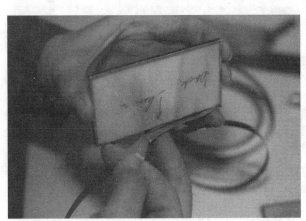

4) Apply the 3/8" foil to the back panel's top edge for the hinge to be attached.

5) Position the long back and a side panel upside-down into the 90° corner of the roofer's square for soldering.

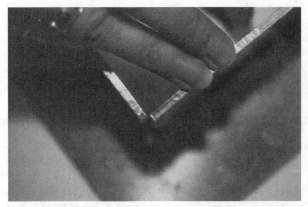

6) *Detail of how the corner edges of the glass should be positioned before soldering.*

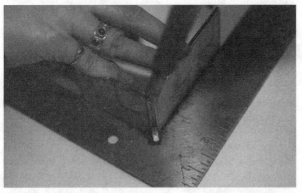

7) *Spot tack the top of the corner before beginning to fill with solder.*

8) *Cut and flow the solder downwards into the side of the V-groove.*

9) *Join the two sections (still upside-down and flush to the table) to form the complete body.*

The body of the box will be flexible until you add solder to the outside corners. Fill the corner grooves by dripping solder onto the foil. Place the flat edge of the iron across the groove and melt solder on top of the iron to allow it to flow into the gap. Move the iron down so the solder drips like candle wax down the foil. Neatness does not count at this time, so if the solder puddles at the bottom of the groove, it is less solder to add to the finished roll.

Once this has been done to the four corners, the body will be firmer and can be propped on a corner. Flux and tin any exposed foil that has not yet been covered. Don't

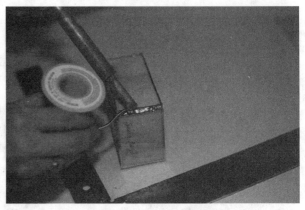

10) *Rough fill the V-groove with solder to build the base for the corner bead.*

11) Building up the solder for the bead.

12) Prop the body for hands free soldering to finish soldering the corners.

run or brush the solder on the corners—cutting and placing the solder gives you control of how much is being applied. Use the round part of the iron tip and hold the iron at a 90° angle to the V-groove as you slice and melt more solder into the corners for final soldering outside. By using the round side of the tip, no ripples are created in the solder. To evenly blend the old solder with the new, go one step (the width of the tip) backwards and two steps forward. Remove the masking tape and solder the inside corners. The foil inside may be only a thin line, so apply a small bead of solder. Now the body can be slightly squeezed into shape if it is not truly squared.

Bottom's Up!

Place the box body (bottom edge down) on top of the 6" x 6" clear or textured glass bottom. Outline the inside and outside of the body with a waterproof marker and draw an arrow pointing towards the hinge piece on the bottom glass. This will be the alley where you'll center the cutter to make the bottom match the shape of the box. It should be large enough not to fall through the corners but small enough to give you a solder seam the same width as the corners. Cut the glass on the smooth side. After cutting the bottom glass, lightly round its corners to fit with the box body's rounded corners.

13) Trace around the body on the outside on the textured side of the glass.

14) This is a heavily textured glass so it's easier to turn the body upside-down and outline the inside on the smooth side of the bottom glass.

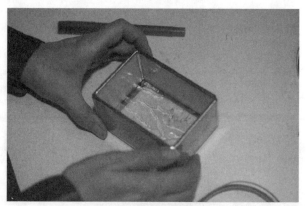

15) Final cut on the box bottom. Look closely—you can see the hinge and arrow marks to help align the bottom to the sides correctly.

17) Check the position of the foiled bottom to be sure enough foil is showing. The foil shown here was trimmed back to about 1/8" from the sides of the body.

Clean and dry the glass (refresh the arrow if needed) for 1/4" foiling. You will double foil the bottom glass by going around it twice. The first time around, position the foil so more is exposed on the glass that will be inside the box. You must allow foil on the inside of the body for soldering. The second time, foil normally, splitting the foil evenly on the glass.

Turn the box body bottom up. Position the glass, aligning the arrow to the hinge side with the extra foil facing down to the inside of the box. Trim the foil if more than 1/8" is showing. Check the fit side-to-side all the way around. It should be centered, fluxed, and spot tacked on all four sides. If there are gaps caused by uneven cutting (not too uneven, we hope), add strips of foil to cover them to prevent the solder from melting through. Pinch a clothespin on one box side, using it as a leg to prop the body up towards you to help position it for soldering. Fill the groove with solder to a finished bead on the outside, then do the same to the inside of the box bottom. Again, the foil showing on the inside bottom may be a thin line, so a small solder bead is preferred.

Fitting the Box Lid

Now that the box body is complete, examine the left-over 6" x 6" piece of opalescent glass for any special effect in the glass that you want on the outside top of the lid. Turn the glass face down on the table and place the box body upside-down on the glass and over the area with the special markings. Trace the outline of the box body with a waterproof marker. Use a ruler to go over the lines to straighten and extend them to the edges of the glass. Make note of and mark the long edge where the hinge will be attached to the body. Cut the glass on the straight lines and lightly round the corners to fit the box body when placed right-side-up again. Align the hinge side to the hinge piece on the box body and center on the body. The edges of the lid should smoothly match the sides of the body but a slight overhang is also acceptable.

16) By adding extra width of foil on the face of the bottom glass, there will be foil to solder on the bottom inside of the box.

Starting on the hinge side, foil completely around using 1/4" foil and then foil the hinge side only with 3/8", overlapping around the corner about 1/4" and trimming the excess to match the 1/4" foil. The extra foil on the hinge portion will support the weight of the lid and the proper amount of solder will give it the strength it needs when the lid is in motion.

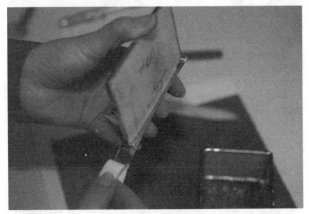

18) Foil the back edge of the box lid with 3/8" to support the hinge and carry the weight of the lid when the box is open.

19) Trim the excess of the wider foil when lapping around the back corners over narrower foil.

Edge Rolling the Box Opening and Lid

Rest the box body on one long side and flux and tin the copper foil on the upper outside face of the box and on the lower inside of the box edge. Add a little more solder to

20) Flux the foil on the lip of the body top outside and inside bottom to begin applying solder for the first step of edge rolling.

21) Build up the solder on the outside of a side panel so it primarily coats the foil but also just hangs over the edge without dripping.

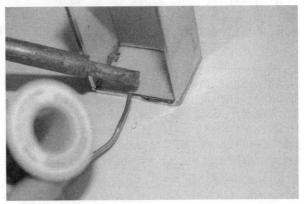

22) Add solder to the inside edge of the side panel to cover the foil and have solder in position for the last step of edge rolling.

23) Melt the excess solder that was deliberately applied to form a U-shape draped evenly over the foil.

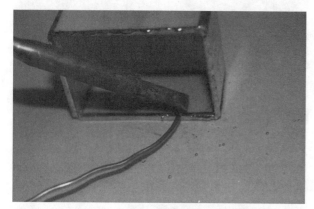

24) Apply solder to the hinge back panel foil and front panel for edge rollling.

the lower inside foil edge so it drips down off the face of the foil and makes a tiny puddle on the lip of the glass. On the hinge portion of the foil, it will take more solder to do this. Rotate the box body so the short sides are presented for flux and tinning outside and inside as done on the long sides. Continue until all four sides have solder on them and return the body to normal position on the table.

With the round side of the iron tip, lightly melt (by keeping the iron on the spot) the solder that is now sticking up on top of the foil. This will flow evenly down left and right over the edge of the foil and set up with a nice round bead. Any extra buildup of solder will run down

25) Add solder to pre-tin foil on the top of the lid for the edge roll.

and off onto the glass and can be removed with care. You can't run or brush the solder—this will remove it from the area you want to build up. If you see the square edge of the foiled glass—cut and place a small ball of solder from the iron tip to the spot and go two steps forward and one step back (remember, a step is the width of the side of the iron tip) to blend the edge roll. The hinge side will take more solder front and back to build up a bead on the face of the glass and edge. This will finish the lip around the box with a smooth bead and keep sharp foil edges down.

Adding the Lid

The foiled lid is now ready to be fluxed and have solder added for the edge roll. Lay it flat on the table, tinning and adding extra solder around the four sides. Turn it over

26) Solder placement on the lip of the edge showing the overflow off the foil.

and do the same again. Pay special attention to giving the wide hinge foil a good bead of solder front and back. When ready to apply or melt the solder that has dripped over the face of the glass, hold the lid with a clothespin to keep your fingers clear of hot solder that may run off. Keep the lid upright front to back and as level on the table as possible. Melt any solder that's there or add solder to the edge all the way around for an even roll. If you have more solder than the foil can handle, the excess will fall off. If a dribble of solder is still attached to the foil, melt it off at the foil rather than take the chance of tearing the foil up by trying to peel the solder off the glass. After this

step is completed, wash the box body and lid with warm soapy water and dry.

The Mystery of Making a Box Hinge

For years the only type of hinge seen on a box was the U-shape. This type was stuck on the back of the box body in the corners and came in two versions. The first type was made by bending two pieces of rod into an L shape, positioning the longer part inside a tube that was soldered to the edge of the lid and anchoring the short ends as close to the corner seams as possible. The second type threaded a rod through a short tube centered on the rod with the extending ends bent at the L-shaped right angle. This made an overall U-shape with a tube loose on the rod for soldering to the lid.

Many times the box body and lid would have only 3/16" or 7/32" foil on the glass edges where the tube was attached, with hardly any solder buildup for strength. The rod would stick out of the back corners at an angle, which spoiled the lines of the box design. The tube was never able to fit snugly into a true 90˚ bend on the rod so the lid would float side-to-side on top of the body. I made only one box with a hinge like that before saying, "There's got to be a better way." I wanted a hinge that didn't have to be anchored in a part of the box body that had no relation to the lid. I didn't like the side slip you get with the lid on the tube-type hinge. My preferred type of hinge is described below.

My Preferred Hinge: Measuring the Tube and Rod

27) Reheat the excess solder to melt smoothly on the edge of the lid.

28) Use the clothespin to hold the lid. This will keep your fingers clear of the hot solder (what is extra will fall off) and flux off your skin.

29) Mark the tube at the 1", 2", and 3-1/4" spots for cutting into three pieces.

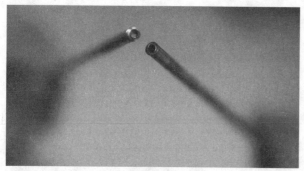

30) The rolled tube ends resulting from using a tube cutter. These trap the rod inside the hinge so it won't come out over time. Hand cutting with a saw requires filing to smooth the ends, enabling the tube pieces to slip over the rod.

Measure the hinge side of the box body between the two soldered corners. This should be about 5-1/4" wide. Mark the 1/8" tube at 5" and cut with a saw. Place the tube next to a ruler and mark it at 3-1/4" and 1". Cut the 3-1/4" length off first. This will be the center of the hinge. File the end straight and smooth if necessary to fit the rod into it. File and smooth the end of the remaining 2" length of tube and cut it in half at the 1" mark. File both ends on the tubes to accept the rod. These are the two outer ends of the hinge. If you are using a mini tube cutter, don't file the end you just separated. You need the rolled ends to act as a cap to stop the rod from slipping out. Measure between the two back corners to determine the length of the three-piece hinge.

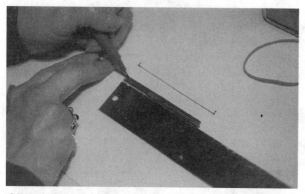

31) Lay the three pieces end to end and place the rod next to them for measuring. Mark the rod to be cut at the 3" line to fit inside the 3-1/4".

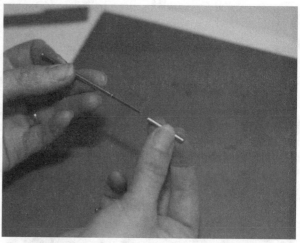

32) Slipping the tubes onto the rod in this sequence—1", 3-1/4", and 1" again to make the hinge.

So now you have three separate pieces of tube. Arrange them end-to-end with the 1" next to the 3-1/4" and the other 1". Lay the rod next to them and mark it at about 4-3/4" long and cut that amount for the hinge rod. File the ends to fit into the center rod and then thread the 1" tube, 3-1/4" tube, and 1" tube into it.

Line up the matching hinge edges of the box body and lid and wrap two rubber bands (parallel) around the body

33) Position the lid on the body to be touching the worktable on top of the panel and even side-to-side on the box body and secure with two rubber bands. Loosen the bands and reseat them if the lid needs to be minutely moved to final position.

34) Place the hinge in the groove between the edge rolls of the lid and extra foil on the back panel.

36) This shows the paper strips for protecting the two end pieces from being soldered accidentally to the lid. The brush is applying flux just to the underside of the end tube.

from side-to-side. Stand the box on the back side and position the lid evenly side-to-side and push it flush with the back panel. The rubber bands securely hold the lid down and in final position for soldering the hinge on. Stand the box so it rests on the front panel so you are looking at the wide area where the hinge will be soldered.

Put the tubes (with the rod inside) in the groove between the lid and the body. As a soldering precaution, place a strip of paper about 2-3/4" wide x 2" long between the center tube and the box body. This will prevent solder from attaching to the body if the tube acquires excess solder. Keep in mind that solder will flow only where flux is, lightly flux the center tube only on the area next to the lid. Don't flux under the tube in the body area.

Heat the center tube in the middle and add a small ball of solder to attach it to the lid. Work your way left and

right of the middle but be cautious of going near the cut seams on the ends of the center tube. Stop soldering about 1/8" away from them. Let the solder cool, then add more solder to dress and smooth the join between the lid and hinge.

Turn the body around, still resting on the front panel so you are looking at the back panel. Slip two strips of paper 2" long x 3/4" wide between the lid and 1" tubes. This will protect the lid from being soldered to the bottom at the end tubes. Again lightly flux the end tubes on the area

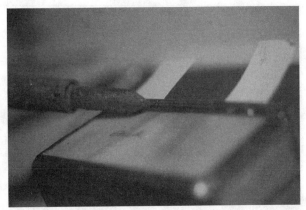

37) Use only the tip of the corner of the iron to preheat the tube and apply a small amount of solder. Again, come in at an angle underneath the tube to prevent solder from contacting the lid.

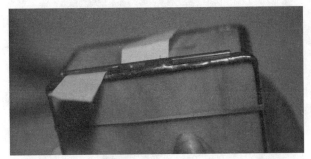

35) The center 3-1/4" tube is soldered in place and the second pass with solder to dress up the joint is half completed.

38) This is a completed solder joint for the tube to the body on the left end.

next to the bottom, staying away from the open ends and the cut seams and add a small amount of solder to attach the 1" tube to the box body. Add more solder to join the tube to the body and let it cool. Then reheat to dress the solder line. Do the same to the other end tube.

Finishing the Lid

Remove the rubber bands and paper strips from the hinge area and see if the box lid opens. Because there's

39) A small dot of solder is added to keep the lid from falling all the way back.

nothing to stop it, the box lid will tend to fall backwards, but don't let it. You may want to attach a chain; if this box lid had a cut design in it, you could attach the chain to a solder seam just inside the edge about 3/16" in from the side and anchor the chain in the bottom seam of the box body near a front inside corner. But this box has a flat uncut lid with no place to attach a chain, so we will use a button.

Turn the box over so you are looking at the hinge again, add a small dot of solder to the center tube, and build up a ball of solder to act as a button to stop the lid from tipping over when opened. It will take several tries to position the ball correctly so it acts to balance the lid weight just back off center when it is opened.

When this has been done, clean the box again. Apply a patina finish to the solder lines and wash with soap and water. Use glass cleaning compound to clean the glass and solder and buff to a low shine. Now you can fill the box with loose change, keys, a deck of cards, jewelry, or any other treasure.

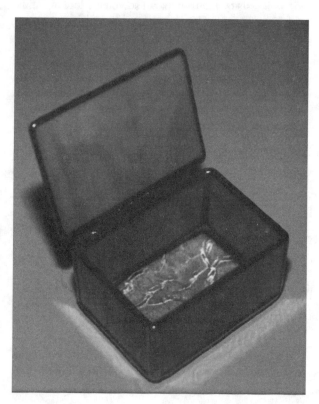

CHAPTER 19
Fundamentals of Fusing

by Darlene Johnson and Judy Lee, Fused Fantasies

Early in 1987, Darlene Johnson and Judy Lee decided to combine their talents to take the fear out of fusing and put some fun into it. As a result, Fused Fantasies was formed. Their books, Enchanted Creations, Simply Stunning, La Fused Boutique, *and* Glass Magic, *are the result of their efforts.* Glass Patterns Quarterly *featured the duo as guest designers in the Winter 1990 issue. The magazine also continues to utilize them as contributing designers.*

In addition to publishing fusing designs, the team is experienced in both traditional and fused stained glass. Both have studios where they teach and do commission work. Their fusing seminar, Fearless Fusing, is offered at various glass festivals.

Fusing is an exciting new direction for the stained glass enthusiast. We invite you to explore with us this new potential for further developing your stained glass interest and skill.

Before you begin to fuse in your kiln, read this entire chapter. It will help you be aware of different fusing terminology as well as special fusing supplies, especially if this is your first experience with fusing stained glass or operating a kiln. The following information will provide you with basic instructions so you can immediately create simple fusing projects and then, building on this information, go on to more complex ones.

KILNS

When thinking about working with a kiln, many envision a fire-breathing monster ready to incinerate all who dare come near. This concept is a myth we hope to dispel. Any kiln that will heat up to 1600°F will fuse glass. This includes ceramic and enameling kilns. Kilns with the elements inside the top of the lid are specifically designed for fusing stained glass. Elements in the lid provide uniform distribution of the heat over the surface of the glass. A small glass kiln with a 10" to 15" shelf provides you with room to expand the variety and size of projects as you gain experience. Mini electric kilns with 4" or 6" shelves that heat quickly are great for jewelry projects.

Firing in Your Kiln

The first thing to determine is how fast your kiln actually heats. The easiest way to do this is to make small pieces of jewelry to fuse—earrings or pins are ideal. Place them on a prepared kiln shelf, vent the lid of your kiln 1/2" and turn the control to high. When the pyrometer reaches 700°F, close the kiln lid. Record the pyrometer reading every 15 minutes until the project is fused appropriately. We encourage you to fuse to at least 1450°F or to a 017 small Orton cone (readily available at most ceramic shops). A safe rate of heating for larger projects is about 10°F per minute.

This can be translated to "an even temperature increase from room temperature to 700°F in the first hour." After the kiln reaches 1000°F the rate of heating may be doubled. After 1000°F you no longer need be as concerned about thermal shock reducing your project to shards of glass and your eyes to pools of tears. If your kiln heats slower than this on high, it's not a problem. You cannot harm your project by heating too slowly (your patience, maybe). If your kiln heats faster than 10°F per minute, adjust your control switch lower so the rate of heating stays within these guidelines.

When your kiln has reached the desired temperature for your project, turn it off. Wearing fusing gloves, use a long handled hook to lift the lid and allow the kiln to cool to about 1100°F. (This is necessary to prevent further change in the glass after you shut off the kiln.) Close the lid and record the pyrometer reading and time.

Firing Guide

The following guidelines will help determine the fusing levels at different temperatures for thin Bullseye or Uroboros and standard (i.e. non-Pyrex) stained glass. Note that thin glass has a narrower fusing range than regular stained glass.

1225°F (020)

Bullseye glass: slight noticeable change in the glass. Pieces are tack fused. Edges are fire polished.
Standard stained glass: no noticeable change in glass. Pieces are not tack fused nor are edges fire polished.

1335°F (019)

Bullseye glass: edges are beginning to round.
Standard stained glass: pieces are tack fused. Color changes are apparent. Edges are fire polished.

1385°F (018)

Bullseye glass: glass is fully fused, edges are sealed, center of fused piece is indented.
Standard stained glass: edges of softer glasses are beginning to round.

1450°F (017)

Bullseye glass: glass is pulled up, pillow effect.
Standard stained glass: softer glasses have lost their sharp edges. Edges of harder glasses beginning to round.

1520°F (016)

Bullseye glass: color is starting to burn out, original shape is gone.
Standard stained glass: edges of harder glasses are rounding. Softer glasses may be fully fused.

1525°F (015)

Bullseye glass: too much! Over fired. Colors are faded.
Standard stained glass: most glass is fully fused at this temperature.

1550°F (014)

Most standard stained glass is fully fused at this temperature.

ANNEALING GLASS

Now that you have turned off your kiln, it's time to discuss the annealing "dragon." This is the other beast of fusing that causes much anxiety for beginning fusers.

Annealing, simply defined, means cooling the glass slowly to avoid stress in the finished piece. Stress occurs when the glass cools too quickly, forming a hard shell around the outside while the inside is still soft and warm. As glass cools, it contracts and will pull against the hard outer shell, creating stress; these forces can cause frac-

tures in your project. Think in terms of cookies when thinking of annealing—your goal is to have the item cool like a Vanilla Wafer, with consistent density throughout the entire cookie. Cooling too rapidly creates an Oreo cookie effect, a hard outer layer surrounding a soft center. Now imagine the white center contracting as it cools, pulling on the hard outside, and you have the basic principle of the stress created by inadequately annealed glass.

A safe rate of annealing for most projects is about four hours from 1100°F to 700°F. This should be a consistent drop in temperature. The critical temperature range where most glasses pass through the optimum annealing range is from about 950°F down to 750°F. It is in this range that you want your kiln to cool slowly to prevent the Oreo cookie effect and achieve the Vanilla Wafer outcome.

You can determine your kiln's rate of cooling by recording the temperature every half hour as it cools. A safe cooling rate is about 50°F every half hour. If your kiln cools faster than this, you will need to add some heat to your cooling cycle by adjusting the control switch. You cannot cool too slowly. The dragon hates a slow cooling because he always loses. It is only when you cool the kiln too quickly that he wins by turning your fused fantasy into a fractured fantasy. Small jewelry pieces require a much shorter time to anneal and will not be damaged by a kiln that cools faster than 50°F per half hour.

FUSING IN A MINI ELECTRIC KILN

Mini electric kilns are miniature kilns that heat with an electric element. Read the manufacturer's instructions before fusing in your kiln. Fire bricks or regular bricks make a convenient fireproof surface to place the kiln on while it is in use and provide a safe surface for the hot kiln top. Keep in mind that you are playing with fire. Never leave your kiln unattended while it is on!

Before you begin to make your project, be sure to have ready a dry, prepared kiln shelf. Preparing the kiln shelf will prevent the project from sticking to the kiln shelf during fusing. Use the kiln wash that comes with the shelf kit or mix your own. (A mix of whiting and diatomaceous earth works well.) Mix the wash according to manufacturer's instructions. Remove any old kiln wash from the shelf by scraping it with a putty knife. Wear a mask to prevent inhaling the dust. Pour the wash into a shallow bowl and dip the shelf into the wash twice or apply it with a soft brush.

Because mini kilns heat so quickly, thermal shock can be a problem with large objects. (With stained glass jewelry, the word "large" is a relative term.) If your project is larger than 1" in diameter, allow the kiln to heat until the pyrometer reaches 500°F. Then unplug or shut off the kiln and let it sit for five minutes before restarting the power. Do not lift the lid.

Glass is usually fully fused at about 1700°F on the mini kiln's pyrometer. It is helpful to start checking its progress at about 1400°F. Note the temperature where the glass begins to change for future reference.

When lifting the lid to check the fusing progress, lift it straight up off the base. Please resist the temptation to just tilt the front of the kiln top back and peek in. This will cause uneven firing.

The amount of time it takes to fuse a project will vary depending on how warm the kiln is when you start to fuse and your electric current capacity (some currents fluctuate wildly) and the type of glass you are using, both as to manufacturer and color. Reds, for instance, may take longer to fuse.

If the kiln is hot, allow the project to sit in the kiln without any power for about five minutes.

Again, remember that glass must be cooled slowly to prevent the finished project from breaking. We cannot emphasize this enough. After the desired fusing range is reached, unplug or turn off the kiln. Wearing gloves to protect your hands, lift the kiln lid straight up from the base to quickly cool down the kiln. This is necessary to prevent further change in the glass after you have shut off the power. Allow the pyrometer to cool down to about 1200°F. Replace the lid on the base. Let the kiln sit until the pyrometer reaches about 200°F before again removing the top. Allow the project to cool to room temperature before removing it from the kiln shelf.

COMPATIBILITY TESTING

Glass is brought into a more liquid state (it is always a liquid, even when solid) by the firing process. This means that it expands as it heats and contracts as it cools. The rate that glass contracts as it cools is what causes different glasses to be incompatible with each other. If one glass piece in your design cools more slowly than another, the project will break. The easiest way to avoid this problem is to use glass that the manufacturer has pre-tested for fusing compatibility. Three such brands are Uroboros, Wasser, and Bullseye. Such sheets of glass are marked "Fusing Compatible" or with the label "Exp. 90."

To check glass that has not been pre-tested for compatibility, you will need a light source and two polarizing lenses. A stressometer kit is available containing these items. Check with your local stained glass retailer for this item.

Chip Testing for Compatibility

Cut and glue 1/2" pieces of stained glass you wish to fuse about 1/2" apart on 1" wide strips of clear glass of the same manufacturer (Spectrum, Armstrong, Wissmach, and Kokomo all have clear glass). Label the glass pieces and 1/2" squares with a fireproof pen (Alton makes an excellent one).

Apply an overglaze (see overglaze section in this chapter). Fire the strip or strips until all the chips are melted into the clear background (about 1550°F or 015).

After the glass is cool, use the stressometer to detect halos around the glass, indicating stress and therefore, incompatibility. Obviously, incompatible glass will have fractured.

To use the stressometer, in a dark room place one Polarized lens on the light source which must be beneath the glass you are observing; hold the strip sample over that lens while rotating the other Polarized lens above it. Stop at the darkest place. A white halo or flares at the corners of the chips will appear around incompatible chips. The chips of glass that do not have halos or light flares at the corners are compatible with each other and can be used in tandem for fusing projects without fear of your project, or you, going to pieces.

PYROMETERS

This is an invaluable kiln accessory since the first thing you need to do in fusing is to determine the accuracy of your kiln's temperature reading. By firing a ceramic cone with or without a project in the kiln, you can determine how accurately your pyrometer is reading.

We recommend firing to about 1500°F since most inaccuracies occur at the higher temperatures. You can use either the large or small Orton cones; be sure to have the correct conversion chart for the size cone you are using.

CONES

We prefer to use cones to gauge our firing temperatures because they react to the time and temperature the same way the glass does. This provides a valuable, consistent firing guide when repeating a project. Initially you may find that your firing success rate is much greater by using the pyrometer only as a starting point for subsequently visually checking the project. There is nothing wrong with visually checking to see how a piece is getting on. We like to begin looking at our projects when the pyrometer registers at least 100°F less than the anticipated final temperature.

If you are using a cone, place it in an area on your kiln shelf where it will be visible through the peep hole. Sound obvious? Well, we hate to tell you...

If you are using a pyrometer, make sure to mark your pyrometer probe so that you always insert it the same depth into the kiln. This will greatly increase the consistency of your temperature readings. Of course, if your kiln has a pyrometer built in, this step is unnecessary.

Approximate Small Orton Cone Temperature Conversions	
Cone #	Temperature
020	1225°F
019	1335°F
018	1385°F
017	1450°F
016	1520°F
015	1525°F
014	1550°F

KILN WASH

The surface your project is placed on must have some type of protection to prevent the glass from sticking to it. It's most economical to use a kiln shelf wash specifically designed for glass, mixed according to the manufacturer's direction. Add enough water to the powder so it is the approximate consistency of thin sour cream. Use a baking brush to generously apply the wash to the kiln shelf. You cannot overuse kiln wash as long as the layers are even. Too little kiln wash will cause your project to stick to the shelf. It is unlikely your creativity can overcome this and breakage will follow. Allow the shelf to dry before you place glass on it.

The shelf may be used for repeat firings until the kiln wash starts to peel off, at which time you should remove all the old kiln wash by scraping the shelf with a broad putty knife. Apply fresh wash as you did the first time.

OVERGLAZES

Overglazes are low-firing glass solutions that can be applied to the surface and edges of your design pieces to prevent devitrification, a complicated physical process that causes glass to crystallize (remember, glass is non-crystalline in clear form) and makes a mess of the surface of your project. Crystallized glass is dull and ugly—the pond scum of glass fusing.

Two overglazes currently available are Super Spray, which does not contain lead and Spray A, which does contain lead. The overglazes are applied using an airbrush and propellant. When applying overglazes, do so in front of a good exhaust fan and wear a mask to prevent inhaling the mist. Your lungs will not like the glass particles and your bloodstream will not care for the lead. A paint brush can be used to apply the glaze to the sides of the glass pieces if you prefer. Do not apply overglaze to the surface of the glass that touches the kiln shelf even if it is covered with kiln wash.

Note: Bullseye, Uroboros, and Spectrum glass does not devitrify, so an overglaze is not needed when fusing using this particular glass.

GLUES

Projects with numerous pieces or several layers need glue to hold the pieces in place so you can transfer the project to the kiln shelf for firing. Currently, the most readily available glue is Elmer's white glue. Use sparingly—too much can cause bubbles and/or small design pieces to float during firing.

IN CONCLUSION

Be willing to explore and experiment. Your own curiosity can lead to some wonderful discoveries and new techniques. Many of the techniques we developed for our projects came from the thought, "I wonder what will happen if..." Of course, we didn't share any of the ideas that didn't make it off the kiln shelf! Those remain our secrets. That's what experimenting is all about, though, isn't it?

FUSING PROJECTS

The following patterns will help you perfect your fusing skills. They range from very easy to more challenging. Since we can only offer a sampling here, if you are interested in more designs for fusing stained glass, ask your local stained glass retailer for copies of our fusing design books, *Enchanted Creations, Simply Stunning, La Fused Boutique*, and *Glass Magic*.

These projects can be made using Bullseye Fusing Tested Glass and/or Uroboros Stained Glass. This eliminates the need for testing for compatibility before you be-

gin to fuse. If you are using a glass other than these two brands, be sure to test for compatibility.

Grape Cluster Pin

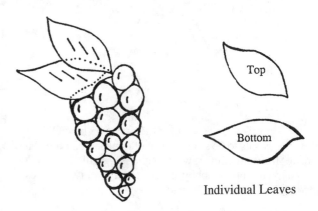

Grape Cluster

Top

Bottom

Individual Leaves

This design uses dichroic glass to create iridescent sparkling grapes. The mini kiln is ideal for making the grapes for the cluster.

From Bullseye magenta dichroic glass, cut the following squares: two pieces 1/2", five pieces 3/8", five pieces 1/4", and two small chips. These cuts do not have to be perfect.

At each corner, use a glass grinder to grind away some of the clear glass underneath the dichroic surface. Do not remove any of the dichroic coating itself. This will help to form a nice round ball. Clean the pieces with alcohol or soap and water, then place them on the kiln shelf, dichroic coating side up. Fire until the squares have formed round balls, about cone 015 to 014. After the balls have cooled, arrange them on a piece of white Bullseye in the shape of a grape cluster. Trace around the balls so you can easily regroup the cluster. Remove the balls and cut around the traced shape on the Bullseye glass for a background piece which should be a little smaller than the actual cluster. After you have cleaned this piece, replace and secure the balls with Elmer's glue applied sparingly.

Cut the leaves from clear, thin rolled Bullseye glass. Place as shown in the design on the cluster. Secure with glue. Fire to cone 018. After the project has cooled, outline the leaves and add their veins with fire-on gold (used for ceramics.) Fire to cone 020.

Black Elegance

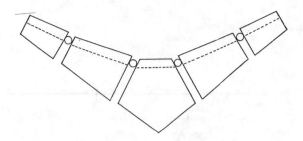

This project needs bead rods to create a channel to allow the pieces to be strung on bead thread. Bead rods are made from nichrome wire. This is usually available through ceramic or hobby shops. It comes in two gauges: 15-14 and smaller 20-18 gauge.

1) Cut the wire into 8" lengths.

2) Mix kiln wash to the consistency of Elmer's glue. Put the wash in a long thin container (an olive jar works well).

3) Dip the wires in the kiln wash. A square of Styrofoam makes a handy place to plant your wires to dry. If you are in a hurry, a hair dryer speeds the drying time.

4) For heavier gauge wire, dip a second time. Allow to dry before using.

Making the Design Pieces for the Necklace

Cut each design piece from the same color of Bullseye glass. (Small circles in the pattern represent gold spacer beads in the finished project.) Clean all the glass pieces. Apply an overglaze to the surface and sides of the Bullseye pieces. Arrange the Bullseye pieces in two rods on the kiln shelf. Put a line of Elmer's glue along the line indicated by the dotted lines in the design. Allow the glue to become tacky. Place a coated bead rod on each glue line. Be sure that no uncoated wire is touching any glass. Place a matching Bullseye piece on top of the bead rod, aligning it with each bottom piece.

Fire until the edges are sealed over the rod, about cone 017. There may be a slight elevation above the rod. After the beads have cooled, remove them from the rods by twisting the pieces and pulling them off the end of the rod.

Finishing the Necklace

Loosely tie a bead on the end of a piece of fish line or beading string. Allow enough extra space at the end of the line to attach the jewelry findings.

Start with an 8mm bead that matches or coordinates with your glass pieces. Alternate with a 5mm to 6mm gold or silver spacer bead until you have a length equal to about 1/3 the desired finished length. Add the glass design pieces, alternating with a spacer bead. String an equal number of beads to match the first side. Adjust the number of beads equally on both sides to create the desired length of necklace.

If you have not already removed the bead that you tied on one end, do so now. Attach each end to a fold-over bead tip. Put a small drop of glue on the knot before you fold over the bead tip.

Attach jump rings and spring rings to the bead tips. Solder the split in the rings to prevent it from pulling apart.

Checker Clock

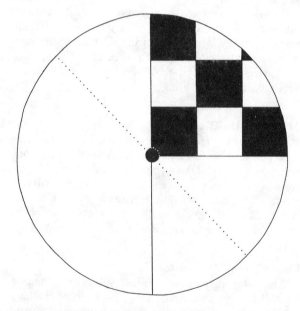

Cut two 6" circles of Bullseye glass. Split one circle in half as indicated by the dotted line. Grind out the 1/4" center hole in each half of the circle. This is the bottom layer for the clock. Split the top circle as indicated by the solid line. Remove the upper right quarter of the circle. Cut the checker board design pieces as indicated in the design.

Clean all the glass pieces. Allow to dry. Apply over-glaze to all the top and side surfaces of the design pieces, including the bottom circle.

Cover a 10" square of cardboard with waxed paper or plastic wrap. Starting with the bottom layer, assemble the clock pieces on this cardboard square. Apply several drops of Elmer's glue along both sides of the center cut line. Offset the two center lines as shown in the design. This allows for stability when you remove the project from the cardboard to place it on the kiln shelf for firing. Be sure to align the two center holes. Use a Bullseye stringer to outline the upper right quarter.

After the clock is assembled and glued, fill the center hole with a fireproof material such as shelf fiber paper. Brush off any excess material.

After the glue has dried, carefully slide the project onto the kiln shelf. Fire until all the seams are sealed, about cone 015 to 014.

Use the 1/4" bit on your grinder to enlarge the center hole to 3/8". Install the clock works according to the manufacturer's instructions (you can purchase clock works in many hobby stores). You may want to paint the hour hands with red airplane paint; the seconds hand with black.

Star Bolo

This bolo is created using star shapes cut with a saw from Bullseye glass, perfect for fusing in the mini electric kiln.

Arrange two large stars and one smaller star as shown in the design on the kiln shelf. Fire until the edges just begin to round, about cone 019.

After the project has cooled, attach the bolo slide to the back of the project using household "Goop" or E-6000. After the glue has dried, loop the bolo cord through the openings. Dip the ends of the bolo cord into the Goop and insert it into the bolo tips.

Fan Frame

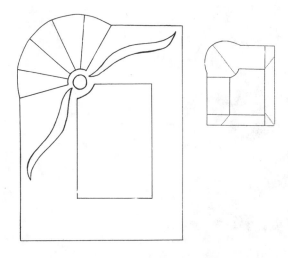

Two layers of glass are used to form the background of picture frames. You may use all Bullseye glass, all Uroboros glass, or a combination of the two glasses.

Cut two solid pieces of glass according to the outside shape of the design. Cut the bottom layer of the background glass as indicated by the dotted lines in the small diagram; the top layer is cut as indicated by the solid lines. These cutting lines enable you to make the picture opening. Put the background back together and move the glued, unfused frame to the kiln shelf for firing. Splitting a solid piece of glass diminishes the cutting line marks in the finished frame.

Clean all the pieces of background glass very well. Lightly coat all exposed surfaces with overglaze. Cover a piece of cardboard with waxed paper or plastic wrap to use for assembling the frame. Assemble and glue the layers together as indicated in the small diagram.

Fuse the background until all the seams have sealed, about cone 015 to 014 for Bullseye; cone 019 to 018 for Uroboros on Bullseye.

Cut the fan portion of the design. Clean all the pieces with soap and water or alcohol. Apply overglaze to all the top and side surfaces of the design pieces. Arrange the pieces on the fused background. Fire until the edges of the fan pieces begin to round, about cone 017 for Bullseye, cone 019 for Uroboros.

Use household Goop or E-6000 to glue the finished frame to an appropriately sized clear, self-standing Plexiglas frame.

CHAPTER 20
Making a Business Card Holder

by Patricia Daley

Business card holders are among many popular smaller glass items that are both practical and aesthetic. They are easily personalized and can augment either the card or the decor. They can provide an immediate first impression that is both stimulating and unique. With such varied inherent possibilities why be satisfied with the bland, impersonal plastic holders that abound in most offices? Here we present one card holder that expresses both the person and the business.

The completed leopard card holder. The white edges of the back glass have been cold painted with black enamel to match the leopard.

Materials

6" x 6" opalescent glass for back and sides

4" x 4" clear glass for bottom and front

2-1/2" x 3" amber cathedral (optional for leopard)

7/32" copper foil

50/50 solder

Reusche black trace paint

medium sable brush (#00)

powdered gum arabic

clove oil

eye dropper

palette knife

tabletop kiln with pyrometer

glass diamond saw

craft knife

This business card holder was a commission piece ordered by a woman who loves cats, especially leopards. I wanted the leopard to be draped across the top of the card holder but avoid a heavy look with the outline of solder. The original concept was to have the back of the card holder amber cathedral glass with the top and side edges contoured to the leopard which was going to be stained, stick lighted, and fired in position on the face of the glass. But due to an almost disastrous accident, the design was changed mid-stream with a surprising result. This accident caused another facet of working with glass to be called upon to complete the card holder that really made this the "cat's meow."

THE PATTERN

The pattern shows the leopard stretched across the top of a 2" x 3-1/2" vertical card holder with its tail dangling down the right side and front right leg extending down the left side.

Place the pattern under the amber cathedral glass on the light table and outline the profile of the cat using a waterproof ultra fine line marker. Extend the straight down lines with the ruler from just under the cat's paw and tail and square off the bottom also.

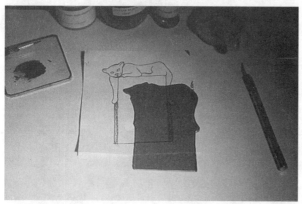

1) The original pattern and cut cathedral amber back for the leopard card holder.

Compound cuts will be necessary to follow the shape of the leopard. Begin by cutting up the left side from the bottom but veer around the paw and head for the exit edge of the glass. Start your score again to come close to the leg but leave extra space around the head outline. Score around the ear area and continue across the leopard's back to the tail. Down the tail and off the edge of the glass near the tip. Come in with another score from the edge under the tail and continue straight to the bottom edge. Square off the bottom and check against the pattern. Use the 1/4" and 1/8" bits on the grinder to shape closer to the paw, head, ears, and tail. Tip the front face edge of the glass down against the grinder and very lightly bevel the edge to remove sharpness. Clean and dry the glass. Be sure to handle it now only by the edges to keep it clean for painting.

MIXING THE PAINT

Measure black trace paint (see Painting on Glass) on a clean clear glass palette. Swirl the paint with a palette knife against the glass to make sure it isn't clumping and sweep it back into a pile. Spread the paint to a thickness of about 1/8" on the glass. Load about 1/8 teaspoon gum arabic powder on the side of the knife and sprinkle it over the paint until it resembles a fine dusting of snow or just turns the black color to pale grayish white. Using the blade of the knife, sweep the paint into a pile and blend the arabic into it. Repeat blending until the color is even. Dip the brush into oil of cloves and gather a large drop on the bristles. Touch the oil to the edge of the paint pile and swirl oil into the paint and blend. More oil can be added with an eyedropper to mix the paint to the consistency of yogurt or almost melted ice cream. You want the paint mixture to be thin enough to flow off the brush but not puddle on the glass.

PAINTING

Place the pattern under the glass again and trace and fill the whole figure of the leopard. Do this by adding brush stroke next to brush stroke and trying not to overlap them. Don't worry about the detail lines to show the face and legs of the leopard—you want to be sure the density of the black paint is solid by removing the pattern and checking your brush strokes against the light by holding the piece up to a window or a source of illumination.

2) Place the cathedral glass on top of the pattern to begin painting with stain. You can tape the glass to the pattern near the bottom to keep the glass from moving while painting.

3) Brushing the black trace paint on the glass, covering the design of the leopard.

Try to place any needed touch up strokes or blending instantly before the paint starts to dry. The black paint will lose its shiny wet look and turn to a matt powder-like finish when it's dry. Overlapping dry with wet paint will make the result fry when fired and flake away from the glass.

DETAIL LINES

Now take a close look at the pattern for detail lines and with the tip of a craft knife, scrape them into the paint on the glass. This is called stick lighting and using the knife tip will give you a thin line to start with.

4) Stick lighting the paint with a craft knife to reveal the leopard's face and body lines. Closely examine the amber lines on the glass to be sure there are no black paint streaks or specks within the line before firing.

Widen the line by scratching the trace alongside the first one. Be careful not to form jagged paint edges by trying to take too much off at one time. Lightly blow the dry paint off the glass if the knife tip has not scraped it clear. If you aren't satisfied with the result, wipe the entire glass clean of paint and paint it over again. You may need several tries, so don't feel discouraged.

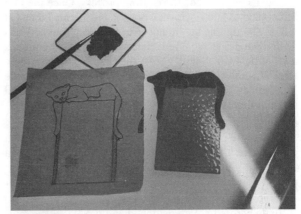

5) The finished stained leopard is ready for firing. The body lines are wide enough to show amber and the paws and tail have been detailed.

FIRING

When the stick lighting is done to your satisfaction, place the glass on the prepared kiln shelf and fire the kiln

6) Peeking in the kiln after firing. Always fire compatible glass and paints at the same time, if possible, to save time and energy.

to 1100-1250°F. You can peek at the glass for a quick moment to see that the paint is evenly red from the heat. Close the kiln lid and keep it down until the pyrometer reads below 500°F.

The near disaster mentioned in the beginning was something I brought on myself by not being patient. Excited by being close to finished and wanting to get onto the next step, I rushed the cooling process. Once the kiln has cooled to 500°F, you can open it and "dump" the heat quickly by tipping the lid upwards for about four seconds or more and then closing it. The kiln shelf itself contains a lot of heat which will "refill" the chamber but at a slow rate. When the kiln is at 300°F or less you can remove the lid completely and let the shelf release the heat and avoid thermal shocking the glass. Unless you do what I foolishly did.

When the glass is fairly cooled to below 150°F, you can remove it with a spatula to a heat proof surface such as another kiln shelf. What I did was slide the room temperature spatula under the glass when it was still about 350°F.

Even before I got it positioned halfway under the middle of the glass it pinged at the bottom edge. I withdrew the spatula and held my breath. The crack started to move up the center of the glass. The closer it got to the leopard the lower my hopes were that it wouldn't just run smack up the middle and split in half. Of course I was thoroughly annoyed with myself for rushing this step when I just plain knew better.

Just before reaching the leopard's belly, the crack took a sharp right turn and stopped under the hindquarters. What to do now—the whole amber cathedral piece was no good because of the crack and after investing that much time and effort I couldn't bring myself to dispose of it. I decided that the only way to save it was to cut the leopard with the band saw as a stand alone object completely out of what was left of the original piece of glass.

Gingerly cutting into the amber from the right side below the tail, I joined the end of the crack and removed half the amber glass from under the leopard. I then completed the cutting so the figure of the leopard was the sole remaining piece of glass.

Since the whole point of painting the leopard was to provide delicate lines as opposed to the heaviness of doing him in the many pieces of soldered foil that would be required, I decided to laminate him to a new piece of glass that would now be the back of the card holder. The modified amount of light coming through the amber glass convinced me I needed a white opalescent background to enhance and dramatize the leopard.

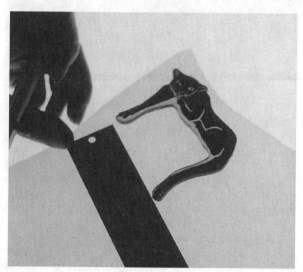

7) After the fired leopard has been cut from the cracked glass, position and measure the leopard for the new back glass.

Draw a 2-1/2" by 3-1/2" rectangle on the white opalescent glass and a second line about 1" above the top of the 2-1/2" line. Position the leopard to lie between these lines. Align the paw and tail so they fall just outside the right and left border lines of the rectangle.

Outline the leopard with an ultra fine pen against the white opalescent glass. Then remove the leopard and cut the shape as it appears, including the rectangle and the leopard outline as one piece. On the grinder make sure the white outline will allow the black leopard to fit exactly without showing any white glass. Mark under the paw and tail for foiling.

Cut two wing side pieces for the business card about 1/2" wide, the two different measurements from the leopard's paw on the right and his tail on the left to the bottom of the holder will determine the height of these sides. Grind them and then foil with 7/32". Add a strip of 7/32" foil on the face of the back glass on the left and right edges under the paw and tail down to the bottom to allow the side pieces to be attached. Foil around the edge of the back glass starting under the paw and ending under the tail. Finally, trim the upper square edge of the face foil to a round corner so it doesn't stick out beyond the side piece.

Tin the face foil on the left and right edges of the back glass and all the edges of the two side pieces. Finish soldering the tops of the side pieces with an edge bead so that step is done before adding them to the back glass of the card holder. Stand the back upright on the work bench within a right angle or roofer's square as a guide and add each side piece flush against the guide and against the pre-tinned face foil.

Spot solder the sides in position, then complete soldering on the inside and outside. Place the back glass with

8) The new back glass and leopard are matched to check the fit on the outside edges. The paw and tail foil start and stop points are marked. The card will fit under the leopard without crowding.

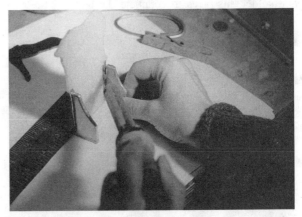

10) Spot solder the wings against the back glass in the upright position to level the bottom.

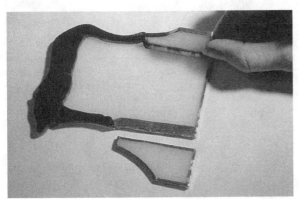

9) Position the right wing so it's on top of the face foil and just under the tail. Note that the foil on the left ends just under the paw.

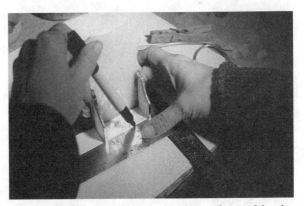

11) Place the holder body on the glass to be used for the bottom and trace the inside area. Use a ruler placed across the side wing pieces to define the front while marking the clear glass.

the two attached sides on a piece of clear glass to provide the bottom. Trace the inside lines and place a ruler across the front edge of the two side pieces to mark the front of this bottom glass. It will fit up and in between the side pieces and the back. Cut, foil, and solder this last piece so its front edge matches the length of the side pieces.

FINISHING

With the card holder on its back, place another piece of clear glass across the projecting section of the two side pieces. This will be the front panel. Mark, cut to size, foil, and solder this piece to complete the body of the card

12) After soldering the bottom in, measure and cut a piece of clear glass for the front and complete soldering.

holder. Clean with soap and water and dry. Add patina, then clean and polish with glass compound.

Check the position of the leopard body on the top of the card holder. It should fit on top, matching to the outside edge of the background glass. When the cards are in the holder, the leopard appears to be reclining on the last four or five cards, so test fit a card to be sure it clears the leopard's body on the three sides, almost touching the box area of the cards.

Brush black enamel paint on the edge and 1/16" in on the face of the white background glass to blend it to the edge of the leopard's body. This will disguise the seam and give the leopard a rounder dimensional appearance. Dab glass epoxy or silicone adhesive under the front leg, center of the body, and under the tail and place it on the background glass. Weight it for about two hours to dry (or per adhesive instructions) before standing the cardholder upright. Trim any adhesive that may have squeezed out from under the leopard and check the level on a piece of glass. If the card holder rocks, add a spot of solder to the bottom, re-patina the area, and wipe clean.

The effect of the raised leopard sprawled across the top of the cards is quite dramatic. The weight shift to the center of the holder adds stability as it stands a little more than 3-1/2" upright and the white glass helps transmit light up through the amber of the face, eyes, and body lines.

The accidental cracking of the panel was a springboard to improving the design one step further than originally conceived. Stained glass is like that. This is one occasion when a leopard almost cracked but still landed on all fours.

CHAPTER 21
Swirls of Color: Kaleidoscope

by Patricia Daley

"I have always been attracted to the colors of cathedral glass moving across the church pews on Sundays. It was a delight to have a small beam of color on my hand and in my palm—to possess it for a brief moment until it moved onto someone else who probably never noticed it."

WHAT'S A KALEIDOSCOPE?

For some people, it's not so much a question of what it is as how to spell it. A kaleidoscope is a tube made of glass (or a number of other materials such as copper or

look through but also to look at, and this is where stained glass kaleidoscopes can compare with the very best of them.

This helicopter kaleidoscope is by Clarity. The eyepiece is in the tail and the mirrors reflect up to the image wheels that make the whirling blades.

Kaleidoscope from Clarity based on a biplane design. The eyepiece is in the tail and the view is toward the prop image wheels.

brass piping, or even a beer bottle) through which you look to see swirls and patterns of color that can be repetitive or of infinite variety. As you look through the scope and turn either the instrument itself or a built in element made for the purpose, the constantly changing blends of hues and designs is almost hypnotic. It has become the practice to create scopes that are not only fascinating to

TYPES OF KALEIDOSCOPES

Now more popular then ever, kaleidoscopes have grown from casual curiosities to accepted "objets d'art." They come in all sorts of shapes and sizes with all sorts of individual modifications, though the basic building blocks are pretty much the same for all. It's all done with mirrors, and like the Indian rope trick, the spectacular end result has to be seen to be appreciated.

There are four categories of kaleidoscopes:

1) The tumble box kaleidoscope, the one we favor, can be filled with just about anything. We like glass chips, but have seen them filled with almost anything, even with small pieces of colored portraits. Whatever you use, light must be able to penetrate it. The box can be round or hexagonal as long as it is in balance and can be turned easily. Here the patterns and the color blends are never repeated.

2) The stationary wheel. Here the viewed objects are fixed in flat disk form, usually foiled and soldered in place, but they may also be epoxied or fused. For best effect in this case, there would be two wheels rotating either in the same or opposite directions, or one stationary wheel and one turning wheel to provide the color and pattern activity. Since the viewed elements are themselves fixed, repetitive patterns will eventually occur.

3) The oil filled wand. This element of a kaleidoscope is a plastic tube filled with shaped glitter, colored granules, or small tumbled gemstones suspended in a clear oil. When the wand is held diagonally the elements float past the range of vision. The oil is thick enough to keep the elements from falling through it too quickly so the eye can be fascinated by the multiple shapes and colors.

4) The marble kaleidoscope. This is the least complicated but also, from our viewpoint, the least effective. It consists of a large marble with swirls of color, that is hand rotated within a wire enclosure. When you look through the marble, the distortion and the movement of color make the patterns. Granted, there is some variety, but when compared with the rich and constant leapfrogging design of the tumble box, this is a pretty passive instrument.

We mentioned beer bottles as novelty item kaleidoscopes. Here the outward show can be more provocative than the inward one. Carefully cut the bottom off a beer bottle using either a hot wire or a bottle cutting kit. Keep the rest of the bottle intact and use the cut-off bottom as a fixed wheel with elements either glued or fused. Glue the new bottom back in place so that the final product still looks, at least from the outside, like your favorite brew container. Affix the mirrors inside by filling around them with tightly packed paper and drill a hole in the bottle cap for the eyepiece. The fun here is a) offering it to someone to look through and watching their reaction as they realize how unique an item it is, and b) drinking the original contents. If you make a number of these at a time you may find your own reaction becoming more colorful.

The finished kaleidoscope with enameled roses and feet.

BUILDING A TUMBLE BOX KALEIDOSCOPE

Materials

6" x12" opalescent glass for the body

6" x 12" clear window glass (or a 3" x 6" textured and 3" x 6" non-textured) for the tumble box

3" x 3" clear glass for the eyepiece

Clarity brand mini-scope refill kit consisting of three pre-cut front surface mirrors, brass axle post, rivets, and felt dots.

copper foil 1/4" or 7/32" (your preference)

50/50 solid core solder

roll each of masking tape and scotch tape

Making the Body

Choose an opalescent glass with distinctive color markings. Measure and cut three pieces 1-1/8" x 8". Make

1) The three foiled 1-1/8" x 8" strips for the body of the kaleidoscope. These roses were painted with enamels and fired for this kaleidoscope.

the 8" cut first to save the remaining 4" x 6" piece for the tumble box end. The glass strips will be assembled in a triangle shape so if the glass has a special spot of color worth highlighting, plan to have that showing on one of the two sides up and decide which end you want it—the object end (where the tumble box is installed) or the eyepiece end (the end you look through).

Planning for the Axle Post

Before foiling the three cut strips, consider what width of foil to use. This depends on the thickness of the glass and your foiling ability. It is important to choose the proper width both for strength and aesthetics. The glass strips form a triangle where you mount the axle post. This post suspends the tumble box.

The axle post may be mounted on the inside or the outside of the body, at the object end, and will be soldered to the foiled edges of the glass. With 7/32" foil there's not much exposed inside the body, but it may provide insufficient edging to solder on the brass axle post. It can be frustrating trying to attach a 1/8" post to a delicate edge of foil. Avoid this by increasing the foiled area by adding additional 7/32" foil to the surfaces of the glass, being careful not to come down too far. With 1/4" foil, you can cover too much surface on thin glass and make the eventual soldered seams big and bulky. Over foiling can cause excessive solder buildup, leading to excessive heat from the soldering process, leading to the glass cracking while you are still in the initial process.

Foiling the Body

Place the three strips of glass face down, side by side, in the sequence you want them in the triangle tube shape that will form the body of the kaleidoscope. For purposes of this discussion, keep the eyepiece ends closest to you. Remove the strip planned for the bottom of the kaleidoscope and set it aside for the moment. Add a strip of 7/32" foil on the left piece of glass about 1-1/2" long, from the right top corner and down the right side, paralleling the edge from the object end.

Place another same size strip of foil on the right piece of glass from the left top corner object end, down the left side of the piece of glass. You should now have two pieces of glass lying side by side with a short foil strip on the face of each piece. These foiled edges should be next to each other.

Now you can foil the three pieces as you normally would, starting on the long side of the glass strips and anchoring the additional foil you have applied on the face of the glass under the foil going around the edge of the glass. Don't over burnish the foil facing up on the glass. This is for the axle post which needs the foil to be tightly adherent. Rubbing it too much will weaken the adhesive surface.

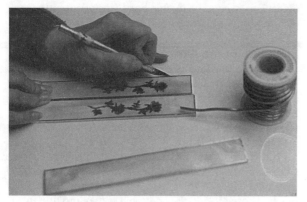

2) Trim the overlap on the foil that didn't match.

Once the glass strips are soldered into the triangle tube shape, you have the base for the kaleidoscope. The top joint will also hold the soldered axle post.

We mentioned that the axle post can be placed within or without the kaleidoscope tube. If you have looked though a stained glass kaleidoscope, you may have noticed a little brass annoyance interfering with the view. This is a rivet. There are two of these that fit in the glass

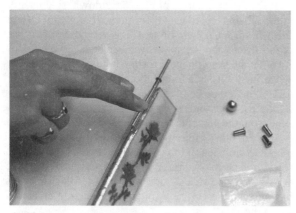

3) If you are mounting the axle rod on the exterior of the body, place the rod with about an inch protruding beyond the body to estimate where to stop soldering.

holes of the tumble box or disk wheel. Their purpose is to protect the glass holes so that as the tumble box turns on the axle post, bare glass doesn't rub them. Unfortunately these rivets tend to show. This annoyance can be eliminated by mounting the axle rod on the outside of the upper corner of the tube rather than inside it. This will raise the rivet enough to be out of eyesight.

Caution yourself by a waterproof mark to leave a space from the front end of the tube when you are starting to solder the upper seam to allow for the post to be added to this area. The post itself can be adequately buried in the solder seam and well hidden with decorative solder techniques.

4) An example of how the axle rod is hidden under decorative soldering on top of the body. Notice the marble foot holding the tumble box off the table.

You now have solved two problems—the extra foiling work previously described for mounting the axle post inside the body and getting the edge of the rivet out of the way. The advantage of putting the axle post inside the body is that you don't have to do the extra soldering required to hide it outside. If your soldering technique is weak it won't show inside. You might want to consider this factor when you choose where to put the axle post, especially if you are making your first kaleidoscope

Body Assembly and Solder Hints

The glass chosen for the body may have a heavy texture or your cutting may not be as precise as it should be resulting in glass edges that don't exactly go together. In short, the equilateral triangle tube, the body of the kaleidoscope, shows gaps along the seams. You can alleviate this problem by repositioning the strips face down and running masking tape over two of the inside seams. This will not only block the flow of solder through the gaps when you turn the strips over and form the triangle, it will hold the pieces together while they are spot tacked into position.

Keep in mind you need to be able to insert a smaller triangle of mirror into the larger triangular body; this is a precise fit and any blockage from solder will interfere with it. While the masking tape can't be removed, it takes up very little room and won't prevent the mirror placement. It also won't show from the outside. The body glass you have chosen is opaque (or should be) and will hide all the inside machinations.

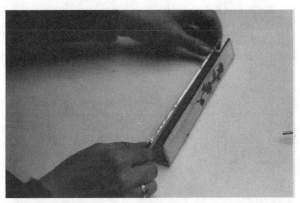

5) Position the glass into a triangle shape and spot tack with solder to stabilize.

Another way to close up gaps after forming the body triangle tube (if this is your first attempt don't let the gaps get to you) is to spot-tack the ends and then add a strip of 3/16" foil atop the foiled V-groove length of the body before adding solder. This method works fairly well if the gaps are not too extensive. If they are, you should re-cut the glass. The drawback here is that adding narrower foil to existing foil surfaces sometimes allows the adhesive from the top layer to boil out. This can pit the solder being applied and foul the new solder bead you are attempting. Hardly an aesthetic joy. One way to prevent this is to use

as little heat as possible on the foil, turning the rheostat control down so the solder will flow but the tape adhesive won't. We usually reserve this method of secondary foiling for the tumble box to insure nothing gets inside.

Filling the V-Grooves

With the body assembled, add solder to fill the V-grooves and to give a nice rounded bead to the edges. The best way I have found is to roughly fill the grooves with solder initially—this will be the base layer to close the gaps and level the solder in the seam. Tin (solder thinly) the edges of whatever copper foil has not taken solder to enable the finishing coat to flow evenly over the sides. Do this to both open ends, but lightly so the eyepiece can be added later and an edge roll can be done to the object end of the body.

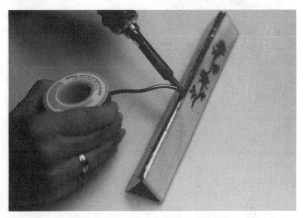

6) Begin to fill the V-groove with solder. If necessary, go over it again to round the solder bead.

Now add the finishing solder bead by cutting and placing solder from the solder roll to the tip of the iron then to the base layer already there. When melting new solder into cooler older solder, you can get ripple effects; avoid this with the "two steps forward, one step back" method. Melt off a piece of solder the width of the iron tip and place it on the seam at the end of the bead and let it flow onto it. Then re-melt the old solder to the width of the iron tip by going backwards and coming forward twice to the end of the bead. Add another slice of solder to the seam and keep repeating the process. This keeps the heat constant so you don't have to fight to blend the solder into a smooth bead. For this process we prefer using 50/50 solder rather than the 60/40 since it solidifies quickly and can be worked without the fear of melt through as can occur with 60/40. Never try to brush or run the solder along the seam, chasing it with the iron. It will get overheated and melt through the seam.

Adding the Eyepiece

You are almost ready to actually look through the kaleidoscope. But you still have a ways to go. Adding the eyepiece brings the finale a little closer.

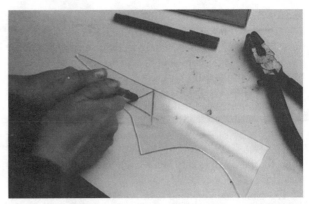

8) Straighten and extend the lines with a ruler before cutting.

This will narrow the opening of the eyepiece to hide the mirror ends and will also focus your vision into the tunnel of the kaleidoscope body. Foil around the glass with 7/32" and place it on the work table. Flux and add solder to the face of the eyepiece and build up the solder to a slight bead. With the foil on the sides overlapping the foil on the face of the glass, there will be the usual problem of the adhesive coming up to the surface. Lightly rub-

7) Outline the shape of the body for the eyepiece on clear pane glass.

Stand the body on the object end and lay the 3" x 3" clear glass we mentioned at the beginning over the eyepiece opening. Draw a triangle shape on the clear glass, splitting the edge of the body glass line down the middle. This will recess the eyepiece within the end of the tube without letting it fall inside. Use a straight edge of the clear glass as a pre-existing side. If you use the center of the glass (perhaps other portions are spotted or otherwise unusable) trace over your hand drawn line with a ruler to extend the lines to the edge of the glass and assure a good straight cut.

Cut this triangle shape and lightly round the pointed ends on the grinder. Clean and dry the eyepiece and lay strips of 7/32" foil on the surface parallel to the three edges.

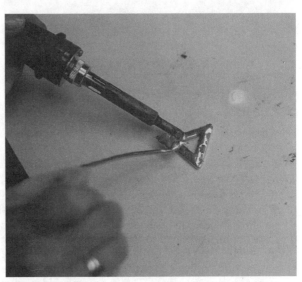

9) Soldering the eyepiece with the added strips of foil on the face of the glass.

bing with the iron tip or digging it out with an X-acto blade can remove it. Patina will also hide small surface flaws if some flecks of adhesive remain.

Wash and dry the eyepiece before placing it in position on the end of the body. Very lightly flux the eyepiece edges on the upended body. Tack solder it in position, then add small amounts of solder to the edges to conclude the sealing process and build up the solder to a finished bead.

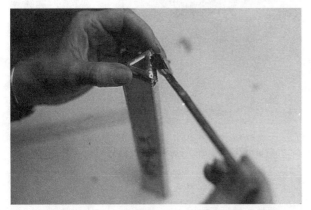

10) Lightly flux the end of the tube before soldering. Another method is to use foil to seal the eyepiece on the tube but that means dealing with more melted adhesive.

Wipe clean with a damp cloth. Now turn the body around and add an edge bead to the object end. Since you have tinned the foil there, add a little more solder to the foil until it just lips over the sides and has a nice raised bead on the open end.

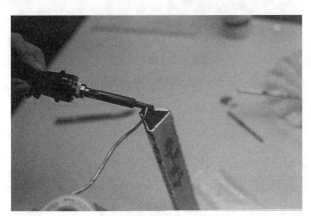

11) Apply the edge roll to the open object end of the body.

Insert a crumpled paper towel into the body to keep the inside dry and wash the flux off the whole body, dry and set it aside.

Making the Tumble Box and Axle Post

The tumble box, as we have said, provides the greatest variety to the patterns seen through the scope. For this kaleidoscope, cut pieces for the tumble box from the remaining 4" x 6" glass used for the body. There are different styles of tumble boxes. In the photo you see four strips of glass being slumped over a form in a kiln to make a round box. Or you may prefer rectangles or octagon or even oversize tumble boxes. The kiln chamber should reach a temperature of 1350°F—enough to bend the glass.

12) The four strips in position on the form for slumping to make the tumble box sides.

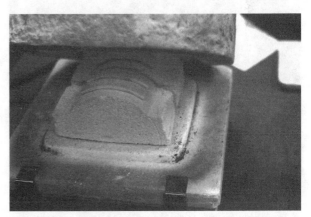

13) Checking the glass in the kiln to be sure it is completely slumped and ready for cool down.

The basic rule of thumb is to keep the box deep enough (at least 3/4") to keep apart the two rivets that pass through the clear glass holes. The finished depth of the sides of the box with the addition of the clear glass surfaces will determine how much of the axle post extends beyond the kaleidoscope body when it is soldered in place. The other consideration is to make the tumble box wide enough to clear the mirrors in the tube, otherwise you will see its edges. The tumble box rim, therefore, should be suspended below the line of sight of the opening at the object end. If using 1-1/8" glass strips to make the body, you would need a tumble box at least 3" in diameter.

Once the tumble box shape is determined, the glass is cut and foiled. Lay the pieces end to end face down against a ruler and tape across the seams with masking tape. This insures that you have one straight rim edge and will help in aligning the desired shape. Pick up the taped pieces and manipulate them to the shape of the box you are making. If you are making an octagon or hexagon shape, be very accurate in measuring these side pieces.

15) Place the strips into the desired shape for the sides of the tumble box and spot tack the seams.

16) Add solder to the seams outside and inside to firm the glass.

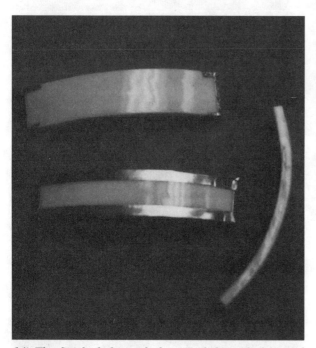

14) The finished slumped glass. Foil the ends first and then double foil the curved surface to have an even continuous face of foil.

Label one piece on the inside of the ring with an A with an arrow pointing down to the table. Slip the 6" x 12" clear glass under the ring and trace around the inside and outside of the ring with a marker. Label it A-inside and mark an arrow pointing to the one on the inside of the ring. Cut the clear glass by running the cutter centered between the two lines drawn around the ring. This will follow the exact contour and automatically center the glass on the ring rim edge. Lightly grind the glass and dry fit it against the rim marked A with the A-inside facing up into the middle. Do the same with a piece labeled B for the other side of the tumble box.

This glass can be textured—a soft open ripple, glue chipped, or hammered will best diffuse the outside light into the box. Also, if there is a visually empty spot in the box, as sometimes happens depending on the amount of material in it, such glass can provide a rather mysterious backdrop. It's your choice how much light to let in: the clearer the glass the more background (and light glare) you will see. The example shown has two clear pieces so you can readily see how much filler to add. The more filler, the fewer empty spots.

Drilling the Center Hole

17) Position the sides on the glass that will be the B diffuser glass.

19) Cut and fit the two clear glasses together and make an alignment mark on the side of the box body to match the glasses with.

18) Trace the inside and outside of the sides on the glass that will be the B diffuser glass.

20) Tape the two clear glasses together and outline them. Find the center point of the circle and mark the glass for drilling the holes.

Take the two pieces of glass previously marked as A and B and place the A-inside and B-inside markings together and tape them securely together with masking tape above and below an imaginary center mark. Then trace the outline of this shape on a plain sheet of paper. Fold the paper in half aligning the outline to find the center line; then crease. Repeat for the opposite half, then fold one more time into a quarter pie wedge and nip a small hole with scissors at the point of the wedge.

Unfold the paper, place the glass on the outline and make a small solid circle on the top glass with a water-proof marker where the center hole was cut out of the paper underneath. This is where the glass should be drilled. You can work a hole into the glass using a 1/8" bit on top of the grinder spindle by lowering the glass at a 45° angle to first start the edge of the bit into the glass. This requires a steady hand to hold the glass firmly in position under the solid circle drawn in the middle. Once the edge is seated, rock it around on top of the bit to flatten the hole and also rock the glass on the bit as it is being ground with even downwards pressure. Occasionally wet the bit with a sponge saturated with router coolant and clean the grinding dust out of the hole you are working on. When you pierce the bottom glass, water from the grinder will get between the glasses but you should concentrate on the bit that will be working through the top glass. As it gets closer to breaking though the glass, ease up on the pressure so the bit does not pop through and chip the edges of the hole.

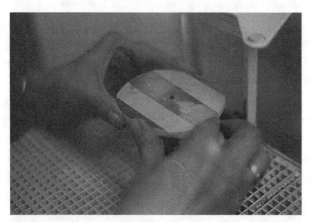

21) The two layers of glass have been drilled and the hole is being adjusted for the size of the rivets that will be inserted.

Once the hole is made, fit one of the rivets though it, increasing the size if needed on the sides of the 1/8" bit. You want the fit snug with just a tiny bit of play around the rivet.

Assembling the Tumble Box Ends

After the hole is drilled, separate the two pieces of glass and clean them one at a time. Dry fit piece A , re-label and make any alignment marks on the outside of the glass. Foil this with 1/4" and then pass the rivet though the hole to protrude to the side that will be inside the tumble box. Flux and add a small drop of solder to the shaft of the rivet to anchor it against the glass.

22) Flux and solder to the side of the shaft of the rivet to lock it down on the glass.

Place this glass face down on the side edges of the rim marked A with the rivet to the inside; then solder inside and outside to a finished roll edge.

23) Place the rivet to the inside of the tumble box, align any marks to match the glass to the sides, and solder it inside and outside.

Re-mark piece B on the outside of the rim sides and clean and patina the inside of the tumble box. If you got patina on the tinned inside edge of B don't worry: the patina will make the inside look finished. Dry fit B, aligning with the B marking on the outside edge of the ring and add the rivet to the hole. Foil, flux, and tin coat with solder as you did with A but do not attach it to the box.

Installing the Axle Post to the Kaleidoscope Body

Dry fit the alignment of B to the tumble box and check the space between the rivets. Work the threaded end of the

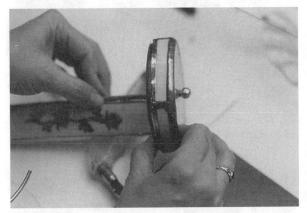

24) Dry fit the tumble box (B is soldered on, A is held in position) for marking the body and tinning the axle rod.

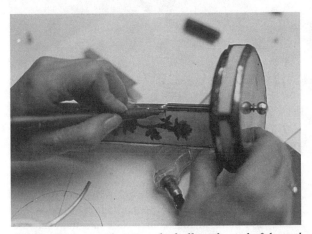

25) Note the space between the ball on the end of the rod and the glass. Mark the body where the end of the rod will be placed when it is seated into the V-groove.

axle post through B into the box and extend it beyond A about 1/4". To secure B to the box and simulate it as compete, tape it with masking tape while you align the axle post through it. It is very important that this be lined up evenly because the smooth operation of the tumble box will depend on it. Once you have extended the post through, screw the round brass ball on the threaded end. Draw it up tight against the glass end of the tumble box and push it out about 1/16". You don't want it tight up against the glass because if you over-tighten the brass ball after the post is installed on the body, you could crack this glass. Mark the post on the long end next to the rivet and withdraw the axle post from the box. The exposed axle up to this mark will be installed in the kaleidoscope body.

Holding the post with pliers or breakers, flux and tin coat the unthreaded end, being careful to keep the mark indicating how far into the kaleidoscope body to place it clear of solder. You might want to wrap a piece of tape on one side of this mark to be sure the area stays clear.

26) Flux and thin coat with solder only the portion of the axle rod that will be sunk into the V-groove.

Position the kaleidoscope body flat on the table and rotate it so the inside upper area where you will attach the axle post is against the work surface. Remember, you placed extra foil against the glass in this area. Lay the axle post within the body of the scope up to the mark, then pull it out about 1/16" to allow slack for the tumble box to rotate. Solder it in place by putting a 1/4" cut piece of solder next to the post. Reach in with the soldering iron tip and melt the solder on one side of the post. Be sure the post is level in the body as you solder it. Allow to cool, then repeat with a smaller piece of solder laid on the other side of the post if needed.

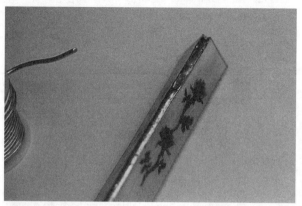

27) Add a small amount of solder to the area where the body was left undone to accept the axle rod.

If you plan to install the axle on top of the body in the V-groove, lay it in the groove and again, position the mark just a little out beyond the body to allow for the tumble box to rotate.

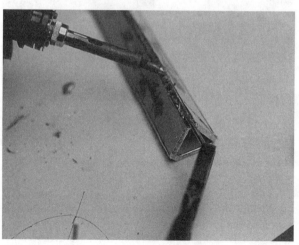

28) Position the axle rod and be sure it is straight left, right, up, and down and heat the rod to sweat-solder it into the small amount added in the V-groove.

Hold in position with pliers and spot tack in the center. Slowly add more solder and allow cooling time as you build the solder up and over on the post.

Finishing the Body

Now that the axle post is in place, do any decorative solder work as desired. We like to add feet to the object end to raise the body to better support the tumble box; this is not only practical, it is nicely decorative.

29) The completed axle installation and the body raised by coins to lift the tumble box off the table.

30) The two matching globs of solder on the scrap glass are done and solder is being applied to the underside of the body on the two corners for legs.

On a scrap piece of glass, melt solder into two equal globs. Roll some solder into a ball and add one to each glob. Add more smaller solder balls into the centers of both globs, building upwards (like stacking ice cream on a cone). On the bottom of the scope, add small solder balls in similar fashion on the seam near the object end. Place the tumble box on the axle post again and shim under the object end of the body with coins to raise the tumble box off the table.

31) More solder has been added to the foot globs to build upwards and the body legs have been built to extend down. The coins under the bottom assure proper height.

When the proper height is set, remove the tumble box and place the solder globs on either side next to the built up areas under the body. When the foot portion is aligned under the leg from the body, melt a little solder to join them at the "knee" and switch back and forth on either side to build up the solder into a thick leg to sculpture melt with the corner of the iron tip into its final shape.

32) Melt the solder at about the knee to join the foot to the leg.

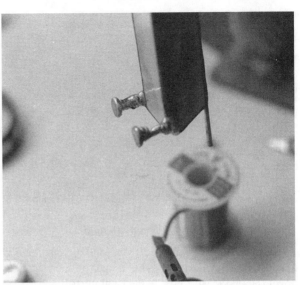

33) Add solder to the thin joint area to build it to an even thickness. The furthest leg has been completed and needs to be shaped by slowly melting and dripping the solder to fine tune it.

Installing the Mirrors

Check the inside of the scope to see if any solder blocks the mirror installation. If so, remove it by heating and drawing it back through the seams by holding the body upside down. Do any patina work and final cleaning with soap; rinse with warm water.

Lay the three pieces of front surface mirror with the protective coating face up side by side. These are special mirrors and you must be careful not to get any fingerprints on them. Most mirrors are silvered on the back surface so light must pass through a layer of glass before being reflected by the silvering. This can lead to some distortion of the image as well as ghost images, especially in a kaleidoscope since the image is reflected back and forth along its barrel. Ordinary mirror in a kaleidoscope would have fuzzy edges. Front surface mirror is made by vacuum depositing a highly reflective aluminum coating on the front of the glass so there is no distortion. The image remains clear and bright.

Under the right mirror, place two strips of invisible tape about an inch from the ends. Place the middle mirror, coated side down on top of the right mirror. Raise the right side of the top mirror as if you were opening a book but be sure that the left side of the top mirror is resting on the left edge of the bottom mirror.

34) Lay the center mirror strip on the left side edge of the right mirror and hold to about a 30° angle.

Raise the mirror to about 30° and pull the tape onto it to attach it to the right mirror. Let it open all the way back down flat on the table next to the right mirror.

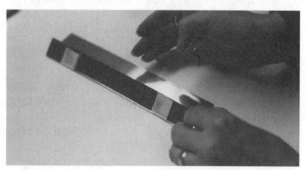

35) Position the left mirror on the now flat center mirror strip and bring the tape up the side.

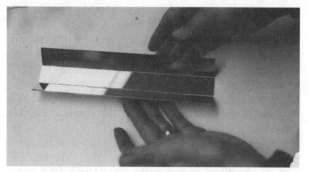

36) Try folding the mirror strips into position. Be sure the proper sequence is followed for the alignment that will give the vanished edge lines.

Add two pieces of invisible tape to the back of the middle mirror about an inch from the ends and repeat the process, placing the left strip face down on the middle mirror and taping it when raised to 30°. You should now be able to fold the three mirror strips into an equilateral triangle with one mirror edge resting on the mirror under it and becoming the bottom for the next mirror to rest on. Lay them down on the table one more time and peel the protective coating off. The best way is to peel down a corner on each strip just a little, gather them together, and draw them all off at one time. Remember not to touch the mirror surface underneath.

37) Once the alignment is verified, peel the protective plastic off the mirrors that will be inside the body.

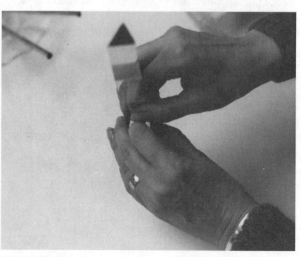

38) Fold the mirrors into the triangle shape and securely tape around the sides.

Fold the exposed mirrors back into the triangle and wrap more tape around them. As an extra, fold metal aluminum tape around the whole length of the mirror tube. The mirror tube should now easily fit into the kaleidoscope body. If it comes out just as easily, add felt dots to the sides to center and hold the mirror in place in the tube.

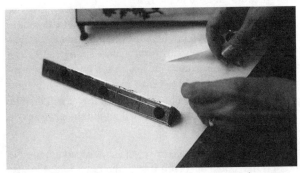

39) If using a wispy body glass or if you want to block any light from the side edges of the mirrors, wrap with aluminum tape. The dots will hold and center the mirror tube within the kaleidoscope body.

Making the Tumble Box Contents

Unthinkable to take a hammer to a pretty piece of glass? Nonsense. The scraps that plague the workshop can be put to good use by smashing them up as tumble box contents. Take a hammer and whack away. Mix colors and densities. Nuggets (glass globs) are especially fun to slam. But be careful. Glass, especially nugget pieces, fly out with considerable force. Put the glass in a shopping bag and roll fold it up several times. An old flatiron is a good anvil, but a cement floor will also do. Strike firmly once on sheet glass, nuggets may take any number of blows.

Don't try to grind the stuff to powder, quit when you have small chunks and chips. Empty the bag over a container so you can sift out what you don't want. There will be a lot of glass dust to be discarded.

Put the pieces into the tumble box. Take out any large ones which may impede the smaller pieces from rolling around inside the box.

To test how well the glass moves, fill the box by covering the whole bottom plus a quarter more with the chips. Hold or tape the B piece back in position and thread the axle post through the rivets. At last you can look though the eyepiece and see what you have accomplished! Turn the tumble box around on the post several times as you look through the eyepiece. If you see a lot of white (clear) space, add more glass to the box. Check the quantity by looking at the end of the kaleidoscope—you shouldn't see back through the box to the mirrors. If you know you have enough glass, check what's acting as a dam to prevent the pieces from tumbling around. It may be a long skinny piece wedged by the axle jamming the rest of the glass. That's the one to remove. Try again. It may take several attempts to get the right combination of shapes to move smoothly. At the same time, watch for one color dominating the overall selection. Try to blend other colors, unless a single color is what you are looking for.

40) Filling the tumble box with multi colored glass chips of different shapes.

41) Now that the tumble box has been checked for color and ease of glass movement, align the glass to any marks made on the outside of the sides and seal the edge of the clear glass to the box body with foil.

Once you've fine tuned the tumble box, it's time to solder B into final position. Be sure it's clean, then position it on the rim. Hold the scope and thread the tumble box on the axle post so B is on the outside end. Fold foil into the crease around the side to seal the edges together

42) Solder the glass to the sides and be careful of flux getting near the rivets and seeping into the box.

to make sure no solder will melt into the tumble box. If you use 1/4" foil, the adhesive may be close enough to the edge of the pre-tinned areas not to be a problem when heated. Remove the box from the axle post and cover the two rivet holes with tape to protect the inside from flux splatter, patina, and glass cleaner. Flux sparingly and neatly solder all around the rim.

Finish by doing any decorative work and then use Kem-O-Pro glass compound applied to a towel to clean the flux and solder. Patina using a small sponge and clean again with the glass cleaner. If you see condensation inside the box, it should soon evaporate unless you have managed to get glass cleaner inside. That you will have to get out the hard way because it will cloud the glass up indefinitely.

Remove the tape from the rivets and thread the tumble box on the axle and secure it with the brass ball. Finally, find a comfortable chair, sit with your elbows propped in the direction of a bright light source, and enjoy the kaleidoscope. You won't want to put it down!

CHAPTER 22
Stenciling and Enameling Nightlights

by Patricia Daley

When stained glass is applied to nightlights the result becomes more than a lighted candle that's better than cursing the darkness. The glow of a friendly nightlight has saved many a shin from a piece of furniture that shouldn't be there and brought security to many a nursery. Designs for nightlights can be wholly of stained glass or painted on a single piece of glass. Painting allows for a more personal nightlight—whether it's a child, pet, place or event—the details can be imparted in a miniature lightbox. Whether it involves the application of stencils for multiple products of the same nature or that one-of-a-kind result, the nightlight has become a formidable sales item.

We use low-fire enamels for nightlights since these transparent paints are easy to mix, overlay readily in different densities, only take a single firing (though you can re-fire for highlighting or dividing lines or to emphasize a shading), and there is a wide range of colors and shades readily available. They also maintain their colors at the slumping temperature of the small glass pieces we use for curved nightlights.

FIRING TEMPERATURES

Enamels are a mix of clear glass (the carrier) and metallic oxides (the colorant) that have been pulverized to the consistency of talcum powder. They are processed to mature at much lower temperature ranges (from 1080°F up to 1175°F) than stained glass paints, which would not cure at the enamel's lower range and would probably flake off the glass.

Temperature range, however, is different for different company's products. Test the enamel's firing capacities before beginning any project. Fusemaster enamels, for example, will not fry at 1350°F, the temperature at which small pieces of glass used for nightlights will slump. It's risky taking enamels much higher than that and for our purposes here, there's no need to. Some enamels might over-fire even at this temperature.

APPLICATION AND TYPES

Enamels are applied to glass by mixing with either a gum arabic solution recommended by their manufacturer (this will extend the drying and blending time of the enamel) or plain water. There are two distinctive types of enamels: lead based and non-leaded. In traditional work, only lead bearing enamel was used (the percentage of lead

---

Materials

small light box to paint on top of or a bright source of light to check enamel density

selection of transparent enamel powders, olive green, black, red

mixing medium (water friendly)

2 small bowls of water (one to add liquid to the powdered enamels and the second for rinsing brushes)

medium line (00 size) and fine line (000 or 0000) sable paint brushes

oval or square of white opalescent glass not larger than 5-1/2" x 5-1/2"

4" x 4" square of clear window pane with ground edges for a palette

6" x 6" clear adhesive or low-tack frisket paper

ultra fine waterproof pen

craft knife

thin tweezers

electric tabletop kiln with pryrometer

---

allowing for the lower firing range) but now non-leaded enamels are made in the same range of colors and are available for general use. Your local supplier may have some on hand or can order some. The non-leaded may be an unusual item to stock.

Different colors of enamels will have different prices—the various shades of red will be more expensive than blues and greens. Enamels come in plastic resealable bags, starting at one ounce.

PREPARING THE STENCIL

The pattern shown here is a rose that will have a colored background on the "canvas" of the white opalescent glass. Remember, enamels are transparent colors. White is used so the glass itself will not influence the color of the transparent enamels. To have a crisp line for the outline of the rose, stem, and leaves, a stencil will be made to keep that area of the glass white while the background color is applied.

As a first step, position the adhesive/ frisket paper under the glass. Outline the glass shape with an ultra fine tip waterproof pen. Cut the paper approximately 1/8" larger than the outline. Center and trace the rose design from the pattern to the plastic side of the stencil material.

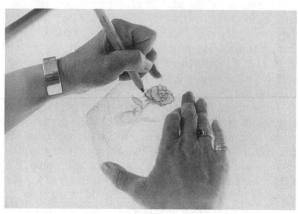

1) Tracing the rose from the final pencil drawing onto adhesive/frisket paper.

Clean the white glass and dry it before applying the stencil. To position the stencil on the glass, make sure it's right side up, then lift a corner of the paper backing and expose the adhesive side by peeling the paper backing carefully from underneath until part of the outline of the

glass is reached. Match the line of the outside of the stencil to the edge of the glass and continue to slowly peel the backing paper away from underneath while smoothing the top plastic onto the glass.

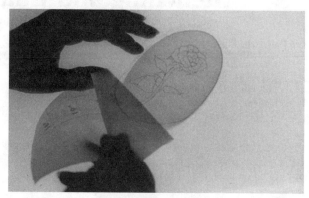

2) Expose the adhesive side of the paper at the top of the pattern and position it on the glass. Peel the paper backing and smooth the sheet onto the glass. Partially lift and smooth again to eliminate air bubbles if necessary.

If air bubbles are trapped or you get off position, lift the stencil and reapply. After you have done this, use the craft knife to carefully cut the shape of the rose, stem, and leaves as individual pieces. Lift off the background area only, leaving the rest covered by the plastic.

MIXING THE ENAMEL

On the blade of a craft knife, measure a small amount of the enamel powder you have selected for the background onto the clear glass palette. Dip the medium size brush into a bowl of water. This water will be the source of clean water for mixing the enamels if you are not using the mixing medium suggested by the enamel manufacturer. When using a small amount of enamel I have found that a brush tip full of water or medium is a good way to control how much liquid is being added to the powder for mixing. Touch the wet brush to the edge of the pile of powder and draw the powder into it, stirring the color around on the glass palette. If it is still not wet enough, add another brush tip full of water. When properly mixed, the enamel will be the consistency of almost melted ice cream, thin enough to flow from the brush onto the glass but not watery. Once mixed, load the enamel on the brush by rolling the brush around on the mix so as to gather the enamel onto the bristles.

APPLYING THE BACKGROUND

Holding the brush at a slant, work in a circular motion from the center out so the denser, darker area will be behind the rose and fading out to the edges of the glass. You can go on top of the stencil if needed to apply enamel into small tapering areas where you may want a consistent color or blend. Try not to let the enamel pile up against the edge of the stencil because a chip out of the edge may occur when lifting the stencil off the glass. If the result is not quite what you envisioned, use your wet fingertip to blend and smooth the area together. Interesting effects are achieved with finger painting in this way, but do it quickly because the enamel will begin to dry as you work it. Don't put your finger to your lips by accident.

When you are done, *immediately rinse your hands* and swish the brush in the second container of water to clean it. The enamel cleaned from the brush will settle to the bottom of the bowl. Using a compatible mixing medium from the manufacturer will slow the drying down and also allow easier blending. Water will evaporate and leave the dried powder thick and less easily blended than if you use medium. If the result does not work the first time, you can brush off the dried powder and reuse it.

PAINTING THE ROSE

With the background in place and dry, you can paint the rose in the top area of the glass. With the point of a craft knife, carefully lift off the center section of the stencil covering the rose. Use the tweezers to grasp and peel

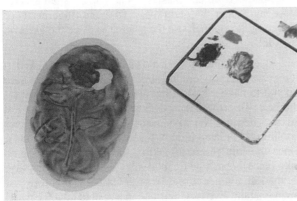

3) The background has been cut away and finger painted, leaving the rose, stem, leaves, and butterfly covered by the paper. Now one petal of the rose has been exposed for painting.

the plastic off the glass. Leave the stem and leaves in place for now. You will have a perfect outline of the rose against the stippled background.

To add the detail of the petals, load a small amount of yellow enamel (much smaller than the background) on the edge of the knife. Use clean water on the brush tip to mix the enamel, then load the medium size brush. Starting in the center of the rose, flow the enamel on the exposed glass, coming as close as you can to the background color without actually touching it. If you touch the dry background enamel with the wet brush, it may absorb some of the moisture and show as a darkened half round area. Don't worry, it should dry the same color if it was just a touch.

When you've finished filling in the rose color, rinse and clean the brush. Draw the bristles into a fine point tip and lay it aside to dry. (Take good care of your brushes and they will take good care of you.)

Use the tip of the knife and the tweezers to lift the stencil off the leaves and stem. Measure an even smaller quantity of green and switch to a fine line brush. Mix and first apply the enamel to the stem and leaf stems. This will require long and short strokes for proper brush control to lay down the enamel. When this is finished, fill in the leaves. Keep the heavier application of enamel toward the edges or maybe 1/2 of the leaves to give you some shading texture; the thinner the enamel the more translucent it becomes. Clean the brush and check what has been done so far.

If you are painting on the light box, you will see your brush strokes as you make them. Use them to indicate light and dark areas if you wish by adding a thin top coat of enamel on the first layer even as you paint it. If you hold the glass up to the light by the edges, you can check the effect. If you are satisfied with the density of the enamels through the white opalescent, go onto the next step of adding the details to make the rose petals and veining the leaves.

If your rose is light colored, petal shading may be achieved by adding another layer at what would be the base and underside of the petals. Small upward curves placed randomly and overlapping will build the shape of the petals. If you have a large selection of enamel colors, you can layer on a secondary color, say orange, on top of a yellow base coat. The change of color will show a definite line, but a little extra wet top coat will allow you to blend this discrepancy. Highlighting by way of adding a wiggly shadow line under the lip of the lighter yellow petal will give depth to the shaded area of the petals. On the leaves, thin center black vein lines can be stroked onto the green directly and fired in place. Extremely thin outlining with the ultra thin brush can be helpful in defining the break between the object in the foreground to the stippled background.

FINAL DETAILS

To accomplish the final details of the rose, clean the fine tip brush and prepare the black enamel. Make it a thinner mix than before, as you want it to flow easily off the tip. You will be drawing rather than brushing with the tip. Load the brush and be sure to roll it to a fine point. Don't load it too heavily with enamel—you don't want to blot out your prior work. To be sure this won't happen, test the flow of your stroke on a clean spot on the palette. When you decide how much enamel to gather up, very lightly draw a slightly curved center line or follow the

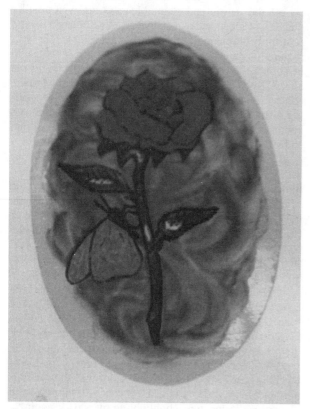

4) *The finished enameled glass. Note the highlight lines on the petals and veining on the leaves.*

contour of a leaf. Add a row of tiny upside-down V-angled brush strokes to give the jagged sawtooth edge of a rose leaf around the bottom half. Randomly draw thin lines from the center line down almost to the edge of the leaf for the veins. The stems can be traced on either side with black, but be careful not to go through an area where a leaf stem comes out. Outline under the leaf stem for shading slightly heavier than you do the top line.

The rose head itself will be suggested by layering color to give it depth. At the very base of the rose, lightly outline the layers of the petals but don't go all the way up to the top of the petal. Where the lip of the petal would fold out and down, just a little wiggle (as a funny smile) will be enough. On the petal coming up from that one, an ultra thin elongated U shape with a slight hump in the center will top the bottom petal and the start of the next one. Use the darker yellow semicircular areas as your guide for petal placement. For the very center where the rose is still unopened, three or four tight curves and semicircles will denote closed petals. Better to be understated with the black lines than trying to outline each petal as an individual element. With that accomplished, clean your brush and point the tip before putting it away. The enamels on your palette can air dry and if the small piles are separate enough, they can be scraped back into their containers with a clean single edge razor blade.

FIRING THE PANEL

Open the tabletop kiln and check the kiln shelf. Use a long spatula to spread plaster of Paris on the shelf as a release and center the glass on it. To avoid fingerprints or smearing the enamel, use the spatula to place the glass on the shelf.

Close the kiln and heat the chamber to 1350°F. When it reaches that temperature shut the kiln off. You can then open it to have a look at the panel and to begin lowering the heat. To protect your eyes from the glow and the hot air and because the kiln needs to be closed for proper cooling, don't keep it open for more than a few seconds. Once the kiln reaches 1200°F, for proper annealing to take place it can't be open at all. Control your curiosity; let the kiln temperature drop to at least 300°F before you open it again. Even so, don't be in a rush to take the panel off the shelf. The difference in the temperature of the spatula and the hot glass will cause the panel to crack within a second or two after the spatula is inserted under it. Best to wait until the temperature is all the way down.

BENDING THE GLASS

If you want to make a curved nightlight, you don't need two firings. The glass can be bent on your mold and the colors matured all in a single firing. It is especially necessary in this case to allow the temperature to come fully down before unloading the kiln because the glass will be under additional stress from being curved.

FINISHING THE NIGHTLIGHT

Hardware is available as part of a socket kit you can purchase for making nightlights. Part of this is a clip with a mounting bar to which the glass can either be soldered or epoxied. A screw and nut (also included) will pinch the clip to the socket. When placed in the wall socket the nightlight should remain upright. If it pitches forward you can slightly bend the clip to balance it.

Three examples of fired and slumped nightlights featuring pets, with Si Isenberg's yellow lab, Champion in the center. The angel is for a specialty gift shop and scenic Portland Headlight at the bottom is fired flat for a panel in a banker's lampshade.

CHAPTER 23
Stepping Stones and Mosaics

by Patricia Daley

The art of mosaic decoration has been around for over a thousand years but has been recently adapted to new uses in decorative glasswork. Colored chips of glass are usually the way to go, but in this instance we are going to use glass cut to follow a specific pattern, then applied and grouted. You'll step lively on this one.

Making Stepping Stones

There are two methods of making stepping stones. In the first, you cast and reinforce cement in a form; in the second, you use an existing cement form to build from.

Method One

Making the mold: Outline the shape of the stone on a two-foot square of 3/4" plywood. Use a basic shape such as rectangle, hexagon, or square. Screw 1" x 2" strips of wood cut to fit against the outline into the plywood. Make another layer of wood strips and screw them through the first layer on the plywood. Cut and screw a third layer of wood strips to the first two. This will build up the sides of the mold to hold the cement. Be sure the sides are flush

Reusable molds come in a variety of shapes and sizes.

even on the inside so the cement will not hang up on edges of the layered wood when the time comes to tip it out

after curing. Cut a piece of reinforcing wire (such as 1/4" square galvanized fence mesh) to fit into the mold. There are now prefab molds available in a small variety of shapes that will eliminate building your own mold, but if you have a certain shape or size you have to make, a custom wood mold is necessary.

Cut paper to fit inside the bottom of the mold to define the pattern size and shape. Mark the paper face down in one corner and turn it over to draw the pattern, leaving a 2" border all around the edges. Use a waterproof marker with a fine tip to finalize the pencil lines. After the pattern is drawn, number each piece along with a direction arrow to align the flow of the glass streaking and swirls and note if a piece is to be light or dark at any particular spot. Make a duplicate copy of the pattern to use as reference when grinding.

Choose opalescent glass to work with because this project will be seen in reflected light, showing the surface color of the glass. Antique glass is nice but needs light coming through it, an impossibility here. Trace the pattern on clear adhesive paper or artist's frisket paper (if needed, tape two pieces side-by-side to fit the whole pattern). Trace the completed pattern on the plastic side and add the numbers. Set aside.

Cut the pattern pieces to the left and right sides of the black lines to make them smaller so the glass pieces will have 1/8" to 1/4" between each of them. Position and trace the pattern on the glass with an ultra fine tip waterproof marker. Cut the glass, grind to fit the pattern piece, and mark with the number on the back side.

Coat the inside of the mold with nonstick cooking spray. This will act as a mold release agent for the cement after it has set up and you're ready to tip it out of the mold.

Peel the paper backing off the adhesive paper or frisket sheet and place it sticky-side-up on the bottom of the mold. Press the numbered glass pieces firmly into place face down (this is why you numbered the back side) on the sticky surface. If the design has too many small pieces to comfortably reposition one at a time, arrange them face up on the table and stick the sheet over the face of them,

1) Cut and fit the wire mesh reinforcing to fit the mold, either before or after the glass is in position.

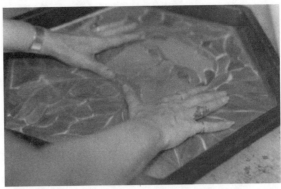

4) Smooth the sheet onto the glass to be sure all the pieces are attached so all will move at once when turned over.

2) The glass has been ground to create wide and narrow lines. The cement will detail the lines of the face and oak leaf veins of the "Green Man" design.

3) Apply the adhesive sheet to the face-up glass in preparation for turning it over and final positioning in the mold. The "Green Man" was made inside the mold and had to be removed for turning.

matching up with the pattern lines on the top. Firmly smooth the adhesive/frisket sheet onto the face of the glass pieces. Support and drag the affixed pieces onto a heavy paper or cardboard in order to flip over and lay into the mold. Finalize the position of all the pieces and over-all space around the sides of the mold.

Mixing the Cement and Reinforcing the Stone

Follow the package directions and mix a bucket of cement (usually about 1/4 the bag). Add the water slowly and thoroughly stir it in with a wooden stick. You want the cement to be slightly thickened when you pour it into the mold. Carefully pour or scoop out a small amount of cement to spread over the glass pieces. Be careful not to dislodge the pieces as you work the cement into the spaces between the glass. After a rough coat is applied, pour cement more freely to fill almost half the mold. Place the wire reinforcement piece into the cement, gently pressing it down in the cement. Add the remaining cement to the mold, being careful not to overfill the mold sides.

Trowel the top of the cement smooth and gently vibrate the surface of the cement to raise the water and air bubbles. At that time, you may want to sign your work on the back of the stone using a blunt pencil or other pointed object before it hardens.

Let the cement rest in the mold for two days to dry before tipping it out onto a firm surface. Remove the adhesive/frisket paper from the glass area and clean off any cement that got on the surface of the glass pieces with a blunt wooden dowel or pencil. Place it on a support that

5) *Partially fill the mold with cement, then add the reinforcing mesh. Push it down as flat as possible without disturbing the glass underneath. Wear protective gloves for easy cleanup.*

6) *The pattern has been carbon copied on a cement patio paver. The pattern pieces and glass are laid on to show spacing.*

will allow air circulation under as well as over it for one day for the final curing.

The advantage to casting the first stone (not in the Biblical sense) is to completely make it one with the glass which is now embedded in its surface. The disadvantage is having an open bag of cement leftover. But then, you still have the mold which you can use again so why not make a few more stepping stones to keep your feet dry and your eyes asparkle?

Method Two

You can skip the mold making process and the masonry work by purchasing patio paving block at the local Saturday hangout for guys—the home improvement/do-it-yourself mega store. These blocks come in a variety of shapes and sizes—round, rectangular, or octagonal. They are mass produced with either a smooth cement like a cinder block or a more open pocket texture similar to popcorn that has been compressed to fit the shape. For the purpose of affixing the glass properly, use a smooth finished one if it is available. The other will work but it takes more adhesive to fill under the glass area.

Trace the shape of the block on paper and draw the pattern, keeping at least 1/4" away from the edge for a border. Follow the same steps for numbering, direction lines, and shading indicators for placing the pattern pieces on the glass as detailed in Method One. Make a copy of the pattern to fit the ground pieces against.

Place the pattern on the block and transfer the pattern by tracing over carbon paper onto the block itself. The more open texture may be harder to trace on but these guidelines are necessary to place the glass on. To prevent smudging the carbon lines after the tracing is done, spray lightly with hair spray or clear sealant. Cut the pattern as in Method One, leaving space between the glass pieces for the grout to be worked around the glass. Grind and fit to the duplicate pattern until all pieces are done.

Use clear latex caulking compound as the basis for the glass pieces. You will need a caulking gun to squeeze the compound onto a scrap of wood or cardboard. Cut the tip of the caulking compound tube to about 1/4". Pierce the inner liner with several small holes and squeeze the rod up to the back of the tube. Draw a bead of compound on a piece of scrap paper and use an old knife to "butter" the back of the glass with the adhesive. If a caulking gun is a tool you can live without, you can buy small tubes of clear silicone sealant at any hardware store. Depending on the size of your project, purchase two or three tubes. They are resealable, unlike the caulking compound which you have to seal with aluminum foil to keep from drying out.

Spread the adhesive on the back of the piece of glass with a little more in the center and tapering to the edges. Using the carbon lines for guides, position the glass and and press it firmly in place on the block. If you are using a block with the more open texture, please add more to help fill the texture under the glass to help level it. Give it a little twist to spread the adhesive on the block, but be

7) *Spread the adhesive thick in the center, tapering to the edges of the glass.*

sure that what may squeeze out from under the glass doesn't fill the space between the glass pieces. Now that you have covered the top of the block with the glass, sight across the surface for any pieces that may stick up over it and press them down by tapping them gently with a small block of wood until they are seated. Check again for the adhesive between the pieces. You should be able to run a pencil down in the space which will help smooth or dig out excess glue. Let the block rest for a day to allow the adhesive to cure.

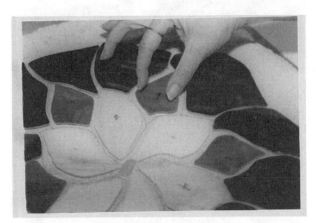

8) *Position the glass pieces and slightly twist while pushing down to force the caulk into the texture of the paver. Watch for caulk coming out from under the glass, filling the grout area. If this happens, clean it off.*

Mix the tile grout to fill in around the glass. There are two types of grout—plain and smooth or with sand added. They come in a variety of colors so choose one that complements the colors of the glass. The instructions on the box will probably yield more grout than you need. The area you will cover is a matter of square inches, not square feet. Spoon some grout into a container and add water a small amount at a time until it's a thick creamy consistency like frosting. If you need more grout, add powder first, then water and mix thoroughly.

9) *The final row of border glass has been applied and the patio block is ready to grout after curing.*

Doing the next step by hand is fun, but gloves are recommended because grout is difficult to get out from under your fingernails and it dries your skin. Gloves will also make cleanup much easier. Scoop out a handful of grout and spread it, working it into one section of the block. Force the grout between the pieces until it comes back up and spreads ahead of its application. Add more grout if your handful is thinning out—fanning out to cover other areas. Don't be afraid to have it lightly cover some of the lower pieces of glass if there is a difference in height. If you used a texture-up glass such as granite or ripple, don't overfill on top of the piece, just fill the gaps around the glass.

After the grout has been applied and is beginning to set, gently wipe the excess off the surface of the glass pieces with a barely damp sponge. Be very careful not to gouge or wear the grout down below the edges of the glass—keep the grout even with the glass surface. You may have to rub a bit forcefully if it has dried too quickly.

Begin cleaning excess grout off the glass with a damp sponge before it dries. The thin haze left on the glass can be buffed off with liquid glass cleaner after the grout firms.

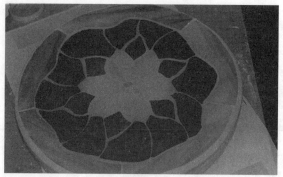

The cleaned and finished patio paver is ready for landscaping. (Jan Goudy class project)

Use a flat wooden tool such as a craft stick, chopstick, or blunt dowel to push the grout off the glass. Using a scouring sponge, soften any sharp areas to a level compatible with the surrounding grout. Let the block dry for an hour or two before buffing the remaining haze off the glass with steel wool and/or Chem-O-Pro. After the grout has completely dried, seal with liquid clear sealer to make it waterproof. Liquid clear sealer can be applied with a small brush just wider than the grout lines.

Indoors or Out?

There are pros and cons about leaving stepping stones outdoors during winter. If you have wire reinforced the cast stone, it may be all right. The prefab blocks from the store are supposed to be weather tough. Our advice (and what we do with our stones) is take them inside. You have worked hard to make the mosaic design. If you have any doubts about the effect of frost and expanding moisture trapped under the bottom of the stone, clean it thoroughly and bring it inside. Prop it up in a corner to enjoy throughout the winter, knowing that the snow will melt someday.

The "Green Man" stepping stone was cut from one sheet of Kokomo-122. It will eventually be used as a tabletop. (Designed and made by Pat Daley)

CHAPTER 24
Working with Stained Glass Beads

by Alice Foster Zimmerman

Along with her partner (and daughter) Kimberly Gingench, Alice Foster Zimmerman is the co-owner of Alice's Stained Glass (ASG) in Glendale, Arizona. This follows a family tradition learned from Alice's grandmother, Ruth Sparrow. Her interest in glass beads began with the desire to further enhance fused glass jewelry, and has grown from there. Her skills rank her among the finest bead makers in the country and her classes in bead making have earned her a national reputation in the stained glass community. She has produced three bead making videos: Lampwork Beads, Lampwork Beads, Advanced Decorating, and Lampwork Beads, Design, Shape and Color.

Many animal species are blessed with natural adornment, but humans have always had to decorate themselves. Beads are the oldest known form of adornment used by humans. They have been fashioned from bones, stones, animal teeth, shells, ivory, wood, precious metals, clay, coral, macaroni, paper, plastic, and glass. Lampwork glass beads stand out among the rest, and in many cultures, are still used as currency and to denote the wearer's wealth and position in society.

There are various ways to make beads from glass but the finest detail and most enduring quality is found in lampworked beads. The name is derived from the "lamps" over which the beads are made. Originally, glass was melted into beads over the flame from the worker's light source—hence the term lampwork. They are also called wound beads, referring to the winding motion used when the beads are made. Once the glass has been melted onto a rod or wire, it is shaped and decorated in the flame while still molten.

The ideal work area for bead making should be compact enough that everything needed is within easy reach. Bead making requires a relatively small area to work in, and surprisingly few tools. The tools used are simple: the torch that provides the flame, the mandrels (metal wires or rods) on which the beads are made, a graphite paddle with which to shape the molten glass, safety glasses, the glass for the beads, and an annealing pan. Other than that, a variety of pliers, a press, and other odds and ends, are all that is needed. A fire extinguisher should also be close at hand.

The work area should be neat and have as many of the various elements to hand as possible. You don't want to have to start looking for things in the midst of working with a hot bead.

The Tools

A lamp or a torch is the primary tool for bead making and provides the flame for melting the glass. An oxygen/propane "surface mixed" torch made to sit on the work bench is the best choice for bead making. Surface mixed refers to the ability to control the mixture of the gasses at the torch rather than pre-mixed at the tanks. A bench torch is preferable for its stability and because comfort is important for the user, it greatly reduces the neck and shoulder fatigue associated with long hours working in the flame.

Although beads can be made using propane alone, oxygen intensifies the flame and provides the cleanest flame possible. Propane torches draft air rather than oxygen to intensify the flame and the consequence can be discolored

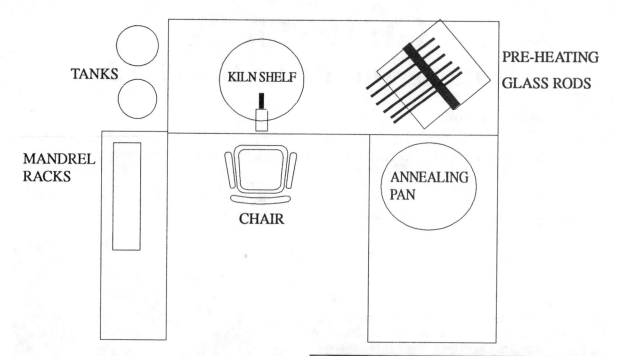

TANKS

KILN SHELF

PRE-HEATING
GLASS RODS

MANDREL
RACKS

CHAIR

ANNEALING
PAN

glass and "burned" spots in the beads. Glass will react differently to the flame, depending on the contents of the glass and an experienced bead maker can adjust the mix of gasses to suit the glass.

An oxygen tank with a dual gauge and a propane tank with a regulator are used to feed the torch. One gauge on the oxygen tank indicates the pressure in the tank and the other adjusts to regulate the amount of oxygen released to the torch. The propane regulator limits the amount of propane released to the torch and is not adjustable. Guidance in the use of gasses and gauges is best obtained from the manufacturers and suppliers of these items. Please allow professionals to handle the setup and testing of all lines and connections for this equipment and follow all manufacturer's recommended procedures for safety.

When preparing to light a bench torch the tank valves are opened, releasing gas into the hoses that feed the torch. The propane is then turned on at the torch and ignited. A flame of about 7" to 8" is desirable. Then the oxygen is turned on and adjusted to the proper mixture. As the oxygen is increased, the visible propane diminishes. The oxygen should be increased until the propane (orange) flame is only about 1/2" to 3/4" long. The remainder of the flame (blue) is oxygen. When shutting off, the process is reversed. First the oxygen is turned off, then the

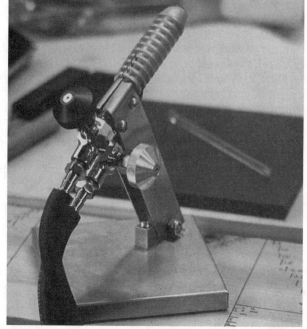

The oxygen/propane surface mixed torch is firmly fixed to the bend and at a height that is comfortable for the worker.

propane. The valves at the tanks are then closed and the lines bled by turning the torch back on.

For lighting the torch a butane "grill lighter" is a good choice. It has a long nose to keep the user's fingers away from the flame and it is lockable. It also has the advantage of requiring only one hand for operation (unlike match books) and lights quickly so gas does not escape into the air any longer than necessary. The case on such lighters is plastic and should not be placed anywhere near the torch area when not in use.

A bead separator to prevent the molten glass from sticking to the metal mandrels is necessary and the mandrels are dipped and then air dried in racks before using. Because wire has an inherent "curl," it is not the best choice for mandrels. Stainless steel rod is preferable because it is stronger, allowing for more aggressive marvering (shaping) and easier removal of the bead. The mandrels that I use and recommend are stainless steel rods in porcelain handles and the larger ones are in wooden handles. Just holding the rod itself is very clumsy because it is so small and a great deal more control is possible with a handle.

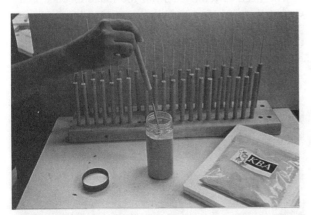

Using the bead separator, the mandrels are dipped and then air dried in racks.

Thermal shock occurs when glass is taken suddenly from one temperature to another. The glass will break and even fly apart if the shock is extreme. A hot plate with a 1/4" steel plate on top to distribute the heat is used to preheat the glass strips or rods. Although it is not essential to preheat the glass, preheating helps prevent thermal shock when the glass is introduced into the flame and is much safer than using cold glass. Since any kind of glass can be used to make beads, preheating is a tremendous time saver when using chunks (like broken bottles). If they are not preheated, a great deal of time is wasted babying them into the flame. An old electric griddle makes a reasonable substitute for the hot plate, but because of the "lip" around the edge of the griddle, it is more difficult to keep glass rods from rolling around.

Coefficient of Expansion (COE) refers to the rate at which different types of glass expand and contract when heated and cooled. Unless two pieces of glass have the same COE, they will expand and contract at different rates and the result will be broken beads. This is also explained by the term compatibility. If two pieces of glass have the same COE, they are considered compatible. If you are making beads from stained glass strips, stick with one manufacturer for a single bead unless you know you are using compatible types. There are rods of glass made specifically for bead making, but they are not necessarily compatible with strips of stained glass. As is the case with glass fusion, if you don't know if the glass you are using is compatible, conduct some tests of your own before putting a lot of time and effort into a masterpiece bead.

Molten glass will not stick to graphite, so a graphite paddle is the tool used to shape or marver molten glass. One that is small and easy to handle is best for bead making. I use two sizes. The graphite is 1-1/2" x 3" and 3/4" x 4" and both have a 6" hardwood handle. The graphite should be smooth and solid black (actually a charcoal color) and not have a grainy look.

When material (metal or glass) is brought into contact with the flame, the resulting "glare" is the incandescence of metal salts. Within this flame is Infra Red (IR), Ultra Violet (UV), and the orange glare which contains Sodium, Lithium and Potassium. IR is experienced physically as heat. Most people do not need protection from IR because they will stop what they are doing if it becomes too uncomfortable. With UV, the damage can occur without your knowledge and protection is necessary. The orange glare is particular to glasswork and will surround the bead, preventing the worker from seeing their work. It may also cause long term damage to the eye. Safety glass protects the eyes by absorbing dangerous rays. Welder's glasses provide some protection from UV but do not absorb the orange glare. Didymium glasses offer *some* protection from UV and absorb the orange glare. The reason I stress "some" is that unless the glasses are rated at least #5, they do not offer complete protection. The bad news for bead makers is that in order to have complete protection, the glass would be so dark that detail cannot be seen.

Because they absorb the orange glare, didymium glasses allow you to see into your work, absorb some of the UV, and are the bead maker's choice. Prescription didymium glasses are costly so I use the lenses from in-expensive "drugstore cheaters" mounted on the front of my safety glasses. I use double-sticky mounting tape to attach them and this works just fine. If you wear more complicated eyeglasses, there is still a simple solution. Order a duplicate prescription without frames and mount them the same way. Whatever you use is your choice and there is some controversy over what is best, but with only one pair of eyes issued to me, I take no chances. Wear some kind of safety glasses. The danger of hot glass pop-ping into your eyes exists so do not work or watch some-one else work without eye protection.

Thermal shock can also occur when the finished bead is removed from the flame. It must be cooled gradually or cracking will occur. I use an oil drip pan filled with ver-miculite on a hot plate, set to high. (Vermiculite is heat treated mica that can be purchased at any gardening cen-ter.)

The term for gradually cooling glass is annealing and cannot be ignored as an important step. The beads are usually in the hot vermiculite for a minimum of one half hour and sometimes for several hours. It depends on the size of the bead and how anxious I am to see it. A large bead takes longer to cool and the need for instant gratifi-cation has killed many a bead. When removed from the hot vermiculite, I place it in room temperature vermicu-lite until it cools completely. Otherwise, I just shut off the hot plate at the end of work and let it all cool down over-night.

Beads can be re-annealed at a later time to relieve inner stress and strengthen the bead. This is done by placing the beads on a kiln shelf, then slowly (around two hours) bringing them up to around 875°F. Then up to 1000°F and shut down. This is an optional step, but if you are making large beads it is a good idea.

An old electric wok makes a dandy substitute for an annealing pan. Put vermiculite in the bottom and just slide the mandrel in when you are done with a bead. The angled sides are perfect for holding the mandrels and a wok gets plenty hot enough to anneal the beads.

The bead is removed from the mandrel once it has cooled to room temperature. To remove the bead, first pinch off the separator from the end of the mandrel. Hold the mandrel behind the bead, turn the bead to break it loose and it should slide right off. If you can't hold it tight

Beads must cool gradually or they will crack. Here is my oil drip pan filled with vermiculite. The beads that are annealing are buried in the vermiculite along the sides of the pan. You can see the handles of the mandrels resting along the edge.

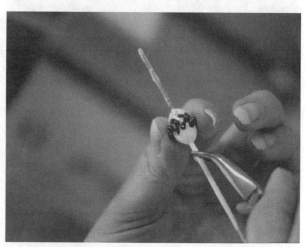

Breaking the bead loose from the mandrel. This requires some patience. Make sure you break away from the sep-arator in front of the bead.

enough, use a pair of pliers to hold the mandrel. If the bead does not readily slide off the mandrel, try soaking it in water for a few minutes. There are differences in bead separators and some do not release as easily as others.

I use special tools to clean the insides of the beads, then rinse them to remove the separator dust and let them dry. Not all bead makers clean the insides of their beads, but I prefer them clean. As long as there is separator in them, dust will collect in trays, on cords, and on clothing.

A variety of small tools are needed for bead making, but they will vary according to personal preference. Most of my hand tools as well as my separator are KBA brand.

Tools and Materials

torch

safety glasses

graphite paddles

rod cutter (for cutting glass rods)

kiln shelf

vermiculite (in pan on hot plate)

butane grill lighter

fire extinguisher (just in case)

mandrels (pre-coated, 12 each in three sizes)

bead cleaners

small bench brush

glass (preheating on hot plate)

slip-joint pliers

stamp tweezers

bent nose tweezers

bent nose pliers

bead press

glass rods and strips, pre-pulled stringers, and other bits and pieces of pre-made decoration.

A corner in a large well ventilated room is the best place for bead making because of the byproduct carbon monoxide fumes created with propane use. An open window is a good idea if the outdoor temperature permits and there is no breeze. A fan can be used to circulate the air but only if the breeze does not interfere with the flame. The smallest draft can start the flame flickering around and make it difficult to work.

The physical strain from bead making is primarily in the neck and shoulders and a work station that is specifically suited to your height and arm length is an important consideration. Your shoulders need to be relaxed, which dictates that your elbows be resting on the bench on either side of the torch. It is essential that the torch be stable on the bench so that your hands are free to work and your body movements will not effect the torch in any way. Never place any tools or materials in such a position that would cause you to reach in front of the flame. A little experimenting with position and height will tell you what is right for your own work station.

My work bench is covered with white building board, which is a flame resistant surface. Under the flame is a large kiln shelf to catch hot pieces of glass and to lay hot tools on. I also have a variety of glass ash trays and other containers to hold all the various chunks, strips, stringers, etc. that are used for decoration.

Making a Basic Bead

Choose the glass for the first bead from your inventory of scrap stained glass or use glass rods made specifically for bead making. It really doesn't matter but the higher the COE number, the faster the glass will melt. For example, Pyrex which is used by lampworkers to make little animals and such, is around 32 COE. It is extremely stiff in the flame and slow for bead making. Moretti glass rod (for bead making) is 104 COE so it is very soft and melts quickly. Most rolled sheet stained glass (Spectrum, Kokomo, Armstrong, etc.) is in the 80s and Bullseye, Wasser, and Uroborous are 90. As the COE gets lower, the glass is less suited to bead making. If you are using sheet stained glass, it is best to strip cut it about 1/4" wide for beads. Strips are easier to work with than chunks, particularly for the beginner. Of course, if you start with something difficult and then discover Moretti rods, you'll think you've died and gone to heaven.

Many hours of bead making have resulted in the way I hold things. I am right-handed and these methods were developed from a right-handed point of view. Please make the necessary adjustments if you are not. Begin by holding the glass in your right hand, heating the end of it high in the flame and slowly work it down toward the torch, always staying about 2" from the torch itself. When the glass is molten it will "ball up" on the end. It is then ready to set on the mandrel.

When the glass is molten it will ball up on the end. The mandrel is right there, ready to receive it.

Using your left hand, heat the mandrel in the flame. I cup the mandrel handle in my fingers and turn with my index finger and thumb. The mandrel will start to glow red in the flame and when it does it is ready to receive the glass. Keeping the glass rod perpendicular to the mandrel, hold it as if it were a pencil and touch the molten ball to the red spot on the mandrel. Slowly turn the mandrel away from you, allowing the molten glass to flow onto the mandrel.

The glass must be molten to flow onto the mandrel and to separate the glass rod from the bead when you are through adding glass. This is done by pushing the bead behind the flame and directing the flame at the point at which you want to separate it.

Don't try to follow the turn of the mandrel with the glass or you will move the glass out of the flame and it will chill. Once chilled it will not flow and the separator will probably break. The glass remains steady in the flame and the mandrel turns away to gather the molten glass.

The first glass onto the mandrel becomes the left end of the bead so it is important that the glass is applied evenly on the left side. Going left to right, glass is added to set the length of the bead. The last glass on the right end of

the bead is also wrapped cleanly and evenly on the mandrel just as the left end was.

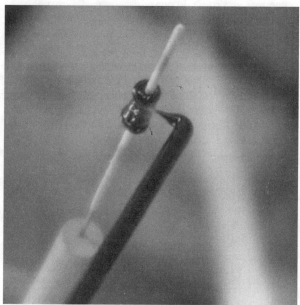

Directing the flame at the point from which you want to separate the bead from the mandrel. Note how the bead is being held behind the flame.

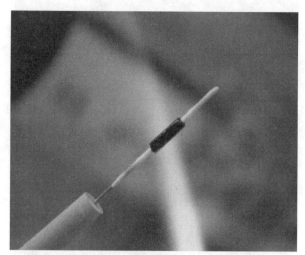

The bead on the mandrel; right and left ends being equally heated by the flame.

The ends are created when the bead is started, not when it's finished, so the first glass onto the mandrel is as important (if not more so) as the last touch of decoration. Thin sharp ends will break very easily, cut thread when strung, and if the ends of a pendant or earring beads are not even, the beads will hang crooked. This is the core of the bead and it should have "shoulders" on which to build the rest of the bead. The core will probably be lumpy and uneven at this point so marvering is the next step.

Lay the glass rod back on the hot plate and switch the mandrel to your right hand. Keep the bead warm and turning at the end of the flame at all times when you are switching hands, picking up tools, or hunting for decoration. If you hold it too long in the fat part of the flame, it will overheat and could drip off. If you let it wander off and cool, it will crack when you bring it back into the flame. You need to keep track of both hands and what they are doing. Having your elbows on the table helps a great deal. If your arms are relaxed, your hands are less apt to drift.

Holding the graphite paddle in your left hand, bring the mandrel out of the flame and roll the molten glass toward you on the graphite to smooth it down. If the glass goes clink when you touch it to the graphite, it is not molten enough. Heat it some more and try again. Heat and roll until it is a uniform cylinder. Take your time, relax your shoulders, and enjoy playing with the glass. A good exercise is to just melt glops of glass and let them drip onto the kiln shelf. This helps you gain a feel for what the glass will do. Just make sure that you have a kiln shelf under the flame to catch the hot drips and don't try to pick them up and examine them. Hot glass looks just like cold glass!

When adding additional glass to enlarge the bead, add it the same way the first glass was started on the mandrel. Concentrate the flame on the glass you are adding, not the glass that's already on the mandrel. If the cylinder gets too hot, it will get out of control and you will lose the ends. Glass tends to pull to the center when heated, and therefore pulls away from the ends, leaving them sharp and pointed. Remember that you are in control of the glass and the flame is one of your tools. Don't become too dependent on it or let it take control.

Round Bead

To make a round bead, first create a core the length you want. The additional glass goes in the center of the core. Continue to add glass until there is enough glass to make the bead as big around as the core is long. Now be-

gin heating and marvering the bead in the same way you did the core.

First marver the glass into a fat cylinder to give it shoulders. Once it is uniform and smooth, continue heating and turning it in the flame and you will see the shoulders begin to round out. The bead will become round very quickly because of the tendency to pull to the center in the flame. When it is perfectly rounded, bring it out of the flame (continue turning) and watch the glow fade. Once the glow is almost gone, the bead can be placed into the vermiculite to begin cooling. If it goes in while it is still soft, it will "dimple" in the vermiculite. If you wait too long it will chill and break.

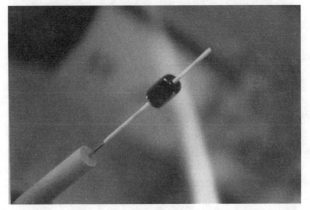

Steps in making a round bead from a fat cylinder. Initial heating and turning of the shoulders of the cylinder.

The cylinder is beginning to round out.

Oval Ellipsoid Bead

Create the core and begin adding more glass only to the center of the core. Help the glass shape to the center by marvering it at an angle from both ends. When angle marvering, take care not to touch the separator with the graphite. This can cut the separator (causing it to break loose) or create pointed ends on the bead. If you picture the ends of the bead as little platforms that the beads need to stand on, it will help keep you from making that mistake. Once the glass is marvered evenly to the center, heating and turning in the flame will allow the center to round and an oval appears.

Marvering a bead into an ellipsoid shape.

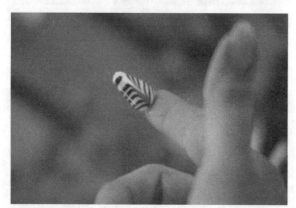

The end of the bead is like a little platform it can stand on. This decorated bead is a demonstration of that.

Bicone Bead

A bicone bead is made the same way as the ellipsoid except that the center is left pointed. A bicone is shaped like two cones stuck together at the large end, so this bead has a diamond shape when viewed from the side. It requires more marvering and more control than an oval to achieve balance and keep the center pointed. Angle the mandrel in the flame to direct the flame at each end as you prepare to marver. This helps you maintain control over the shape by heating only the area you intend to marver and not overheating the rest of the bead. If the bead is off balance it is easy to add a little more glass to even it out. It's not as easy to take it off, but it can be done. Stamp tweezers are the tool of choice. Find the spot where there is too much glass, get it hot and pinch some off with the tweezers. When using metal tools on molten glass in this way, do not heat the metal before using it. This will cause the glass to stick to it.

Heating the bicone bead.

Tabular Bead

Tabular beads are very popular, especially for pendants. Tabulars are beads that have been flattened. If you flatten an oval or a round, you will have an oval or round tabular. If you start with a bicone, you will end up with a diamond shaped tabular. The most important thing about making tabulars is that the shape must be balanced before flattening. A bead press is used for many other things in bead making but its primary use is for tabulars. Once the bead is the appropriate shape, it should be heated thoroughly and uniformly, then quickly flattened with a *cool* press.

Using the bead press to flatten a tabular bead.

The chill marks left by the press have the appearance of thumbprints on both sides of the bead. Although they may be sort of cute, they are indicative of sloppy bead making and need to be fire-polished out. Aim the flame at both sides, taking care not to overheat the bead, until these marks are gone. Marvering should never be the last thing you do. Even one last little touch of the graphite can leave chill marks which must be polished out before removing the bead from the flame.

Firing the chill marks on a tabular bead.

Decorating

Most decorating of glass beads begins with the simple stringer, which is a thread of glass. Stringers are pulled by taking two preheated rods (or strips) of glass and heating the ends of them in the flame. Once they begin to melt,

push them together and continue heating. As you push them against each other, a molten ball will form between them. Once you have a ball approximately 3/8" in diameter, bring the rods out of the flame, toward you, and gently pull them apart. The length and thickness of the stringer is dependent on the size of the ball and the speed with which you pull. With some practice, you can control the size of the stringers to suit your own needs.

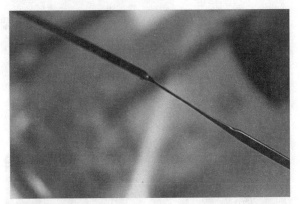

Making a stringer. The two rods are being gently pulled apart.

Hold short rods or strips with pliers to heat the ends and turn them into longer rods by welding them together. The same technique is used as in pulling stringers, just don't pull. Please remember that when welding short rods together, the welds will stay hot for quite some time.

Dots

Dots are the first step in decorating. Pull a few black stringers for practice. Then make a small round or oval white bead to be decorated. Practice decoration is best done using black and white. They are easy to distinguish in the flame and make it clear how well you did at decorating when the bead is cool.

Keeping the bead warm and turning in the tip of the flame, melt just the very end of a stringer. It will ball up on the end and the size of the ball will determine the size of the dot. Bring the bead out of the flame toward you and touch the molten ball to the bead. Push the bead back through the flame and pull the stringer away as the dot passes through. Placing dots can leave tails on the stringer which need to be melted back into the stringer or snapped off (tap it sharply on the kiln shelf). A good way to prac-

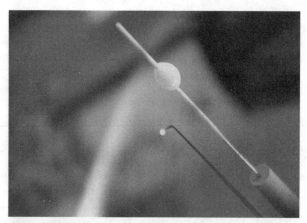

Preparing a bead for dotting. Step 1: The bead is being heated in the flame. Note the stringer behind it with its balled end ready to do the dotting.

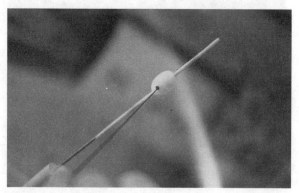

The bead at maximum heat now ready to have the stringer applied for dotting.

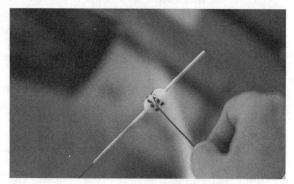

After practicing making dots, try lining them up in even rows.

tice this technique is to place dots all over the bead with no particular design in mind, just to get the feel of the stringer. Then make another bead and line the dots up in even rows or in a planned pattern.

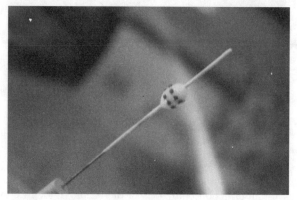

The finished dotted bead still on the mandrel.

Feathering

Feathering is raking or combing the surface of the bead to distort stringer decoration. A simple feathered bead can be made by starting with a double row of contrasting dots around it. After marvering them into the bead, feather between them to turn the dots into teardrops or flower petals. There is no really good tool for this job—a sturdy short stringer works just fine. The secret is to barely catch the surface of the bead and do not heat the stringer, just the spot on the bead to be feathered.

Try some dots on dots. Using black and white stringers on a white bead, place black dots then white dots in the center and then black dots again until you run out of room. Then feather the bead. There are many variations of this technique, but it does require some practice to become accurate.

Spiraled Feathered Stringers

Working high in the flame and using the flame to soften the stringer rather than actually melt it, turn the mandrel away from you and allow the stringer to spiral on to the bead. Marver the stringer into the bead and then feather it by pulling a sturdy stringer through the bead in one direction, then the other, making quarter turns around the bead.

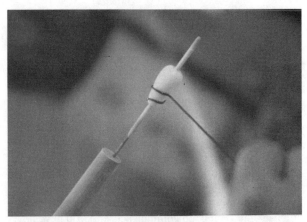

Spiraling the stringer onto the bead.

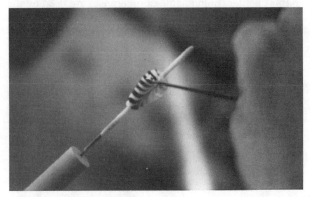

Completing the spiral.

Troubleshooting

Beads breaking: There are several points in the process when breaking can occur. The first is in the flame. If you are distracted (looking for a tool or stringer) and the bead wanders out of the flame for too long, you may hear a cracking when you bring it back into the flame. Detailed decoration can also be a problem. If you spend a lot of time at one end of a long bead, the other end can cool enough that it will crack when you get it back in the flame. It is a good practice to move the bead through the flame from time to time, to keep the whole thing hot when you are decorating. After you have spent a lot of time working in the flame, you will find your own rhythm and it becomes something you don't really have to think about.

If you do get a crack in an unfinished bead, continue heating until the crack has disappeared and don't make the same mistake twice. Along that same line—no you cannot put a finished cracked bead back on a mandrel and reheat it. It isn't worth the effort.

The obvious stage at which beads break is when taken from the flame to the hot vermiculite. You can't sit there and admire the bead. Admire it later when it's cool.

If a bead offers resistance when removing it from the mandrel, don't force it! If the bead will turn on the mandrel, it will come off. If you are using wire, it may be the curl that's preventing the bead from sliding. A burr on the end of the mandrel rod can stop a bead and crack it if you use force. If the bead turns on the rod but still won't release, try soaking it in water for a few minutes. Make sure you are using a good separator—specifically a bead release or separator, not kiln wash or shelf primer.

Separator breaking: When beginners making their first beads, the most common problem is breaking separator. Keep in mind that this substance is used to release the bead from the metal rod. Therefore it has to be somewhat fragile to start with. If you handle it with this in mind, you will do less damage. When adding glass to the mandrel, it must be molten! It must flow onto the mandrel.

Uses for Finished Beads

Beads need not be used exclusively for jewelry. Some other uses include watch fobs, key chain fobs, rearview mirror decoration, lamp finials or pulls (make the hole large enough to pass the ball chain through), window decoration, and sewn onto clothing.

Safety

Naturally you would not touch a hot plate when its elements are glowing red. But remember that the annealing pan and the steel plate on top of these hot plates are hot too, even though you can't see the elements. Be careful around them and do not allow small children into your work area unsupervised. People are going to want to watch you work, but before they watch make them aware of the things that may be hot and require that they wear safety glasses.

Make sure all electrical connections are sound and avoid the use of extension cords. The power strips should go directly into the wall outlet to be safe. Keep in mind that a hot plate pulls about 15 amps, and therefore two hot plates may overload a power strip. Power strips usually have their own circuit breakers—don't try to override them. They tell you when you are overloading the circuit. It is best to plug one hot plate in to one power strip and each strip into a separate circuit in the building. This will avoid blowing circuit breakers and causing an overload.

When you finish working, always turn off the gas tanks and bleed the lines. Once the flame is extinguished at the torch, turn off the valves on the tanks. Then turn on the torch, (just as if you were going to use it) and light the flame. Let it burn out on its own while you watch. Never leave the tanks turned on and the torch unattended. Never leave a lit torch burning while you answer the phone or hunt for something. It only takes a second for a pet or a child to get into trouble.

Oxygen and propane tanks should be strapped to a wall. Plumber's tape (a metal strap with holes in it) can be placed around the tanks and then screw the ends into a wall. This prevents them from accidentally being knocked over. The connections on the tanks should be checked for leaks, even if you can't hear or smell any leaks. Do this by mixing a soapy water solution and applying it to all of the connections. If there is leaking, you will see bubbles. All connections should have Teflon tape on them to prevent leaking.

Remember to allow for ventilation of the carbon monoxide fumes associated with gas use. You should work in a large unconfined area or an area where the fumes can dissipate. The area should also be clear of any flammable liquids or other flames (gas appliances) that could cause ignition if gas were released into the air.

Make sure the work surface and the surrounding area is protected from the hot glass. The small hot pieces that can pop off the ends of the rods are hot enough to scorch and even cause flame. Protect yourself from this possibility by wearing clothing that will not melt (manmade fibers will melt, rather than burn). Keep a fire extinguisher within easy reach and know how to use it.

There will always be broken glass, chips, chunks, etc., around any glasswork area. As a glassworker, you are probably used to it. Don't overlook the possibility that someone observing could be cut and keep the area clean.

Please follow all manufacturer's instructions for safety and use your own good common sense. If you have never worked with gas flame before, have the experts set it up and check it for safety. The tools and materials mentioned in this chapter (brand name or otherwise) are used by the author, but that does not constitute a recommendation. No warranty is implied for these products and neither the author, publisher, or the manufacturers are responsible for injury resulting from their misuse. Because of the nature of this art medium, injury could occur and the users of these products take the sole responsibility for their own safety, as well as any individuals injured by their misuse of products, carelessness, or failure to follow manufacturer's recommendations.

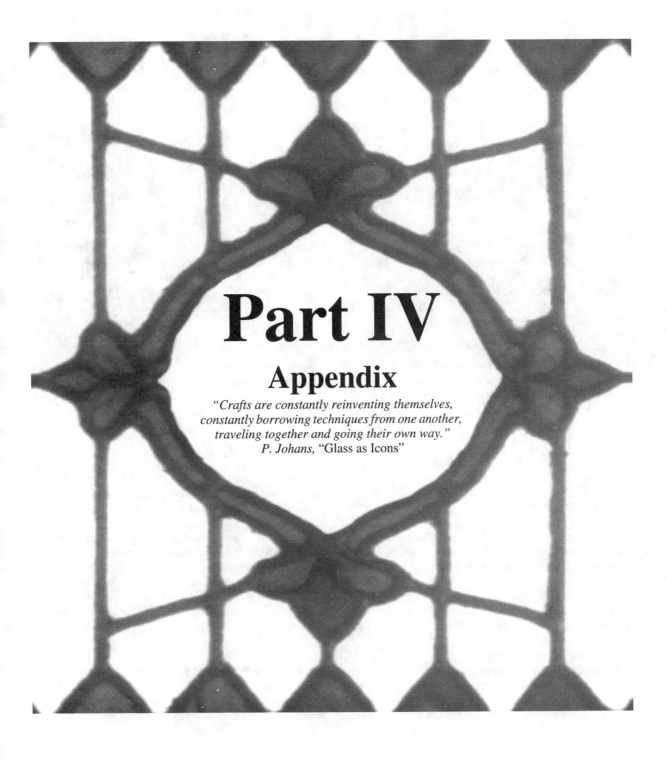

Part IV

Appendix

"Crafts are constantly reinventing themselves,
constantly borrowing techniques from one another,
traveling together and going their own way."
P. Johans, "Glass as Icons"

CHAPTER 25
Learning and Teaching Stained Glass

Joyce Morrisette displays a panel designed by herself for a wine cabinet door. The bottle was painted and fired and the grapes were foiled nuggets. The wine in the glass was foiled behind the clear wine glass as a plating method.

John Silver with a sign he foiled from individual glass pieces for his wife's office. He wanted to try this for a first project. It turned out to be his fourth.

LEARNING

Finding a Teacher

Selecting a qualified person to teach you stained glass is the first step in the learning process. There are several questions you might ask when making your choice. You will probably want to ask these over the phone but before signing up you should meet the teacher face to face. Communication is a variable process and you want to at least get an impression of how informative a person this is and how well you will understand his or her teaching method.

How Many in the Class?

Is the class geared to one-on-one instruction (most expensive) or is it in a group setting? If it is a group, how many students will be admitted? If it is a continuing education/recreation program, be sure to ask about numbers.

Many such classes sign as many students as possible, allowing little time for individual attention and a lineup for grinders and other shared tools. One teacher, no matter how capable, has a limit as to how many students he or she can handle; usually one can work with up to six students comfortably. If there are ten or more students, ask if the teacher has an assistant to help with the class. If so, how good is the assistant? Glass studios may offer instruction at a higher fee but limit the number of students to allow for personal attention. That saves you money in the long run.

How Long are the Sessions?

Optimum class time is at least two hours. Less than that and not much will be accomplished, longer and most student's attention span seems to lapse.

Investigate the Workspace

The way the work surface is situated will depend on how effectively you will work. If it is a classroom, you'll be sitting down and working on little desks attached to the seats. We have always found this a poor working condition.

Ask to see the workspace where the class is to be held. If the person teaches out of their home, is there a room specially set up for stained glass? If your teacher is a friend who is willing to show you on the kitchen table, that's one way to learn, but if it's a stranger teaching you and half a dozen others in her kitchen, that's going to be a cramped space and a poor way to learn. Most studio workspaces use professional tables and leave plenty of room between students.

Lighting and Ventilation

Soldering produces fumes and bad light leads to eyestrain. Avoid working in a small closed room in dim light. The area should have not only tables at the proper height for cutting, but a plethora of fluorescent lights and fans or other ventilation to allow for fumes.

What's the Cost and What Does it Include?

The fee for most courses does not include tools, glass, or other supplies but are there tools available for rental or can you use class tools at least until you decide you want to buy your own? Often some tools belonging to the teacher can be borrowed for the initial session but if you are going to the expense of taking a course in glass, you should include in that cost at least a pair of pliers, a glass cutter, and a soldering iron. Get a rough figure of what the total cost will be so you know what you are getting into.

What Can You Make?

What is the project? Is it chosen by the teacher or can you work on something you want to make? If the first project is completed before the end of the class sessions, is there another available to fill the remaining sessions? And what happens if you miss a class?

What are the Teacher's Qualifications?

Who is the teacher and how long has he/she been teaching stained glass? We've known of instances where someone just completed a beginner course themselves and immediately became a teacher. Are there examples of work by the teacher to be seen? What is the method of teaching: does the teacher demonstrate and then have you do the work, does the teacher merely explain without demonstrating, or does the teacher do most of the work for you while you look on?

Is There Storage Space for Your Work?

Generally there won't be because most studios need all the space they can get for their own storage. If storage space is available, how safe is it? Will the teacher be responsible for your project? If there isn't storage space, how difficult will it be for you to get your project to your car? Is there parking nearby?

What About Advanced Instruction?

Does the teacher have advanced classes or are the classes only for beginners? Suppose you want to continue with more sophisticated projects? Are classes ongoing or are they arranged in groups?

There are many other questions you might think of before you start learning about glass. But at least consider some of those above. The answers can help you select a class perfect for your comfort and ability.

TEACHING

If you enjoy working with glass and with people you can make some money and enjoy watching your students apply the principals you impart toward creative ends. It takes patience, concentration, and time to teach and in addition there are the unexpected factors that will challenge your tact and resilience. However, teaching is a job you can always quit once you stop enjoying it. The main thing to keep in mind is that teaching is a business and should be run as one. Here are a few basic guidelines from our experience.

Get Paid for the Full Course

Money may be the root of all evil but it's an evil we all have to live with. Get yours up front. Space and knowledge are what you are selling. A student who only comes and pays on an irregular basis is taking up space that could sell on a regular one. A student who wants to pay even weekly is a risk factor; if he or she doesn't show up, again there is space wasted. Sell your classes in six or eight week increments and get paid for the entire set when the student comes in to register. Then if the student misses a week you aren't out financially.

Don't Take Registrations Over the Phone

Meet your prospective students face to face. This allows them to get an impression of you and certainly helps you find out what they are going to be like in class: quiet, know-it-all, dependent, intense, etc. Obviously you can't make out someone's entire character at one meeting, but all you want now is a hint. Sometimes that's enough to spot a potential troublemaker or total incompetent and then you can figure a way to prevent him/her coming in. At this time, get your fee in full.

Age Limit

It's best not to accept any youngsters under the age of 16 without a participating parent and no one under the age of ten. There is really no top age limit, but older students may require more assistance. Be prepared to lend your hands and eyes to these students to help them work things out.

Who to Decline

Don't accept pregnant or nursing women. No exceptions. If the child develops problems, you may have the finger pointed at you whether you are responsible or not.

A Time to Start and a Time to End

When the student signs up be sure it is understood what the time limits are. Students who come in ten to 15 minutes early and "just want bring their stuff in before class" will shortly take advantage to start working and ask for advice. The door to the studio should be kept locked until the appointed time arrives. The same rule applies to closing the class. Even though everyone may be having a good time and going strong, you should call time at least ten minutes before the end to allow the students to get ready to go. Otherwise some may try to stay all night. At Christmas, it may be necessary to stay overtime to have gifts finished in time, but even that's a bad habit to get into. Of course you can't be late opening class; if you are make sure you make up the time at the other end.

Storage Space

Best advice: don't store anyone's work. Automatically you will be responsible for anything that occurs to it or that doesn't occur but the student thinks it did. Storage also takes up space that you need for your own work. And suppose the student doesn't return? How long do you keep this extraneous glass and lead and copper hanging around? If you do store, make sure the student signs a note stating that if a month goes by and he or she doesn't return for it, the material will be dumped.

The Missing in Action Student

Anyone can get sick or go on vacation in the midst of a paid group of classes and they should not be penalized for that—provided they call and let you know. True, they have paid for the space they will be unable to occupy, but you are entitled to know if they will be there or not. If the absence continues over a period of weeks, the missing classes should then count as paid up and the student would have to re-register should he or she wish to return. This should be explained to the prospective student at the time of signing up.

Safety

No one, without exception, should be allowed to poke into the scrap glass bin or pull glass from the shelves. You may have bandages around for minor cuts from working on the bench, but the bins and the scrap glass box can inflict very bad cuts that no bandage can fix. If a student wants a particular piece of glass from either of these two places, you should get it. Make this a hard and fast rule and play it safe.

Grinders should always have the proper shields in place, but offer safety glasses as well. Keep an eyewash on hand in case something gets in an eye. Students should not wear sandals; glass pieces do fall off the table. No smoking, no food allowed.

Students Take Priority

If you are teaching—do it! There will be times when everyone is busy grinding, foiling, or soldering, pretty much working on their own. Don't go off in a corner to do your own work and ignore your students. If someone has a question, they may feel shy about bothering you and resent that you are not attentive. You have been paid to teach and you have that obligation. However, if you have a small project of your own, it may be a good time to work on it alongside the students, keeping them in view, but showing them perhaps some technique they haven't seen yet. Show them briefly what it is and what you intend to do. It shows off your technique and provides incentive for progress.

Two Difficult Types

Students learn from you and from each other. They listen to what you say and watch what their neighbor is doing and most try to work on their own. But occasionally you can have a student who constantly wants your exclusive help on every move. Don't be trapped into building the project for this type, which is possibly what he or she is aiming for. Set up a step to be done and demonstrate how it's done. Mark the next one for the student to do. Check it and encourage but get up and walk away. Check back in a few minutes. You may have to re-do the entire process, but keep walking away once you do. If you stay alongside such a student you will never be able to check others in the class. Some students want you as a personal investment. You have to break that grasp.

The second type is the know-it-all; the one you hear telling others in the class his or her methods and shortcuts. You have to nip this in the bud immediately or you will have lost your leader status.

Structuring a Class

Some classes run an average of six weeks for about two hours. We have run ongoing classes two ways—for eight weeks with three hour classes and for six weeks with two hour classes. We may let the student pick the initial project or we give them a choice of three possibilities.

On the whole we prefer a six week session with two hour classes where students choose an 18 to 21 piece 8" x 10" panel geared to be completed in that time. The first class teaches how to handle the tools and how to cut on single strength windowpane as well as pattern prepara-

tion. If possible, have students cut some of the project glass before they go home. The second and third class involves cutting and grinding. The fourth class should see the end of the grinding and fitting process, and allow time for the students to do some foiling before they leave with the project. They should finish the foiling at home before class next week. The fifth class is devoted to soldering and the final sixth for any solder touch up, cleaning, patina applying, applying channel edging, and final cleaning.

If a student wants to work at home, we explain what can be done on his or her own to move the project along but ask them to stop if they have problems or questions and in that case, to wait for class. Above all, be ready with the next project if the beginner's panel is finished early.

Advanced Classes

So much for beginner classes. For advanced classes, you might provide dimensional work as a panel shade or building something within a framed space to get the students used to going by measurements. Be careful that you don't offer patterns that are too complex. A third round of classes could involve making a box or kaleidoscope. The fourth could become individualized with the student's choice.

In this way you are always offering something new, something to look forward to and you can keep your students coming, happy, and involved.

CHAPTER 26
Glass Sculpture

by Hugh Naggar

Although the thrust of this book is stained glass, the field occasionally overlaps to ancillary modalities. To be perfectly frank, it has been somewhat difficult for us to stay out of the glass blowing arena, since colored glass certainly plays a part there as well and glass blowing is quite an experience. What we couldn't resist, partly because this field is so self-contained, was providing at least a beginning look at lamp working, where glass rods are shaped into amazingly complex and winsome forms. Even here, stained glass has a place since the rods used may be colored either by the addition of a chemical while working them, or of themselves. If the joy of working with glass is extended by acquiring new ways to work with it, combining the various methods and techniques to form a personal aesthetic, certainly this mini type of glass blowing will add to that joy. So we couldn't leave it out.

Scientific glasswork can evolve into pleasurable glasswork. At least that's what Hugh Naggar found when he enrolled in a three month course in that field. Since that time 21 years ago, he has been creating, through his studio Crystal Creations, his own glass products. They have been chronicled on television, in exhibitions, arts showings, and charitable auctions. For the last five years he has directed his energies to teaching this rather mystical art form. The classroom has given him a refreshing new perspective which he carries over into this introductory chapter.

PREFACE

Glass sculpturing is a medium that has mystified people for centuries. While it requires a great deal of energy, in the form of intense heat, to set the process in motion, once in motion, it is subject to the force of gravity. These two factors captivated my interest for the first 21 years of my involvement with glass. Then I began to focus on the exciting notion that I am the lead in a dance with molten glass and I have become a vehicle for the creative force.

The goal of this chapter is to present in photos and text the knowledge for an opportunity to have a hands-on experience in sculpting molten glass. I will show you some opening steps in the dance, hopefully beginning your own creative flow. I do not intend to imply that these steps are

Materials	
(approximate cost for equipment $400)	fuel regulator
lampworking kit	heavy-duty rubber hose with B style fittings
hand tools and equipment	18" x 24" x 1/4" cem-fill work surface
National hand torch	oxygen and fuel gas check valves
single hole tip for hand torch	flint lighter
National torch holder and base	1-1/49" x 2" x 3/8" graphite paddle with handle
didymium spectacles with plastic frames	1/8" and 1/4" brass tubing (available at any hobby shop)
needle nose pliers	cobalt blue glass
oxygen regulator	fire extinguisher

easy to achieve, for they require fairly good finger dexterity and a high level of motivation. However, and most importantly, the true prerequisite to mastery is your desire to practice lampworking in your own workshop. Complete each piece until you are comfortable with the procedures. Remember, repetition is the mother of skill.

SETTING UP YOUR WORKSHOP

The work bench should be a minimum of 35" x 45" of clear open space, on top of which you need an 18" x 24" x 1/4" cem-fill work surface. The torch should be securely fastened to the leading edge of the work bench in front of where you will be sitting and facing—nothing flammable (curtains, lampshades, etc.) should be close to this area. An economical way to fasten the torch to the table is by using an L-shape angle iron made of aluminum and two C-clamps. One clamp holds the aluminum to the table and the other holds the torch to the metal. The National torch holder and base are also available.

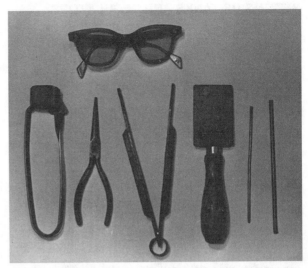

Didymium spectacles, needle nose pliers, flattening tweezers, graphite paddle with handle, 1/8" and 1/4" diameter brass tubing.

The torch has red and green knobs. The red should be on your right while the torch is pointing away from you. The flooring beneath and around the bench should not be carpeted. A four by eight foot sheet of 1/2" plywood is recommended. Invariably, some hot glass will drop and cause burn marks. The hosing that originates from the regulator and goes to the torch should be snaked underneath the work bench, out of the realm of being touched by hot glass. With an open flame, a fire extinguisher should always be nearby. Glass is inherently difficult to photograph. Instead of contending with the brightness of the flame hitting the glass, I indicate the flame by an illustration. The arrow head represents the light blue tip. The distance the glass is from that point is to be noted. (All these tools are available through Wale Apparatus, Hellertown, Pennsylvania.)

The tools should be placed by your dominant hand with the stock Pyrex glass rods on the opposite side. Unlike metal, glass is a very poor conductor of heat. If you remove the end of a glass rod that was in the torch while it is still a bright orange glow, you can touch the rod within 3" of that end before you begin to feel the heat. However, since glass does not conduct the heat, it retains it. When it stops glowing and it looks like all the other glass rods, it can still hold temperatures as high as 1000°F. Depending on the size, it can take up to ten minutes before the glass can be safely handled.

National hand torch and 0X-2 tip with C clamp mount system. The flame is set for normal working flow.

SETTING UP TANKS AND REGULATORS

The oxygen and propane tanks should be used in the upright position and secured to something firm and stable (wall, pole, or work bench). Teflon tape should be used on the threads before installing the regulators. The one-way check valves go between the regulators and the hosing. Apply soapy solution to all junctions to detect any leaks in the system. The main valves on the tanks are opened first, then the valves on the regulators are opened (clockwise) to allow five to seven pounds of pressure to go to the torch. A set of safety steps and procedures are available at the welding supply house and should be strictly adhered to in setting up and closing down the equipment for the day. At the end of your work session, all valves should be closed, any propane in the line should be burned off, and the oxygen released using the green knob.

LIGHTING THE TORCH

The propane fuel should be lit first by turning the red knob towards you (counterclockwise). Next, ignite the tip of the torch with the flint lighter. If the yellow flame is separating from the tip of the torch, there is too much pressure. Slightly close down the red knob (clockwise) until the flame reconnects with the tip. Now start to open the oxygen. If the yellow flame is too small, it will blow out when the oxygen is introduced. When the proper balance is achieved, you will see a blue flame with a light blue flame in the center. Familiarize yourself with the three sizes the OX5 tip offers: 1) small and narrow for heating small areas without deforming the surroundings, 2) average used 95% of the time, and 3) soft and bushy for annealing.

The tip of the light blue flame is the hottest part of the torch (3500°F). Most of your work will be done about 3/4" from that tip. When turning the torch off, first shut down the propane, then the oxygen. If you hear a popping sound from the torch when both knobs are being shut off or if there is a tiny flame on the tip of the torch, the valves underneath the knobs are not seating properly. Some investigation is in order.

HOLDING AND MANEUVERING THE GLASS ROD IN THE FLAME

Note: Any time you place glass in the flame, you must be wearing the didymium spectacles. Start with an 8mm Pyrex glass rod about 15" in length. Hold the rod horizontally and in the center with your palm facing down. As you balance the rod with your fingers, begin to smoothly and slowly rotate it about 200° in both directions. While maintaining the rotation, insert about 1/2" of the rod into the flame. Be careful not to move the end of the rod in and out of the flame, instead imagine a pivot point about 3/4" in front of the light blue flame. With proper movement in the flame, the glass will go from clear to orange to yellow and begin to flow. It will behave like a thick syrup and be subject to gravity. The rotation in the flame not only distributes the heat evenly around the glass, it also counteracts the gravity to allow the glass to bead up and create a sphere. Practice this rotation with your palm up.

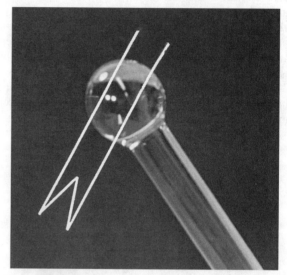

A 3/4" sphere on the end of an 8mm Pyrex rod.

You can increase the size of the sphere by positioning the rod a little more vertically (about 45°) while the ball is still in the flame and rotating. Alternate the heat between the neck and the bottom of the sphere. If the glass becomes bright yellow in sections, you are rotating it too slowly and/or you are too close to the light blue flame tip. When the glass is yellow, it is more fluid and difficult to control. Move the molting sphere up the flame away from the light blue tip to decrease the heat and slow down the movement—now you begin to lead in the dance! Your goal is to create a close to perfect sphere with a 3/4" diameter. I recommend that you create two or three of these spheres to familiarize yourself with the rhythm and flow of the glass. You will be able to use these glass balls in the next project.

MAKING A MUSHROOM

I chose the mushroom because it is a simple piece that effectively demonstrates the important role gravity plays in this medium. The first step is to make a holding rod called a "cold stick," which is a way of gripping the piece you are working on with another glass rod. When the piece is done, it can be snapped off the holding rod quite effortlessly. It will leave a small mark on the finished piece which can be fire polished in seconds. The holding rod should be made first so when you are ready to use it, the working piece does not have a chance to cool. Heat the end of a 5mm rod to yellow and, holding the end of the 8mm rod in the flame, remove a portion of the molten glass with another glass rod in a scooping manner to form a rounded end with a 1/8" diameter.

Now you can begin making the same 3/4" sphere you made in the last exercise. If you decided to use the same ones, which by now have cooled, please introduce them to the flame very slowly. Glass, even Pyrex, that has been heated, cooled, and suddenly reheated, will shatter—often sending razor-like shards of glass through space. You must start on the very outskirts of the flame and slowly bring it closer to a light blue flame in the minimum time of two minutes. Once you have made the sphere and it has stopped glowing, maintain the rotation of the rod and position it vertically while hitting the top 2/3 of the ball with the flame.

The head of a mushroom beginning to form while the rod is rotated vertically and the top 2/3 of the sphere is being heated to a yellow glow all the way around.

The glass will start to droop over all the way around the rod and create the head of the mushroom. When you begin to approach the shape you want, remove it from the flame and continue the rotation for three to five seconds to maintain the shape. The head of the mushroom should be kept very hot—about 3" from the light blue tip. Heat the point of the holding rod you made earlier to yellow, then remove it from the flame while the head of the mushroom is close to it. As the tip goes from yellow to orange, place it on the crown of the head of the mushroom and pull it very slightly apart while rotating both rods in the same direction. This motion is done without much hesitation so as not to allow the holding rod to solidify crooked. That juncture point between the holding rod and the head of the mushroom should have a diameter of 1/8". When properly executed, the two rods should be as one long, straight rod with the head of a mushroom in the middle.

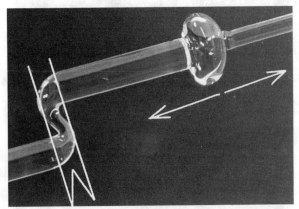

A 5mm holding stick, mushroom head and rod making one straight line. The torch hits break point 2" down from the head as the ends overlap.

From the head of the mushroom, go down the rod 2" and begin to heat the glass to yellow. Within the flame, pull apart by 1", overlap the ends of the rods by 1/2" without touching one another, and twirl them around each other.

This will give you a clean break in the rod without turning the glass into spaghetti. At this point, place the holding rod with the head of the mushroom on it in your dominant hand with your palm facing up. Begin forming a ball on what will become the bottom of the mushroom.

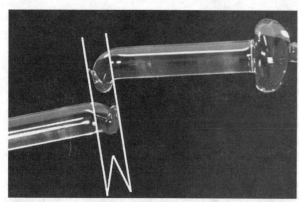

The break has happened in the flame as the ends were twirled around each other. This avoids the long spaghetti like glass when the ends are just pulled apart.

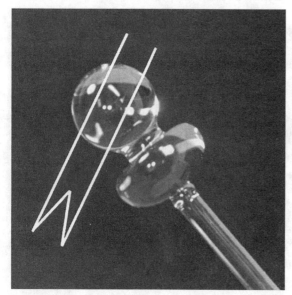

Forming the bottom ball of the mushroom at a 45° angle to increase the size. Allow it to come within 3/8" of the head before bringing the rod horizontal.

As in the previous exercise, you are going from a horizontal position to a 45° angle to increase the size. When the ball has grown bigger and closer to the head of the mushroom (within 3/8"), begin to bring the rod to a vertical position (90°) with the mushroom on the bottom. Since your palm is already facing up, there will be a natural flow of motion as it faces toward the torch.

The bottom ball should be kept at an orange glow by moving up the flame. It will start taking the shape of a teardrop with a fairly thick stem just below the head.

While glowing orange, keep rotating it, bring the rod to vertical. Move up the flame to slow the movement of the teardrop shape.

The rotation is continuous while the glass is in and out of the outskirts of the flame. Achieving symmetry is important to acquiring control of the movement of the glass. Practice this to gain confidence in dealing with gravity. At this point, bring in the very bottom of the mushroom to the light blue flame.

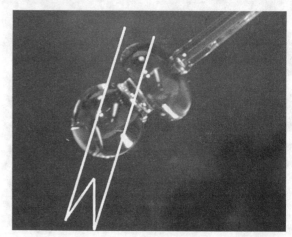

To soften the bottom of the mushroom, allow it to face the torch while rotating to let the yellow reach all around the edge.

As you rotate the glass, the yellow glow will begin to reach all around the apex of the bottom sphere. Remove it from the flame and swiftly and gently press on the fireproof tabletop.

Flatten on the tabletop without creating a "foot" like the mushroom on the left. Don't apply too much pressure.

Apply enough pressure to flatten the base without forming a foot at the bottom of the stem. Annealing the piece in the flame is recommended. To anneal, rotate it in the bushy part of the flame for about one minute.

Removing the Mushroom From the Holding Rod

To avoid shocking the glass, slightly warm up the top inch of the needle nose pliers on the outskirts of the flame. Grip the neck of the mushroom firmly with the needle nose pliers in one hand. With your other hand, hold the 5mm cold stick. In a downward motion, hit the junction on the narrowest point of the metal torch tip. To fire polish off the mark, bring the mark to 1/2" of the light blue flame in a swirling motion for about three seconds. Be careful not to let that part of the flame hit the needle nose. Congratulations! You have made your first completed piece.

MAKING AN ICICLE FROM A FLAT DISK

With an 8mm rod, make a 3/4" sphere, as done previously. When the ball is in the yellow glow mode, place it on the clean, fireproof surface and flatten it with the graphite paddle.

Flattening a 3/4" ball with a graphite paddle.

For best results, execute this movement without hesitation and with a fair amount of pressure. You now have a flat disk on the end of a rod. Fuse the end of a 5mm rod to the bottom of the disk and, as it solidifies, rotate both rods in the same direction to keep them as one long straight rod with a disk in the center.

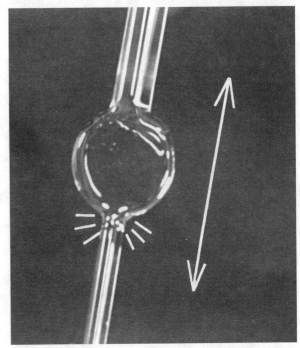

A 5mm rod fused onto a flattened disk and making one long straight rod, with the disk in the center.

Alternating the heat to both flat surfaces, bring the disk to a yellow/orange glow. Remove from the flame, pull apart slowly, and begin to spin the 5mm rod while holding the 8mm rod steady.

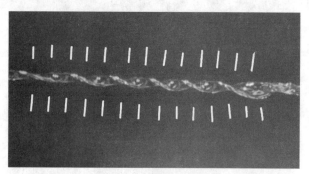

After heating both flat surfaces of the disk and while the whole disk is glowing, begin to slowly pull apart while spinning the 5mm rod.

Without hesitation and with the proper amount of orange glow, you will have about five seconds of spinning motion. With practice, the icicle will taper down to the 5mm rod. Once it solidifies, don't force the issue.

Placing a Loop on the Top

Heat the wide end of the icicle to an orange glow. Remove from the flame, pull up and over, and connect the bottom part of the loop.

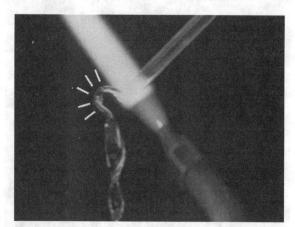

After heating the top part of the disk, remove from flame, pull the molten glass up and over to form the loop to suspend the icicle.

This is done right near the flame to burn the rod at the junction of the loop. Hold the loop with needle nose pliers and remove the 5mm rod. This is your second completed piece.

Double Rod Icicle

Hold a 15" 8mm rod in each hand. Rotate one end of each rod in front of the light blue tip for a few seconds, just to heat 1" of the respective rod. After they have both been heated by taking turns in the flame, repeat the process, only this time allow 1/2" of each rod to molten. When one end is glowing, move it up the flame and start heating the end of the second rod. Be sure they do not touch! Alternate the ends in and out of the light blue tip, keeping the end that is not in the hot section slightly above the light blue tip, but still in the flame. Continue until the ends bead up to just a bit larger than the diameter of the rod.

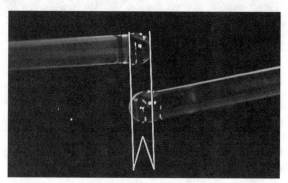

Both rod ends in the flame, alternating in front of the light blue flame. They will start to bead up just slightly bigger than the diameter of the rod.

When both ends are yellow, overlap them by 1", then touch the molten glass ends to the sides of the respective rods. Keep the rods parallel and touching each other on the length of that section.

To secure those ends to the rods, heat each one to yellow and press it into the rod with the torch tip. These steps should be done at a steady pace while keeping that entire area heated. Once the piece resembles the photo, begin heating the wide surfaces of the parallel section. Go back and forth over that 1" section. Alternate the heat between the two sides until the parallel section becomes uniformly red and behaves like a wet noodle between the two rods.

Overlap the rods and connect them as shown, making sure the two rods are touching the length of that 1" overlap.

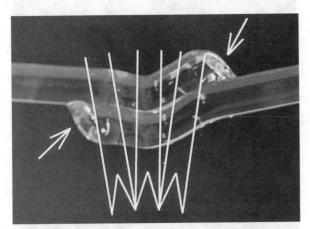

Press the glowing ends into the rod with the torch tip. Heat the length of the 1" overlap to a glow by alternating the heat on the wide side (the wet noodle look). If the rods separate, bend them into each other.

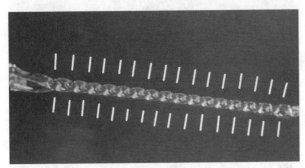

Start to slowly pull the two rods apart while rotating one of them.

When this occurs, remove them from the torch and start to pull apart for 7" while rotating one of the rods.

Insert photo #Sculpt-18

You will have about five seconds to accomplish this. Repeat the process of placing the loop on whichever end you choose (refer to instructions above). You have now completed your third piece. If this procedure is done with 8mm rods, it would be a small horn for a unicorn.

MAKING A SWAN

Start with a 20" 8mm rod. Rotating the rod in both hands, begin to heat the center. As the glass becomes orange, press the glass together creating a ball in the center.

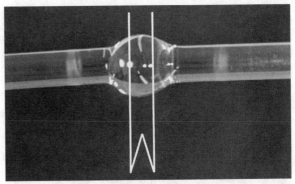

Making a ball in the middle of one long rod. The start of the swan's body.

This piece requires that both hands work in unison for the rotation. The angle and pressure applied, along with coordinating the balance, will dictate how symmetrical the ball will be. Work at making a 3/4" diameter ball in the flame. Once you have that size ball in the flame and both ends of the rod are in the horizontal position, remove them from the flame and maintain the shape until it solidifies. Now the task is to turn that round shape into a football shape.

Heat half the ball and slightly pull apart. Maintain the rotation with both hands moving in the same direction. (To stay in the driver's seat, be aware of the coloration of the glass and where you are in the flame.) Repeat for the other half of the football. Continue with the rotation out of the flame, so you have a straight rod with a football in the center. The ends of the football should be about 1/4" in diameter.

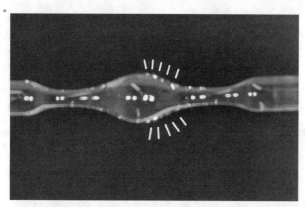

Heat each side of the ball separately and slowly pull apart to shape a football in the middle of one long straight rod.

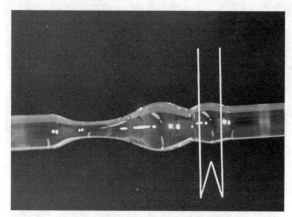

On your dominant side of the football, heat up the juncture while pushing the rod in. The end will grow from 1/4" to 1/2" and remain glowing while you remove it from heat and shape the neck.

To make the swan's neck, go to your dominant side of the football and turn the 1/4" diameter into one approximately 1/2" in diameter.

Feed the rod into the body of the swan while keeping it in constant rotation. within the flame. Keep this section glowing. Remove from the flame, pull slightly out, then back over the body of the swan.

This move may be a little challenging, but you will find if the glass is in the reddish flow and proper viscosity, it will be like painting three dimensions.

Now, you should have a swan's neck with a rod attached where the head will ultimately be placed. At this juncture, heat into the rod about 3/8" and all the way around the rod. Position the rod perpendicular to the head and rotate counterclockwise (if you're right-handed).

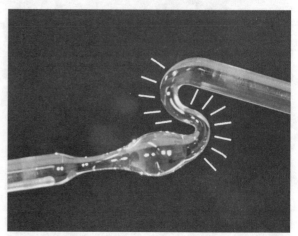

Keeping the 1/2" diameter, red hot, remove from the flame. Pull slightly away from the body, up and over the back of the swan. Head is tilted down.

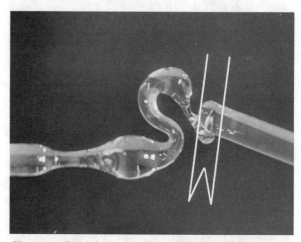

Heat into the rod about 3/8" and all around it. Turn the rod perpendicular to the head of the swan. Right-handed people should rotate counterclockwise. Pull the head away from the flame, creating the forehead and beak.

In this rotation, you are pulling the soft glass on the front part of the head down and away, shaping the forehead down to a pointed beak.

In creating the wing, you will use a technique known as a fold. To do this, you must soften the end (3/8") of the 8mm rod, not allowing it to grow in volume beyond the diameter of the rod. With the hot body of the swan facing away from you and close to the torch, begin to spread the molten glass from the back to the front.

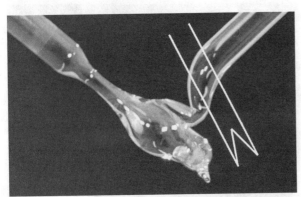

Starting the fold. Spread the glass from the back to the front, pause and rotate to heat up more glass. Then fold by reversing the direction to the back.

Keeping the end of the rod in the flame and reddish, pull away and to the front of the body, fold it back down, then pull to the back of the body and up.

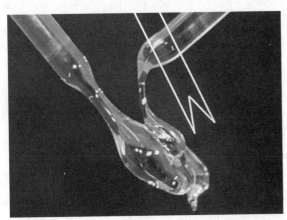

As you make the fold and start towards the back, press down to the body then away and up to shape the wing tips.

Allow the glass to taper to a tip. You have created a wing! Not being ambidextrous, I turn the swan upside down and repeat the process. However, this time I go down where before I went up.

Rotate the swan on the bushy part of the flame for about one minute to make sure it is uniformly hot. Soften the bottom of the swan and flatten. Place the eyes on the head by positioning the space where the eye is to be set very close to but not in the flame.

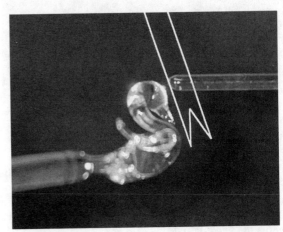

Placing the eye is done by a quick touch to that spot with the tip of a 5mm rod. The same technique is used for buttons and nose using different colored glass.

The molten tip of the 5mm rod comes out of the flame, places the eye, then goes back into the flame. Practice this quick little move. Once the eye is in place, it may have to be touched by the flame to bead up and appear more orb like. This method may also be used to place the nose and buttons on a teddy bear using a blue glass rod. Now you have completed your fourth piece.

MAKING A TEDDY BEAR

This will be the last piece, however it entails a procedure that may be used in a variety of other projects—adding limbs.

With a 15" 8mm rod, make a 3/4" ball similar to the one in your first exercise. Place a cold stick on the end, creating a straight rod with a ball in the center—the body of the bear.

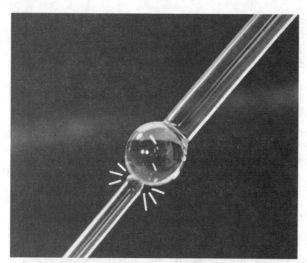

The 5mm rod is attached to the working piece cold stick. You must see the juncture seam. The sphere is very hot, but not molten when the rod is attached to it.

Burn off the rod just the way you did with the mushroom, only leave about 3/4" of the rod on the sphere. Rotating this section in the flame, allow it to bead up into a ball a bit smaller than the one it is attached to. You have created the head of Teddy!

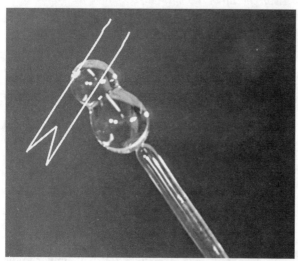

As you make the fold and start towards the back, press down to the body then away and up to shape the wing tips.

To create the arm, heat about 1/2" on the end of the 8mm rod. Allow it to bead up slightly larger than the diameter of the rod. Keeping this end red hot, bring the hot body of the Teddy to the fire. Start to heat the area (where you are applying the arm) to a yellow glow. Bring in the red hot end to the arm socket and, while in the flame, connect the two. Remove to just outside of the flame and softly pull to shape the arm.

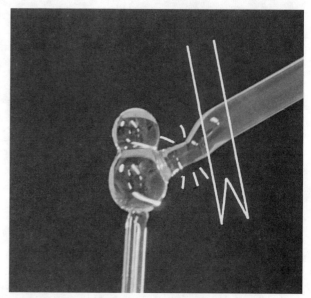

After heating up the arm socket, bring in the molten rod and fuse together. Pulling slowly, form the arm and leg.

The faster you pull, the thinner the arm gets. The slower you pull, the thicker it stays. (Remember, teddy bears need stocky arms for hugging!) When the arm has solidified, burn off at the desired length and press the soft glass on the side of the torch tip to create the paw. On the same side of the body, repeat the process for the leg.

It is recommended that you have different colored glass available. Perhaps cobalt blue for contrast. At this point, without the interference of another arm and leg, you can place two buttons on the belly. How about a nose and eyes? Do this the same way you did the eyes of the swan. Once the blue is used, repeat the process for the arms and legs.

Choose the desired length arm. Burn off the rod and press on the flat side of the torch tip to make a paw.

Place equal size balls on both sides of the head. Heat separately and flatten with tweezers. Notice the buttons and eyes.

Using a 5mm rod (and the same steps for attaching arms), place a tail on the back end of Teddy, along with a couple of the same sized balls for the ears on the head. After these have been placed and solidified, heat just the ears (individually) to red, then flatten them to face front.

Warm up the needle nose pliers, hold on to the neck, and snap off the stick. Soften the bottom and flatten. Please be careful, teddy bears do not like deformed posteriors.

This chapter has been written to give you a taste of what I believe to be an intriguing medium. If the techniques and procedures described herein are practiced with even moderate determination, it will open up the world of lampworking to you. These procedures can be applied to a wide variety of pieces. For example, with a minor change in timing and heat, the swan's body can become a jumping dolphin. A fold can be fashioned for the fins. The neck of the swan can be transformed into the trunk of an elephant. Whatever you conceive, you can achieve.

CHAPTER 27
The Work Area

Working in stained glass can take very little room or quite a lot of room. It depends on the scope of your endeavor. You can work at home on a kitchen table or in the basement or garage, or you can put aside an entire shop for your craft. Many small (and not so small) stained glass businesses have developed from what were essentially "kitchen table" beginnings. Where you work is certainly important to your convenience and morale but it isn't quite as important as how you work. That depends on how you utilize the space at hand. Whatever space you set aside for stained glass, certain features should be included.

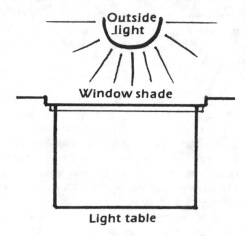

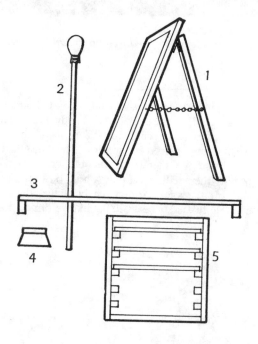

Good lighting is essential for a work area designed specifically for painting on glass. All reflected light should be subordinate to that coming from below or behind the glass. Too much reflective light can make it hard to see what you are doing.

A few necessary items for a workshop where painting on glass is done: 1) easel set on a table near a window; 2) mahl stick; 3) bridge; 4) side view of bridge leg; 5) palette box.

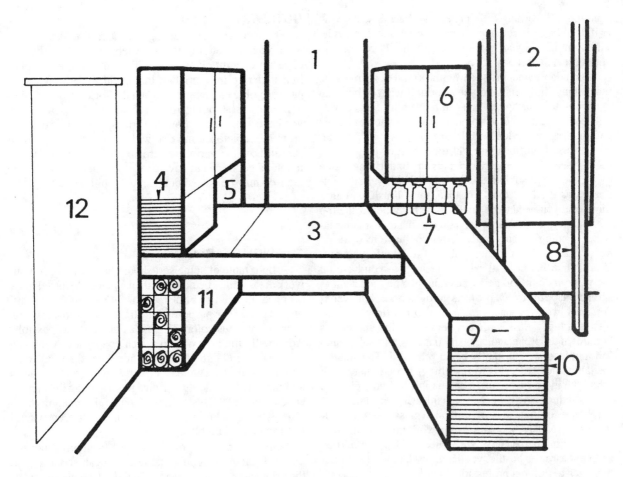

An ideal studio setup for painting on glass: 1 and 2) windows; 3) light table; 4) palette box; 5 and 6) storage; 7) trace and matt paints; 8) easel; 9) brush storage; 10) rack for cut, traced, and painted pieces; 11) cartoon rack; 12) cartoon mounting for viewing during while painting on the easel.

THE WORK TABLE

Not the kitchen table by any means, the work table should not be a surface you are going to be eating on. We prefer our work table surfaces made of 3/4" plywood covered by 1/4" luan (three-part wafer plywood) with one side finished smooth and sealed with varnish to make it less porous to chemicals and also easier to keep clean. You can make such work tables yourself. The luan should be secured to the plywood with multiple small brads rather than glue. Brads allow it to be replaced when it gets beat up from use.

Varnishing should be done late in the day and left to dry overnight. Usually a single coat is sufficient, but two coats certainly won't hurt. For a work table base you can go simple, as in two sawhorses propping up the surface, or complex by creating a support of multiple level shelving with hinged areas, trap doors, pop-up supporting rods, drawers, and what have you. Some work tables we have seen are almost habitations.

However you build your work table, remember to make it comfortable to work on. The top should be approximately 36" from the floor; an average height for standing and working without getting a backache; however if you are a short person there's no hard and fast rule. The point is, it's your work table and should conform to your ease and abilities.

If you don't want to use saw horses (and they aren't the most stable supports) and yet you don't want to build an extension to your house, you can make a frame out of 2" x 4" boards. This allows for some storage shelves below and makes a very sturdy table. Again, our own work tables utilize a full four by eight foot sheet of plywood as the surface which usually overlaps the underlying frame by a good couple of inches all around. This overlap is important as it allows tools, dustpan, table brush, and anything else you need to be handy to be hung below the top without getting in your way. You can make a smaller table depending on how much room you have to work in, but we advise you to make the largest table you can. You'll find that no matter how much room you have on the work table, it will never be enough. You may want to spread out with several projects going at once, but even if you only work on one, tools seem to multiply on their own and hide; glass is always being selected and pieces laid down atop one another, and patterns and solder and foil and lead are constantly being retrieved. The smaller the table, the harder it is to find things buried under each other, the more frustrating it can be just to find a place to put something down where you can easily reach it.

As you continue to work in stained glass you will modify your premises, including your work table, to express your working personality. We've seen tables so modified as to appear user-hostile, yet the individual working on it manages to turn out professional work.

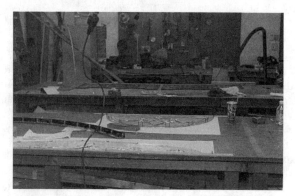

Work tables and tool pegboard. (Stained Glass Connection, Sarasota, Florida)

OUTLETS

You can never have enough of them. We like to run a multiple strip outlet to the work table itself, one that accepts up to eight plugs. You will need this many to plug in a soldering iron, grinder, lamp, and so forth. It's a lot easier to plug something in when the socket is waist-high than to keep stooping for baseboard outlets. Of course you have to be careful how you arrange the cord from outlet to the tabletop so no one will trip over it and also be careful how the various electrical cords lie on the table; it's not a good idea to have one lying where a hot soldering iron may be placed or chemicals spill on it.

THE LIGHT TABLE

A light table of some sort should have a place in your work area. It may be no more than a piece of frosted glass propped on two fire bricks with a fluorescent bulb lighting the glass. The purpose of the light table is to allow you to match various colors of glass as precisely as possible. Admittedly the best way to match colors is to view any glass by natural light, but this is not always possible on a continuing basis. The least effective way to match hues and tones is by holding various glasses up against an incandescent bulb. This will give you a false reading every time. The light table is a compromise between natural light and a bare bulb.

Some of the best light tables come from print shops—they call them "stripping" tables. You can scout around the print shops in your area to see if they are getting rid of an old stripping table. Again, size is dependent on the amount of room you have, but get the biggest light table you can fit in your space.

If you can't locate a light table already built, you can build one yourself. Essentially a light table is a box with reflective surfaces inside and several fluorescent bulbs spaced 12" to 18" from the top glass. The reflective surfaces can be aluminum foil spread to cover the entire inside portion and the bulbs attached to a fixture placed upside-down on the bottom. The glass top must be frosted to get the proper spread of light. To get the right amount of surface light, you'll need to experiment with such factors as size of box, strength and amount of light source, and depth of the arrangement. Once you have built the light box, don't use it as just another flat surface to pile things on or you may have to build another one for function.

Light table and pattern storage area. (Stained Glass Connection)

GLASS BINS

Glass storage is one of the most frustrating problems you'll encounter. Because stained glass reduces itself to so many different sizes and shapes, no matter how uniform the pieces are when you purchase them, maintaining these remainder portions can tax anyone's ingenuity. The best storage method involves the use of bins. Start with newly purchased glass in sheets cut to size, or portions of sheets cut to size. For the larger sheets, ask your supplier for any unused shipping cases he may have.

Glass bins made of shipping crates. (Stained Glass Connection)

These come in different strengths and functionality, depending on the company that knocked them together (and that's putting it mildly). At best, you'll get a case that could foundation a house; at worst, one that is so feeble it splinters as you look at it. Or one that looks to attack you with nails sticking out in all directions. Obviously you will take the best you can get, but even some of the worst cases can be rebuilt as glass bins depending on how much work you're willing to do.

Dedicate one of the walls in your work space to glass bins. The larger bins go on the bottom, smaller ones on

Square foot glass and smaller panes divided by manufacturer and sorted by glass number. The bins were originally for plate storage at a local printing company. (J&P Stained Glass, Scarborough, Maine)

top. *Note:* Don't place any bins higher than you can comfortably reach to pull out a sheet of glass. If you are stacking bins, be sure the bottom bins can support the weight of the top ones—not when they are empty, but when they are full of glass. Not all glass cases are the same size so if you are using them as bottom bins you will find variances in height that will transfer to those bins sitting atop them. There's nothing wrong with this, provided you have enough support to maintain the arrangement. Not only should glass be stored according to size, but also according to color and, if possible, according to manufacturer. Not all of us have space to allow for this convenient breakdown, but such a system will help you find just that right sheet at the right time for the right project.

It's much less sloppy looking to have all bins the same size, and you can easily do this by cutting them to match or just forgetting the cases and building a row of bins out of wood from the lumberyard. This will take longer than just throwing some glass bins together but you only have to do this once and you can cut and measure everything so it matches the odd sizes of glass you will have lying around as well as standard sheets. This doesn't mean you can store every piece of glass that will be left over from various projects. There comes a time when this simply doesn't pay. That's where the scrap box comes into the picture.

THE SCRAP BOX

There are workers who can't bring themselves to throw out even the smallest leftover shards and there are those who toss pieces large enough to be used in other projects. For the former, the wastebasket is too large; for the latter it is never large enough. Which one are you? Best to be in the middle here. Keep a wooden box, not a deep one, not a large can, for scrap glass. You don't want it deep because then you'll fill it and have to rummage through the levels for that one piece you suddenly need. This can be dangerous. You don't want a cardboard box because the glass will eventually eat through it.

Our advice is to just keep one scrap box, certainly no more than two. If you allow more than that you'll soon have an entire floor full and that's counter-productive. Once your scrap box gets full, it's time to sort through it (carefully) and discard any pieces you don't think you will ever use again—odd-shaped pieces, pieces smaller than 5" x 5", hard to cut pieces, or pieces of dark, difficult to see through tones. Throwing away glass pieces can be a traumatic experience for some people; it was for us. We

ended up with ten good size garbage cans full when we finally took the time to sort through storage bins in the basement of our studio. The garbage men were not happy.

This cabinet has 32 pull-out drawers of scrap glass that has been sorted by type and color. (J&P Stained Glass)

Some studios sell their scrap glass. You may want to do this, assuming you have a working studio and have customers who want the stuff. Don't let anyone go through your scrap box no matter how insistent they are. If they cut themselves, you are to blame and you don't need this kind of problem no matter how well insured you

An unusual retail display where the racks can be backlit to show how glass would look in a shade. Three racks contain 6" x 12" panes of Spectrum sorted by number. (J&P Stained Glass)

may be. Take the time to pull out pieces yourself. Most scrap glass sells by the pound, so have a scale ready. Don't wrap the sellable pieces in newspaper. Most scrap will be odd-sized and pointed in various directions and someone will probably get cut as the pieces jiggle about. Either wrap them in cardboard or put them in a box. The idea is not only to protect your customer, but yourself.

The key to a well functioning studio or work space is organization. When working in glass, organization is vital if you don't want to spend most of your time hunting for things.

Indoor/outdoor carpet covers the cutting board using glass crates as a base. (Stained Glass Connection)

STORING TOOLS

You can use a tool caddy, pegboard, or individual drawers but whatever you use, make sure you use it. We've seen workers with tools all over the work table with empty pegboards and caddies that seem to be decorative items. Keep in mind that as you work in this medium your collection of tools will grow rapidly. Nothing is more frustrating than not being able to find a tool because it's buried under something on the table.

Keep your work table neat, not just for looks but for ease of use. Replace each tool after you are done with it. This will not interrupt your work flow; on the contrary it will enhance it. Keep a roll of paper towels handy for spills and for wiping your hands. The less time you spend walking around your work space looking for things, the more time you'll have for the work in hand. We can't emphasize this enough.

WINDOW SPACE

This is a luxury item which, if you are working in a garage or basement, you may not be allowed. As soon as you can, try for a space with a window. Not only will you be able to choose your colors better, you will find the entire ambiance of the work space will, literally, lighten up. After all, stained glass is dependent on natural light. It's an airy, free flowing medium and shouldn't be cribbed or confined in a space where the light of day cannot realize its potential. While a light table is a fine working tool to get your colors to blend, the only real effect a piece of stained glass can accomplish is in league with natural light.

CHAPTER 28
Selling Your Work

While the majority of individuals enter the stained glass field as a relaxation, a hobby strictly for their own enjoyment, the temptation occasionally arises from the compliments of friends, to make a business out of it. Nothing is wrong with this but there are two strong considerations: 1) Most important, can you turn out work some stranger will be willing to buy, and 2) Are you willing to function under the stress of someone else's demands and uncertainties? If you unequivocally answer yes to these prerequisites you may want to take the chance of starting your own studio.

WORKING ON COMMISSION

You may enter the business of stained glass without even noticing that you've taken this step. As you continue your progress in the field, word gets around and friends and relatives will begin to ask you to "make me something." Eventually you will begin to realize that being paid with compliments for these somethings, while good for the ego, leaves a certain fiduciary embarrassment since you have paid for the glass, lead, copper, and time that you've provided gratis. You can start by putting a minimal price on your creations. From this, it may be only a small step to larger projects, and eventually to making a window for someone's home. If you can carry out this project to yours and your customer's satisfaction, you can consider yourself a pro. However, there are a lot of missteps to be avoided along the way.

In many cases a customer, whether a stranger or a relative, won't know anything about glass or what they want, and will depend on your knowledge. Be prepared to offer advice without overwhelming the client with your preferences. Clients who are totally unsure of what they want and who just "go along" with what you like may be unhappy with the final result. If they are unhappy, you certainly will not be hearing from their friends. A stained glass project, whether lamp or window, fire screen or stepping stone, comes into being through an interplay between customer and artist. It is not the least important part of the work to guide your customer so the two of you understand fully what is practical, as opposed to what the customer anticipates.

GUIDING THE CLIENT

Consider a stained glass window. Many people who want one for their home aren't sure what kind of design would be best. They know they don't want a "churchy" window. They may have some preconceived notion of the costs involved. They may assume you are going to totally rework the embrasure where this window will fit. Their assumptions can cost you the job if you mishandle them. You must straighten out all the details involved before cutting a single piece of glass. Not the least of these is cost. We've had customers come into our studio with books of color pictures under their arms to show us the elements they want incorporated into their window. Once they find out the cost, they can lose a bit of color themselves. But it's important you be up front from the start. The worst thing is to allow your customer to anticipate something you don't realize they are considering because you have not nailed down precisely what is going to be built.

Nailing the project down involves putting it on paper. Use sketches, acetates, design elements, whatever, and be sure to give copies of these to your customer to take home to show husband or wife or the neighbors. Some workers object to this, fearing the customer will take these to another studio and have the work done there. We're not suggesting you give a prospective client a full scale drawing of what the window will be like; this comes later after a contract has been signed. But sketches and measurements have likely been already obtained from other studios before the client has come to yours and if not, such rough estimates are part of your relationship with your customer and show good faith. They should be nothing another studio can't do in a few minutes and they allow your customer to take you home with him or her and consider all the points you have discussed in a familiar environment, one in which the work will be installed.

PRICING

In general, professional studios cost out a window based on its square footage (the amount of glass and came needed) and the complexity of the design (the amount of time needed). The more complex the design, the more labor, the more time, the higher the cost. Square footage is achieved by measuring the length and width of the work and multiplying the two together in inches and dividing by 144 inches. But this is not the final calculation in most instances. Added to the measurements, pricing varies from less costly diamonds or any strictly repetitive pattern to pictorial designs, single or double glazing, three-dimensional effects, painted details, use of bevels, etc. all of which can add considerably to the base price.

There's also the cost of you, the artist, and you may be very pricey because you are very good and have a fine reputation. On top of all this cost is the type of glass being used, whether it's antique or cathedral, imported or domestic, Bullseye or Spectrum or Wismach or something you produce yourself from melted down coke bottles in your living room glory hole. Pricing can be based on painstaking evaluation of all these elements to arrive at a fair price, or on the fact that you need the work and are willing to cut corners (literally) to get the job.

It is important to remember that the ordinary person has little idea, and cares less, as to the amount of creative effort and training involved in producing even a simply designed stained glass window which he or she considers mainly ornamental. Such a customer may be taken aback at any price you quote, though to you it may seem lower than reasonable. Yet this same individual would probably not react in this way if the work was a painting or a piece of sculpture since that is considered art. Not the least element of stained glass pricing is getting the public to realize that stained glass is also art. Fortunately, thanks to such individuals as Ludwig Shaffrath and Narcissis Quagliata and others in that category, stained glass is beginning to reach that pinnacle. But the trickle down effect is still much to be desired. The best pricing is probably what you honestly consider fair. You'll find out just how fair your pricing is by how busy your studio becomes.

THE PLANNING STAGE

If you have examples of previous work you've done (and it's always a good idea to keep a picture file of completed projects—never get lazy about this) show your customer the file. It's not only good to have something in front of you that can be discussed, it's comforting to the customer to realize you've done this before. If this is your first customer you are at somewhat of a disadvantage in this regard but you can still show pictures of generic windows and patterns out of books. We have found that customers are mainly interested in their window anyway and not necessarily those of other people; they've come to talk about what they think they want and anything you can show them that applies, even peripherally, to their dream window will help. We like to show samples of various stained glasses along with some basic patterns which can be modified to suit a taste. You should have enough choices to give your client a good idea of where this project is going.

Once this has been decided, draw up a contract to that effect and get a deposit. This can be from 25% to 50% of the total, or can be divided into stages, paid as each stage of the project is completed. Specify in the contract that once glass cutting has begun, no further changes of design are possible. Otherwise you may end up doing this one window for the rest of your working days.

ACETATES AND TRANSPARENCIES

Another method of showing clients what their projected window will look like both in design and (so far as is possible) in color is to make up an acetate. This involves painting a small exact replica on clear plastic. It's a time consuming project and we don't advise doing it unless the project is extensive and a good deal of money is involved. We have had to go to this extreme when dealing with a group of people rather than a single individual. Church windows, library windows, anything involving a committee (heaven help you) generally calls for more specific indications of what the finished work will look like than your ordinary client will insist on.

Acetates are more involved in the making than a drawing and should be charged for, the amount depending on what you think your time is worth. An acetate must be drawn to scale and painted to resemble as closely as possible the completed window. There are special enamels that can be used to paint on plastic; check with your supplier. In some cases the customer may want to keep the acetate even after the window has been completed and installed. Since he or she has paid for it, why not? If not, you can add it to your portfolio to show your next customer with the proviso that it is not a routine part of the contract but an extra. Acetates by their nature are much more "stained glassy" than slides and also help to show off your technique in painting miniatures. If you've never painted on plastic we advise you to practice fairly extensively before trying it on a prospective customer who will judge your overall technique by this specific one. We have always found that creating an acetate of a window helps the sale, but a poor example of an acetate can lose a sale.

Color transparencies (slides) are another way to show off your work; we take color slides of all the work we do preferring them to color prints even though they are somewhat more awkward to exhibit. We find the colors are more precise with slides. We always have a viewer handy for customers to use so we don't have to go scrambling for one. Also, the three-dimensional effect is much more exciting than the flat look of a bunch of color photographs in a book. And slides are more involving. With slides the customer must physically get involved with each example, picking up one slide and then the next. You want the customer to spend time with your work. And slides are, of course, a natural adjunct to any group presentation. That doesn't mean you can't have color photographs as well. The optimum situation is to have two cameras, one for slides and one for pictures. Remember, your past work is the best sales modality you can have (assuming that it works for you, not against you).

THE WORK IN PROGRESS

Usually there is a stipulation in the contract as to when the work will be completed. Most clients want their project completed yesterday; the time involved is something else they must understand. Be wary. No matter how sure you are you can complete a project by a projected date, you should always leave some safety time in there for something to go wrong. If nothing does (and hopefully nothing will), you are ahead of the game. But all too often something unplanned happens, whether it's a misplaced shipment of material or some family event or dividing your time between too many projects. It's less stressful to have a little more time than you may think you actually need. The last thing you need is to have your creativity stifled by a cramped due date and late penalties.

Sometimes a client will want to visit the workshop to see how the project is coming along. Here is where your assessment of your customer will decide whether or not this is a good idea. If your client fully understands the nature of the construction and you have a good relationship, fine. If your client is picky, uncertain of what they actually want, nervous as to the final design, and generally interfering, it's probably best to keep them away from the shop. First of all, they aren't going to see much since the window will be flat down on a table being leaded; second they might start wanting to change things, regardless of any contract. Any contract is only as good as the people involved. We all know people who vary with the moment. The best way to keep a difficult client at a distance from the shop is to say your insurance won't allow anyone not working there to be in the shop and to show the window only in its final state when, after all, it will appear at its best and any objections would (hopefully) be moot.

CHAPTER 29
Photographing Stained Glass

When photographing stained glass, including step-by-step instructions, some guidelines may be helpful to the novice photographer. Very often you will want to keep a photographic record of your work either as black and white sequential shots of an important project, or color prints or slides of something wonderful you made to sell. Good quality photographs will enhance your portfolio and provide you with a better resource for potential customers.

The components necessary to take good pictures are a good quality 35mm camera, film, lights (or flashes), a sturdy tripod, colored paper or fabrics, and a surface to place the items (such as a card table) or a means of hanging larger stained glass objects to be photographed. Photographing stained glass is difficult enough; when bevels are also involved it's like photographing air. By preparing in advance, you will save a lot of time and frustration when you come to the actual photo session.

CAMERA

You don't need a Hasselblad, though if you have one, by all means be our guest. Any quality single lens reflex 35mm camera in good working order will suffice. Do not use a range finder 35mm camera, as it will make it difficult to properly focus and frame objects. An older 35mm camera or a camera in questionable condition should be checked by a reputable repairman before use. Finding out that none of your photographs came out because of camera malfunction is a tragedy.

Ideally, you should have several lenses: a standard 50mm lens, a wide angle lens (24 to 35mm), and a zoom lens (80 to 200mm). A standard 50mm lens is essential. A wide angle lens will be very helpful if you are photographing large objects (an extensive window, for example) and have limited space. A zoom lens will help you get closer to the object (in the camera's viewfinder) and get a better picture without having to move the camera and tripod constantly.

If you will be photographing small pieces of glass, a micro or macro lens is a must. Macro and micro lenses

(they do the same thing) allow you to focus within inches of the object (and fill the frame), which is essential with small highly detailed pieces. A 55mm to 105mm macro or micro lens is suitable. If you don't have a micro or macro lens and need one, check the local camera shops. They may rent a suitable lens that will match your camera. This is also true for other equipment you may need. Many camera shops in metropolitan areas and their suburbs rent equipment by the day or week for a reasonable fee.

Alternatives to macro or micro lenses are diopters or close-up lenses that attach to the front of the camera lens. These lenses are the same size as filters and provide the same effect as the macros and micros. Check the camera shop for details. These are inexpensive and you may want to purchase a set to add to your camera equipment.

FILM

For color photography, slides are preferable if you ever want to publish your work or present them at craft shows or any other event. We suggest using Kodachrome or Ektachrome color slide film (both made by Kodak) or Fujichrome T (from Fuji). Medium speed film (with an ASA/ISO rating of 40, 50, 64, 100, or 160) will provide excellent enlargements with good detail and fine grain. If you are planning to use black and white film, Kodak T-Max 100 or Kodak Plus-X (with an ASA/ISO rating of 125) are preferred for essentially the same reasons. Due to improvements in ASA/ISO 400 speed film, it is acceptable to use this speed in color slide or black and white.

Take the exposed film to a reputable film processor or camera shop. Only take black and white film to a shop that is experienced in black and white processing and printing. Don't trust the corner drug store to provide good processing and prints to be used in a publication. Ask a knowledgeable photographer or call a professional photo studio and ask for recommendations.

LIGHTING

If you have access to a studio lighting setup (strobes, soft boxes or umbrellas, power pack), terrific. Such set-ups can be rented from many camera shops for a moderate fee. However, you can take professional quality photographs using special light bulbs (250 or 500 watt) placed in clamp-on light fixtures with reflectors (available at hardware stores). Typically, these reflectors can handle 250 watt bulbs, but they cannot endure the heat of 500 watt bulbs. If you are planning to use tungsten balanced film (Ektachrome or Fujichrome T), use 250 watt ECA bulbs or 500 watt ECT bulbs (available from the camera shop). Use blue bulbs (250 or 500 watt) for Kodachrome (or other daylight balanced) film. Avoid using fluorescent light or illumination from standard light bulbs—fluorescent light requires special filters and standard lamp bulbs create a reddish hue with color film and do not provide enough light to be useful. Any of the bulbs suggested will be fine with black and white film. Remember, if you use 500 watt bulbs, you must use a fixture that can handle the heat without melting or risking an electrical fire.

Use two lights for the photo setup, placing them in front of and at 45° angles to the object. You may also want to back light it. We take pictures with and without back lighting and determine later which are best. Clamp the lights to chairs or secure them in some other fashion that will allow easy movement. Do not place the lights too close to the object, as the heat from the lights may crack the glass. Don't place the lights too far away either, or you may not have enough light to produce an adequate picture. The lights should be slightly above the object being photographed (at a 45° angle) to avoid strong shadows behind the object. You may place one light a few feet closer to the object than the other light to add texture.

A SIMPLE STUDIO SETUP

If the objects to be photographed can be moved easily, move them to the studio. Set up a sturdy card table and place a roll of colored paper (four foot wide rolls are available from the camera shop) or a large, unwrinkled piece of fabric so it forms a seamless background for the object. For black and white photography, a light tone of gray paper or fabric is fine. Use fabric or paper that will provide a reasonable amount of contrast to the object shown. For color photography, use a light blue or other soft unobtrusive and reasonably complementary color for the background. If you can show the object in its context (a window in its embrasure), do so but keep the picture uncluttered. Don't add a lot of extraneous and unrelated objects that take attention away from the focal point. As a rule, provide some background on all four sides of the ob-

ject in the photograph and be careful not to inadvertently cut off any portion of the object. In other words, leave some blank space on each side of the object.

When using lights (not flashes), set the camera on a tripod and use a cable release to keep the camera steady. This is necessary because you will need to use a fairly small lens aperture to allow for good depth of field. When using a small aperture (f-11 should be sufficient), you will need a slow shutter speed (1/8 to 1/30 second). Take the light reading directly off the object and take a picture. (On most cameras, light readings are given in the viewfinder by a centered needle or LED readout.) Then bracket the shot one f-stop above and one f-stop below the light reading and take a picture at each setting. When using slide film, bracket the shots in 1/2-stop increments.

When using a flash or flashes as the light source, shoot at 1/60 second (or 1/250 second if that is your camera's flash sync speed) and set the aperture at f-11.

If you are photographing a person doing various steps in a project, use flashes. Don't try to use lamps—your photographs will be blurred (because of the slow shutter speeds necessary with such lights) and your subject will be uncomfortably warm.

PHOTOGRAPHY UNDER DIFFICULT CONDITIONS

You won't always have the luxury of shooting in convenient and controlled situations. You may have to photograph important items under trying circumstances. We have photographed Tiffany windows both outside and inside buildings from impossible angles that did nothing for the end result. Don't try to shoot everything in sight just because it's there; better to get one roll of usable pictures with clear, well-defined objects or steps that are informative than to shoot ten rolls of film that are not usable.

If the day is overcast with little or no breeze and no threat of rain, you can take the objects and studio outside and work there. An overcast sky will provide soft even lighting and allow you to work without the lights. Use a gray card for light readings when using color film outdoors—it will provide better and more accurate measurements than taking readings from the objects themselves. Gray cards are inexpensive and available at all camera shops. Another way to get soft lighting indoors is to bank the lights off white mat boards (or other large pieces of cardboard or similar material) onto the object. This will provide softer and more even illumination.

When shooting under less than favorable conditions, such as at a show, museum, or store, you will probably have to use an on-camera flash. *Note:* If you are planning to take photographs in a museum, check the museum's rules before snapping any pictures.

SHOOTING TIPS

When there is a great deal of immobile or unavoidable clutter around the object you wish to photograph or if the object itself can't be moved (such as a large window), position a white or other uniformly colored sheet or seamless paper behind the object. (If you're feeling ambitious, iron the sheet before leaving home or at least try to keep it reasonably wrinkle-free.) If it's possible to move a large stained glass object without injuring yourself or the object to be moved (and the owner agrees), do so. You want to show the item in clear detail. The less it has to fight with clutter, the better.

Try to keep people out of the background and make sure they are not reflected in the glass you are photographing. Politely ask people to move or wait until they move away. In the same vein, avoid making a self-portrait in the reflection from the glass you are shooting. It will often act as a mirror. Position yourself so you can't see yourself or the camera in the glass. If that means crouching down or standing to the side, do it.

When photographing an individual doing step-by-step instructions, set the flash at angles that will avoid shadows. Get close to your subject and focus on the hands. Make sure that what the person is doing will be clearly shown in the photograph. Show the involvement of the person's hands in the work and keep necessary tools in the picture. However, don't allow the person's hands to block or obliterate the visibility of the action being shown and don't completely show the tool being used if it means you will have to back up and lose a clear tight view of the work. Before beginning the step-by-step process, lay out all the tools and photograph them. When the work is ex-tremely delicate and you need to get very close to show a step, do so, but don't block the flashes with your body or the camera.

Use a small step ladder to photograph objects that cannot be moved.

Always bracket the shots. This is especially important in situations when you have little control over the conditions and general lighting.

If you will be photographing small objects, take a card table and a few rolls of paper or fabric to use as backgrounds.

If you are photographing small objects that lay flat, use a copy stand (if you have one available).

PRINTS

It is essential that black and white prints be of the best quality and clarity possible. Both glossy and matt finish prints are acceptable. Ask the camera shop or other film processor and printer for flat toned, low contrast prints (from black and white film). Low contrast prints provide the best reproduction for publishing purposes. Again, make sure printer is experienced in black and white work. Recommendations from professional photographers can be helpful. Call a local studio if you can't find a reputable shop on your own.

Prints should be no smaller than 4" x 5" for clarity. We prefer 5" x 7" prints. When marking prints with figure numbers or other forms of identification, do not use magic markers, felt tip pens, marking pens, or rubber stamps on the backs of the prints. These will bleed through the photographic paper or smear when another print is placed on top. Either way, the prints will be unusable. Avoid using ballpoint pens and pencils on the backs of the prints as well, as they will ruin the surface of the prints. Your best bet is to write whatever information is necessary on an adhesive label and then affix the prepared label to the back of the print. You may use a pen or pencil on the label.

CHAPTER 30
Repairing Stained Glass

The above lamp is definitely worth repairing. In this case, cost was a factor as always, but also involved was the intrinsic worth of the lamp. Repair was not the only consideration; a lot of rebuilding was necessary because the weight of the shade was beginning to fracture struts. A case for repair and rebuilding. (see page 325)

The above lantern was brought in for repair. Is it worth repairing? Should it be rebuilt? Should it just be junked? Its fate often depends on you, the expert glass-worker.

A FEW CAUTIONS

If it's your own creation you are repairing, it may not be fun but at least it's a meaningful job to you or you wouldn't have created it in the first place. This holds true whether the piece is a panel with several broken portions or a lamp with a missing panel. It's still your baby. If you're doing repair work for others it's even less fun. Not only can such work be tedious and difficult, but most objects brought in for repair run the gamut from soiled to filthy—with stained stained glass, rusted re-bars, oxidized lead, and splintered wood frames. As you clean the glass and scrub the corroded leads, you may even break a piece of sound glass. With all this, you can't even charge as you would for a new creation.

It's not true that it costs more to rebuild than to repair. In many cases rebuilding a shattered window adding whatever materials can be salvaged would save time and money. More time may be wasted tediously disassembling such a disaster while trying to begin a repair than starting from scratch. You should realize this and charge by the hour to make up for it, but more important, your customer should realize it. Anything short of rebuilding may be a poor compromise. Unfortunately, your customer doesn't want to pay for a rebuilding. He feels, and will state, that he could buy a brand new whatever it is for what you want to charge for redoing his old one. Where stained glass is concerned, most people don't understand the work involved in making a new piece, much less fixing an old one.

Then there's the fact that many times repairs on stained glass objects leave scars. If subjected to careful scrutiny, the piece may always look repaired. Again, this is something your customer should understand.

The beginner repair craftsperson is often tempted to quote a low price just to get the job. Unfortunately, he may then be tempted to take shortcuts to match the fee and the resulting piece may be to no one's satisfaction.

Let the customer know that a repair is not a restoration. Restoring something implies that it will be brought back to a state of pristine creation, while repair involves merely replacing a portion of the object so it will once again be functional and decorative. But it will not necessarily be perfect. People may be willing to pay the price of repair, but they often expect restoration for their money.

REPAIRING WINDOWS

Obviously the easiest windows to repair have pieces that are broken out near the borders. But this is not a rule of thumb. If the window is brought in with its wood frame, the fact that it has broken border pieces is modified by the fact that it must be taken out of its frame before any work can be done on it. We rarely accept a window in its frame because we aren't going to get paid for the time involved removing and then resetting it. There are exceptions. We recently had to repair several inside pieces in a stained glass door which was the main entrance to a house. Taking this large stained glass center section out (it was built in quite solidly) and replacing it would have taken hours and we had to do the repair and replace the door before dark, eight hours from the time we picked it up. In this instance, we worked on the piece in its frame, awkward as it was.

If you want to do repairs, try to work as clean as you can without doing a spit and polish job. Clean the glass around the breaks with glass cleaner and be careful when passing a rag over the surface of any old panel so you don't inadvertently stick yourself on a piece of turned-up lead or an old copper wire that was used to join a reinforcing rod. You can easily cut a finger to the bone by cleaning a piece carelessly. Once the window and the leads are at least cleaner than they were, cut away the border lead near the broken piece. You will probably have to cut it at the corners or, if you're lucky, you might get away with just cutting that portion of it at the glass break and bend-ing it back. If it's old and corroded, you may not be able to solder it back in place once the new piece of glass has been placed. So you likely will have to replace the entire border lead anyway. The broken glass should be pulled gently out of the surrounding came with glass pliers, not your fingers. It may not be easy to do this if the piece has been puttied in; very likely it has and you'll have to dig it out with your lead knife. Once it's out, use the point of a lead knife to scrape inside the lead channels to make sure no small pieces remain inside that will not allow the new piece of glass to seat properly.

To get a size and shape of the space for the replacement glass, place a piece of pattern paper beneath the opening surrounded by the open lead (aside from the border piece), and with a sharp pencil trace the shape. Do this exactly to the point where the border lead has been cut away and use a ruler to join the two ends of the design to take the place of the border lead. Enlarge the design very slightly, perhaps 1/16" all around to allow for the lead channels where the new glass will fit. Cut out this pattern with regular scissors and check the pattern in the space, holding it on top of the leads to allow for the channel spaces. Finally, when the fit looks good, cut a piece of glass to shape. The glass should fit exactly into the empty space, snapping into the waiting channels of the lead with the least bit of tapping from a lead knife handle. You can then replace the missing portion of border lead and solder it to the lead on either side or, if that's not possible, cut away the entire old border lead and replace it, being careful not to disturb all the glass pieces that utilize it along the way (shudder).

In many cases, you will find old putty in the empty leads surrounding the broken glass. This should be thoroughly cleaned away with the lead knife blade or any tool that will fit and once the new glass is back in place, new putty should be applied. Never skip this important step. So much for breaks along the border.

Center Breaks

For windows or panels that have pieces broken out in their centers, the repair is considerably more complicated. Several methods may be applied here.

The Tinker-Toy Approach. This involves taking the entire window apart to the point of the missing piece or pieces. You must cut away the border lead and work your way through all the sound glass pieces between the border and the area you must fix. In complicated windows, this can involve a great number of pieces of glass and lead, for all the lead must be cut away as the glass is removed.

There is the additional risk of breaking glass pieces. There is also a lot of putty scraping involved, since before any of the glass pieces can be removed, you must pass the point of your lead knife under all surrounding caming to break away the hard putty. This must be done on both the front and the back of the panel, and the more pieces you get out, the more difficult it is to turn the panel back and forth. It's a cumbersome method, but once you get to the area of the break, you can fit the new glass exactly. You then back out the way you came in, replacing leads, glass, and putty as you go. As with most repair jobs, the most difficult part is preparing the object for repair, not the repair itself.

This approach involves time and effort and you should get paid according to the complexity of the work. Usually, we use this technique only on windows that are very expensive or museum pieces, where the owner understands the amount of labor involved and is willing to pay for it.

The tinker-toy approach requires a good craftsman with a steady hand. If the window has a fairly complicated design, make a pattern before taking it apart to make certain the pieces all go together again the way they were before. An easy way to make a pattern is to press a piece of craft paper over all the lead lines. This will indent the paper and when you lift it, you will have a rubbing of these lines with the design and exact spacing of the glass. You can then darken the lines with a magic marker.

Be gentle when removing sound glass. If you break a piece, you may not be able to match it. Keep scraping your knife into the leading around each glass piece, sinking it progressively deeper to get the putty out so the piece can be wiggled free. Be careful that the old glass doesn't suddenly snap and your hand flies back against a neighboring piece of glass. This is one of those all too frequent accidents that accompany repair work. Another is having your lead knife slip into a carelessly placed bracing hand.

The Lead Flap Approach. The lead flap approach is used in repairing central portions of broken panels. Flap up the edges of the surrounding lead came as best you can so that the top flanges are at right angles to the surface and fit the glass as closely as possible, approximating it to the space left for it. This procedure works best for diamonds, squares, or rectangles. It will not work with freeform pieces or pieces with sharp points or acute inner or outer curves since the came will be too difficult to pry up along its top surface.

1) With the point of a lead knife, thoroughly explore all surfaces of the came surrounding the break. If they are torn or if the leads are in poor condition, they must be cut loose from the window and replaced. This must be accomplished before any repair is done. When cutting old leads away, be careful not to crack any of the glass they support. Very gently with the lead knife, first cut one came surface to the glass and then turn the panel over and cut the other. Pushing the came from behind with your knife blade, you should be able to pry the old lead loose. With the lead knife, scrape the exposed piece of glass to remove all putty from its surface, and replace the lead with a new piece, soldering it to its neighbors. Make sure all the leads are firm and the channels completely empty.

2) Start your repair. What you will have is a space surrounded by came with empty channels. With glass pliers, bend the uppermost surfaces of the leads around the break upright so they end up as close to a right angle to the surface as possible. Cut these surfaces at the joints if necessary to allow them to be raised. It is necessary to do this only on one side of the panel. The channel surface below (on the other side) should be left alone to form a shelf for the new glass to rest on. You now have a hole surrounded by came, with a bottom surface below in a horizontal position and the surface above in vertical position.

3) Place a piece of pattern paper under the opening. With a sharp pointed pencil, make a pattern of the existing space. You must enlarge this pattern to compensate for the horizontal shelf of lead below so that the glass will be about 1/16" larger than the pattern.

4) Cut the glass to shape after enlarging the pattern and smooth all edges. If you cut your pattern correctly, you should be able (with the help of a lead knife) to pry this new piece of glass into the opening. It should sit firmly on the bottom flanges of lead.

5) With the lead knife, check to make sure the glass is sitting properly. Using the blade of the knife or a putty knife, smooth down the raised flanges of lead so they now cover the upper edges of the glass. The area should be re-soldered where you've cut the leads to allow the channel surfaces to raise. Once this is done, the piece should be seated firmly back in the leads. Try to use smooth glass pliers when bending the channel surface up and down; otherwise the grozzing

teeth will leave marks in the lead which are impossible to remove.

The difficulties with this procedure are what you might expect. The glass cutting must be absolutely precise and no matter how precise your glass cutting is, if your initial pattern isn't correct, you will still have trouble fitting the glass into place. While the paper pattern may seem to be sitting properly, this is only an illusion because of its thinness as opposed to the thickness of the piece of glass that is to follow it. Don't be discouraged if you've cut your glass precisely to pattern and it still doesn't fit. You will have to back and fill, placing marks on the glass with a glass pencil at the areas of contact and grozzing these until the glass finally falls into place.

At the same time, be careful you don't over-grozz. The grozzing must be done a bit at a time. If you do too much grozzing in any one area, when the glass sits in you will have a hole between the glass and the lead at that point, and the whole piece will have to be redone. Grozz and fit, grozz and fit, and eventually the glass will go in the space. However, this may still not be the end of your troubles, for the lead rim that has been dislocated upwards may not want to come down again without looking crumpled. Lead so treated tends to look ragged when placed back over the glass and your repair will be noticeable. You can avoid this ragged appearance by bringing the lead both up and down very gently and a little at a time. Patience is the key.

All the same, you may find that no matter how much patience you exercise, you're left with a piece of lead that looks tattered and worn. This is one of the difficulties of this technique. Try to lessen it by smoothing the surface with a lead knife or putty knife blade over and over. Watch the amount of pressure you apply. When you bend the lead channel surface up, cut it with a lead knife at the corners where the tension is at its worst, rather than letting the lead tear away at these areas. This will not only allow for a neater solder joint at the site when you're done, but it takes a lot of the strain off the central portion of the flange so that the whole flap can move as a unit. Above all, don't use any tool other than wide jaw glass pliers to bend the lead up so that you are grasping as much of the channel surface as possible.

The Half a Lead Replacement Method. A third technique for replacing these difficult central portions of broken glass starts by using a lead knife to cut away all the leads surrounding the space to be restored. This leaves the empty space surrounded by borders of glass. Place pattern paper under the space to be filled and trace the pattern on it with a sharp pencil. However, here the pattern need not be enlarged since you don't have to compensate for existing lead. Once the pattern is cut, fit it into the space to see how closely it matches. If it doesn't match, mark where it's off and cut a new pattern. Once the pattern fits accurately, cut the replacement glass to match. Holding the glass from below, push it up into the space. It should fit as closely as possible to the bordering surfaces of glass, leaving only the space for the lead heart between.

Make a plasticene clay mound under the glass space to support the surrounding pieces. It should be thin enough so it doesn't lift the panel away from the table surface, but thick enough to keep all pieces of glass from moving. Press the new piece of glass into the space and on the clay bed. With a toothpick, remove any plasticene that oozes up between the pieces. Measure the leads, always remembering to match them to the type of lead used throughout the rest of the panel. It can be embarrassing to have a perfect repair with the wrong leads. Cut the leads to size, then cut them in half through the heart. Don't mix up these matching halves. Mark them so you can match the top and bottom surfaces. On half of each piece of lead, run some permanent glass adhesive down its side. Then place each piece on the panel covering the spaces between the glass pieces. Press each piece down firmly and allow a few moments for the adhesive to hold. Solder the ends of these half leads to their neighbors and immediately wipe away any glue seeping out from beneath the channels.

Allow at least an hour for the adhesive to set, then turn the panel upside-down, remove the clay bed, and clean the under portions of the glass. Carefully place each remaining matching half lead on top of its former half piece in the same direction it was cut and repeat the process of adhering these half leads to the glass. You will end up with a neat surface that has an apparent single H lead holding two pieces of glass together. This type of repair gives the best appearance for the least amount of work.

Difficulties. You may have trouble shaving the old lead from the glass if it's still in place. Make sure your lead knife is sharp. Lead will peel away if you nick a corner firmly with your knife and run your blade through the heart along the surface of the glass.

If you mix up the two halves of any of the came or place them the wrong way, they won't match and you'll have one side standing away from the glass.

The replacement glass itself may be the problem. If your cutting has been so close that one surface of glass touches another, you won't be able to force the lead heart between them. Conversely, if the glass edges are too far apart, you may find that the lead came is not wide enough to cover the space. You have no choice here but to re-cut the glass. Make sure to size the cut glass piece against the space provided before beginning the leading process.

REPAIRING BUCKLED WINDOWS

In a buckled window, the old bracing has given way and the leads have allowed the glass to buckle, usually outward. Leaning on the buckled portion on the work table to push it back into shape is dangerous though it seems logical. You can break glass and get cut. Windows that are badly buckled must be taken apart and completely re-leaded. There is no other way to fix them. If the buckling is just beginning, you might get by with a new reinforcing rod, pulling the old lead cames back into place against it. However, chances are that once the window begins to buckle in one area, it will probably begin to buckle in another.

Re-leading any window involves a certain amount of unleading. This is the most extensive part of the repair process. When you quote a price, don't neglect this. Consider how much work you will have to do before you can actually start the work that the customer feels he is paying you to do.

REPAIRING SUNCATCHERS AND MOBILES

These are usually simple. The back-to-back lead (1/16 U) allows for a good deal of mobility in moving pieces around. Just cut the outside lead and all struts to the broken part, bend them aside, slide the broken pieces out, and replace them. Then bend the piece back into shape and solder the bordering leads. If the object is smashed in several areas, it is not worth repairing.

REPAIRING LAMPS

Straight Panel Lamps

Repairs may be necessary for long pieces of a skirt or paneling or for some of the small pieces within the skirt. Small pieces must be removed and replaced, which means also removing and replacing the surrounding pieces. Since most of these pieces are foiled, you must take the area apart and rebuild it. Such skirts are not deep and there are usually only a few pieces of sound glass between you and the fractured area.

Repairing lamp panels can be accomplished best by stripping away the top surface of two adjoining H cames.

This allows you to lift out the broken glass. Cut a new panel to the shape of the space and place it on the half leads remaining below. Cut away as much of the heart of a new half lead as possible, cutting with metal shears right to the flat surface of the lead. Put the half lead over the edge of the new piece of glass. It should match the half-lead below, whose lead heart projects upward between the new panel and the neighboring panel. Before replacing the new half lead, stretch it so it will be firm and straight. Run some glass cement under it so it will firmly adhere to the glass.

This type of repair is usually easy. The heat of the bulb won't disturb the glass cement, which can take high temperatures.

Bent Panel Lamps

Bent panel lamps are the most difficult of all repair jobs. The problems vary with the number of curves involved in the bent panel, whether it is a U-curve or an S-curve, and whether the panel is held to the frame by metal clips or metal channels, either of which may be missing. Metal clips can be cut from new metal (either brass or copper) and replaced, but metal channels and their filigree coverings are another matter. In some cases old missing channels and missing filigree can't be matched to those still there and you have to find something reasonably close or tell the customer you will have to either substitute for what's missing or redo all the metal framework. In this case, it may be cheaper for your customer to buy a new shade.

Panels held by metal clips are easier to fit than those held by metal channels. Make the new panel using one of the existing panels as a guide (you will have to remove it from the shade) and fit it into the clips. It should fit accurately if your mold was made correctly though it may take some grinding to get it to fall into place. Fortunately with clip-in shades you have some room to maneuver because the metal overlay shields edges of panels not perfectly aligned. Even S-shaped panels will fit reasonably well into a clip-in frame. However, S-shaped panels held in a metal groove frame are difficult to work with and repairs should be done only with the understanding that the end result will not be perfect. In addition, any soldering that must be done on the old brass may show no matter how you try to disguise it chemically with any of the solutions available for the purpose.

You may have to cast four or five panels before you get one that will come close to fitting, especially if the panel is S-shaped. Even at that you will probably have to grozz or grind the panel here and there to get it right. Grinding a bent panel, especially a newly fired one, is a risky business because of the stresses already within the glass from firing. You may try to grind off the smallest amount from one edge and find that the panel has broken in half. That's always a thrill. However, without grinding to a greater or lesser extent, you probably will not get the panel to fit. One reason bent panel replacement is so expensive is the amount of breakage that can occur.

When bent panel lamps were originally made the panels were bent on steel molds pressed from above and variations in their dimensions, if any, could be taken up throughout the fabrication. There is no way to move the panels around during repair to allow for modifications in the various panels. And chances are that your replacement panel, if you are working on a metal rim shade, will not fit perfectly in the metal groove that held the old broken panel. To alleviate this, copper foil the new panel after smoothing the edges. Widen the old brass channel to take the copper foiled thicker edge. To enable the metal to accept solder, rub it with a stiff brush until it shines. Flux and run solder between the foil and metal so the panel is locked into the old rim.

SOLDERING OLD LAMPS

All new soldering must be aged to match the existing metal. This is done either with a manufactured solution or your own preparation of copper sulfate or a mixture of hydrochloric acid and sulfur, a noxious concoction that should be used only in a well-ventilated area. Don't do this until you finish soldering; once you've used any solution on a soldered surface you will no longer be able to solder along this surface. With S-shaped panel repair, the best you can hope for is a panel that will not stand out too badly from its neighbors and that will be held in place by the pressure of the lamp frame. Such repairs should only be done by experts.

If you're not certain of your ability to repair stained glass, limit yourself to fixing only your own projects or those of friends (you may lose friends this way). You can probably only make money in repairing if you work on several jobs at a time. If you split the time among several projects, repairs can be worthwhile. Most repair procedures involve waiting periods (for instance, waiting for the glass cement to dry when using the half lead method) and this time may be spent on another repair job. In this way you will be able to make such jobs pay, thus financing your more creative endeavors.

The lamp on page 320 was made in 1910 and repaired in 1926 and 1937 by other studios. Here it has had its top section (cone) with its two small pieced base layers removed as part of a massive rebuilding operation. Nicholas the cat checks out our replacement of the initial small pieced layer of all new glass pieces. The lamp was also out of round so we wrapped it with string and pulled the ends firmly but a little at a time to reactivate the proper shape. Twelve gauge wire was then soldered to the bottom inside skirt base to maintain the shape.

CHAPTER 31
Safety First and Last: A Checklist

Although we have taken some pains throughout these chapters to indicate that precautions must be taken when working with chemicals, hot irons, sharp pieces of glass, noxious fumes, and lead oxides on the skin, it seemed judicious to recap much of this in a final note. We want to stress that stained glass work is not a dangerous occupation provided that common sense and reasonable concern for your own skin and for that of others outweighs enthusiastic disregard. The same principle applies to driving a car.

PREGNANCY AND CHILDREN

Under no circumstances should a pregnant or nursing woman work in stained glass. This seems so obvious that it is surprising how often we have had to turn down students who fell into this category. Nor should babies be allowed in the workshop. Again, we've had prospective students who wanted to take class but couldn't get a babysitter and wanted to leave the infant in a basket or crib in the studio while they worked. The presumed exposure of the child to anything in the air or on the table may leave the unwary teacher who wants to do a favor in a very unfavorable position down the road.

TOXINS AND FLAMMABLE SUBSTANCES

The degree of risk from exposure to toxins depends on the material or substance used, length and frequency of direct contact, and personal sensitivity. Risk is exacerbated by careless handling or improperly arranged working areas. Skin irritation is the most common problem experienced by glassworkers, with respiratory trouble and poisoning next.

Always use utmost caution when working with solvents such as toluene and xylene, benzene, and other hydrocarbons, or with lead. Don't breathe fumes during the soldering process. One way to avoid potential health risks is to use a less dangerous substance that will do the same job, even if the product is more costly. The same applies

to the choice of process or technique. If two methods are available, choose the least dangerous. For example, wet grinding is preferable to dry because it doesn't throw off large amounts of dust into the air. Never use any material that is not well labeled. Read labels for a complete list of ingredients, easily understood instructions for handling, and descriptions of safety hazards. In general, if a product smells bad, burns the eyes or causes tearing, irritates or bleaches the skin, or causes an itchy nose or coughing, assume it's dangerous.

HANDLE THINGS THOUGHTFULLY

You can always obtain information about ingredients by writing to the manufacturer for a Safety Data Sheet and product description. But certain things should be self-evident. For instance, flammable substances should be kept away from heat. Hot objects should be allowed to cool before picking them up. Disposal of waste chemicals should be performed immediately after they accumulate. Always follow the instructions provided when mixing chemicals. All spills should be cleaned up immediately. A leaky container should be replaced, not patched. Where possible, unbreakable containers should be used.

Good personal hygiene is essential. Eating, drinking, smoking, or applying cosmetics should never be done in the work area. Accidental splashes on the skin should be washed with water immediately. Eye splashes should be flushed with water for at least 15 minutes and a doctor consulted.

Styrofoam presents the greatest fire hazard of all the polymers. If methyl chloride has been used as the foaming agent, sawing or cutting the foam may release methyl chloride vapors and produce serious health effects, including damage to the liver, kidneys, bone marrow, and central nervous system. Heating Styrofoam for any purpose (molding usually) is extremely dangerous because it releases noxious vapors. Never heat a polystyrene.

EPOXY RESINS

Wear protective clothing when working with resins. Curing agents, or hardeners, can cause serious skin irritation or even burns if you get splashed and pay no attention. In addition, these resins are flammable. Smoking increases the inhalation effects of any exposure to these materials and also creates a potential fire hazard.

LEAD CAME/SOLDERING

Soft soldering, which employs an electric iron, as opposed to hard soldering or brazing, does not present a significant lead exposure if proper ventilation is provided. Proper ventilation is an elastic term, however. For one individual it may mean a fan ten yards down the hall; for another 15 open windows in a three foot circumference. Use common sense. If you're working in a closet you're liable to get hung. If you have a space the size of a garage (which is where many hobbyists work) you should be all right, assuming you don't have a group of friends also working in this space, all soldering at once. Check the Tools chapter for devices that can help you get rid of noxious vapors wherever you work.

The fumes from soldering are only part of the problem. The lead itself is poisonous. When working with it, keep fingers out of your mouth, wash your hands before eating, cover any cuts or sores, and store lead and other dangerous materials away from children or pets. Many of the paints and stains used in the stained glass field contain lead. Since these come in powder form, a certain percentage of paint dust will be in the air. You might want to wear a mask when working with this material. Lead-free paints and stains are available and you should consult your local supplier about their efficacy as compared to their leaded counterparts. Our own experience with non-leaded paints have been disappointing.

It's a good idea to have a blood lead test every six months or so. Consult your family doctor and tell him you are working with lead and follow his advice. We have worked in the stained glass field for over 30 years, have followed all the precautions we suggest, and our blood lead tests have always been within normal limits.

A SAFE WORK AREA

The kitchen isn't one. It is a bad substitute for a workshop or storage area. Contamination of food is inevitable.

Your work area should have built-in safety features, such as a source of running water, an eyewash kit, a first aid kit with a lot of bandages, and a fire extinguisher. Hopefully you'll never have to use any of them. The best way not to have to use them is to have them available. Physical hazards such as cluttered walking space, floor spills, or inadequately grounded or overloaded electrical equipment should be eliminated. Be careful of long hair, loose sleeves, or hanging jewelry that might catch in equipment, especially in these days of advanced technology when everything seems to be rotating, cycling, punching, slicing, and generally in motion.

VENTILATION

We keep coming back to this, but we want to emphasize that adequate ventilation is absolutely essential in the workshop. Adequate ventilation means that fresh, uncontaminated air moves past your face and away from you with sufficient strength to clean the toxic fumes from your breathing zone. As a test, a wet finger should be dried by evaporation within two to three seconds. Properly placed window fans or exhaust and blower fans may do the job in conjunction with an open window.

GLASS

To reiterate another point: Glass is no more dangerous than the individual working with it. Of course some individuals are more dangerous than others. Glass reacts to your stimulus. The simplest way to avoid having it embroider your skin is to not take it for granted. Any large piece of glass should be tapped lightly with your knuckle to test for vibration before it is lifted or carried. A rattle is a warning, a solid ring means the piece is safe to handle. Small pieces should be checked for beginning fractures, not against an overhead light, but by supporting them with two hands in front of you before a window or good light at eye level. Don't use your body as a brace for the piece of glass you intend to cut.

Be careful how you store glass. It should never be stored above shoulder height. If you have to reach over your head to a glass bin—or worse, climb a ladder to reach it—you are asking for trouble. The best way to work with glass is to keep both feet on the ground, literally as well as figuratively.

A FINAL WORD

None of these warnings, dire as they may sound, should discourage anyone from working with stained glass. A similar set of concerns could be expressed for just about any hobby or profession. The purpose of pointing out hazards is not to discourage you but to maintain your physical well being so you can continue to enjoy the craft. We want you to stick around, buy supplies, and use them in good health.

Knowing your materials and using them intelligently is as much a mark of sophisticated purpose as the product they will help you produce. Our point is that unless you heed the first part, you may not get to the second. That would be a shame, considering how much fun you'd be missing.

Glossary

abrasion The process of grinding away the top surface of a piece of flashed glass. A grinding wheel or burr may be used.

acetates Scaled down treatments of windows of stained glass done with special paints on heavy plastic to get a "see through" effect.

antique glass Glass that is made by the old method of hand blowing. The glass is blown into cylinders and the cylinders cut and flattened into sheets.

breaking the score Separating a piece of glass into planned sections along a marked line.

breaking and entering It is more difficult for a burglar to get into a home through a stained glass window than through one of window or plate glass.

cartoon The blueprint for a work of stained glass containing all cut lines and possibly all paint lines.

cathedral glass Machine-made, transparent stained glass. Uniform in thickness; about 1/8".

composition The overall design of a finished piece containing the proper balance of color and linear flow.

cut line The borders of cut edges of glass demarcated in a cartoon.

cylinder One of the steps in the production of antique glass sheets.

dalle A thick slab of stained glass for use with epoxy or cement. Broken pieces of dalles, or "chunks," may be copper foiled into windows or lamps to give a faceted effect.

epoxy Clear, fast-drying glues for joining glass to glass.

etching This process is done with hydrofluoric acid, the only acid that attacks glass. The purpose of etching is to save cutting and leading of tiny pieces. Etching can be done only on flashed glass.

Favrile A word coined by Tiffany to describe his glass. His methods of production of this glass are still unknown.

flashed glass A sheet of glass where one color is laid on top of another. Any color may be flashed on top of another provided the two are not mutually exclusive of light. Such glass is used extensively in etching, but it can be used as is for the particular hue it presents.

flints Planned breaks in a diamond or rectangular window, usually in the form of a curved triangle, to break up a strict geometric design.

fusing The art of adhering glass to other glass surfaces or melting one glass directly into another. The heat necessary for this is best applied in a kiln, though a torch may be used with very small pieces.

gemmaux A process whereby small pieces of colored glass are glued and then grouted to an underlying piece of clear window glass to form a pattern.

glass bending Sagging or draping glass over a mold, then heating the glass blank in a kiln until it either sags into or drapes over the mold.

glass globs Thick, rounded pieces of stained glass of varied colors and sizes used as glass "jewels" to enhance a design.

glass jewels These may be faceted, hollowbacked, reflective, or bulls-eyed. Unlike globs which are allowed to assume their own shape, or chunks which are hacked off a dalle at random, jewels are formulated in a mold of Swedish steel and then polished.

glass thickness Anywhere from 1/8" in machine-made (cathedral) glass to nearly 1/2" in certain heavy antique glass. Thickness in antique glass may not be uniform within the same sheet. This is liable to cause a rocking of the glass on the cutting surface, which must be compensated for by the worker.

granite-backed glass A form of textured glass with one side roughened (also called pebble glass).

grisaille A process developed in the 13th century for windows having the bulk of the glass white or gray with extensive leading. The most famous example is the Five Sisters window at York Cathedral.

grozzing Wearing away the small pinpoints and chips of glass along a cut surface using a fine tooth pliers especially made for the purpose.

hammered glass A type of textured cathedral glass with multiple small indentations.

hydrofluoric acid The only material that attacks silica (a basic constituent of glass). It is used for etching.

joint The area where one lead line meets another. Such joints usually butt one against another.

kiln An oven made of firebrick. Kilns can be electric, gas-heated, or wood-burning.

knapping The process of faceting slab glass by chipping away at the edges with the slab glass hammer.

lead came Extruded pure lead that is channeled to specific dimensions either on one or both sides. The channels then accept and hold the glass to shape.

leaded glass Glass held together by lead cames.

leading Assembling a work of stained glass where lead came is the holding material.

millefiore Beads of glass heated in a kiln and spread out into whorls of color. The use of this material dates back to ancient Egypt.

mold High temperature firing shapes into which glass can be sagged or over which it can be bent or folded.

mold release A substance applied to the surface of a mold to prevent the glass from sticking to it at high temperature.

mosaic glass An opaque glass where the colors have been heavily mixed (also called puddle glass).

Murano An island off the coast of Venice; traditional home of famous glassworks.

opalescent glass Non-transparent glass; the colors are seen by reflected light.

oxidation The tough, outer coat on lead came that must be wire brushed before soldering.

pattern A paper (or thin sheet metal) template from which the glass pieces are cut.

ponce bag A piece of tied up rag with whiting inside used as a stencil.

pontil The blowpipe used in gathering and blowing molten glass.

pot metal The medieval name for the molten glass batch. It was heated in a large pot and metallic oxides were added for color.

reamies Sheets of antique glass containing faint and delicate streaks of color.

reinforcing rods Galvanized steel rods used to span a window to prevent it from bowing.

resist material Used to protect areas of the glass to be left unchanged, as in etching and silkscreening. Asphaltum and beeswax are resist materials.

rolled edges Usually found only on antique sheets where the cylinder of glass was cut. This has smoothed over from the oven and bulged somewhat from the surface. It must be cut away before the sheet can be worked.

sandblasting Another form of glass abrading.

score The line imposed by a glass cutter or diamond upon the surface of a piece of glass. The fracture line weakens the glass along its length.

semiantique glass Machine-made glass with little movement or texture but with brilliant tones.

silver stain Really an etch; it imparts a golden color to clear glass.

streakies Glass sheets with streaks of color running through them. Colors may be many and varied against a background of yet another color, either opalescent or antique.

tapping One of the techniques of breaking out a score. A ball-ended glass cutter is used, though the heavy end of a regular cutter is also effective. Glass must always be tapped from the bottom.

tinning Soldering completely over the surface of another metal either to stiffen it or to allow its color to be changed.

tints Lightly colored hues and tones of stained glass.

tracer A special brush used in painting on glass.

Sources

Manufacturers Only

The companies listed below make the products used in the craft of stained glass. They will not sell directly to individuals but will recommend the nearest dealer/supplier in your area. Due to space limitations, this is a partial list of the many companies that make products used in stained glass.

Glass

If you are traveling or in the area of one of these glass manufacturers, contact them regarding the availability of plant tours to see how glass is made. It is a fascinating process to see!

Armstrong Glass Co.
359 Hood Rd.
Jasper. GA 30143

Blenko Glass Co.
PO Box 67
Milton, WV 25541

Bullseye Glass Co.
3722 SE 21st Ave.
Portland, OR 97202

Carolina Glue Chip
PO Box 237
North Wilkesboro, NC 28659

Allen H. Graef-Dichroic Glass
3823 E. Anaheim St.
Long Beach, CA 90804

Kokomo Opalescent Glass Co.
State & Market
PO Box 2265
Kokomo, IN 46901

Lins Glass Foundry
PO Box 236
Fort White, FL 32038

Oceana Sheet Glass Co.
2720 Rodeo Gulch Rd.
Soquel, CA 95073

Spectrum Glass Co. Inc.
24305 Woodinville-Snohomish Hwy.
Woodinville, WA 98072

Uroboros Glass Studios
1313 SE 3rd
Portland, OR 97214

The Paul Wissmach Glass Co.
PO Box 228
Paden City, WV 26159

Youghiogheny Glass Co.
2621 W. Crawford Ave.
PO Box 800
Connellsville, PA 15425

Copper Foil

Edco Copper Foil
326 36th St.
Brooklyn, NY 11232

Venture Tape Corp.
30 Commerce Rd.
Rockland, MA 02370-0384

Glass Cutting Saws

Diamond Tech International, USA
4002 West State St.
Tampa, FL 33609

Gemini Saw Co.
3300 Kashiwa St.
Torrance, CA 90505

Gryphon Corp.
101 East Santa Anita Ave.
Burbank, CA 91502

Tools

GlasStar Corp.
20721 Marilla St.
Chatsworth, CA 91311

Inland Craft Products
32052 Edward
Madison Heights, MI 48071

The Cooper Group
Lufkin Rd.
PO Box 728
Apex, NC 27502

Fletcher-Terry Co
Spring Lane
Farmington, CN 06032

American Hakko Products
25072 Anza Dr.
Santa Clarita, CA 91355

Mika International
6000 North Baily Ave. Suite 3
Amherst, NY 14226

Sandblasting

Rayzist Photomask
2105 Industrial Ct.
Vista, CA 92083

PhotoBrasive Systems
4832 Grand Ave.
Duluth, MN 55807

Solder and Came

Canfield Technologies Inc.
1 Crossman Rd.
Sayreville, NJ 08872

Fry Metals - Stained Glass Division
4100 6th Ave.
Altoona, PA 16602

Chicago Metallic Came
4849 S. Austin Ave.
Chicago, IL 60638

Cascade Lead Products
1614 West 75th Ave.
Vancouver, BC V6P 6G2

Kilns

Paragon Industries
2011 South Town East Blvd.
Mesquite, TX 75149-1122

Jen-Ken Kilns
3615 Ventura Dr. W
Lakeland, FL 33811

Denver Glass Machinery Inc.
3065 S. Umatilla St.
Englewood, CO 80110

Paints and Enamels

L. Reusche & Co.
1299 H St.
Greeley, CO 80631

Thompson Enamels
PO Box 310
Newport, KY 41072

Fusion Headquarters Inc. (Fuse Master)
7402-A SW MacAdam Ave.
Portland, OR 97219

Eastman Corp. (Color-Magic)
7447 Via de Fortuna
Carlsbad, CA 92009

Lamp Forms

H. L. Worden Co.
118 Main St.
PO Box 519
Granger, WA 98932

Bradley B. Corp.
1610 Rock Ave.
Yakima, WA 98902

Publications

Glass Patterns Quarterly
8300 Hidden Valley Rd.
PO Box 69
Westport, KY 40077

Glass Craftsman Magazine/The Glass Library
64 Woodstock Dr.
Newtown, PA 18940
www.glasslibrary.com

Stained Glass Quarterly
Stained Glass Assoc. of America
1125 Wilmington Ave.
St. Louis, MO 63111

Index

C

Came cutter, 111
Came cutting pliers, 64
Canfield Co., 45, 47
Canopies, 172–173
Carbide cutters, 55, 56
Carbide glass bits, 68
Cartoon, 146
    for slab glass, 214–215
Cascade Metal, 93
Cathedral glass, 16–17
Chagall, Marc, 13, 17
Chain, 173
Chain pliers, 64, 173, 175
Chartres windows, 23
Children and stained glass work, 326
Chipping hammer, 214
Chipping in glue chipping, 225
Chip testing for compatibility, 241–242
Chunk glass, 19
Cingria, Alexandre, 13
Circle cutters, 57–58
Circles
    breaking out, 36–38
    measuring, for multi-paneled lamps, 159
Cleaning
    in silkscreening, 22–223
    stained glass, 125
Client, guiding, 314
Coating chamber, 81–82
Coating process, 81–82
Cobalt, 22
Coefficient of Expansion (COE), 281
Colonial games, 116
Color
    adding, 15–16
    developing sense of, 93–94
    and the light table, 94
    in stained glass design, 15, 94
Color Magic, 71–72
Commission, working on, 314
Compatibility testing, 241
    chip testing for, 241–242
Compressor in sandblasting, 178–179
Cones, 242
Connick, Charles, 13

Cookie cutters, 80
Cooper loops, 127
Copper, 22
Copper braid, 156
Copper foil, 118–124
    background, 118
    beading, 123
    combining with lead came, 124
    common problems with, 123–124
    and foiling machines, 124
    size and thickness, 119–120
    soldering tips and irons, 123
    step-by-step directions, 120–123
    technique, 118–119
Copper foiled multi-piece panel shade, 167–171
    foiling, 167
    soldering, 167–168, 170–171
    tapping, 168–170
Copper-Mate, 47
Copper wire, 93
Cornering, 111
Corners, designing, 92
Corrosive fluxes, 47
Coventry Cathedral, 13
Crackle glass, 18–19
Cracks, repairing, 127–128
Craft paper, 71
Cram, Ralph Adams, 13
Crushed glass, 79–80
Crystal, 15
Cutter, scoring with, 214
Cutter wheel lubrication, 56
Cutting, lead came, 110
Cutting force and speed, 29–30
Cutting stance, 30
Cutting surface, 30
Cutting wheels, 29
Cylindrical beads, 22

D

Daley, Patricia, 227, 247, 253, 269, 274
Deep cutting, 177
Dental drills, 70
Deoxidizing, 43
Desoldering, 52–53

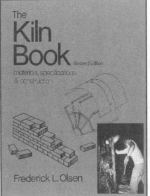

DOZENS OF PROJECTS WAITING FOR YOU

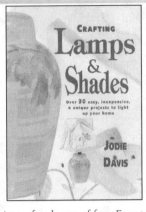

CRAFTING LAMPS & SHADES
Easy, Inexpensive and Unique Projects to Light Up Your Home
by Jodie Davis
No matter what decorating style you prefer, from country or contemporary to sweet or sensational, one of the 30 lamp and shade projects in this book will turn boring into beautiful in just a few hours of fun. Easy-to-follow step-by-step instructions and illustrations demystify the wiring process.

Softcover • 8-1/4 x 10-7/8 • 144 pages
50 color photos and 150 illustrations
LASH • $21.95

PAPER PLUS
Unique Projects Using Handmade Paper
by Nancy Worrell
Enter the exciting world of creative papermaking with this detailed guide. Simple step-by-step instructions walk the user through sheetmaking, handcasting and sculpting with a variety of papers. This start-to-finish guide puts the art of papermaking at your fingertips.

Softcover • 8-1/4 x 10-7/8 • 128 pages
80 illustrations • 50 color photos
CHPP • $18.95

STAMPCRAFT
Dozens of Creative Ideas for Stamping on Cards, Clothing, Furniture, and More
by Cari Haysom
Any surface is up for grabs with stamping. Large and small-scale objects alike take on new dimensions when customized stamping takes over. See just how easy and versatile stamping is with these 40 examples, perfect for beginners and stampaholics alike.

Softcover • 8-1/4 x 10-7/8 • 128 pages
color throughout • **STCR • $19.95**

ENAMELS, ENAMELING, ENAMELISTS
by Glenice Lesley Matthews
Here's everything you'll need to know to enamel on silver, gold, copper, aluminum, and other metals, from preparation to application to firing to safety procedures. Techniques covered include graffito, cloisonnè, grisàille, pliquè-a-jour, and more.

Hardcover • 8-1/4 x 10-7/8 • 192 pages
30 color photos
EEE • $29.95